THE CONSTANT CIRCLE

Fire Ant Books

The Constant Circle

H. L. MENCKEN AND HIS FRIENDS

by SARA MAYFIELD

INTRODUCTION
by Edmund Wilson

THE UNIVERSITY OF ALABAMA PRESS
Tuscaloosa and London

Originally published by the Delacorte Press, 1968.

Typeface: Caledonia, Bulmer, and Grayda

∞

The paper on which this book is printed meets the minimum requirements of
American National Standard for Information Science-Permanence of Paper for
Printed Library Materials, ANSI Z39.48-1984.

Library of Congress Cataloging-in-Publication Data

Mayfield, Sara, 1905–1979
  The constant circle : H.L. Mencken and his friends / Sara Mayfield ; introduction
by Edmund Wilson.
    p. cm.
"A Fire Ant book."
Originally published: New York : Delacorte Press, 1968. Includes index.
  ISBN 0-8173-5063-2 (pbk. : alk. paper)
  1. Mencken, H. L. (Henry Louis), 1880–1956. 2. Mencken, H. L. (Henry Louis),
1880–1956—Friends and associates. 3. Authors, American—20th century—
Biography. 4. Journalists—United States—Biography. 5. Editors—United States—
Biography. I. Title.
  PS3525.E43Z68 2003
  818'.5209—dc21   2003007998
British Library Cataloguing-in-Publication Data available

$\mathcal{C}$ONTENTS

*T*HE AFTERMATH OF MENCKEN

Edmund Wilson

IN THE SPRING OF 1912, just before graduating from prep school, I somehow happened to pick up a copy of the *Smart Set*, a trashy-looking monthly,
and was astonished to find audacious and extremely amusing critical articles by men named Mencken and Nathan, of whom I had never heard. I
continued to read the *Smart Set* through college, at first with a slight feeling of guilt, for it was making fun of everything respectable in current
American drama and literature. But the "American Renascence" had already begun, and I was already dissatisfied with the traditional critics. I
had never paid any attention to William Dean Howells in *Harper's*, and
The Nation was dominated by Paul Elmer More, who seemed to be opposed on principle to any contemporary of talent, whether American or
English. When, at college, I discovered a book by W. C. Brownell called
American Prose Masters, it was with a hope (because that was a time when
we wanted American literature taken seriously; as was said of Noah, we
prayed for rain and were deluged), a hope which was followed by disappointment. Brownell disapproved of Poe, and though it was he who, as an
adviser to Scribners, had had them bring out the New York Edition of
Henry James, he did not seem really much to believe in him. He had, as I
learned afterward, rejected Van Wyck Brooks's *America's Coming-of-Age*,
which was eventually to become a landmark, on the ground that it was still
"too early" to call attention to the weaknesses of our supposed classics. But
Mencken, quite outside the New England tradition, to which he was sometimes unfair, was not constrained by its inhibitions and was honestly attempting to sift out what was valuable from the rubbish of our own very
second-rate period—from the eighties to the early 1900's—and as he became more self-confident in his heresies he steadily became more impres-

sive. I was led to reread *Huckleberry Finn* and to look up *What Maisie Knew*, which Mencken had described as "a passionless masterpiece."

The strange history of the *Smart Set* has been told in detail and most entertainingly by Mr. Carl R. Dolmetsch in his *The Smart Set: A History and Anthology*, with a personal memoir bv S. N. Behrman. The magazine was founded by Colonel Mann, the blackmailing owner of *Town Topics*, as "the Magazine of Cleverness," and was then aimed at an appeal to social rather than intellectual snobbery. It became involved in Colonel Mann's scandals, but was later bought by someone more respectable and edited by Mencken and Nathan and Willard Huntington Wright—that somewhat mysterious character who began as a high-powered intellectual but later turned into "S. S. Van Dine," the popular writer of detective stories. It was abandoned by Mencken and Nathan in 1923, when the then owner forbade them to print a disrespectful squib about President Harding's funeral train, and fell into the hands of Hearst, who dropped it at the time of the Depression. This history has now been followed by a volume of Mencken's contributions to the *Smart Set*, *H. L. Mencken's Smart Set Criticism*, very well selected and edited by William H. Nolte. This last cannot, of course, carry with it all the atmosphere of the old *Smart Set*, which was something quite special, created by the unique combination of the editors with the magazine's variegated past. There was the cover, with its young man and woman in evening dress, he bowing, she curtsying with a fan, watched from the background by a masked devil, who was snaring them with long strings prettily baited with winged hearts. As the magazine became more and more a vehicle for the editors' ideas and for superior stories and poems, this cover became incongruous; it underwent many transformations in order to bring it up to date, but it basically remained the same and came to seem one of the jokes of Mencken and Nathan, who were informal and recklessly mischievous. They had a department called "Americana," in which they reprinted absurdities from the press, and another called "Répétition Générale," which was devoted to ideas and epigrams that they thought they might use later. There were dialogues, in which each wrote his own lines and in which they were represented as walking along Fifth Avenue or in some other local setting. They invented a character called Owen Hatteras, to whom some of these features were sometimes ascribed; he was supposed to have become a major in the First World War and was afterward given that rank. Owen Hatteras was the purported author of a pamphlet called "Pistols for Two," in which actually each of the editors was writing—sometimes fantastically—about the other. "He dislikes," wrote Mencken of Nathan, "women over twenty-one, actors, cold weather, mayonnaise dressing, people who are always happy, hard chairs, invitations to dinner, invitations to serve on committees in however worthy a cause, railroad trips, public restaurants, rye whisky, chicken, daylight, men who do not wear waistcoats, the sight of a woman eating, the sound of a woman singing, small napkins, Maeterlinck, Verhaeren, Tagore, Dickens, Bataille, fried oysters, German soubrettes, French John Masons, American John Masons [John Mason was then a well-known American actor], tradesmen, poets, married women who think of leaving their husbands, professional anarchists of all kinds, ventilation, professional music lovers, men who tell how much money they have made, men who affect sudden friendships and call him Georgie, women who affect sudden friendships and then call him Mr. Nathan, writing letters, receiving letters, talking over the telephone, and wearing a hat." "His table manners," wrote Nathan of Mencken, "are based upon provincial French principles, with modifications suggested by the Cossacks of the Don." Mencken had been trained as a journalist on the Baltimore Sunpapers, and so was never oppressed by the American academic standards, which he continually ridiculed and denounced. And even as a journalist he was very much at his ease. On one occasion, limited for space, he cut off an article in the middle of a sentence.

One finds in Mr. Nolte's selection the original reviews, then so unconventional, of Conrad, Huneker, and Dreiser which were afterward used as material for the solider essays of *A Book of Prefaces*, of 1917. I am glad to find old pieces I remember and that Mencken never collected—especially the summaries of periods in his life, such as the "Taking Stock," of March 1917, written to celebrate the occasion of his "one hundredth mensual discourse in this place" in which he tells us that in the course of the eight and a third years he had "grown two beards and shaved them off; I have eaten 3,086 meals; I have made more than $100,000 in wages, fees, refreshers, tips, and bribes . . . I have been called a fraud 700 times, and blushed at the proofs . . . I have had seventeen proposals of marriage from lady poets . . . I have been abroad three and a half times, and learned and forgotten six foreign languages . . . I have fallen downstairs twice. I have read the *Police Gazette* in the barbershop every week; I have shaken hands with Dr. Wilson; I have upheld the banner of the ideal; I have kept the faith, in so far as I could make out what it was," etc., etc. This frankness had the effect of making the *Smart Set* pleasantly informal: you might almost have been drinking with him at Lüchow's. It is at once funny and rather irritating to find this old German Nietzschean in one of his favorite Nietzschean phrases, describing Anatole France as "still fit for dancing with arms and legs." How else is it possible to dance? But can one imagine either Nietzsche or Mencken or Anatole France performing any such antics as this suggests? Mencken, however, got tired of the *Smart Set*—as he said, of its gray paper, its cheap format. The *American Mercury* followed, a much more attractive-looking production. It was this that most people, I think, read when Mencken's reputation was at its height. But it was otherwise not as attractive as the *Smart Set*. The break with Nathan left it deficient both in humor and in what Mencken called "beautiful letters," and the writers on current affairs tended all to give the impression of having been so processed by the editor himself that their work seemed practically to have been written by him—an impression which he later tried to explain away as having been created by the necessity he found himself under of remedying the bad writing of many of them. And it is therefore very much worthwhile to have Mr. Nolte's collection of Mencken's earlier, more spontaneous work.

There is in English no satisfactory biography of Mencken, no sound, comprehensive book. Van Wyck Brooks's chapter about him in *The Confident Years* is, from the literary point of view, the best thing I know. I was interested to hear Brooks say that he thought it was one of the best things he had ever written. His and Mencken's temperaments were so much unlike that this makes it a great tribute to Mencken's influence. *The Irreverent Mr. Mencken*, by Edgar Kemler, and *Disturber of the Peace*, by William Manchester, are both undistinguished journalistic jobs (the second much fuller and more valuable than the first). *H. L. Mencken: A Portrait from Memory*, by Charles Angoff, who worked with him on the *American Mercury*, has its interest as a personal memoir but gives a disagreeable impression. It seems obvious that Mr. Angoff was a rather humorless young man and that Mencken was constantly kidding him—he called Angoff "Professor"—and that Angoff is having his revenge in very much the same way that Anatole France's secretary Jean-Jacques Brousson did in his books on his late master. This Mencken is made to sound like a wise-cracking, insensitive bully talking nonsense at drunken parties or, in his office, propounding outrageous opinions that one feels, when one has gauged Mr. Angoff's intelligence, must have been specially intended to shock him. The daughter of a Baltimore friend of Mencken to whom I lent Angoff's book said that she was quite unable to recognize the man who used to come to their house. I find difficulty in believing, as Mr. Angoff asserts, that "it was no secret that during a great part of their relationship they [Mencken and Nathan] were little better than friendly enemies." It is true that the partners broke up over the policy of the *Mercury*—Mencken's ambitions as a serious thinker were, I believe, getting a little beyond him—but it was only at the time of the *Mercury* that Angoff knew the editors, and their friendly relations were later restored. My impression on the few occasions when I visited the *Smart Set* office was that they worked together in their comedy act, in person as well as in their writings, on a not at all inimical basis. Mencken was likely to be carried away into developing one of his paradoxes, irrelevant to the business in hand, in a way not much different from that of his written monologues, and Nathan would cut short his digression by interjecting some brisk little question of a more or less illogical kind which would stop his partner in his tracks. It would take Mencken a moment to grasp it, and there was no way to make a sensible reply.

But there does now exist in French a large-scale study of Mencken that is superior, as far as I know, to anything else that has been written: *H. L. Mencken—L'Homme, l'Œuvre, l'Influence*, by Guy Jean Forgue, a professor at the Sorbonne, who formerly worked at Yale and has edited a volume of Mencken's letters. Though written in French for the French, this study attacks the subject in a more serious and scholarly way than any of the books by Americans. M. Forgue goes into Mencken's origins, German as well as American, and analyzes, in relation to them, his ideas and his attitudes, which present so many contradictions, with the systematic thoroughness so characteristic of French criticism and a sense of the American background that is astonishing in a foreigner. He explains the importance to Mencken of his immigrant Prussian grandfather, who was proud of his relationship to the Bismarcks and looked down on other Baltimore Germans; the grandson was an enthusiastic Nietzschean, adored German music to the exclusion of other kinds, wrote an admiring article about Ludendorff at the time of the First World War, loved to talk about the *Polizei* and the *Gelehrten*, and idealized the German nobility. His opposition in both the wars to the championship of England by the United States and his interest in the "American language" in contradistinction to the English were evidently the results of his loyalty to Germany. Mencken was a curious example of the second generation American who, in the freer life of the United States, retains the strong social prejudices of the people that he still belongs to, though his family have left them behind, and the situation in his case is complicated by the Menckens having come to the South, so that Henry liked to defend the Confederate cause in its quarrel with the Washington government. His strong colloquial flavor and knockabout verbiage cannot be conveyed in French, but it is remarkable that a Frenchman who has lived in this country for a relatively short time should appreciate these so well and translate them as accurately as he does.

And we have also now a memoir of Mencken which brings us closer to his personality than any other has yet done and which should be read as an antidote to Angoff: *The Constant Circle: H. L. Mencken and His Friends,* by Sara Mayfield. After the death of Mencken's mother, with whom he had lived all his life and on whom he was much dependent, he married, at the age of fifty, Sara Haardt, also of German origin, and set up a new establishment. Sara Haardt was already gravely ill, and she died, five years later, of tubercular meningitis. She grew up in Montgomery, Alabama, and Miss Mayfield was a close friend of hers from her girlhood. Miss Mayfield's book deals primarily with this episode in Mencken's life, and her story is interesting in several ways. Besides presenting a unique intimate record of the private personality of Mencken, which M. Forgue so carefully distinguishes from the legend of himself he created, Miss Mayfield gives a lively account of the Montgomery in which she and Sara Haardt and Zelda Sayre (later Fitzgerald) and Tallulah Bankhead grew up. Montgomery had been the first capital of the Confederacy; Jefferson Davis had taken the oath of office in the Capitol. The girlhoods of Zelda and Tallulah are described as having been just what one had always imagined. They were both the daughters of important local citizens: Zelda's father and Miss Mayfield's father were associate justices of the Supreme Court of Alabama; Tallulah's was a congressman, and an uncle a senator. In New York, they gave the impression of young barbarian princesses from a country where they were free to do anything—though Miss Mayfield tells us that Tallulah was eventually sent away to an Academy of the Sacred Heart to keep her out of trouble. I recognized the type in bud when I once came up from the South on the train, sitting across from a pretty blond belle in rolled stockings with her feet on the opposite seat, who played jazz on a phonograph all the way. She might have been Tallulah or Zelda in the phase described by Sara Mayfield. Zelda, says Miss Mayfield, "two years younger than Sara, was still tomboy enough to stride the guns [of the Capitol], slide down the banisters of the famous circular staircase in the rotunda, and climb over the minié balls, piled up in pyramids like oranges in the fruitstands." "Her only rival" was Tallulah Bankhead, who "could bend backward far enough to pick up a handkerchief from the floor with her teeth, stand on her head, and turn a fancy cartwheel," as well as imitate one of their teachers—who wore high net collars and long black dresses and attempted "by prim bearing and quaint methods . . . to instill the aristocratic manners of the old school into us—in a way that made us rock with laughter." Tallulah was genuinely witty and Zelda had some literary ability. Sara Haardt, "fragile, lovely, and flame-like," was less obstreperous and was more serious-minded. Like Miss Mayfield, she went to Goucher, where they both wrote short stories. Through these short stories, a prize for one of which Sara Mayfield won in a contest in her freshman year, these girls got to know Mencken when he came to make the award and spoke to them on "How to Catch a Husband." Apart from her Saxon ancestry, her having grown up, like him, in the South, and her interest in literature, Mencken must have been attracted to Miss Haardt by something of the same kind of charm—which Miss Mayfield says was irresistible—that made Zelda and Tallulah popular. She became a regular solace and companion of Mencken after his mother died (the talkative bachelor's indispensable woman friend), and though he fought marriage off for a time, having avoided and disparaged it all his life, it was inevitable that he should marry her. Miss Mayfield, in telling about this, brings out Mencken's considerate and sensitive side in a relationship which seems to have been unique for him. He was certainly much shaken by Sara's death. One had the impression after this that he was left more disagreeable and bitter, becoming rather nasty in his arguments with such opponents as Upton Sinclair, in a way that had not been characteristic of his hard-hitting but good-humored ridicule. Sara died in 1935, and the situation was made for him much worse when his ideal of Germany was contradicted by the behavior of Hitler and the Nazis, of whom Mencken had never approved but of whom he had always predicted that the Germans would soon get rid.

This memoir by Sara Mayfield is well done and a valuable document. It is a good thing that someone has survived to write it. (I must protest at a small point, however. A story has persisted from volume to volume—I find it also in Manchester and elsewhere—that "with the diary [Zelda's] in hand, Scott [Fitzgerald], Edmund Wilson, and John Peale Bishop besieged Nathan in his apartment in the Royalton until he finally invited them in to have a drink." As for my own part in this alleged exploit, I never saw Zelda's diary,

I barely knew George Nathan—at that time I had not even met him—except in connection with some articles that he wrote for *Vanity Fair*, and I was never in his apartment in the Royalton. I do not think it at all likely that he would allow himself to be "besieged"—he was a pernickety and snubbing little man—or to behave in the expansive way that, in another version of this story, he is made to. Now that I am old enough to see biographies of people I remember and descriptions of occurrences that I knew at first hand, I have come more and more to distrust the statements found in writings on literary figures on which the authors have been unable to check. I have even been inaccurate myself—as I have found on consulting my journals—in my memoirs of old friends. Did Trelawny tell the truth about Byron and Shelley? Was Edmund Gosse reliable about Swinburne? Later investigators say definitely not.)

When Mencken died in 1956, after his years of disablement and silence, he was cheerfully looking forward to the publication of a book which he had got together before his stroke and later, after his stroke, forgotten till it was found by his secretary. This was *Minority Report: H. L. Mencken's Notebooks*, published in the year of his death. It is a scattering of reflections on all sorts of subjects tossed off in the course of years. "It will be nice to be denounced again," Miss Mayfield reports him as saying. In spite of my great admiration for Mencken, which is usually revived when I reread him, this book, when first I read it, rather repelled me. Here you have to take account inescapably of his habitual confusion in thinking and his dogmatic German brutality. In a note, at the end of the volume, on the development of his own style, he declares that "the chief character of my style . . . is that I write with almost scientific precision—that my meaning is never obscure." It is true that *Minority Report* is written in plain enough English, with little Menckenian embroidery, but the statements in the methodically numbered paragraphs do not always hang together, and since they are rendered clearer than usual by the simplicity with which they are put, we are relatively little distracted by the writer's tremendous entertainment value. On one page, he is recommending that, although the Pure Food and Drug Act is "falling into the hands of uplifter-bureaucrats" and "bound to become arbitrary and oppressive," it is "sound in principle" and should require "that everything for human ingestion that is offered for sale should show a label indicating its ingredients." On another, he lays it down that "No one ever heard of the truth being enforced by law. Whenever the secular arm is called in to sustain an idea, whether new or old, it is always a bad idea, and not infrequently it is downright idiotic." He is always demanding freedom, but he regards as "one of the most irrational of all the conventions of modern society . . . the one to the effect that religious opinions should be respected." This convention protects the theologians, with whom one would first have to deal (what does this mean? Aren't all religious opinions theological?), "so they proceed with their blather unwhipped and almost unmolested, to the great damage of common sense and common decency. That they should have this immunity is an outrage." Should religious opinions not acceptable to Mencken therefore be whipped and molested—that is, should they be suppressed? What else can you do about them? After all, one is not forced to accept them. "If all the farmers in the Dust Bowl were shot tomorrow, and all the share-croppers in the South burned at the stake, every decent American would be better off, and not a soul would miss a meal." Note the use of "decency" and "decent" in the last two of these quotations. One may admit that it is uncomfortable to hear about the poor and that any great solicitude about human life, except where oneself is concerned, has lately gone by the board, if it ever widely existed. But will decent people really be gratified and "better off" at hearing about other people being burned at the stake?

Mencken's attempt to stave off such criticisms as this is to be found in item 429, where he argues against his critics: "If you were against the New Deal and its wholesale buying of pauper votes, then you were against Christian charity [which Mencken often told us he was]. If you were against the gross injustices and dishonesties of the Wagner Labor Act, then you were against labor [which Mencken very often was]. If you were against packing the Supreme Court, then you were in favor of letting Wall Street do it. If you are against Dr. Quack's cancer salve, then you are in favor of letting Uncle Julius die [Uncle Julius is evidently a German]. If you are against Holy Church, or Christian Science, then you are against God [the whole idea of a Divinity has been discredited on another page]."

These paragraphs, then, after all, are not so very much different from the jottings in the "Répétition Générale" in the pages of the old *Smart Set*. But these contradictions are so obvious that they have never really mattered. We never expected coherence of Mencken. He was a poet in prose and a humorist, and in his time, in certain departments, one of the bringers of light to "the Republic."

May 31, 1969

THE CONSTANT CIRCLE

$\mathcal{B}$ALTIMORE DAYS

As HE MOUNTED THE ROSTRUM in Goucher Hall one evening in the spring of 1923, H. L. Mencken was as innocent of any vernal impulse as I was of acting as a catalyst in the matrimonial liquidation of the most vociferous bachelor in America. The week before, in advising me that I had won the Freshman Short Story Contest, my English instructor at Goucher College, Harry T. Baker, had announced, "My old friend Henry Mencken, who is to make the award, has asked us to go to supper with him later in the evening."

But, having stammered my thanks, I added on second thought, "I'm afraid the dean would faint if I asked permission to go out with Mr. Mencken." For, in the cloisters of Goucher, the literary achievements of *The Smart Set*'s editor had been eclipsed by his antics as the Bad Boy of Baltimore. Had he not excoriated the Sacred South as "The Sahara of the Bozart," persuaded Alfred Stieglitz to entitle a photograph of a horse's posterior "Spiritual America," and collaborated with George Jean Nathan on *Heliogabalus,* said to be the most scandalous play ever written? To the Baltimoralists, as he called them, particularly the academic contingent, Mencken was a roistering, Rabelaisian critic, who lambasted the charlatanry of the learned and delighted in calling pedagogues "fools" and "jackasses" and describing their mentality—or lack of it—in terms that undoubtedly curdled the blue blood of Dorothy Stimson, dean of Goucher.

"You'll have to have a chaperone," Mr. Baker conceded. "Suppose you go talk it over with your faculty adviser."

It would be wiser to consult with Sara Haardt first, I decided, as I charged up Charles Street to her room. For she had taught me in prep

1

school in Montgomery, Alabama, before she became instructor in English at Goucher, and she was nearer my age and point of view than my faculty adviser.

"Why certainly you'll go, goose!" Sara said. "Wear some of your Paris clothes and bowl Mr. Mencken over."

The idea of a freshman just turned seventeen captivating a middle-aged iconoclast, the literary lion of the time, hailed as a new Juvenal, another Dryden, the Voltaire of America, evoked an uneasy laugh from me. "I wouldn't know what to say to an editor if I met one. Besides, I'd have to have permission and a chaperone—not that I'd need one with a critic that probably has gray whiskers and walks with a cane, but you know this place."

"They'll doubtless imagine he intends to stick a hypodermic needle in your arm and make off with you." It was Sara's time to laugh. "But don't worry. Emily Clark, the editor of *The Reviewer*, says he's a very nice, amusing man."

"Since you're so intrepid, suppose you come along and chaperone," I suggested.

"Wait," she hedged, "until I talk to Dean Stimson and see what she says."

Sara could charm the birds out of the trees when she tried, and by dinnertime she had cajoled the dean into giving me permission to go to supper with Mr. Mencken and Mr. Baker, provided that Sara agreed to act as chaperone. Overawed by the prospect of an evening with so erudite a critic, and in a quandary as to what to say to him, I set off to the library to learn all I could about him.

Forewarned and forearmed with the results of the research on the life and works of H. L. Mencken, I was prepared to beard the lion, though not without some trepidation. On the evening of the award, dressed to the nines and hoping that an urbane exterior would conceal the butterflies underneath it, I slipped into a seat beside Sara in Goucher Hall. Promptly on the stroke of eight, Mr. Baker appeared with the lion in tow.

At forty-two, Henry Mencken looked no more like the Bad Boy of Baltimore than the gray-bearded pundit I had imagined him to be. His neat blue serge suit, stiff collar, and hightop shoes gave him the appearance of a professor from Johns Hopkins rather than a high-flying, hardhitting idol smasher. He was five feet eight inches tall, stocky and broad in the beam, with a large leonine head. His blond hair was parted a little left of center; his cowlicks were carefully slicked down. But his eyebrows were bushy, untamed, and singularly expressive. He had a large, ruddy button of a nose, a firm, well-shaped mouth, and round china-blue eyes that brimmed with amusement as he surveyed the audience that he was to address.

After a brief introduction, Mr. Mencken strode to the lectern and looked over the top of his horn-rimmed glasses at the assembly—"two hundred and fifty virgins," according to the charitable estimate he later made. As he took his notes from his coat pocket, his eyes rested on Sara Haardt. When Sara graduated from Goucher, she was described in its yearbook as a "soulful highbrow." She was tall, slender, and willowy, with something of both the *femme savante* and the *femme fatale* about her—a strikingly beautiful woman as well as a charming and intelligent one. She had a fine head, regular, rounded features, and slender, sensitive hands. Her hair was like burnished bronze, curly and crinkled with gold highlights; her eyes were very large and of a soft deep brown; her skin was as fair as the petals of a white japonica. There was both a fragility and a subtle power in her beauty, and it caught and held Mencken's eye.

He abruptly stuck his notes on "The Trade of Letters" back in his pocket and launched into a lecture on "How to Catch a Husband." In women's colleges, he pointed out, the longing for a career was now epidemic and even the yearning for service had begun to make progress, but under both those aspirations there still lingered the immemorial desire to catch a handsome and a solvent husband. He made short shrift of careers for women, particularly in journalism, which he said was no trade for a lady. Marriage was the only safe and secure haven for a Christian girl. A woman should find a suitable husband, preferably a banker or broker. Babbitts were more easily domesticated than movie actors or college professors. Take a tip from the Canadian Mounted Police: Get your man.

This was puzzling advice from a rock-ribbed bachelor—and doubly puzzling because he omitted specific instructions as to how to accomplish such a feat. Once a woman made up her mind to marry a man, he argued, the sucker was as good as hooked. For the moment, he forgot that he had once advocated a dollar-a-day tax upon bachelors, on the ground that it was worth that much to be free, and remembered only his *obiter dictum* that the allurement that women hold out to men "is precisely the allurement that Cape Hatteras holds out to sailors; they are enormously dangerous hence enormously fascinating." If they were taken away, a man's existence would become as flat and secure as a milch cow's. "The most disgusting cad in the world," he added, "is the man who, on the grounds of decorum and morality, avoids the game of love."

But for all his bold words, Mr. Mencken was himself wary and cautious. Having made his opening gambit and, inadvertently or not, fired the first shot in a romantic campaign that he was to wage for the next seven years, Mr. Mencken awarded me the prize, a twenty-dollar gold piece, and quickly extricated himself from the Goucher girls who crowded around him. "Shall we go?" he said, taking my arm and steering me down Charles Street, leaving Sara and Mr. Baker to follow us. He walked briskly, with his toes turned in and his legs slightly bowed, setting a pace that made it difficult for them to keep up with him.

As we waited on the corner for a cab, I asked, "What's your advice to a young writer, Mr. Mencken?"

He looked down at me with amusement in his eyes. "Wait until you're old enough to know something to write about," he replied. Then, reaching over, he turned my coat collar up against a raw wind whipping off the Chesapeake and added gently, "And wear warm clothes so you'll live to do it."

With a wave, he flagged a taxi and handed us into it. "I bought a car once," he explained to Sara. "It was almost a fatal experience. Besides, it was expensive and a nuisance. So I sold it. I find I save time and money by using taxis."

Before we were well on our way to his favorite *kaif*, the Schellhase Palazzo, it was clear that Mr. Mencken was trying to angle Sara into casting a line his way. He ushered us into the restaurant, ordered a round of Pilsner, and with the grin of a small boy showing off before his girl, opened his throat and downed a stein of it in a single gulp. Thus primed, his conversation sparkled. He described George Jean Nathan's technique for handling importunate actresses, Mrs. Pat Campbell's affair with Bernard Shaw, and the strange friendship of Lawrence of Arabia with Mrs. Shaw—a rich spinster, he added slyly, who captured G.B.S. when he was slowed down by a lame foot. As Mr. Mencken talked—and coruscated—over his cracked crabs and beer,

Sara listened with the rapt attention she reserved for those marked for conquest.

Once, when he paused to light an "Uncle Willie," his favorite brand of cigars, I edged in an ingenuous question. "Mr. Mencken, what do authors talk to editors about?"

"Money," he grinned, amused at the naïve query. He sat back and rolled his cigar from one corner of his mouth to the other as he studied Sara and me, half smiling, one brow lifted, his eyes popping in an expression of fascinated incredulity. "Imagine finding a pair of lovelies at Goucher!" he said. "I'd always thought that higher education muddied a woman's complexion."

Then, turning to Sara, he tried a new gambit. "Come to think of it, Miss Haardt, didn't you send me a story for *The Smart Set* once?"

"Yes, and you read it very promptly." Sara was unfailingly diplomatic and skilled in the soft compliment.

"As I recall, I found it most impressive. Unfortunately, it didn't fit our needs just then. Send me some more stories and mark them for my personal attention. Keep at it! All young writers have to collect enough rejection slips to paper a room before they learn to write. Scott Fitzgerald told me that he once had a hundred and fifty of them pasted up in a frieze around his room. I accumulated a wheelbarrow load of them myself. I shiver to think of the hack work I did before I hit my stride— covering the police court, writing medical articles, even ghosting a book on *What You Ought to Know About Your Baby*."

Whatever Mr. Mencken may or may not have known about bringing up babies, that evening was the beginning of long years of experience in the care and feeding of young girls. He was a most considerate host and interrupted himself frequently to see that we were supplied with food, drink, and cigarettes.

After the waitress brought another round of beer, he said, "I suppose you girls knew Zelda Fitzgerald in Montgomery."

"Yes," Sara replied. "We grew up with her."

"What a girl! Cleverer than Scott, if the truth were known. I've no doubt but that she startled the booboisie in the Bible Belt. She and Scott have acquired a Babbitt's *palazzo* in Great Neck, Long Island, and a secondhand Rolls-Royce. I see them now and then in New York with Nathan."

"How did you like *The Beautiful and Damned*?" Sara inquired.

"Better than *This Side of Paradise*. There was a good deal of Scott and Zelda in Anthony and Gloria and more of Nathan in Maury Noble. Scott's jealous of Nathan's devotion to Zelda, I think. He went on an epic bender not long ago and quarreled with George. An odd fellow, Scott—erratic and undisciplined—but he writes well," he added.

"Indeed he does," Sara agreed, "as long as Zelda supplies the copy."

"Joe Hergesheimer told me that when Zelda's baby was born, Scott stood by, pencil in hand, taking notes. By the way, Joe's coming down here soon and you must be sure to meet him. A charming fellow. Scott's inclined to make light of Joe. He calls him 'the best people's best novelist' because Joe's gotten rich writing and lives in West Chester like a Pennsylvania satrap. When Fitzgerald told me that he himself had made and spent thirty-six thousand dollars last year, I called him Mr. Fitzheimer; and I think he's still miffed with me about it."

"I hear that Scott said that, like Aristides, you would soon be exiled because people would grow tired of hearing your praises sung." Sara's smile transformed Fitzgerald's quip into a compliment. She was charming in her softness, in the delicate line of her profile and the richness of her coloring. Under her reserve, there was a playfulness, a piquancy of expression, a flash of ironic humor that appealed to Mr. Mencken.

They chatted on of this and that—Mencken with wit and penetration, Sara with smooth assents and wide, admiring eyes. And so the evening passed with Pilsner and polite conversation, with no disturbance of the peace, no idols smashed, and no levantine dissipations. At eleven-thirty, Mr. Baker pushed back his chair. "This is pleasant indeed," he said, "but we have to get Cinderella back to the dormitory before twelve."

"Then we'll adjourn till next time." Mencken paid the check and clapped on his fedora. Mr. Baker took Sara home; and, despite my protest that they could escort me to the dormitory, Mr. Mencken insisted on doing it.

When I thanked him for his kindness, he said, as he left me at the door, "We must do this again soon." He lifted his hat—straight up from his head as only gentlemen in the South still do. "I'll drop you a line. Good night."

Instead of going to my room, I slipped in to give a classmate a glowing account of the supper at the Schellhase. I reported that Sara and I had discovered, as many young writers have before and since, that H. L. Mencken was one of the kindliest, most courteous of men.

The editor of the Goucher *Weekly* asked me to do a piece for it on Mr. Mencken, and I consulted a young reporter who, since he came from a family of newspapermen and worked with Mr. Mencken on the Baltimore *Sunpapers,* was certain to have some interesting sidelights on him. I might as well have asked James Boswell about Samuel Johnson.

"The Menck is the greatest guy in the world," he declared. "Ask any newsman who knows him. When I went to see him about getting a job on the *Sun,* he was so damn polite you'd have thought he was running for office. 'Well, what kind of work do you do, young man?' he asked.

"When I told him I wanted to write editorials, he didn't even laugh. He just rolled his cigar from one side of his mouth to the other and said, 'Good, but editorial writers have to begin as reporters. Now, fill me in on your education and experience.' Where people get the idea that he's a fire-eating ogre, I don't know."

"Why don't you write an editorial, 'In Defense of Mencken,'" I suggested.

"Well, I would, but I'm still confined to reporting the doings of the police court," he confessed.

In the course of further inquiry at the Goucher library, I found that Henry Louis Mencken was a native Baltimorean, born on the south side of Lexington Street, near Fremont, in 1880—on September 12, which is Old Defender's Day, a Maryland festival commemorating the defeat of the British in 1814 at North Point. He was the eldest son of August Mencken, Sr., and Anna Margaret Abhau, the daughter of a master cabinetmaker who, like Henry's grandfather, Burkhardt Mencken, had emigrated from Germany to Baltimore in 1848. Anna Abhau came of German and Scotch-Irish stock; August Mencken, from a distinguished Saxon family of scholars, philosophers and lawyers. Although Henry once boasted to Theodore Dreiser that he too was part peasant, his German ancestry was predominantly Junker. Through his grandfather, Burkhardt Mencken, he was related to the Bismarcks, and one of the most profound influences of his youth derived from the

achievements of a distant cousin, Otto von Bismarck, the Iron Chancellor.

Burkhardt, who had served his apprenticeship to a cigarmaker in
Saxony, began life in Baltimore, as his grandson Henry Louis was to
do, at a tobacco bench, rolling cigars. August Mencken, Henry's father,
was, like Burkhardt, a freethinker, an arch-conservative, and a hard-
headed businessman. In his photographs, he appears as a prosperous
merchant, handsome, well built, well dressed, wearing a derby, a
heavy gold watch chain with a Shriner's emblem, and a virile brush
mustache. After serving an apprenticeship at Burkhardt's tobacco bench,
August struck out for himself and founded his own cigar business, "Aug.
Mencken and Bro." The firm, fragrant cigars turned out at 368 West
Baltimore Street were labeled with the coat of arms of the scholarly
Menckenii, which he had copyrighted as a trademark and which Henry
Louis later appropriated and had stamped on the covers of his books.

After the birth of Charlie, Henry's brother and his junior by twenty
months, August Mencken bought a three-story red brick house with
an elegant fanlight, a white stone stoop, and a walled garden behind it,
on Hollins Street, opposite Union Square. Henry and his family moved
there when he was three years old, and when I met him he was still
living there with his mother, his sister Gertrude, and his brother Charlie
and August, Jr. Of his home at 1524 Hollins Street, Mencken said:

> I have lived in one house for forty years. It has changed in that time
> as I have—but somehow it still remains the same. No conceivable deco-
> rator's masterpiece could give me the same ease. It is as much a part
> of me as my two hands. If I had to leave it I'd be as certainly crippled
> as if I had lost both legs.

Henry's childhood there, of which he was to write so vividly in
Happy Days, was one long boisterous adventure. At that time, by his
account, he was "a larva of the comfortable and complacent bour-
geoisie," who was "encapsulated in affection and kept fat, saucy and
contented. Thus," he added, "I got through my nonage without acquiring an inferiority complex." Two days before his sixth birthday, he was
put aboard a horsecar and delivered into the hands of Professor
Knapp. He spent his grammar school days at F. Knapp's Institute,
where he earned excellent marks in English and drawing but, curiously
enough, not in German, though his letters to his parents, written iu
that language, are models of composition, as well as filial piety.

Despite a lack of manual dexterity, so marked that he never mastered the mechanics of tying a bow tie, even under George Jean Nathan's expert tutelage, he learned to play the piano and handle drafting instruments. Since he was slightly color-blind, painting never attracted him, nor did he ever evince any great interest in the visual and plastic arts. However, at Knapp's Institute he did develop a consuming interest in anatomy and physiology. Chemistry and photography also attracted him; but his deepest love was for music, and after a brief period of instruction from his father's bookkeeper, he began to perform in public and to compose waltzes.

Although his father was a self-styled agnostic and his mother only conventionally religious, Henry was sent to a Methodist Sunday school at an early age and was later confirmed in the Lutheran Church. Convinced that in addition to his religious and intellectual education Henry needed physical training to cure his scholarly stoop and make "a kind of grenadier" of him, his father sent him to the YMCA. But all that the rings, trapezes, and stuffed horses accomplished, Mencken remembered, "was to fill me with an ineradicable distaste not only for Christian endeavor in all its forms but also for every variety of calisthenics."

At the age of eight, he claimed to have "bloodied" his first book. As a Christmas present in 1888, he demanded a toy printing press. When it came, he found that all the lowercase *r*'s of the type were smashed. Therefore he was forced to discard his first name in favor of his initials. "Other presents came and went," he once said, "but there was never another that fetched and floored me like 'Dorman's No. 10 Self-Inker Printing Press' "—the little set that gave him his first whiff of printer's ink and his famous signature, H. L. Mencken.

From Knapp's, Henry entered the Baltimore Polytechnic Institute. After his graduation from the Polytechnic, he was put to work in his father's factory, rolling cigars and studying Spanish to prepare him for handling the Cuban affairs of the firm. From his father he had inherited a taste for Havana tobacco, St. Louis beer, and Moselle wine. He had also derived from his father a sturdy, independent skepticism and a strict honesty in intellectual as well as financial affairs. His father, he said, divided all mankind "into two great races: those who paid their bills and those who didn't."

Henry's adventures with Dorman's No. 10 Self-Inker had led him to prefer the smell of printer's ink to that of Havana leaf and the copy desk to the cigar bench. He took a correspondence course in writing and began to write both poetry and prose in his spare time. But in obedience to his father's wishes he continued to work at the tobacco bench until the death of August, Sr., on January 13, 1899. As the eldest son, Henry then became head of the house. His first act on returning from the cemetery was to take down a crayon portrait of his father, a bad likeness done by a "saloon artist," by which he did not want his father remembered, and burn it in the back yard. The following Monday, he dressed himself in his best suit, looped an Ascot tie about his high, stiff collar, and trudged through the rain to the offices of the Baltimore *Morning Herald* to apply for a job as reporter.

Max Ways, the city editor of the *Herald*, pushed up his green eye-shade and asked Mencken to fill him in on his experience—but, alas, he had none. Mr. Ways had no openings for inexperienced cubs at the moment. However, he suggested that Henry stop by to see him again. For a month Mencken haunted the *Herald* office. Finally, one bitter, snowy night, to be rid of him, Mr. Ways sent him out in the country to find one of the *Herald*'s stringers, who had not been heard from for six days. Toward morning, Henry made his way back through the blizzard with his first news story, a brief item about the capture of a horse-thief. Having acquired "experience," he was put to work on the *Herald* and given a salary of eight dollars a week.

Finding himself with a press card, "at large in a wicked seaport of half a million people, with a front seat at every public show, as free of the night as of the day," the eighteen-year-old Mencken absorbed "earfuls and eyefuls of instruction in a hundred giddy arcana." At the turn of the century a newspaper reporter in Baltimore had a gay and gaudy time of it. It was, as he looked back on it some forty years later, "the maddest, gladdest damnedest existence ever enjoyed by mortal youth."

Although he soon discovered that the public position of a reporter in those days was slightly above that of a streetwalker but considerably below that of a police captain, Mencken was irrevocably committed to the fourth estate. Fortunately, he was not dependent upon his meager earnings from the *Herald*. For, he explained, he belonged to an "inferior subclass of the order of capitalists." He was not rich but his ease and comfort depended upon the scarcity of wealth. Hence he was admittedly a shameless "admirer of the Constitution of the United States in its original form" and "a Tory in politics" to the end of his life.

An independent income, however, did not prevent him from trying to supplement his earnings by writing short stories, verse, and advertising pamphlets. He also began a novel on Shakespeare but abandoned it when he found that he knew too little about the background of the period. After steeping himself in Elizabethan stage lore, he attempted to do a play, the scene of which was laid in the Globe Theatre on July 16, 1601, the opening night of Hamlet. But again he found that he knew too little, and he also abandoned the play.

In 1903, when three of Mencken's friends founded the Illustro-Press, they came to him for suggestions. "I naturally suggested a book of my own compositions," he said. "They preferred verse to prose, and so verse it was." There was a certain tradition of poetry in the family, as Mencken explained many years later in a letter: "Since 1556, when the Menckenii were converted to Christianity, the family has produced no less than nine head of poets. All were bad."

With the appearance of *Ventures into Verse*, Mencken became the tenth poet of his tribe. Many of the poems included in it, written under the influence of Kipling and Austin Dobson, dated from his teens. The majority of them had already been published in the *Herald*, *The Bookman*, and *The Smart Set* before he incorporated them in the slender volume of verse. A hundred copies of the poems were printed. Since Mencken had paid either thirty dollars or sixty dollars—accounts differ—toward the cost of publishing the book, he took half the copies and the owners of the press took half. Mencken kept only a few of his fifty copies. The rest he distributed among his newspaper friends. For *Ventures into Verse* was not intended to sell, but to show off the work of the Illustro-Press and secure more work of that kind for it. When Mencken first saw the little book, bound in boards with a red spine, as he noted years later in a copy belonging to a Washington lawyer and bibliophile, Frank J. Hogan, "I damn nigh bust with delight."

But before the book was issued, Mencken had stopped writing verse. Had he felt inclined to continue versifying, the reviews were encouraging. However, although it was widely noted, and in some quarters highly praised, the only purchaser was a bookseller in Portland, Maine, who ordered two copies—the total sales of Mencken's first book.

The year after the publication of *Ventures into Verse*, Mencken won his journalistic spurs by getting out an edition of the *Herald* in Washington after its Baltimore plant had been demolished by the Great Fire of 1904. A few months later, he called on Theodore Dreiser, then editor of Butterick Publications, to discuss a series of articles that a Baltimore doctor had employed the young journalist to ghost for him. Mencken was to say of Dreiser's second novel, *Jennie Gerhardt,* "It is an accurate picture of life and a searching criticism of life, and that is my definition of a good novel." He further credited the novelist with "having lifted the obvious to the inexplicable." But he added that Dreiser was "a genius who doesn't know how to write or when to stop." Dreiser's first estimate of Mencken was even less flattering:

> There appeared in my office a snub-nosed youth of twenty-eight or nine whose brisk gait and ingratiating smile proved at once enormously intriguing and amusing. I had, for some reason not connected with his basic mentality, you may be sure, the sense of a small town roisterer or a college sophomore of the crudest yet most disturbing charm and impishness who, for some reason had strayed into the field of letters. More than anything else, he reminded me of a spoiled and petted and possibly over-financed brewer's or wholesale grocer's son who was out for a lark. . . . "Well, well," I said, "if it isn't Anheuser's own brightest boy out to see the town."

By this time, "Anheuser's own brightest boy" had become something of a prodigy in the publishing field. He had been made city editor of the Baltimore *Morning Herald* at twenty-three; two years later, he was promoted to editor of the *Evening News.* After its failure, he landed a job as Sunday editor of the Baltimore *Sun* on July 30, 1906, at a salary of forty dollars a week. His articles and short stories had appeared in half a dozen popular magazines of the day. He had also published *The Philosophy of Friedrich Nietzsche* and written an introduction to Ibsen's *Little Eyolf* and *A Doll's House.*

Early in his newspaper career, to alleviate the dismal round of a police-court reporter's duties, Mencken had wandered into the Enoch Pratt Free Library, a favorite resort, which he had frequented ever since he was five years old. There he stumbled on a learned publication called *Dialect Notes,* through which he discovered a hobby that was to set him on the road to his monumental *The American Language.* With his ear cocked to the speech ways of Baltimore, he began to study common parlance there.

Shortly after his visit to Dreiser, Mencken and George Jean Nathan were asked to join the staff of *The Smart Set,* which, Henry reported, had refused more than forty pieces of his poetry before offering him the job of literary editor "with the rank and pay of a sergeant of artillery." On a trip to New York to discuss the terms further, Mencken met the man who was to become his "local Laertes" there, George Jean Nathan, a handsome, dapper boulevardier, who was then drama critic for *Harper's* and *The Bookman*. His first impression of Nathan was that he looked exactly like "a West Indian doorman." Never were two men outwardly so different to form such a fast friendship. Nathan was slight, dark-haired, dark-eyed, swarthy, and Semitic; Mencken was stocky, blond, blue-eyed, ruddy, and Nordic. Henry was two years older than George. Nathan had graduated from Cornell, where he had been a member of Kappa Sigma, the Quill and Dagger, and the Masque, had won a fencing championship, and had edited the Cornell *Widow*. After taking his degree there, he had attended the University of Bologna and traveled extensively abroad. Mencken had never gone to college, nor had he yet made his maiden trip to Europe.

At first their only common ground appeared to be the baseball diamond. Mencken's father had once owned an interest in the Washington ball club; Nathan's father had owned an interest in the Fort Wayne, Indiana, team. But over a cocktail together the two young critics soon discovered that they shared a deep aversion to uplifters, politicians, civic-minded numbskulls, and flatulent educators, as well as an ardent admiration for Ibsen, Dreiser, Ambrose Bierce, and Mark Twain. After they launched on an editorial partnership at *The Smart Set*, their firm was known as "Mencken, Nathan, & God."

Eventually, without the help of the Deity, they worked out an arrangement by which Mencken, who resisted all efforts to lure him to New York, could carry on his duties on *The Smart Set* from Baltimore. Nathan gave the manuscripts sent to *The Smart Set*'s Manhattan offices a first reading there, winnowed out the worst of them, and forwarded the rest of them to 1524 Hollins Street in Baltimore. Mencken had grumbled at having to make three trips a month to New York, "that third-rate Babylon," and remained firmly anchored on the shores of "that immense protein factory of Chesapeake Bay," where he could indulge his taste for crabs, shrimp, and oysters.

Human relationships in Baltimore, he maintained, tended to assume a solid permanence. There the friends of today remained the friends of tomorrow. His circle of friends in his home town had become "a sort of extension of his family circle." His contacts were with people who were rooted as he was. They were not continually moving from one place to another and so were not always changing their friends. In such a constant circle of friends, he said, "abiding relationships tend to be built up, and when fortune brings unexpected changes they survive those changes."

Being as averse to the clique as he was to the cliché, Mencken avoided literary cliques in Baltimore. Many of his friends were on the Johns Hopkins University faculty. One crony, Willie Woollcott, was a prosperous glue manufacturer; his wit excelled that of his brother Alexander. Most of the *Sunpapers'* staff were Mencken's personal friends as well as his business associates. But to him, in the early days, the constant circle revolved around the members of the Floristan Club, an association of gourmets, and the amateur musicians of the Saturday Night Club.

The Saturday Night Club grew out of a trio composed of Sam Hamburger, violinist, Al Hildebrandt, cellist, and H. L. Mencken, pianist and virtuoso of the loud pedal. Before Prohibition, the club met in a back room over Hildebrandt's music shop. After the concert, its members dined together at Miller's Restaurant, frequently on its famous "cannibal plate"—a mixture of raw eggs and raw beef, seasoned with Mencken's accounts of how the choicest morsels in it had been obtained through the courtesy of a friend of his, a surgeon in the dissecting room at Johns Hopkins. After the passage of the Volstead Act, however, the club was forced to meet at the homes of its members and to depend upon Henry as *Braumeister*. As a result, it was reported that anyone who entered his cellar at 1524 Hollins Street risked bombardments of broken glass from exploding bottles.

Before Major Ambrose Bierce, "our one genuine wit," as Henry once called him, disappeared into Mexico, he frequently came to Baltimore to drink beer at 1524 Hollins Street. "Bitter Bierce's" disgust with modern America and its democratic politicos was exceeded only by his contempt for "yokels" and "louts." To Bierce all reformers were "anarchists" and all farmers "peasants"; and from him Mencken derived many of his aristocratic prejudices.

On his trips to New York, Henry usually spent his evenings with Nathan, Willard Huntington Wright (better known as S. S. Van Dine, the creator of the Philo Vance detective stories, whom Mencken had lured to *The Smart Set* as assistant editor), and John Williams, a theatrical producer. Through Williams, H.L. met Philip Goodman, an advertising man who occasionally produced plays. At the time, persuaded that he could make a fortune by selling books through drug stores, Goodman nourished the ambition of becoming a publisher. As Mencken and Nathan were dissatisfied with the John Lane Company, which then printed their books, Goodman's scheme appealed to them. Eventually, after a hearty lunch at the old Hofbrau House on Broadway, they both agreed to let Goodman take over the publication of their books.

At lunch, Goodman, a Gargantuan eater, had wolfed down a huge steak with all the trimmings, topped off with four or five of the sandwiches sold for a nickel each at the Hofbrau bar in lieu of free lunch. He not only had the enormous paunch but the bawdy wit of Falstaff. Both he and Mencken enjoyed good food, good drink, and a good story. For many years they corresponded constantly, spicing their letters with some of the most pungent Rabelaisian humor ever penned.

During the early *Smart Set* days, Goodman and James Gibbons Huneker were Mencken's favorite companions at Lüchow's in New York. To H.L., Huneker was the most colorful and charming of the New York literati. He later remembered the old man's talk as a veritable debauch of "sly and stimulating scandal," overflowing with fantastic anecdotes, usually apocryphal but always amusing—the last authentic words of Walt Whitman, the topography of Liszt's innumerable warts and wens, the secret of Zola's asphyxiation, the truth about Tschaikowsky's suicide, the talents and virtuosity of Lillian Russell's husbands and lovers—conversation that "made his books seem almost funereal." Rabelais was a lady missionary in comparison, but there was always a colossal wit in his ribald anecdotes. Mencken planned to publish the old man's bawdy letters—after the Comstocks were safely lynched.

For his part, Huneker was one of Mencken's most exuberant admirers and enthusiastic press agents. The best beer comes from Bohemia, he announced, the best prose from Paris, the best poets from England. "But the best fried oysters and terrapin and literary critic—from Baltimore! By God!" In urging Mencken to accept a sinecure with the Munsey newspapers for which he had recommended him, Huneker said, "You owe it to your country. You are the big critical center now. You should have a wider audience—though the Lord knows you can't sneeze in Baltimore without rattling the window panes in Chicago."

Joseph Hergesheimer's friendship with Mencken began when H.L. reviewed the novelist's first book, *The Lay Anthony,* in the December 1914 issue of *Smart Set* and wrote him that he hoped they might meet soon. After some correspondence, Hergesheimer came to Baltimore to see him, and they took a ride in a Studebaker that Mencken had just bought. "It was," Hergesheimer said, "the damnedest ride any man ever survived." Henry was talking fast and driving faster, gesticulating with both hands and looking at everything but the road. Once he had started the car, he seemed to feel that he had no further responsibility for its conduct; it lurched and skidded along with the curtains flapping while its driver talked to Hergesheimer, frequently letting go of the wheel to make a forceful gesture in emphasizing a point. The car careened from one side of the road to another, veered off into a field, spun around, and miraculously regained the pavement, where it missed an oncoming truck by a fraction of an inch, caromed into a telephone pole, and, blessedly, came to a full stop. Hergesheimer always maintained that the ride was the most terrifying experience of his life—wars, riots, and revolutions not excepted.

If Hergesheimer liked to tease Henry about his car and his driving, Mencken delighted in ribbing Joseph about his clothes and his opulent way of life. Upon one occasion, he reported that the novelist had passed through Richmond wearing an eight-hundred-dollar leopardskin chasuble; on another that he had met him in the Algonquin "sporting a plug hat that cost sixty bucks" and that had a music box inside it that played *"Gott erhalte Franz den Kaiser."* Even more far-fetched were Henry's accounts of Joseph's trip to the West Coast in 1922. He alleged that Hergesheimer was robbed of his diamond-mounted toothpick in Seattle; poisoned by wood alcohol in Portland; won seventeen dollars shooting craps in San Francisco, which he squandered on a hand-painted silk shirt; and had a roaring time in Los Angeles, where he drank forty cocktails in forty hours.

A frequent recipient of Mencken's fables about Hergesheimer—and vice versa—was the Irish critic Ernest Boyd, whom H.L. had first met while the Irishman was British vice-consul in Baltimore. Boyd had married Madeleine Reynier, a dark-haired, vivacious French woman, whom he had met while she was teaching at Trinity College, Dublin. Mencken was impressed with her cleverness, and he and she formed a friendship that outlasted her marriage to Boyd. When the Vagabond

Players were founded in an empty grocery store in Baltimore, Madeleine, who was on the board of directors, persuaded them to open with a "first," a satirical play, *The Artist*, which had been published in Dreiser's defunct *Bohemian* magazine and written by a famous Baltimorean, H. L. Mencken.

In preparation for the opening, the Vagabond Players decided to spruce up their makeshift theater by varnishing the seats. When Mencken arrived to watch the dress rehearsal, he had dressed for the occasion by putting on a starched shirt and his new pin-striped suit. The manager ushered the author of the play toward a newly varnished bench. Mencken thanked him and took a seat. A moment later, feeling something wet and sticky seeping through the seat of his pants, he let out a howl. When he tried to rise, he found himself firmly glued to the bench. After the rehearsal, having extricated the seat of his trousers from the seat of the theater by a series of contortions, he assured the Vagabond Players of his good will but did not show up for the opening the next evening. But, as evidence of his continued support, he forwarded all the suitable dramatic scripts that came into the *Smart Set* offices to the directors of the theater and offered them his own *Heliogabalus*—a play "full of Maeterlinckian subtleties," in which the setting for one of the scenes was a bed that held thirteen people.

The Smart Set was subtitled "A Magazine of Cleverness." Both Mencken and Nathan had the ability to recognize talent when they saw it, and after they were put in complete editorial control of the magazine, under their policy of encouraging new authors and promptly replying to contributors, *The Smart Set* was flooded with plays, verse, and stories. James Branch Cabell, part of whose *Jurgen* was published serially in *The Smart Set*, also appeared in its pages for the first time as a dramatist. Lord Dunsany and Eugene O'Neill both contributed plays to it. Dreiser, Edgar Lee Masters, Maxwell Anderson, Sara Teasdale, and Lizette Woodworth Reese all wrote poems for it. Mencken and Nathan also published some of the early stories of Thomas Beer, Sherwood Anderson, Ben Hecht, Ruth Suckow, F. Scott Fitzgerald, and Edna St. Vincent Millay, whose first story, "Barbara at the Beach," appeared in the November 1914 issue.

At Ernest Boyd's instance, the editors of *The Smart Set* introduced the short stories of another noted Irishman to the American public;

James Joyce's "The Boarding House" and "A Little Cloud," his first publications in this country, were printed in *The Smart Set* in 1915. Joyce afterward claimed that he was never paid for them, but his assertion appears to be untrue in view of the unimpeachable honesty of the magazine's editors as well as the existence of a letter from Mencken to Joyce of July 24, 1915, saying that he had sent a check for the American rights to the stories to the Dubliner's English publisher.

At a time when Somerset Maugham's stories were selling at two thousand dollars apiece and up, Mencken and Nathan bought a rejected, dog-eared manuscript of his, called "Miss Thompson," at exactly one-tenth of his minimum price. When the story was dramatized as *Rain*, Tallulah Bankhead coveted the role of Sadie Thompson in it as a part that had "guts and swagger and shock." Maugham, always cool toward the dramatization of the story, refused to let Tallulah play the part. On seeing a new story of his, "The Man Who Wouldn't Hurt a Fly," she wired her manager, "THE MAN WHO WOULDN'T HURT A FLY IS CRUCIFYING ME." Her manager offered her the lead in *Tarnish* to console her, which, said Tallulah, was "adding incest to injury." She then appealed to the editors of *The Smart Set* to use their influence with the author of "Miss Thompson." But Maugham remained adamant, and it was not until *Rain* was revived later that Tallulah made a name for herself in it as Miss Thompson.

In view of the limited budget on which the magazine was operated, Mencken, who had been Joseph Conrad's chief promoter in this country, solicited a story from him, asking him to let him have it as reasonably as possible. After many months, Conrad's agent wrote H.L. to say that he now had a story available for six hundred dollars. In reply, Mencken cabled him, "FOR SIX HUNDRED DOLLARS YOU CAN HAVE THE SMART SET."

After Frank Harris, at various times editor of *The Fortnightly Review, Vanity Fair, Saturday Review,* and *Pearson's*, pronounced Bernard Shaw and Henry Mencken "the only two wholly righteous men in the world," H.L. wrote Harris asking him for an article on "How I Discovered G.B.S." On the day that the issue of *The Smart Set* containing the article he had requested from Harris came off the press, Mencken discovered to his chagrin that a rival magazine had already appeared on the stands carrying the identical piece. To Mencken's vociferous protest, Harris replied that he considered the story good enough to merit printing it twice.

To increase the difficulties of *The Smart Set* during World War I, the hazards of magazine publishing became so great that in order to keep *The Smart Set* going Mencken and Nathan resorted to putting out what they called their "louse magazines"—*The Black Mask*, a sensational pulp, now a collector's item; the daring *Parisienne;* and *The Parasite.* In wartime even the cheapest pulp paper, which was used for all four magazines, became so expensive that Mencken complained to Dreiser that only the rich could afford to have diarrhea.

Despite their trials and tribulations during the war, by 1920 Mencken and Nathan had made *The Smart Set* into the most civilized and sophisticated magazine in America. Henry's editorial duties kept him oscillating between New York and Baltimore, where his "Freelance" column in the *Sun* had earned him an enviable reputation as a columnist as well as an editor. In the "Freelance" he enjoyed "stirring up the animals" by attacking the advocates of Prohibition, civic crusaders, Christian Scientists, single-taxers, the American booboisie, and the skulduggery of the politicians they sent to Washington.

Forced to choose between a world run by the Teutons or one run by the YMCA, Mencken would undoubtedly have preferred the German regime. However after the United States entered the War to End War in 1917, against his "advice and consent," he imposed a voluntary censorship on his newspaper work and abandoned his "Freelance" column. Silenced on the political and diplomatic fronts, he turned again to philology to become, as he was fond of saying, a lexicographer, which by Samuel Johnson's definition was "a maker of dictionaries, a harmless drudge." By the spring of 1918, while still carrying on as co-editor of *The Smart Set,* he had begun *The American Language.* He had also published *A Little Book in C Major* and *A Book of Burlesques.* In 1918, *In Defense of Women* appeared, and in 1919, *Prejudices: First Series,* "a general slaughter of the literary gods in America." It was followed a year later by a second volume of *Prejudices,* in which the field of slaughter was extended to include politicians, humanists, "Women as Spectacles," and "The Woman and the Artist."

Mencken had long contended that any man who married after thirty was a damn fool and simply issuing an engraved invitation to trouble.

He was almost thirteen years past his own nuptial deadline and a confirmed bachelor when he met Sara Haardt. In 1923, he was out of love with all his old girls and disenchanted with *The Smart Set*. The first subscriber on its list, he snorted, was an Elks' Club. Further, *The Smart Set* had become as "righteous and decrepit as a converted madam." Nowadays it was largely read by "the higher ranges of kept ladies," whose intelligence was superior to their virtue. And by the time Sara and I met him, he was already preparing to assassinate *The Smart Set*. In the summer of 1923, he and Nathan sold their stock in the magazine at a profit. In July, he wrote Sara:

> Confidentially, I am making plans to start a serious review—the gaudiest and damndest ever seen in the Republic. I am sick of the Smart Set after nine years of it, and eager to get rid of its title, history, advertising, bad paper, worse printing, etc.

In a letter to her on August 17, 1923, he added:

> I am working night and day on my new review. Knopf is to be the publisher, and it will be very sightly. Why not send me some ideas for it. Anything that interests you—the South, the American University, the Anglo-Saxon, anything. Our aim is to set up an organ of educated Toryism, avoiding the chasing of liberal butterflies on the one hand and the worship of Judge Gary on the other. I hope, in an early number, to print an article denouncing Abraham Lincoln.

The probable title of his new magazine, he announced, would be *The American Mercury;* its format, the most chaste and dignified possible; its contents, dedicated to liberating the serious young writer as the little magazines had liberated the young poets. Despite its grave purposes, it would, he hoped, have overtones of the "atheistical and lascivious." Absolute freedom of speech would prevail in it, he promised, so long as it was annoying to right-thinking men.

CHAPTER TWO

*M*ONTGOMERY DAYS

SARA HAARDT'S BACKGROUND was, in its way, as interesting as Mencken's. When she was born in Montgomery, Alabama, on March 1, 1898, the ghosts of the late Confederacy still walked its somnolent oak-lined streets. Her fellow citizens carried their heads high, for a nation had been born there in the Cradle of the Confederacy, and its first flag had been raised from the staff of the State Capitol.

Montgomery was a city of tradition and taste, built like Rome upon seven hills, high on the red bluffs above the Alabama River. Its early settlers, Sara's maternal forebears among them, came from Virginia and South Carolina; or, like her paternal ancestors, from Europe. The ties between Montgomery and the old countries were very close.

During the "Roaring Forties," the riches of the Cotton Kingdom and the free and easy life in Alabama brought a wave of German settlers. Among them was Johannes Anton Haardt, a scholar and a lover of liberty who had fled from vineyards of the Rhine-Pfalz in 1842 to find freedom in the blacklands of Alabama. In 1848, the same year in which Burkhardt Mencken came to Baltimore from Saxony, Johannes Anton Haardt settled in Montgomery, bringing his slender patrimony with him. There Johannes met and married another native of the Rhien-Pfalz, Philippina Norheimer, who bore him ten children between 1849 and 1866. His son John was Sara Haardt's father.

Sara was seven years my senior, and my father constantly held her up to me as a model of decorum, intelligence, and tact. Father was a great favorite with her and she with him. Although they adhered to the Episcopal church, which he favored because "it doesn't interfere with people's religion or their politics, either," they were both what the fundamentalists call "freethinkers"—liberal, skeptical, and tolerant. In their discussions of religion and politics, books and people, Sara always maintained her points steadfastly, yet so diplomatically that when I argued with Father somewhat more vehemently, he would always remind me, "Sara Haardt's as suave as silk; she never crosses anybody."

In our early years, the aristocratic tradition was still in force, and "snob" had not yet become one of the more abusive four-letter words. The arbiters of elegance in Montgomery had come originally from Charleston. Hence, their fiats followed the "Charleston say-so," according to which "Peace and privacy are the greatest luxuries that money can buy," and further, "A lady's name should never appear in print but three times: when she's born, when she marries, and when she dies." As a result, there is little record of Sara's early years in the files of the Montgomery newspapers.

The summers in Montgomery were hot, sultry, and humid. But as the long evenings deepened slowly into the powder-blue dusk, the scorching days left behind them a cool, enchanted hour, known as "first dark," which appealed to Sara and her playmates as a wonderful time for catching lightning bugs, putting them in bottles, and making little lamps of them; for acquiring the treasured carbons discarded by the lamplighters who replaced them in the streetlights; and for playing Pop-the-Whip, Prisoner's Base, and I-Spy.

On Sunday afternoons, Sara liked to go to the zoo at Oak Park or to Pickett Springs, where there was an amusement area, marked off by whitewashed trees that appeared to be wearing spats on their trunks. Under the trees there were barbecue pits, popcorn stands that gave off a delicious buttery smell, a gaudy merry-go-round, and the red, blue, and yellow caravan of Leota, the gypsy palmist, whom Sara, for all her skepticism, consulted now and then. Another favorite excursion of Sara's was to the wharves along the river. Whenever the steam calliopes of those fabulous floating castles of white gingerbread-work known as pleasure boats were heard above the steamboats sounding as they rounded the bend, she and her friends took out for the landing at the foot of Commerce Street.

Commerce Street ran from the river to the Confederate Fountain; Dexter Avenue from the Confederate Fountain to the State Capitol—a beautiful Greek Revival building with stately Corinthian columns and

an imposing dome, which stands on the green slope of "Goat Hill"—
was a favorite playground for Montgomery youngsters. Flanking the
long flight of stone steps leading up to the Capitol were two Confederate cannons and several large piles of minié balls that served the
same purpose in our youth that jungle-gyms do today. Sara, who was
too dignified for such gymnastic antics, perched demurely on the cannons or stood awed beside the brass star that marked the spot where
Jefferson Davis had taken the oath of office as President of the Confederate States. But "Baby," as Zelda Sayre, the future Mrs. F. Scott
Fitzgerald, was called, being two years younger than Sara, was still
tomboy enough to stride the guns, slide down the banisters of the
famous circular staircase in the rotunda, and climb over the minié balls,
piled up in pyramids like oranges in the fruit stands.

"Baby" was a rebel and a daredevil from the word go. Her only rival
in derring-do was "Dutch," better known today as Tallulah Bankhead.
After Tallulah's mother died, she and her sister Eugenia were packed
off to her aunt, Marie Bankhead, the wife of my cousin Dr. Thomas
M. Owen, who presided over the Department of Archives and History, which then occupied the north wing of the Capitol. My father
and Judge Anthony D. Sayre, Zelda's father, who were both associate
justices of the Supreme Court at the time, had their offices on the floor
just above it. While Sara was still in her teens she began to work in the
afternoons at the Capitol, where Father kept me busy in his office.
Consequently, she and I had a grandstand seat for the song-and-dance
routines, the dramatic performances, and gymnastic exhibitions that
Zelda and Tallulah staged at the Capitol, given half a chance and a
minimum audience.

Tallulah could bend backward far enough to pick up a handkerchief
from the floor with her teeth, stand on her head, and turn a fancy cartwheel. But even more amusing to us were her imitations of Miss
Gussie Woodruff, who ran a dames' school in Montgomery for forty
years. She was a white-haired maiden lady and always dressed in high
net collars and long black silk dresses with a pince-nez pinned to them
by a gold fleur-de-lys. Tallulah could take off Miss Gussie's prim bearing and the quaint methods by which she attempted to instill the aristocratic manners of the old school into us in a way that made us rock
with laughter. Not only was Tallulah a gymnast and a mimic but a
song-and-dance specialist—and such a born entertainer that her arrival

in the neighborhood was heralded by the cry, "Lock up the piano, here comes Tallulah."

Zelda wanted to be a dancer from the time she was old enough to walk and always took top billing when she appeared in the ballet recitals at the Grand Theatre. As a childhood photograph of Sara in costume attests, at one time she too went in for ballet. But as she was reserved by nature and completely devoid of Tallulah's and Zelda's exhibitionism, she soon decided that her talent was for poetry rather than for dancing. One of the most vivid of my early memories of her is of hearing her read her verses aloud—"trying them out on the dog," she called it. I was frequently impressed into service as the "dog" and delighted in the office. For her voice had a lovely lilt to it that was like a musical accompaniment to her verse. She not only had a brilliant mind, quick in its perceptions and keen in its analyses, but she was also a good student and a thoroughly conscientious one.

As Miss Gussie Woodruff's curriculum did not extend beyond the grammar grades, my mother persuaded Margaret Booth, a young teacher, to start a private school for girls. In 1914, the Margaret Booth School opened its doors in her home at 117 Sayre Street, not far from where Zelda lived. Zelda, however, who even in her early teens was "the belle of Alabama *and* Georgia, too," elected to go to Sidney Lanier High School, a coeducational institution. Further, she was outspoken in her sympathy for the girls whose parents immured them in the cloistered schoolrooms at 117 Sayre.

Miss Margaret limited her enrollment to a hundred girls, ostensibly selected on the basis of their being the best fitted to be turned into what she termed "college material." She herself taught Latin, English literature, and history of art. Mademoiselle Marguerite Dognon drilled French into us by a rigorous system of *précis, dictées,* and *cahiers.* A unique cultural feature of the Margaret Booth School was the morning convocation, at which the Lord's Prayer was said, the *Marseillaise* sung in French, and the roll call answered with quotations from Robert Browning. One of Sara's favorite responses, frequently repeated tongue in cheek in after years, was:

> Only grant that I do serve
> Else why want aught further of me . . .

Another was the line that so aptly characterized her revolt against what Mencken called "the thread-bare Confederate metaphysic":

One who never turned his back but marched breast forward . . .

About the time Sara entered Margaret Booth, Tallulah, in the interests of decorum and public safety, was immured in the Academy of the Sacred Heart in New York. One saving grace in the situation, as far as Tallulah was concerned, was that she was allowed to go to the theater now and then. After she saw *The Whip*, nothing could deter her from a career on the stage. When, at sixteen, she finally got a small part in *The Squab Farm*, the papers headlined her triumph, "Society Girl Goes on Stage." The Cradle of the Confederacy was shaken by the news; Cousin Marie, shocked into what was known in those days as "a state," wired her, "REMEMBER YOU'RE A BANKHEAD." Through a slip in the telegraph office, the message Tallulah received read, "REMEMBER YOU'RE A BLOCKHEAD." Tallulah was amused—and delighted—by the reverberations in Montgomery.

After the United States declared war on Germany on April 6, 1917, Montgomery was overrun by soldiers from the nearby cantonments at Camp Sheridan and Camp Taylor. Old economic barriers and social distinctions were swept away. At the Beauvoir and Country Club dances, Sara's local beaux were joined by officers from all walks of life. Southern sharecroppers, Midwestern Babbitts, and rich Yankees stood cheek by jowl with Montgomery bluebloods in the stag lines.

The "New Freedom" had begun to burn in Montgomery with a flame that dimmed the phosphorescence from the decaying ethos of the late Confederacy. Many years later in "The Love Story of an Old Maid" Sara remembered a teen-age club of her youth called The Breakers, every member of which was supposed to be a breaker of something— a breaker of laws, or traditions, or, preferably, a breaker of hearts. She and her contemporaries were all rebels, born in a smug time and an ultraconservative place in which revolt was long overdue.

Zelda, endowed with the conviction, shared by many of her aristocratic contemporaries, that, as she later said of Alabama Beggs in *Save Me the Waltz*, she could "do anything and get away with it," carried a torch for the "New Freedom" in the vanguard of flaming youth. Although Sara smoked an occasional cigarette or took a cocktail now and then, her intransigence, by and large, was intellectual. Zelda and Tallulah rebelled along more unconventional lines. Once out of the convent, "Dutch" lived alone at the Algonquin Hotel in New York, where in place of a chaperone she employed a French maid—just as effective and far more useful. To prove it, at twenty, Tallulah was still, in her phrase, "a technical virgin." As long as a girl retained the somewhat equivocal virtue of a technical virgin, she could, however, under the "New Freedom," have a very gay time—if she kept quiet about it. From the Confederate point of view, the sin was in the saying.

But Zelda and Tallulah could never resist the temptation to tell a good story, particularly if it was on themselves. Both of them embroidered, embellished, and retailed their exploits until the end products kept the gossips' tongues running overtime. They bobbed their hair, used makeup, raised their hemlines to the knee, danced cheek to cheek in the toddle, did the shimmy, the Charleston, and the Black Bottom. But Sara confined her dancing to the more dignified measures of the waltz, the fox trot, and the tango. She had her full quota of beaux; but unlike Zelda and Tallulah in their younger days, she was as interested in books as in boys and did well in her studies at Margaret Booth. Her talent for verse was recognized there when she was asked to write the class poem and the school song:

> Margaret Booth School, Alma Mater,
> To thy praise we'll sing,
> For ideals so lofty o'er us,
> To thee we will bring—
> Love, devotion, truth, and honor,
> All to which we cling,
> Margaret Booth School, Alma Mater,
> E'er to thy praise we'll sing.

On the evening of May 24, 1916, Sara was graduated from the Margaret Booth School. Fragile, lovely, and flamelike, she came forward to lead the class in singing the "Alma Mater" she had composed. Six years later, she had the misfortune to discover that the "lofty" ideals of the school that she had hymned in it existed in theory rather than in practice, a discovery that led her to write the bitter story "Commencement," which Mencken published in *The American Mercury* in August 1926.

In the autumn of 1916, Sara entered Goucher College in Baltimore.

There she elected to major in history. But under the influence of Dr. Ola E. Winslow—or Miss Winslow, as she preferred to be called—Sara's interest was diverted to English and composition. Miss Winslow's gentleness, her shy charm, her intellectual integrity and sound scholarship, and her impeccable taste in literary criticism inspired one of the deepest and most enduring affections in Sara's life. Encouraged and tutored by Miss Winslow, she won the Freshman Short Story Contest with a story that appeared in *Kalends,* the Goucher literary magazine, for April 1917. She soon added to her literary reputation by her contributions to *Weekly* and became an editorial assistant on its staff and that of *Kalends.*

Among her co-workers on the Goucher publications were a lively pair: Louise Baker, who was short, dark, and keen; and Anna Pearce, who was tall, fair, and bland. Anna lived just a block away from Gimle Hall, where Sara occupied a single room on the second floor overlooking Charles Street. In the absence of Anna's stepmother, the Pearce house at 2105 North Charles offered a haven from the austerities of Goucher, a place where Sara, Louise, and other members of the publications staffs could smoke and drink Coca-Cola while they read proof and made up dummies. Later they were joined by a charming imp, Margaret Fishback, who became "the Poet Laureate of Manhattan" and the author of those plaintive lines, doubtless inspired by the difficulties of doing one's laundry at Goucher:

> I wonder where, I wonder where,
> I can hang up my underwear.

When a tall, rangy, Down-Easterner named Harry T. Baker came to the faculty at Goucher after having been reader for *Cosmopolitan* and *Good Housekeeping* and literary editor of *Country Gentleman,* he recognized Sara's gift for words and encouraged her to channel her stories and poems toward more remunerative publications than *Weekly* and *Kalends.* In Sara's sophomore year her grandmother, who had been sending her to college, died. Even with the help of a scholarship from the American Association of University Women in Montgomery, Sara had a hard time making ends meet. When her literary efforts failed to yield anything more profitable than experience and rejection slips, she was forced to supplement her funds by taking a part-time job as college postmistress. As a history major under the direction of a stern authoritarian, she was compelled to spend long hours in the library, doing the outside reading required. Between overwork and the Spartan diet of the wartime Goucher commons, she began to lose weight and grow pale.

Sara had never been strong. Physical effort tired her; she danced well and enthusiastically, but beyond that she was allergic to exercise in any form. "I was never in dramatics!" she noted in her copy of the Goucher annual, *Donnybrook Fair,* "or athletics!" She never learned to swim; and when she was notified that she must report to the college pool and be taught to do so, she openly rebelled. Nor would she don the ungainly blue serge bloomers that were mandatory for basketball and field hockey. By pleading that she was not strong enough to undergo physical training, she managed to dodge the required sports and gym classes for four years, during which she and the head of the medical staff waged an interminable feud over her refusal to comply with the athletic regulations.

At the end of her sophomore year, Sara was elected editor-in-chief of *Donnybrook Fair.* Her first essay, an attack on Philistinism, was printed in *Kalends* in 1919. In its June issue, there appeared a poem of hers, which under the influence of the Imagist movement showed a simpler, easier, more fluent technique:

> Love is a wild thing;
> It frightens white flowers;
> It warms cold hearts;
> Red roses quiver under its fierceness.
>
> Love is a gentle thing;
> It smoothes velvet petals;
> It softens gray hearts;
> Pansies remember it in their breath.

Since Sara was at Goucher while Mencken was writing his famous "Freelance" column for the *Sun,* she undoubtedly knew of it. But the first time I ever heard of the "Freelance" or its author, it was not from her but from my uncle, who was then in command at Fort Howard, just outside Baltimore. Like the Menckens, he came of German stock and commended Mencken for his opposition to Wilson's determination to involve us in World War I and for the blows "Freelance" had struck for freedom of speech, freedom of the press, and freedom from intolerance of everything Germanic, from Bach to beer and pretzels. It was due, in large measure, he thought, to Mencken's influence that during the war hysteria no one in Baltimore had yet been jailed for denouncing Wilson's idealism or his Great Crusade to make Europe safe for democracy.

Even so, the temper of Baltimore was uncomfortably chauvinistic for its large German colony; particularly for Mencken, who was admittedly against the war, against sending the AEF to pull the British chestnuts out of the fire, against conscription, against being drafted, or having his brother August drafted. Beyond that, he maintained a strict neutrality; and after this country entered the war, he voluntarily discontinued his attacks on the Wilson administration. Nevertheless, after the new firm of Alfred A. Knopf took over from the John Lane Company and published Mencken's *A Book of Prefaces* in 1917, the literary editor of the New York *Herald-Tribune* trained his siege guns on its author, whom he alleged to be pro-German, and launched a war within a war against him. The charges that Mencken was an agent of the Wilhelmstrasse were groundless, senseless, and libelous. Nevertheless, Knopf took alarm and a temporary break occurred between him and the Sage of Baltimore. As Mencken had pasted together *Damn! A Book of Calumny* during the first part of February and *In Defense of Women* during the following six weeks, he turned the manuscripts over to Goodman. Both books, which were brought out by Goodman, met initially with rough treatment from the critics. *In Defense of Women,* a backhanded lampoon of feminine strategy in the war of the sexes, brought new blasts from the Baltimoralists, though at least one conservative Confederate critic found it "hilarious and every word of it true." The professional reviews damaged its sale; and Goodman, whose scheme of selling books through drug stores proved premature, was unable to dispose of more than nine hundred copies. When he fell behind in his royalty payments, he was glad to turn from the hazards of publishing that he knew not to the hazards of Broadway that he knew and to let Knopf handle the books.

Meantime, Mencken, who had been co-editor of *The Smart Set* since October 1914, had acquired stock in the magazine. Consequently, he was forced to spend a considerable portion of his time in New York. Because the war had sent the price of living there skyrocketing, H.L. was in need of money. Shortly after returning from his tour of Europe as a war correspondent, he signed a six-month contract with Edward A. Rumley, publisher of the New York *Evening Mail,* to do a series of three articles each week for his paper. Mencken studiously avoided discussing the war or its issues in the articles, which included some of his best-known essays, his account of the suppression of Dreiser's *Sister Carrie,* "The Sahara of the Bozart," and his inimitable bathtub hoax. The trouble began when Mr. Rumley was arrested for concealing the German ownership of the *Evening Mail.* On July 23, 1918, Mencken wrote Ernest Boyd:

> I daresay you have heard of the Evening Mail débâcle. Rumley, who ran the paper, is jailed on a charge of taking money from the Wilhelmstrasse. Whether or not he did it I don't know. My notion is that, if he did it at all, it was only after his own money had become exhausted. He started out with a good deal, all inherited.
>
> My own connection with the paper was slight, and fortunately of such a character that I had nothing to do with Rumley and his financing. The articles I did were not started until after the U.S. had got into the war, and had no relation to the war whatsoever. I was induced to do them, not by Rumley, but by Cullen [John Cullen, managing editor of the *Evening Mail*], an old acquaintance here in Baltimore. Cullen is still on the job under the new management. This management now tries to wiggle out of the contract with me to save the expense, but I am in hopes of collecting my money. Altogether a sweet-smelling episode.

Mencken, who was completely innocent of any complicity with the Wilhelmstrasse, obtained two hundred and fifty dollars from the *Evening Mail* in settlement of his contract. But he was understandably vexed by the hubbub caused by the unfortunate incident and the resultant damage to the sale of his books.

When I returned to Montgomery, my ears were full of Mencken and I hastened to pass *In Defense of Women* along to Sara. She was amused but only mildly interested; her current enthusiasm was for Sherwood Anderson, whose stories, many of which were published in *Winesburg, Ohio* the next year, had already begun to appear in the little magazines. However, after she met Mencken, she returned to *In Defense of Women* again and again—with a great, even a vested, interest.

Later in the summer, we were to hear more about Mencken from Lieutenant F. Scott Fitzgerald of the Forty-fifth Infantry, Ninth Division, U.S.A. Fitzgerald had introduced himself to Zelda at the Montgomery Country Club one sultry July evening. She was seventeen at the time, a golden blonde whose summer tan and high cheekbones gave her the look of a fair-haired Cherokee princess. Her skin was the color of a ripe peach; her eyes Confederate gray. She had the nose of a young falcon. Her features were cleanly modeled over the kind of bone structure that comes from generations of breeding—a face that Scott remembered as that of "a saint, a Viking Madonna." As he came in the door, Fitzgerald, who had escorted two of his superior officers to the dance, caught sight of Zelda, barricaded behind the stag line.

Zelda was beautiful, vivacious, fascinating—made for love—and so fantastically popular that she presented an immediate challenge to the competitive spirit in Scott. Without troubling to excuse himself from his companions or ask for an introduction, he marched over and broke in on Zelda. Before he could ask her name, one of the stags cut in. Scott broke in again and again. He was irritated, intrigued, ready to fling the gauntlet down at the stag line.

At the time Scott looked like an Arrow-collar advertisement in a Brooks Brothers uniform. His blond hair was parted in the middle and slicked down. He had a fresh-scrubbed look. His skin had taken on a healthy tan under the meridional sun. At times, his eyes appeared to be blue; at others, green and hard as chalcedony. He danced well, borne up by what Zelda remembered in *Save Me the Waltz* as some "heavenly support beneath his shoulder blades," his head cocked a little to the side, held up not by some heavenly support but by the high collar of his tunic. He impressed Zelda "as if he secretly enjoyed the ability to fly but was walking as a compromise to convention," and she was undeniably fascinated by him.

About a month afterward, Sara and I had stopped in the rotunda of the Capitol to talk to the watchman, and as we came out on the portico, Zelda was showing Scott the star on the steps where Jeff Davis had taken the oath of office. She introduced him to us, and he told us that his name was Francis Scott Fitzgerald and that he was a great-grandson of Francis Scott Key, who had written "The Star Spangled Banner." He could give the Confederates and the New Englanders both cards and spades and beat them to the draw in bringing out the family tree. When his claim met nothing more than a polite "How interesting!" from Sara, he tried another tack. Was Mencken still writing for the Baltimore *Sun?* Mencken and Dreiser, he said, were the greatest living writers in America. He had a story, "Babes in the Woods," that he was going to send Mencken for *The Smart Set* as soon as he polished it up a bit and a novel, *The Romantic Egotist*, that he wanted him to see.

As we took leave of them and walked on down the steps, I was laughing. "What's so funny?" Sara asked.

"Boots and spurs on an Infantry lieutenant." Fresh from an army post, I had been quick to note the crossed rifles on the collar of Lieutenant Fitzgerald's tunic and the spurs on his cavalry boots, significant details that revealed an amusing facet of the character and aspirations of the author of *The Romantic Egotist*. Scott, as he afterward confessed, had come to the Deep South convinced that if the girls there would lose their heads over a man with shoes on, as he'd heard, they would certainly toss their bonnets over the White House of the Confederacy for one who wore boots, and he immediately took advantage of the regulation that permitted him as a member of a headquarters company to wear them instead of the usual puttees.

To Fitzgerald's discomfiture, after Sara went back to Goucher, two of her admirers gave Zelda such a rush that Scott's courtship was stymied for a time. Little as Scott cared for his local rivals, they cared less for him. It may be, as Fitzgerald and his biographers intimated later, in the twilight of chivalry, when Freud was in favor and sexuality in flower, that Zelda was permissive in her youth, but the evidence from Zelda's Montgomery beaux is against them. As Zelda said of the flapper:

> She flirted because it was fun to flirt and wore a one-piece bathing suit because she had a good figure, she covered her face with paint and powder because she didn't need it and she refused to be bored chiefly because she wasn't boring. She was conscious that the things she did were the things she had always wanted to do.

Zelda spearheaded the revolt against the "outworn Confederate metaphysic" and established an *entente cordiale* with the Yankee officers at Camp Sheridan. There the Boswell of *The Beautiful and Damned*, the laureate of the flappers and jellybeans, was waiting in the wings. Zelda put on her choicest pair of earrings and a great deal of audacity and rouge, refused to buckle her galoshes and let them flap, and so created a new type in American fiction that was to furnish both Scott Fitzgerald and Sara Haardt with material for many of their early stories. "Zelda," Sara maintained, "was the first flapper. All the others are imitations."

In October, Scott's unit was sent to Camp Mills and ordered overseas. The Armistice was signed while Scott's division was still at Camp Mills; Scott's disappointment at not getting overseas ended in a drinking marathon. His conduct at Camp Mills "had been so erratic that his commanding officer confined him to quarters." He slipped off, went AWOL to New York, and liquidated his sorrows in the Knickerbocker Bar. With his usual luck, his unit was ordered back to Camp Sheridan. The series of disasters that made up his military career ended not with a bang but a major contretemps. As aide-de-camp to General J. A. Ryan, he rode beside him in a dress parade. Despite his boots and spurs, he had no knowledge of horsemanship; given the opportunity to use his spurs, he made the best of them and was thrown from his horse. From General Ryan's point of view he was easily the most expendable man in the regiment and the second to be demobilized. After he was discharged on February 14, 1919, he drifted to New York and then back to St. Paul to rewrite *The Romantic Egotist* into *This Side of Paradise*. Five days before it was published there appeared in the Montgomery *Advertiser* of Sunday, March 21, 1920, a formal notice of Zelda's engagement.

On the front page of the society section in the same issue of the *Advertiser* in which Zelda's engagement was announced, there appeared the headlines: SARA HAARDT ELECTED TO PHI BETA KAPPA. On her graduation in June, the Goucher yearbook hailed her as "a soulful highbrow" and eulogized her in verse:

> The quietude of genius and the strength
> Of high endeavor mingle in her eyes;
> Not of the spirit only is her life—
> Her cool, sane judgments, wholesome humor, too,
> And power of execution. . . .

CHAPTER THREE

*J*AZZ AGE DAYS

ALTHOUGH MENCKEN WAS Fitzgerald's first commercial publisher, having bought "Babes in the Woods" for *The Smart Set* in June 1919, Scott later said: "It was not until I got the proofs of my book from the publisher that I learned of Mencken. I happened across *The Smart Set* one day and I thought, 'Here's a man whose name I ought to know. I guess I'll stick it in the proof sheets' "—a strange lapse of memory, for *This Side of Paradise* was not accepted, much less printed, by Scribner's until September 16, 1919. By that time the issue of *The Smart Set* carrying the story was on the stands, and Mencken had bought "The Debutante," a playlet, which, like "Babes in the Woods," Fitzgerald had reworked from an earlier version, written while he was at Princeton for the *Nassau Literary Magazine.*

With the thirty dollars that Mencken paid him for "Babes in the Woods" Scott bought a pair of white flannel trousers for himself and a magenta feather fan for Zelda, whose influence upon the revised versions of the story and the playlet is unmistakable. In turning *The Romantic Egotist* into *This Side of Paradise*, Fitzgerald used portions of both pieces, parts of Zelda's diary, and excerpts from letters written to her by other men. "Plagiarism," she quipped, "begins at home."

Before Scott left Montgomery, he borrowed the diary from her, took it to New York, and gave it to a Princeton friend, who read it and found it "a very human document." With the diary in hand, Scott, Edmund Wilson, and John Peale Bishop besieged Nathan in his apartment in the Royalton until he finally invited them in to have a drink. Fitzgerald, who proposed to turn Zelda's journal into a novelette called *The Diary of a Popular Girl*, asked Nathan to read it and give him his opinion of it.

Nathan was so impressed by it that he wanted to publish it—and to meet its author. But in June Zelda broke her engagement to Scott. Consequently, finding himself in an embarrassing position in regard to publishing her diary, he quietly diverted it to his own purposes in *This Side of Paradise*.

After Zelda rejected him, Scott spent the day drinking martinis at the Princeton Club, where he threatened to jump out of the window. But instead of committing suicide, he embarked on a marathon spree, which ended only with the advent of Prohibition on July 1. Having given up his job with the Barron Collier advertising agency, he retreated to St. Paul to rewrite his novel. It is improbable that he met Mencken before its appearance. For, although he knew Nathan, relations between the co-editors of *The Smart Set* were somewhat strained at the time as a result of Nathan's neglect of his editorial duties.

In January and February of 1920, *The Smart Set* published two more of Fitzgerald's stories. The following month, six days before the publication date of *This Side of Paradise* on March 26, Scott sent Mencken a review copy of the novel with a holograph note on the flyleaf:

> This is a bad book full of good things, a book about flappers written for philosophers, an exquisite burlesque of Compton Mackenzie with a pastiche of Wells at the end.
>
> F. Scott Fitzgerald,
> March 20th, 1920

But Mencken does not seem to have acknowledged the book or reviewed it until after Nathan introduced him to Scott and Zelda the following summer.

A few days after Scribner's accepted his novel, Scott had written Zelda, telling her of his success and asking if he might see her again. She replied casually that she would be glad to have him come down and reminded him to bring a bottle of gin because she hadn't had a drink all summer. "Zelda was cagey about throwing in her lot with me before I was a money-maker," he said later. "She was young and in a period when any exploiter or middle-man seemed a better risk than a worker in the arts." Innately the more prudent and the more sensible of the two, Zelda refused to marry him until he had visible means of supporting himself and her.

In November, Scott went to Montgomery and persuaded Zelda that he was going to be a famous writer who could open for her the glittering gates of wealth and success. Early in January, Zelda agreed to marry him, but Judge and Mrs. Sayre opposed the match. Scott, they felt, was unstable. They were also dubious about his ability to provide for Zelda. Besides, she was an Episcopalian, he a Catholic. But, if Scott did not have what he considered "the two top things"—money and position— he had an Irish tongue; and in the end he got "the top girl" and won her parents over.

"Zelda has had several admirers," her mother wrote him, with more than Anglo-Saxon understatement, "but you seem to be the only one to make anything like a permanent impression. . . . A good Catholic is as good as any other good man and that is good enough. It will take more than the Pope to make Zelda good: you will have to call on God Almighty direct."

A week after the appearance of *This Side of Paradise*, the personal column of the Montgomery *Advertiser* noted that Zelda and her sister Marjorie had left for New York. Judge and Mrs. Sayre did not accompany them—fortunately, for what they found would certainly have dismayed them. Fame and fortune had come to Scott almost overnight. In the money now, and out to prove it ostentatiously and alcoholically, he went on a monumental bender. Bellboys were called up to bathe him. He left the taps on after one of his luxurious ablutions and flooded the hotel. Five-dollar bills he used to light cigarettes; five-hundred-dollar ones he carefully folded to show the figures and wore in his vest pockets. When Zelda arrived, he made short shrift of the frills and furbelows in her trousseau and sent her out to buy a wardrobe that he considered more suitable for New York, where a number of sophisticated parties were being given for them. However, their marriage on April 7, 1920, in the Rectory of St. Patrick's Cathedral, was by contrast a quiet affair.

The Fitzgeralds took the New York literati by storm. Nathan was enchanted with Zelda, who flirted lightheartedly with him, as she did with all attractive men. After the Fitzgeralds took a cottage in Westport for the summer, Nathan wrote her gallant *billets doux*, addressing her as "Fair Zelda," "Sweet Souse," and "Dear Blonde." On July 12, 1920, he asked her and Scott to come in for a party, since Mencken, with whom he was now on better terms, was arriving on Wednesday. A fortnight later, he added that he had laid in three cases of gin for the party and that he would like to have her meet Mencken.

Afterward, Zelda reported that she could hardly sit down as the result of an injury sustained at Nathan's party. In a bathtub some-where—nobody seemed to remember the exact locale—she plumped down on a broken bottle of bath salts and had to have three stitches taken in her rear end. It must have been quite a party, even for the Jazz Age, for on his return to Baltimore, Mencken complained that he had to go back to New York the next Tuesday as he was forced to work a double shift at the *Smart Set* office because Nathan was suffering from acute alcoholism. Prohibition was killing him. Every apartment in New York, H.L. explained, had become a barroom, and neither he nor Na-than ever got any sleep.

Nathan's apartment in the Royalton was just across 44th Street from the Algonquin, where Mencken kept a suite and entertained when he was in New York. On his trips to Gotham, he occasionally lunched at the Algonquin with a group of Broadway and Hollywood celebrities who were more or less regular customers there: Robert Sherwood, Marc Connelly, George S. Kaufman, Harold Ross, Robert Benchley, Heywood Broun, Alexander Woollcott, John V. A. Weaver and his wife Peggy Wood, Dorothy Parker, Edna Ferber, and Neysa McMein. At the beginning of the high-living, loose-talking twenties, when hard liquor and easy money first began to undermine New York's staid brownstone traditions, H.L.'s friend Edmund Duffy, then cartoonist for the Brooklyn *Eagle,* had done a caricature of the literati at lunch in the Rose Room of Frank Case's Wayside Inn and titled it "The Al-gonquin Round Table." The Round Tablers referred to themselves as "The Vicious Circle," and their barbed wit and chill ferocities were too far removed from the genial humor and warmth of Mencken's con-stant circle in Baltimore to attract him. Besides, he secretly believed that all literary cliques were composed of "childish gossips and idiots." He distinctly preferred to spend his evenings out in Baltimore with his musical cronies of the Saturday Night Club rather than with the card sharks of the Thanatopsis Literary and Inside Straight Club, a branch of the Round Table, which met on the second floor of the Algonquin.

For Mencken was no gambler. On the rare occasions when he did sit in on a poker game there, it was usually for the purpose of rib-bing Willie Woollcott's brother Alec when he returned from a Broadway opening. After such an event, Alexander Woollcott would arrive at the Algonquin not only completely dressed, but dressed as he felt befitted his station as drama critic of the New York *Times,* in a high silk hat and opera cape. Whenever Mencken could catch him in such an extravagant outfit, he would shake his head and complain, much to Woollcott's embarrassment, "I'm ashamed of you, Alec, for turning up so richly and ostentatiously appareled while your poor brother Willie doesn't have a clean shirt to his name. Despite his dire need, my spies tell me you throw away a fortune on croquet and cards."

Mencken was grossly exaggerating, of course, although the Round Tablers' stakes sometimes ran so high that after an evening's losses left Robert Sherwood looking more than ever like Abe Lincoln after the Battle of Bull Run, he observed gloomily, "Only the brave *chemin de fer.*" Equally famous for her wit was Dorothy Parker, whose quips at the expense of Clare Booth Luce have become classics. The distinction of being one of the few wags who ever topped one of Mrs. Parker's witticisms belongs to Tallulah Bankhead, whom Mencken met at an Algonquin party, at which the length and strength of the drinks emboldened Tallulah to give a benefit performance of some of her acrobatic routines. Caroming about in a series of backbends, Tallulah crashed into a table of glasses. After a misplaced cartwheel shattered a chair, a committee was appointed to escort her back to her own room. As they steered Tallulah out, Mrs. Parker peeped out from the closet in which she and her dachshund had taken refuge and asked mildly, "Have they taken Whistler's mother home?"

When her question was repeated to Tallulah next day at lunch, she looked ruefully into the mirror of her purse. "Sad to say," she groaned, "the less I behave like Whistler's mother the night before, the more I look like her the morning after."

When Mencken met Zelda he was as charmed by her as he had been by Tallulah. After his enthusiastic review of *This Side of Paradise* appeared in the August 1920 issue of *The Smart Set,* acclaiming it as "The best American novel I have seen of late" and Scott as "a highly civilized and rather waggish fellow," the Fitzgeralds invited him to visit them at Westport. Since Mencken was rather a waggish fellow himself, when Scott sent him a copy of a collection of his short stories,

Flappers and Philosophers, published six months after *This Side of Paradise* appeared, the Sage enjoyed teasing him in a letter of September 4, 1920, about the use of his name in Scribner's publicity:

> Dear Mr. Fitzgerald:
> Thanks very much for the book. I'll read it with the utmost delight, despite the fact that hay-fever and alcoholism have knocked out one of my eyes and my hands tremble with the palsy. By a characteristic act of God it reaches me too late for my November book article.
> William Lyon Phelps is much flustered by the fact that he and I are quoted by Scribner in conjunction. He is a charming idiot.

And again on September 9:

> The other day I had a letter from William Lyon Phelps referring to Scribner's use of his name and mine in their announcements of "This Side of Paradise" on the ash-cans. Phelps said he was willing to refrain from legal proceedings if I was.

It was not long after Mencken met Fitzgerald that T. R. Smith, the managing editor of the *Century* magazine, invited the editors of *The Smart Set* to come up to his apartment for a drink. Nathan recalled:

> When we got there, we found with Smith a tall, skinny, paprika-headed stranger to whom we were introduced as one Lewis . . . [who] strangling us and putting resistance out of the question, and yelling at the top of his lungs, began: "So you guys are critics, are you? Well, let me tell you something. I'm the best writer in this here gottdamn country and if you, Georgie, and you, Hank, don't know it now, you'll know it gottdamn soon. Say, I've just finished a book that'll be published in a week or two and it's the gottdamn best book of its kind that this here gottdamn country has had and don't you guys forget it! . . ."
> Projected from Smith's flat by the self-endorsing uproar—it kept up for fully half an hour longer—Mencken and I jumped into a taxicab, directed the driver to speed us posthaste to a tavern where we might in some peace recover our equilibrium and our ear-drums, and looked at each other. "Of all the idiots I've ever laid eyes on, that fellow is the worst!" groaned Mencken, gasping for breath. . . .
> Three days later I got the following letter from Mencken, who had returned to Baltimore:
> Dear George: Grab hold of the bar-rail, steady yourself, and prepare yourself for a terrible shock! I've just read the advance sheets of the book of that Lump we met at Schmidt's and, by God, he has done the job! It's a genuinely excellent piece of work. Get it as soon as you can and take a look. I begin to believe that perhaps there isn't a God after all. There is no justice in the world. Yours in Xt., M.

The "Lump" was a future Nobel prize winner, Sinclair Lewis, and the book was *Main Street*. In the midst of the fight over the suppression of *Jurgen*, Mencken took time out to tell its author, James Branch Cabell, that Lewis' book had amazed him mightily. He had, he admitted, always heard that Red was a talker, who planned good books but wrote bad ones. However, he found that *Main Street* was full of genuinely distinguished stuff and its story extraordinarily good. He suspected that Cabell had been coaching Lewis along.

Early in autumn, Scott and Zelda arrived in Montgomery, filled with enthusiasm for Cabell and Mencken. The Sage had suggested that he and Fitzgerald "drop honorifics"; Scott now spoke of him as "Menck." Delighted by his review of *This Side of Paradise*, Fitzgerald declared that he had rather have him like his books than anyone in America.

For all the enthusiasm he brought with him, Scott labeled that visit to Montgomery as one of his most unpleasant trips. He and Zelda had electrified the Cradle of the Confederacy by turning up in a ramshackle Marmon. Their cars, Zelda explained, were always "secondhand and romantic," and this particular back number was so dilapidated that it inspired Scott to write "The Cruise of the Rolling Junk." By contrast, their clothes were ultramodern for 1920. They had had matching white knickerbocker suits made for themselves, designed for coolness, comfort, and presenting a solid front rather than for startling the Confederates. But when they appeared in them at the country club, a shock wave rippled over Zelda's friends. One of them amused Sara Haardt and irked Zelda by remarking that she "left here in long dresses and came back in short pants."

Scott always felt that he was never properly appreciated in Montgomery, and probably he was not. On their precipitate return from Alabama, where they had been forced to leave the ramshackle Marmon, the Fitzgeralds tried rusticating in Westport again, breaking the monotony of suburban life by frequent trips to New York to party with the Boyds and the Van Vechtens or with Nathan and Mencken.

Jazz Age parties in New York had a flavor all their own. At one of them, given by Joe Hergesheimer and "policed" by his wife, Dorothy, Mencken reported that Joe kept him up until three A.M., in a lavender suite, complete with grand piano, at the Algonquin, trying to bulldoze him into asking Rabindranath Tagore, the Hindu poet, who was staying in the hotel, to come play jazz for them on the piano. Unlike

Dorothy, Zelda never learned the gentle art of "policing" her husband's parties. Instead, she rode with him on the tops of cabs, drank toasts to him from her slipper, and flirted with his friends, particularly with Nathan, until Scott, in a jealous rage, let fly at George Jean with a roundhouse right.

After Mencken described Fitzgerald's *Flappers and Philosophers* in *The Smart Set,* in November 1920, as "a sandwich made up of two thick and tasteless chunks of *Kriegsbrot* with a couple of excellent sardines between," Scott did an admiring review of Mencken's *Prejudices: Second Series* in *The Bookman,* but entitled it "The Baltimore Anti-Christ." More amused than offended, Mencken told Fitzgerald:

> I find your encomium on reaching New York. You drench me with vaseline, cocoa butter, oleomargarine, and mayonnaise. God will curse you for it through all eternity. "Moon Calf" actually is a far better book than *Prejudices II.* Dell steals more intelligently than I did.
> When do we meet? I kiss the hand of the fair madonna.

Despite the exchange with Mencken, the Fitzgeralds continued to see him and his friends. Just before Christmas, Zelda wrote to James Branch Cabell, enclosing a picture of herself, asking him if he would do a favor for "a young and pretty girl," and explaining that "under pretense of intoxication" she had attempted to purloin Nathan's first edition of *Jurgen* for Scott's Christmas present but came off with a fencing foil instead, which she would gladly exchange for a copy of the book. In reply, Cabell wrote her a charming note and sent her a copy of *Jurgen,* which had become a rare item after the New York Society for the Suppression of Vice declared it an "offensive, lewd, lascivious book" and had Robert M. McBride and Co. indicted for selling it.

When Scott began work on *The Beautiful and Damned,* in which Nathan appears, thinly disguised, as Maury Noble, Mencken offered to tell him of an episode, undoubtedly fictitious, in which George Jean had been involved with "La Schapiro, a typical Grand Street flapper." For his own part, H.L. claimed that he not only deprecated the gifts of the Greenwich Village poets but the pulchritude of its flappers. Indeed, he swore that he had long since taken oath never to make love to any lady author who was not published by either Harper, Scribner, or Henry Holt.

Although he usually avoided Village parties, Mencken was present, along with Ernest Boyd, Llewellyn Powys, Sherwood Anderson, and

Carl Van Vechten at a famous soirée given by Dreiser in his apartment on St. Luke's Place. It began as a very dull affair in the novelist's bare sitting room, with no diversion except his lumbering attempts to engage his guests in conversation and nothing to drink except home brew. Boyd and Van Vechten, both famous wits, sat silent on their hard chairs, the latter "drooping like an ageing madonna-lily that has lost its pollen and has been left standing in a vase which the parlour maid has forgotten to refill with fresh water." Then Mencken, described by Powys as "a veritable tweedledum, with curtailed schoolboy jacket," began "making schoolboy jokes and talking schoolboy talk with a kind of boisterous *bonhomie.*" Toward the end of the evening, Van Vechten said, "an uninvited Scott Fitzgerald appeared with a bottle of champagne" and "furnished the town with gossip for a week." He arrived very drunk, Mencken added, and introduced himself to his host by saying, "Mr. Dreiser, my name is Fitzgerald. I have always got a great kick out of your works." Dreiser took the bottle of champagne and carefully put it away in the refrigerator for future reference, leaving its donor to drink yeasty beer. In his *Memoirs,* Sherwood Anderson declared that Dreiser shut the door in Fitzgerald's face as he had in his a few days before. But below Anderson's account in Mencken's copy of the book, there is an indignant note in H.L.'s handwriting: "Another lie! Fitz came in and was politely treated by Dreiser."

Dreiser's party was by no means the only occasion on which Scott's behavior created conversation in New York. He tried to outdo the scantily draped chorines at the *Scandals* by shucking off his clothes in an orchestra seat, dived into the Pulitzer fountain in front of the Plaza, insulted his hosts and those that refused to serve in such a capacity, and passed out with his head on Zelda's shoulder at literary teas.

As a result of the injuries sustained in a night-club fracas, he and Zelda had to postpone their 1921 trip abroad for a week. After a whirlwind visit to England, France, and Italy, Scott concluded that Europe was a vastly "overestimated place." In August he and Zelda went back to St. Paul to await the birth of their daughter, named for Scott, despite a wire from Mencken advising that they name her Charlotte after Charles Evans Hughes. Scribner's published Scott's second novel, *The Beautiful and Damned,* in March, and the Fitzgeralds left at once for New York to celebrate. Whereupon, on March 21, 1922, Mencken wrote Cabell:

Fitzgerald blew into New York last week. He has written a play, and Nathan says that it has very good chances. But it seems to me that his wife thinks too much about money. His danger lies in trying to get it too rapidly. A very amiable pair, innocent and charming.

Disappointed in the sales of *The Beautiful and Damned*, the Fitzgeralds had now gone back to St. Paul, where Scott was to revise his play, *The Vegetable*. By fall, the Fitzgeralds were back at the Plaza, which Zelda described as "an etched hotel, dainty and subdued, with such a handsome head waiter that he never minded lending five dollars or borrowing a Rolls-Royce." There Zelda and I compared notes on the experiences of innocents abroad, while Scott talked to producers about *The Vegetable*. "It's going to be a money-maker," he predicted. He was very much excited about it; and Zelda was excited about the curtain for the New Greenwich Village Follies, on which she was pictured in a favorite pose—diving into a fountain.

Within two years' time, in one way and another, Scott and Zelda had made a name for themselves as the Fabulous Fitzgeralds, the legendary and eponymous figures of the Jazz Age. Scott was now a successful novelist, Zelda was celebrated as a beauty and a wit. The very air of Manhattan was heady with prosperity, bootleg liquor, and jazz. In urging Cabell to join him in New York, Mencken warned him not to delay his visit too long because soon or late the place would be consumed by a pillar of fire from Heaven. The parties there with the Fitzgeralds left me with a similar impression, and I departed without regret the first week in October to join Sara at Goucher, where she was to be an instructor in English and I a freshman.

Although Sara was the youngest instructor at Goucher, she commanded great respect and affection from her colleagues. Her closest friend and confidante on the faculty was Dr. Ola Elizabeth Winslow. Born in Grant City, Missouri, Miss Winslow's charm was not that of the Midwest but of New England. She was reserved, modest, selfless; but for a delightful sense of humor, she was almost prim in her demeanor—a shy little spinster with the steady, thoughtful eyes of a contemplative. Her hair was ash blond, flecked with gold, her mouth, mobile and easily twisted into a smile. It always amused Sara to remember that Miss Winslow, now an authority on Jonathan Edwards and a Sanskrit scholar, had done her dissertation at the University of Chicago on "Low Comedy as a Structural Element in English Drama" before she came to teach at Goucher. Teaching was a calling with her rather than a profession or a livelihood, and she kept open house for her students. On Sunday evenings, Sara, Dorothy Hancock Tilton, who was a class ahead of me and as Brahmin as I was Confederate, Anna Pearce, Louise Baker, and I frequently met at Miss Winslow's apartment on Charles Street for tea and talk that ranged from the epigrams of H. L. Mencken to the epigrams of Pantanjali.

All of us learned a great deal about writing from Miss Winslow, and Sara learned so rapidly that she was beginning to win literary recognition. In July 1922 a series of her character sketches, "Strictly Southern," appeared in *The Reviewer*, founded in Richmond the year before, when someone at a party said, "Let's start a magazine." One of its founders, Emily Tapscott Clark, the daughter of an Episcopal minister, who combined the talents of editorial Lorelei Lee and a Jazz Age Jane Austen, had parlayed equal parts of charm and soft soap into a publication that became the herald of the literary renascence in the South. Delighted with Emily and her little magazine, Mencken took, as she said, "a hectic interest" in it. He, Hergesheimer, and Cabell not only rendered editorial advice and contributed to it gratis but helped Miss Clark secure free will offerings from other well-known writers. Carl Van Vechten, Ernest Boyd, Arthur Machen, John Galsworthy, Louis Untermeyer, Gertrude Stein, Amy Lowell, Robert Hillyer, Babette Deutsch, Julia Peterkin, DuBose Heyward, Gerald Johnson, Hervey Allen, Hansell Baugh, Frances Newman, and Burton Rascoe had all published in *The Reviewer*; and when Emily Clark printed "Strictly Southern," Sara's name appeared among a notable list of contributors.

As a result of "Strictly Southern," however, she and I both found ourselves in the ill grace of many of the unreconstructed Rebels at Goucher. For they regarded anyone who wrote or even intended to write about the Sacred South except in eulogistic terms of roses and romance, moonlight and magnolias, as guilty of *lèse-majesté*. In due course, since Miss Haardt and I were known to them as Big Sara and Little Sara, I too was convicted of the same offense as guilty by association with the author of those realistic sketches of small-town characters in the South. Therefore Sara and I found a more appreciative audience in our friends from above the Potomac, especially after Emily Clark published another of Sara's Southern short stories.

On the morning after Sara received the news of its acceptance by

The Reviewer, we met her at the college drug store and toasted her in "Confederate champagne," better known as Coca-Cola. The restrained celebration of such a momentous event was possibly due to the fact that printed on the inside cover of *The Reviewer* was a warning composed by James Branch Cabell: "The payment for such mss. as may be found available will be in fame, and not specie."

A few weeks afterward Mr. Baker introduced us to Mr. Mencken. The first humdrum semester at Goucher was over. Our next year in Baltimore was to be so gay and exciting that its occasions were celebrated with Moselle and Veuve Cliquot instead of Confederate champagne.

$\mathcal{T}$HE DAYS OF GRACE

FROM THE VICIOUS CIRCLE at the Algonquin, where Emily Clark had been warned not to open her mouth except to put food in it because everything that was said there was instantly repeated and generally repeated wrong, the young editor of *The Reviewer* had heard stories about Mencken, chiefly thrusts that he ascribed to Nathan's inventive mind, but which nevertheless made her a bit wary of the Sage before she knew him. Her turbulent friendship with him began with his enthusiastic response to her appeal for contributions to *The Reviewer*. He averaged, she said, a letter a week of advice, whether she replied or not. On the heels of two such unanswered epistles came a personal note from him, which made her realize for the first time that "he was a human being," and aroused her curiosity about the man from whom it came.

Louis Untermeyer had told her that Mencken was "a real aristocrat with men but afraid of women except of a certain kind," to which Carl Van Vechten added, with even greater inaccuracy, that H.L. had "never known any kind of women well except the Broadway kind and middle-aged intellectual ones like Edna Ferber and Zoë Akins," two well-known playwrights with whom he sometimes lunched at the Round Table. He himself said that he knew very few women in New York at the time; and one of them, at least, who could be called neither literary nor middle-aged was Neysa McMein, the glamour girl of the Round Table, a warmhearted, earthy artist with tawny eyes and taffy-colored hair. But whenever Mencken stopped by her apartment in the evening for a drink, he found Alec Woollcott there.

For Miss McMein had inspired a strange love in Woollcott, who, despite his much publicized impotency, had asked her to marry him. Egged on by Mencken, one of the Round Tablers inquired what Woollcott's intentions were in proposing to her. "Oh," she laughed, "Alec just wants somebody to talk to in bed." For all that, Woollcott regarded her as his fiancée at the time; and it was a point of honor with Mencken never to become involved with other men's girls. True, he sometimes called on Kirah Markham, an actress who became Dreiser's companion, and "Gloom," Estelle Kubitz, one of Miss Markham's many successors in the novelist's inconstant affections. But Mencken's attentions to them, as well as to Lillian Gish, Nathan's Dulcinea, were of a distinctly fraternal and platonic order.

Indeed, Madeleine Boyd says, "He did not have very many serious girls in those early days." He was too busy for them, as he himself told one of his biographers. He had long since outgrown the little blond German girl with whom he had fallen in love at the age of fourteen and the red-haired Genevieve of his youth; the only enduring attachments of his *The Smart Set* period that Madeleine remembers were to Bee Wilson McDonald, a young newspaper woman; to Fanny Butcher, who ran a bookstore in Chicago and wrote reviews for the *Tribune* there; and to the mysterious "Miss Bloom or Blum," about whom Carl Van Vechten gossiped to Emily Clark.

Marion Bloom was an occasional contributor to *The Smart Set*. Mencken met her shortly after he became editor of the magazine. Later, when she went into business as a literary agent, he wrote Ernest Boyd and a number of his other friends, suggesting that they let her handle their manuscripts. Although she says Henry was not in love with her, he spent many of his evenings in New York with her. One cold November night in 1915, he took her with him to visit Kirah Markham and Dreiser in their Greenwich Village apartment. Afterward, Mencken reported to the novelist that "the fair Bloom, having venerated you from afar and as if you were some gaseous E flat amateur Jesus, emerged from your presence in a state bordering on maryolatry." After Gloom, who was Marion's sister, supplanted Miss Markham in Dreiser's ménage, Bloom was with her so constantly that Mencken jocosely referred to Dreiser as his brother-in-law.

Between 1914 and 1916, the friendship between the two men was at its height. Dreiser had given Mencken the manuscript of *Sister Carrie*, asked him to act as his literary executor, and confided to him that after

pondering for some years over what his last words were to be had now
definitely decided upon "Shakespeare, I come!" However, Dreiser resented Mencken's attack upon his novel *The "Genius"* in *A Book of
Prefaces*. H.L. made a gift of the manuscript of his *Prefaces* to Marion
Bloom, but as his relationship with Dreiser deteriorated, he became
temporarily estranged from her too. In 1918, when she sailed for
France, where she served as a nurse during the war, she reflected ruefully that Mencken was so afflicted with hay fever that their parting
seemed "to be rather a secondary thing"—so secondary, in fact, that on
receipt of a cable from her after she landed, he complained to Ernest
Boyd about the cost of his reply.

While Bloom was abroad, Mencken had an open quarrel with
Dreiser. However, despite the fact that H.L. had consistently panned
The "Genius," when John S. Sumner of the New York Society for the
Suppression of Vice succeeded in having it banned as blasphemous
and obscene, Mencken and John Cowper Powys drafted a protest and
obtained the signatures of many other writers on it. Mencken sent out
some twenty-five letters a day requesting authors to sign it, among
them the oft-quoted plea addressed to a minor novelist, Henry Sydnor
Harrison, urging him to reconsider his refusal to support the protest
and thus "give public notice that the authors of the United States, putting aside their personal likes and dislikes, are united against the
common enemy, as authors of France were in the Zola case." Not only
did Mencken work day and night over the protest himself but he also
spent three hundred dollars of his own money in fighting Dreiser's
battle against the Comstocks. Having cautioned Dreiser to avoid enlisting the help of the radicals lest he alienate the support of the five
hundred respected editors and writers who had already signed the
protest, Mencken was enraged when Dreiser flouted the Author's
League and sought the support of "jitney geniuses" and Greenwich
Village radicals.

In the midst of the ensuing uproar, Dreiser sent Mencken, who was
always wary on the subject of perversion, a four-act play he had written, *The Hand of the Potter*. Mencken warned him that nothing was
more abhorrent to the average man than sexual perversion and that
it would wreck their efforts to defeat the Comstocks if it were staged.
Fully half the signers of the protest, he pointed out, would demand to
have their names removed. Dreiser filled him with ire, he added. He

damned the novelist in every European language. Dreiser, he complained, had a positive genius for doing foolish things. One step more and he would be writing sex-hygiene books for use in nunneries. When Dreiser proposed to have the play printed, Mencken said:

> In brief, the publication of it would be a docile baring of the neck—highly delightful to the moral mind. They will not stop at more accusations of polluting the innocent. They will seize on the perversion, roll it on the tongue, and quickly get you into training as the American Oscar Wilde. And against that there is no defense. I am opposed to hopeless fights. They not only injure a man; they make him ridiculous.

Just before the case of *The "Genius"* came up in court, Dreiser, ignoring Mencken's remonstrances, sold an option on *The Hand of the Potter* for a thousand dollars to Charles Coburn, who planned to produce it at the Greenwich Village Theatre. Mencken threw up his hands.

Between Mencken's estrangement from Dreiser and Dreiser's from Gloom, by the time Marion Bloom returned from France the quartet had broken up. Henry reported that he and Bloom had "agreed to adjourn *sine die*." In despair, she wrote Gloom that to go on without him was virtually impossible. Mencken soon discovered that he missed her, too; it was simpler to go on together than not. In 1922, he sent her a note with a presentation copy of *The American Language,* saying that the book was almost as much hers as his own. She had helped with the research and stood by in the library while he sweated and cursed to keep the girls from flirting with him. After she moved to Washington and opened a shop there, he saw her frequently until she married in 1923.

In *Pistols for Two,* Mencken claimed to detest literary women. Yet, on the whole, he put in a great deal more time with them than with "women of a certain kind." He bestowed his editorial attentions on Willa Cather, Thyra Samter Winslow, and Ruth Suckow among others. Nancy Hoyt, Elinor Wylie's sister, was one of his favorites during the early twenties. He was a great admirer of Dr. Louise Pound, a distinguished linguist and Professor of English at the University of Nebraska, saw her whenever she came East, and corresponded with her for many years. Another staunch friend among the literati was Blanche Knopf, the wife of his publisher. Alfred Knopf once said of Mencken in his early days, "Even then he had the reputation, chiefly with those who did not know him well—and I didn't yet know him well—of being a burly, loud, raucous fellow, rough in his speech, and lacking in refined manners. How mistaken this opinion was I learned a little later, when on a visit to Washington, I introduced Blanche Knopf to him. He met her with the most charming manners conceivable. Manners I was to discover he always displayed in talking with women."

Emily Clark's aunt, who lived in Baltimore, disapproved of Mencken "so frightfully" that Emily inclined to share her views until she met him and, like the Knopfs, discovered that the Baltimoralists' opinions of "Horrible Harry," as they called him, were undeniably mistaken. After Mencken sent her his "Morning Song in C Major," an appraisal of the literary reawakening of the South, for *The Reviewer,* Emily was so pleased that she urged Hergesheimer to bring the Sage to see her. Mencken agreed to accompany him on a barnstorming trip to Richmond as soon as he had covered the Disarmament Conference in Washington.

James Branch Cabell and his wife, Priscilla, furnished Emily Clark with much of her literary gossip. It was rumored that this quiet, shy Virginia gentleman with the primness of a schoolmaster had once been hopelessly in love with Amélie Rives, a cousin of his, sixteen years his senior, then married to Prince Pierre Troubetzkoy, a fashionable Russian painter. Amélie, a descendant of the first families of Virginia and the owner of Castle Hill, one of Virginia's most beautiful estates, had spent most of her life abroad. To her fame as an internationally celebrated beauty, she had added the distinction of becoming a successful novelist and playwright. Realizing that his attachment to Princess Troubetzkoy was a hopeless infatuation, Cabell in 1913 amazed his friends and relatives in Richmond by making a marriage of convenience with Mrs. Emmett A. Shepherd, the widow of a lumber dealer.

According to Emily, he always wrote about modern Virginia, but the things he wanted to say about it were so dreadful they terrified him, and, therefore, he called it Poictesme. Mrs. Cabell she described as "sort of edgy, like Dame Lisa in *Jurgen.*" After Priscilla, alias Dame Lisa, had several teeth pulled and was telling everyone about it with her usual candor, her visit to the dentist, Emily predicted, would "beyond doubt be retailed in some mythological form in Mr. Cabell's next book." Guy Holt, Cabell's publisher, maintained that, like the woman in *The Cream of the Jest,* Mrs. Cabell actually gave her husband herring for breakfast every morning instead of eggs.

On learning that Mencken and Hergesheimer had decided to visit

Richmond, Cabell invited them to Dumbarton Grange. "We are giving a dance for the younger set," he explained, "it would be a very great comfort in tribulation if both of you would come. I shall reserve the library for the literary guests so that we can withdraw utterly from the dancers." As he told them later that it would be "an addition to the party, I candidly confess, should you bring something on the hip, as by force of circumstances the affair will be Saharan." Mencken arrived with a trunkful of wines and liquors. But whether they had been forewarned of the drouth enforced by Priscilla or the herring she served for breakfast, H.L. and Joe decided to avoid the hazards of hospitality and stay at the Jefferson Hotel.

Hergesheimer said that they had the time of their lives in Richmond. On the evening of their arrival, fortified by a drink at the Jefferson, they dined with Emily Clark and her stepmother. "The afternoons," he continued, "we spent with James in a stark dwelling beside the railroad tracks on Richmond's periphery. This, however, was Dumbarton Grange, invested with the pride and circumstance of its title." Although Mencken protested that he had not danced since the minuet went out, he donned a dinner coat and went to the dance, taking along "a supernal Baltimore rye" to console his host. "I danced like mad," Hergesheimer admitted. But neither James nor Henry "deviated from a pattern of being wholly apposite and circumspect" with the debutantes.

On a subsequent trip to Richmond, Cabell introduced Mencken to the Prince and Princess Troubetzkoy, who were so charmed with him that they invited him to visit them at Castle Hill; in the course of the years he was several times their guest there. As the Princess had been Cabell's inspiration for so many of the charming ladies in his biography of Manuel, Hergesheimer was surprised that she "gave Priscilla, a plain-looking wife, no concern whatever." Mrs. Cabell's view of James, like Dorothy's of Joe, was "notably without nonsense." Priscilla, Hergesheimer added, was an "outspoken wife. She drove a heavy white automobile with conspicuous daring and as vigorously attended James." She was so right for him that "she made no bones of her inability to read his books. She treated me with the indulgent brevity reserved for a minor James."

Mencken, with his usual gallantry toward women, withheld comment on Mrs. Cabell. Sara, who went to Richmond some seven years later to do an article on her, was more charitably inclined toward her than Emily, whose tart accounts of her were doubtless prompted by the veneration in which the editor of *The Reviewer* held Mr. Cabell.

In March, Emily saw Mencken in New York. "He is really splendid," she said, "and I like him lots, but he bursts out now and then with something that seems to terrify him, and then he walks on eggshells . . . for a while, and it amuses me. He forgets and walks on the inside of the street too." She also met Nathan while she was there. But she found that she liked Mencken much better. He was so "ingenuous and full of gusto." Moreover, she said, "He's so big and knows so much about everything, and yet, in a way is so innocent." It was not long before he began to rival Hergesheimer and Cabell in Emily's literary affections. After a visit to Baltimore, she announced:

> I had lunch with Mr. Mencken yesterday. He grows on me tremendously and I like him better than in Richmond and New York. I can only see him alone here, because he won't go to anybody's house or the Country Club. He says he can't make acquaintances here because he lives here and they would bother him. Aunt Rosa [Mrs. John S. Tapscott] disapproves of him so frightfully that I didn't tell her I lunched with him.

After Mrs. Tapscott told Emily that "No one in Baltimore meets Mencken," Emily retorted that she was narrow beyond belief. Mencken was very much sought after by such impeccable Baltimoreans as Senator Bruce's son David, Harry and Van Lear Black, part owners of the *Sun*, and Rosamund and Frank Beirne of the *Sun* staff. But Mencken "wouldn't be bothered by Baltimore people because he lived there and couldn't shake them." While that was one of Emily's exaggerations, Mencken himself said that when he was in Baltimore he was so infernally harassed by telephone calls from bores that he could never get any work done. The town, he grumbled, was full of imbeciles who gave dinners with nothing to drink. He never went to them; but the dinner givers had thick skins and it took time to escape from them. They did not invite him because he was a pretty fellow, he explained, but because they seemed to think that literary gentlemen were always glad to get a free meal. So they were—but not a dry meal.

When Emily learned that he had actually gone to a tea given in honor of a Harvard professor by one of the impresarios of the Baltimore elect, Mrs. Arthur Kinsolving, wife of the rector of St. Paul's, she declared that it was the most extraordinary thing she ever heard of. She predicted with amazing accuracy that Mencken would eventually join the Maryland Club and go to the country club on Saturday evenings. After Mrs. Kinsolving put her cachet on the Bad Boy of Baltimore, Mrs. Tapscott was forced to remove her objections to him, and Emily was able to lunch with him at Marconi's without having to give Aunt Rosa the slip. Mencken praised Emily's essays, sent her autographed copies of his books, and introduced her to his literary friends in New York. Just as she began to have the same proprietary feeling about him that she did about Cabell and Hergesheimer, Frances Newman appeared on the horizon as her rival for the literary affections of all three gentlemen.

"Frances, not the Cardinal," as Miss Newman described herself, was at that period dividing her time between writing book reviews for the Atlanta *Sunday Constitution* and acting as head of the lending department of the Carnegie Library there in her native city. Widely read, intellectually astute, and possessed of a pungent, biting wit in her acrimonious reviews, Miss Newman had trod an astringent, corrosive oil from the ripe olives of American literature. Her piece on *This Side of Paradise*, she had afterward admitted to Scott, was "assault with intent to murder." When Fitzgerald wrote her that her review had made him as angry as his book had evidently made her, she told Cabell, "I feel as if I had pulled a spoiled baby's curls and made him cry."

Nor did she spare the author of *Jurgen*, whom she attacked for lack of inventiveness. Later, however, she recanted after a visit to him at Dumbarton Grange, "the cockpit of American literature" as she called it. She had arrived aflame with indignation at Mencken's "Sahara of the Bozart," dressed (as usual) all in purple, with a list of questions she wished to ask Cabell written out on a sheet of mauve paper. Despite Mr. Cabell's contention that Mencken was "one of the very few indisputably great men now living," she had dealt harshly with him, adding in a letter to her host that she had gone the evening before to hear Fritz Kreisler but found that instead of listening enraptured, she had merely used the *Liebesfreud* and *Liebeslied* as a pleasant stimulus to the invention of epithets concerning Mr. Mencken.

The winning of Frances Newman began six months later, on September 12, 1921, when Mencken wrote her to the effect that if she happened to be a graduate of one of the more eminent women's colleges, *The Smart Set* would like to have an article about it from her for a series its editors had planned. Miss Newman replied tersely that since she had not had the advantages of a college education, she could not write the article. With consummate tact, Mencken congratulated her and assured her that no Vassar girl could possibly write as well as she did.

A month later Emily met Frances Newman at a *Reviewer* meeting in Richmond and reported to Hergesheimer:

> Miss Newman is clever, of course, but so silly for a woman of her age. She drawls and coos and says your books and everybody's books that she likes are "darling" and "sweet." I hope if I get that way at her age somebody who really likes me will kill me with a club. I don't like her writing as much as Mr. Cabell does, do you? It's so dreadfully erudite and full of slop. Miss Newman has been corresponding with Mr. Mencken about her work, and they've made an appointment for lunch this week. I think he's going to be badly jarred when he sees her.

Far from being jarred by Miss Newman when he met her in New York a few days later, Mencken found that "as a person she was singularly attractive, mainly because of her uncommon courage." She was, he added, "pawkily malicious, vivid, and unconventional" and "possessed of a feline cleverness that was completely feminine, but beside it ran a shrewd and tolerant humor that was almost masculine." After H.L. read the first episode of the novel Miss Newman was writing, *The Hard-Boiled Virgin*, he numbered her among his "Violets in the Sahara," adding: "Miss Newman has a tight, glittering, extremely uncommon style, and more learning than fifty professors." By the time he returned from Europe in the fall of 1922, he and Miss Newman were on friendly terms and his letters began "Dear Frances" and concluded *"Ich küss die Hand."* Nevertheless, he continued his attentions to Marion Bloom in Washington, to Fanny Butcher in Chicago, and to Emily in Richmond. Impressed by Emily's satirical essays on *Virginia* in *The Reviewer*, in the spring of 1923, he urged her to incorporate them in a book to be called *Stuffed Peacocks*, which he recommended to Knopf for publication.

It was at this point that Sara Haardt appeared on Mencken's horizon.

On the morning after we first met Mr. Mencken, Sara turned up at the Chelsea Pharmacy with *In Defense of Women* on top of a pile of blue exam books. "Well, hussies, let me read you what our host of last evening has to say about us." She was laughing as she leafed through the book, but evidently she was not too amused by the passage she read:

> The female body, even at its best is very defective in form; it has harsh curves and verily clumsily distributed masses; compared to it the average milk jug, or even cuspidor, is a thing of intelligent and gratifying design.

"And listen! Wait till you hear this!" she went on.

> Ninety-nine men in every hundred, when they go a-courting, fancy that they are the aggressors in the ancient game and rather pride themselves upon their enterprise and daring. Hence we find in Don Juan a popular hero. As a matter of fact, says Shaw, it is the woman that ordinarily makes the first advances and the woman that lures, forces or drags the man on to the climax of marriage.

"What would you do with a man who's written things like that?"

"Run, probably, but not too fast if I liked him," I said.

"Not on your tintype. Marriage is out of my line," she maintained. "There's a certain elegance in celibacy and an unquestionable dignity in the cloistered life."

"Have it your way, but before you take the veil, remember that Mr. Mencken is a nice, eligible bachelor, who by his own admission has reached the age when the advantages of marriage begin to outweigh its drawbacks."

"Why?" she asked quickly. "What did he say on the way back?"

"Oh, nothing except that we must meet again soon. But somewhere in the book from which you've taken your text, he argues that first-rate men usually marry late in life when the disabilities they suffer from marriage begin to diminish. He's evidently no gynophobe, and, apparently he likes the savor of romantic comedy."

At all events, he was too astute not to wait until the stage was properly set to make his next entrance. We heard no more from him until Joseph Hergesheimer came to town. The week before Mr. Hergesheimer arrived, I had a note from Mencken asking me to have lunch with him at Marconi's the following Friday and to bring my friend Miss Haardt, "to cheer up Joe."

On our arrival at Marconi's our host called for a round of cocktails and briefed us on the Pennsylvania Petronius. In his salad days, Hergesheimer, he said, had been poor and virtuous, a kind of American Villon, an out-of-pocket painter, living on beans and Uneeda biscuit, nourishing his soul on the gaudy dream of a contract to paint the canvases for a sideshow. But fortune and Wall Street willed otherwise. He was tempted and fetched with demonic subtlety by the powers that be. His artist's eye fell on Dorothy Hemphill, beautiful, blue-eyed, and intelligent, but, alas for him, the daughter of a Pennsylvania millionaire. He was enchanted; he was in love; he was lost to art.

Somewhat dashed when the lady's family set the dogs upon him, Hergesheimer quickly recovered his aplomb and gave ear to the call of Vox Mazuma. He pawned his palette and maulstick and bought a gold-plated Corona, slightly used but still serviceable and highly impressive. Once he hung out his shingle as another Henry James, he found a High Church rector from Wall Street to publish the bans. Unfortunately, tying the matrimonial knot did not end his financial entanglements—a thing that was not accomplished until he sold his soul to the *Satevepost*. Now he was rolling in wealth, foundering in luxury, parading in brocaded dressing gowns of burnt orange and pajamas of cerulean and glass green—glorying in his shame. He now had an early American palazzo in West Chester, crammed to overflowing with bibelots and *objets d'art*—carpets from Baluchistan and Persia, diamond-studded safety razors, solid platinum dog-collars, Hepplewhite cocktail-shakers. In it he entertained Russian grand dukes, Long Island millionaires, the editors of *The Saturday Evening Post*, the more conservative United States Senators, and such members of the literati and cinemati as had aseptic table manners.

If Mencken was not the most accurate cicerone in the wilds of contemporary literature, he was, by all odds, the most amusing. When Mr. Hergesheimer arrived, he presented him to us with the warning: "Joe has a raccoon coat but don't let that mislead you; he's overage for it; he's really a knowledgeable fellow, and otherwise civilized enough to have become a kind of stockbroker's Shakespeare."

"He's given you a new title, Mr. Hergesheimer," I said, for Sara was lending her attention to Mencken and leaving me "to cheer up Joe," who didn't look as if he needed any such charitable service. "I thought you were called the Sargent of the American Novel."

Mr. Hergesheimer smiled as he emerged from his raccoon coat, a plump figure in well-cut tweeds, with an embroidered silk handkerchief in the pocket of his coat, a Charvet tie, and a handmade shirt. He was an impeccably groomed, immensely dignified Pennsylvania Dutchman, nearing fifty. His close-cropped poll was already gray. He had bland, chubby features and a full sensual mouth. Behind their steel-rimmed glasses, his round, solemn eyes were inquisitive and discriminating. He looked more like a wealthy patron of de luxe hotels, chic clubs, and fashionable racing meets than a writer. Under his stolidity and opulence, it was difficult to discern the artist, the novelist with an exotic imagination, the exquisite craftsman of *The Three Black Pennys, Java Head,* and *Cytherea.*

Nor was it easy to imagine how the affluent *bon vivant* beside me had emerged from a Presbyterian childhood and a long harsh struggle for recognition. His grandfather, he told me, had been a Presbyterian lay preacher—a man of immense energy and vitality who had helped establish the first type foundry in Philadelphia and had written two books, one a collection of verse, the other *The American Printer.* Hergesheimer's father was a well-known cartographer, whom he remembered as always bent over his drawing board, working with a crow-wing quill in an aroma of camphor and india ink, copying faded seventeenth-century maps in beautiful muted colors. His son Joseph, a fat, shy, sensitive boy, took the money his grandfather left him and escaped from a narrow life in Philadelphia to study painting in Italy. There he met and married Dorothy Hemphill. Through her influence, while recovering from a breakdown, he began to try to write. From his artistic training, he brought to his new craft a feeling for color, a delight in form and texture, a passion for luxurious fabrics and ornaments. But his sensuous prose netted him nothing but rejection slips.

With an ironical twinkle in his eye, he said, "My first published piece was *Cavolo Repetana,* a recipe for stuffed cabbage that appeared over Dorothy Hergesheimer's signature in *Good Housekeeping.* After I finally sold three potboiling articles to *Forum,* I dug in out in the wilds of western Virginia to write *Mountain Blood.* When Mitchell Kennerley told me he was going to publish it, I cried for twenty-four hours from sheer relief."

While the Fitzgeralds were in St. Paul, awaiting Scottie's birth, Hergesheimer had run into the author of *This Side of Paradise* at the Kilmarnock Book Shop. Scott, his ardor for the profession of letters having been somewhat chilled by the reviews of his first novel, complained, "A writer's life is full of bitterness, frustration, and despair,

Mr. Hergesheimer. I'd rather have been born with a talent for car-
pentry, hadn't you?"

Hergesheimer's eyes snapped. "Good God, no! And you talk to me
about frustration and despair. I wrote and rewrote for fourteen years
with nothing but rejection slips to show for it. I spent years living
on hominy and cornfield peas in the mountains of Virginia, hammering
away on a broken-down typewriter, before I sold a damned line."

As we listened to Mr. Hergesheimer, it occurred to us for the first
time—but by no means the last—that the trade of letters was an arduous
and discouraging profession. Only later were we to learn that writing
is not a profession but an obsession. Writers, as we were to discover
from long experience with them—a large part of it of the hard, home-
made variety—are born with some strange, built-in compulsion that
makes them write for the same reason that roosters crow or hens lay
eggs. Driven by that irresistible urge, Hergesheimer had pounded away
at his ramshackle typewriter until he became one of the highest-paid
writers in America. As soon as he could afford a home, he and Dorothy
bought the Dower House, a pre-Revolutionary farmhouse in West
Chester, Pennsylvania. Collecting furniture, china, and glass for it had
become a hobby with him; and while Sara and Mr. Mencken were
engrossed in their conversation, Mr. Hergesheimer talked of Sheraton
and Chippendale, Stiegel glass, Lowestoft china, and the antique shops
in Charleston and New Orleans. "I want to do a book about the South,"
he announced. "The old South, I mean."

"Come down, and we'll show you what's left of it," I promised.

The waiter arrived with more cocktails, served in after-dinner coffee
cups out of deference to the prohibition laws. "To Andrew J. Volstead!"
Mencken lifted his little cup in a mocking toast.

"To Mabel Walker Willebrandt," Sara replied.

"To the Watch and Ward Society," Hergesheimer added. "Knopf tells
me that the boobs in Boston regard *Cytherea* as in a class with *The
Sheik* and are selling it from under the counter."

"A dozen barkers couldn't do more to plug it," H.L. assured him.

While Mr. Hergesheimer had been chatting with me, Sara and
Mencken had been engaged in exploratory talks. They shared a distaste for evangelists, gospel singers, Holy Rollers, actors, literary fakirs,
politicians, athletics, Prohibition, terrestrial redemption, the Oxford
movement, the New Humanism, and other such non-Euclidean theol-

ogies. Both of them were intellectually avant-garde, iconoclastic, ostensibly cynical about love and marriage, but basically romantic, sentimental, and emotionally Victorian.

Mr. Hergesheimer studied the two of them. "They'd make a good match," he decided before the dessert was brought on.

"Excellent," I agreed. But later the thought of what would happen to their household if a fuse blew out gave me pause. Although Mencken eventually mastered the trade of bricklaying and Sara the intricacies of opening a can, both of them had a marked lack of manual dexterity and an aversion to machinery, even of the simplest domestic varieties. Neither one of them would drive a car, operate a Mixmaster, or manipulate a dial phone if there were any way to avoid it. Part of their attraction for each other, I suspect, was derived from the numerous aversions and prejudices that they shared.

Mr. Hergesheimer evidently sensed that there was a romantic attachment between them and was inclined to further it. For he said as he told me goodbye, "I want you and Sara to come up to the Dower House for a weekend soon. And be sure to bring Henry along!"

"I see that Joe'll need chaperones," H.L. grinned. "I'll arrive with two duennas and three trained nurses in addition to a valet and private secretary."

Mencken went about his self-appointed task of looking after the pair of us with the same Teutonic thoroughness and precision with which he tackled his research. He often spoke of himself to us as "the old Ironmaster," which was only one indication of the Iron Chancellor's influence upon him—an influence reflected in his broad intellectual interests, linguistic ability, militant conservatism, championship of minorities, and even in his handwriting and his attitude toward women. Once when Dreiser asked, "Does the average strong, successful man confine himself to one woman? Has he ever?" Mencken replied brusquely, "Did he argue that Otto Von Bismarck was not a strong, successful man? If not, then he should have known that Bismarck was a strict monogamist—a man full of sin, but always faithful to his Johanna." Mencken himself was not only a staunch advocate of monogamy but was offended by promiscuity. Beyond the fact that he was convinced that the Freudians and the novelists vastly overrated sex, there appeared to be very little basis for his reputation as a misogynist.

Without exception, the women who knew him well found him kindly, courteous, compassionate, even tender in his attitude toward them. As a friend, he was thoughtful, generous, devoted, and loyal—despite his epigram "Loyalty is the virtue of a dog." Rosalind Lohrfinck, who was his secretary for twenty-two years, once remarked on how surprised she had been to find the man so different from his writings. "He was soft-spoken," she said, "always considerate of others and the very personification of politeness." Never once during the thirty-three years of my friendship with Henry Mencken did I ever know him to be impolite, inconsiderate, or guilty of the slightest impropriety where any woman was concerned, nor have I ever heard any woman allege to the contrary. If he ever inclined to "those of a certain kind," he had outgrown them by the time we knew him; in fact, the only one of the species to whom I ever heard him refer was the girl from Red Lion, Pa., the subject of one of his favorite after-dinner stories.

His fleeting acquaintance with the girl from Red Lion dated back to 1903, when the daughter of a Dunkard farmer arrived in Baltimore on the milk train and startled the Scotch hack driver on duty at the Union Station with the request, "Please take me to a house of ill fame." Since it was not his to reason why, the dumbfounded cabbie drove the young lady to the studio of one of Baltimore's toniest madams, Miss Nellie d'Alembert. The astonished proprietor of the bagnio pumped the girl's story out of her and tipped off Mencken, then city editor of the Baltimore *Herald*. He sent a reporter around, who called back to say that, while the girl was no bucolic Lillian Russell, she was a personable milkmaid with a story so fantastic that Mencken had better hear it for himself.

When H.L. arrived at Miss Nellie's establishment, he found the madam and the goggle-eyed reporter listening to the apple-cheeked girl from Red Lion, who confessed that, carried away by the urbane love-making of a swain named Elmer from the city of York, she had in an unguarded moment reverted to the antique custom of bundling and awakened to find that she had lost her good name. At daylight she went out to milk the cows, her eyes so full of tears that "she could hardly find their spigots." Convinced that there was nothing for her to do but leave home and lead a life of shame, she had run away to Baltimore and applied for a position on the resident faculty of Miss Nellie's academy. Eventually, with Miss Nellie's help, they persuaded her that not since Victorian times had young girls been condemned to a life of shame by such inadvertent slips and advised her to go back to the farm and marry Elmer. Whereupon they made up a purse, Miss Nellie prepared a box lunch to be eaten on the train, and the girl from Red Lion, Pa., was diverted from the primrose path and returned to the farm none the worse for her unique experience in the stews of Baltimore.

From Mencken's plaint that, sad to say, most men's amorous adventures began with a "slavey" and his boast in *Pistols for Two* that he had never seduced a working girl, the inference is that even in his younger days he inclined to be discriminating about the kind of women on whom he bestowed his favor. If "the Broadway kind" amused him in his *The Smart Set* period, he became wary of them as he grew older; and, if he *was* afraid of women, which is doubtful, his fear of them confined itself to the predatory Broadway variety.

By the age of forty, despite his expressed distaste for literary women, he was seldom seen in public with any other kind. He had a distinct preference for escorting young ladies who came from "the noblesse of their respective neighborhoods"; and when he invited them to meet his friends, he wanted them "to put on their noblest finery." Neither he nor Joe Hergesheimer cared for intellectual girls in frumpy clothes. When they took ladies along with them, they wanted them to be knowledgeable enough to act as an audience and sufficiently ornamental to serve as window dressing.

While writing is necessarily a solitary profession, Ben Hecht to the contrary, no author I've ever known was less a lonely man than Mencken. Gregarious and friendly by nature, he was popular both with men and women, always in demand among his numerous friends, constantly entertaining and being entertained. Between his sessions with them and the immense amount of work he devoted to laboring over his books, doing his articles for the *Evening Sun*, sending out some forty letters a day soliciting contributions for his magazines, reading and editing manuscripts, I often wonder how he found time to put in the amount of it he did with Sara and me.

Once or twice a week, he'd take us to the Schellhase for beer, to Marconi's for lunch, or, on special occasions, to the Rennert Hotel for terrapin and chicken à la Maryland. He constantly reminded us to eat enough food, dress warmly, and wear galoshes in wet weather. Further, he screened our beaux with a vigilance never equaled by our Alabama grandmothers. Into the bargain, he acted as our literary adviser and introduced us to the swarm of writers, editors, and publishers that were continually descending upon him. As often as not, he prefaced these introductions with a jocular warning—"You'll have to watch him, he's a garter snapper," or "Be careful, he's a leg pincher," or "He's a charming fellow but a chicken-chaser."

But there were no such jocular remarks about the author of *Jurgen* when Mencken persuaded him to stop over in Baltimore on his way back from a visit to the Dower House. The Sage had more respect for Cabell as a man and as an artist than for any of his literary friends. "Cabell," he said, "mirrors the disdain of a defeated aristocracy for the rising mob. He is the only articulate Southerner who is a gentleman by Southern standards; all the rest are cads." When *Jurgen* was suppressed as obscene and indecent through the efforts of the New York Vice Society, Mencken had protested vigorously that not only was Cabell's book not pornographic but that it was the best piece of writing done in America in a dozen years; in fact, a work of art.

Certainly, no man ever appeared less like the author of "an obscene and indecent" book or the subject of Emily Clark's literary gossip than Mr. Cabell did. Hergesheimer contended that Mr. Cabell affected "the drab attire of a contemporary Virginia gentleman with a black ribbon at his eye" as a mask for the creator of Dorothy la Désirée and the other sirens of Poictesme. His suit was sober gray; so was his hair and the eyes behind his austere, professorial pince-nez. His finely modeled features were cast in an academic mold; a close observer would have known that he was a scholar without seeing the Phi Beta Kappa key on his watch chain. He was easy and urbane in his manner, yet there was an inscrutable, enigmatic quality about him. Even so, it was difficult to imagine him as the biographer of Manuel and the creator of Poictesme.

In the process of overcoming tragedies that would have crushed a lesser man, Mr. Cabell had acquired the self-possession and detachment of an Indian swami. Princess Troubetzkoy once said that he lived securely barred within his ivory tower. Yet upon occasion he would emerge from his intellectual fasthold to make a brilliant observation on the human condition or a humorous sally about his friends. H.L.'s galvanic zest and infectious gusto constantly amazed him. "Mencken," he said, "is a phenomenon somewhere between electricity and influenza." When Emily Clark reminded the Sage that Virginia was peopled by Episcopalians—to such an extent that she knew only one Methodist who moved in Richmond society—and demanded to know why he thought the South was controlled by the fundamentalist clergy, Mr. Cabell sighed, "Ah, if Mencken could only acquire the *Southern Churchman* and so reach the public that has the actual and dire need of him."

With her engaging voice, flattering manner, and talent for gossip, Emily Clark was as vivacious and ebullient as Mr. Cabell was reserved and nostalgic. She had a good figure; her legs, a friend quipped, were as much admired as her brains. A columnist once delighted her by saying that she wore her clothes in the way that Hergesheimer had tried in vain to make his hard-boiled heroines wear theirs. Her tawny hair and clear green eyes led Carl Van Vechten to tell her that she looked like "a child of the Divine Sara's by a yellow leopard"—a fanciful but perhaps more accurate description of her than Mencken's, who called her one of the "Violets" in the Sahara of the Bozart.

While Mencken was discussing the future of *The Reviewer* with its editor, Sara was taking Emily's measure—and she was taking Sara's. Between two Violets of the Sahara, H.L. was bouncy, jocular, and thoroughly pleased with the situation. With a wave of his cigar, he dismissed the troubles of *The Reviewer* as common to all periodicals, offered his aid and assistance, and promised to write Alfred Knopf again about the book of sketches that Emily Clark was doing.

Mr. Cabell's family and mine were connected in some dim, distant way, and while the discussion of *The Reviewer's* prospects was going on, we chatted of our Virginia cousins and of Ellen Glasgow, whom I had met in Richmond the year before. Every now and then, Mr. Cabell would cut his eye at his host and look as if he too were amused by the triangulation. "Mencken has a way with the ladies—for all he's had to say about them. He even won Frances Newman over," Mr. Cabell observed.

"It must have been a formidable task if what Scott Fitzgerald says about her is true," I replied.

I gathered that for the last year, despite the avuncular aid of Cabell, Mencken, and Hergesheimer, *The Reviewer* had been having financial difficulties. At a time when it appeared that even if it were published as a quarterly instead of a monthly, nothing short of a miracle could keep it afloat much longer, Edwin Swift Balch, a wealthy lawyer from Philadelphia, who had deserted the bar to become an explorer, mountain climber, and author, descended on Richmond. He was, Emily said, "rich, fat, and aristocratic, and rather nauseating at times"; and when he became sentimental with her in the garden, it was, indeed, "very terrible." But after he brought to pass the needed miracle by buying half the stock of the magazine, three thousand dollars' worth, and putting it in her name, her attitude toward him underwent a drastic change. "Mr. Cabell," she wrote Hergesheimer, "thinks it doesn't matter who you marry and I'm wondering if that may not be true, and if it isn't sensible to do it for continental reasons just as he did." The more she wondered, the more sensible it seemed. In less than six months, she became Mrs. Edwin Swift Balch and abandoned *The Reviewer*.

One of the few lions of the time that she never persuaded to contribute to that remarkable magazine was Theodore Dreiser. Not long after Horace Liveright made the premature announcement that he was bringing out *The Bulwark*, begun in 1914 but never finished until 1945, we were having luncheon with Mencken at Lüchow's when Dreiser came in. He and the Sage had had one of their periodic breaks after Liveright used a fabricated quotation from Mencken in the abortive publicity for *The Bulwark*. Mencken protested that if he had said in it "the big power of Dreiser's massive impetus is evident," that he was certainly drunk and he threatened to punish Liveright for misquoting him by writing twenty anonymous letters to John S. Sumner, executive secretary of the New York Society for the Suppression of Vice, condemning Van Loon's *The Story of Mankind*, recently published by Liveright, as obscene.

Dreiser lumbered past our table with the briefest of greetings to Mencken, obviously embarrassed to see him again. Henry, he knew, disapproved of his variegated amours, his radical Greenwich Village cronies, and his communistic leanings. To a rationalist like Mencken, Dreiser's adventures with the ouija board, his preoccupation with spiritualism, numerology, and theosophy, like his socialistic schemes, were but little short of imbecility. Dreiser complained that Mencken refused to take him seriously. It would be nearer the truth to say that while the Sage conceded that Dreiser at his best was a first-rate artist, he found him increasingly impossible as a man. Nevertheless, Mencken, innately forbearing and quick to be reconciled with friend or foe, sprang up, shook Dreiser's hand, and insisted that he join us in having some sauerbraten and knackwurst. Dreiser sat down reluctantly, waiting for H.L. to scold him about the invented blurb.

"The Great American Primitive" was a massive man with a well-filled waistcoat wrinkling over his paunch. He had the head of a decadent Roman Emperor. His deep-set eyes were kindly and observant if a bit owlish behind the round, gold-rimmed pince-nez that he kept popping off and on. One of his eyes had a cast in it, so that he appeared to be looking both at you and beyond you. For a man who was so fluent, even verbose, on paper, he spoke with difficulty, pausing and groping for words and coming up with clichés and platitudes. He was patently nervous at having unexpectedly come face to face with Mencken. Taking out his handkerchief, he folded it into a small square, took it by the ends, drew it out, twisted in into a ball, and carefully folded it again. His anxiety was needless, for Mencken quickly put him at his ease and dismissed the spurious quotation by assuring him that it was "just one of those things"—and one which was happening with ever increasing frequency.

The lengths to which authors and publishers would go to get a blurb for an advertisement from Mencken were truly amazing. One of the most persistent of his clients for such items was Sinclair Lewis. After three years at Yale, Lewis had quit to fire furnaces in Helicon Hall, Upton Sinclair's brummagem utopia in New Jersey. But Red soon left to dig in on the upper floor of a cold-water flat in New York's gashouse district and write. As he was unable to sell enough stories to eat regularly, he worked first as a reporter on a newspaper, then as reader and publicity man for a publishing house. He wrote three undistinguished novels before he hit the jackpot with *Main Street*. He dedicated the book to Cabell and Hergesheimer. After it became a best seller, Lewis grumbled to Hergesheimer that the irony of its success would make excellent material for a short story. "Hell's sweet bells," he exclaimed, "here is divine comedy! An earnest young man, yankee of physical type, comic and therefore the more humorless, writes a long book to slap the bourgeois—the bourgeois love it, eat it."

Lewis's next novel moved Mencken to write Cabell that Lewis's *Babbitt* was superb, miles beyond *Main Street*, and that his picture of the hundred-percent go-getter could not be mellower or more accurate. But, unhappily for its author, it moved the bourgeois to slap back and it was reported that Lewis had had to leave Hartford, where he was then living, because he kissed the wife of the president of the Rotary Club. Whatever the reason for his departure was, he suddenly pulled up stakes and turned up, alone and quite drunk, in Baltimore, where he wanted to see H.L.'s friend, Paul de Kruif, professor of bacteriology at Johns Hopkins.

Mencken had suggested to Lewis that he do a full-length portrait of an American college president instead of a scientist in his next novel. Disregarding his advice, Lewis had persuaded Dr. de Kruif to accompany him to Barbados to help him work up the scientific background for *Arrowsmith*. H.L. was not pleased with the idea nor with the state in which Lewis appeared in Baltimore, where he had made a hole in the well-stocked cellar at 1524 Hollins Street before he left for the West Indies to escape Prohibition. He felt even less happy about the book and its author after he learned that Lewis and de Kruif had disagreed over the amount of credit to be given the latter on the title page of *Arrowsmith*.

On his return from Barbados, Lewis blew into the Schellhase one night while we were having a beer there with the Sage. He wanted to get a puff for the *Arrowsmith* advertising from Mencken, who told him that since he had from five to ten such requests a week he'd been forced to make a rule against giving out blurbs. Moreover, although he had not yet seen the manuscript, he said that Lewis's plan for a bacteriological novel was the damnedest nonsense that he had heard of in years. Such a book would not only be dull reading but scientific tripe.

"For God's sake, Hank!" Lewis exploded. "It's the best goddamn book I've turned out! Best goddamn thing ever written about a scientist. And I want you to say so!"

"Watch your language, Red." Mencken objected strongly to Lewis's use of profanity in our presence. But I think we were less astonished by his language than by his appearance.

In describing himself, Lewis once complained that he did not look so "damned soulful" as the large-eyed yearning photograph in the *Transcript*, for in real life he was rugged, with considerable nose—the thin, chinless Lincoln type. He was tall and lanky; his movements were so stiff that in sitting and rising, he reminded me of a jackknife opening and closing. The trousers of his ready-made suit were too short, and its coat sleeves left two inches of his bony, freckled wrists bare. His hair was carrot-red, unruly, and uncombed; his triangular face tapered to a point at the chin; the skin was stretched so tightly over it that it revealed the outlines of his skull. He was three sheets to the wind when he arrived. His cheeks were flushed and pitted from acne. Whether Mencken called him "Red" because of his hair or his face, I don't know.

He impressed me as a contradictory, paradoxical man who had imposed a rather transparent veneer of sophistication on a more genuine core of Sauk Centre pine, and by doing so had created a deep division within himself. Despite his affectations, he was not without a kind of homely charm. He was a glib talker with a talent for mimicry. His imitation of Paul de Kruif's measured, scientific approach to writing a novel struck Mencken as inordinately funny. Seeing that he had put Mencken in a good humor, Sinclair Lewis whipped out a notebook, got the blurb he wanted, and wrote it down. Then he began to tell us how well his books were selling. He sounded more like a book salesman drumming up trade for his novels than a writer. Each time we saw him, he went through the same routine—a routine that left the impression that we had been listening to a literary promoter who was to belles-lettres exactly what George F. Babbitt was to real estate.

By contrast, we found Sherwood Anderson quiet and rather shy. He had been living in New Orleans and had stopped over in Baltimore on his way to New York. Mencken told us before Mr. Anderson arrived that he had been a prosperous paint manufacturer in Elyria, Ohio. One day in the midst of dictating a letter, he walked out and went to Chicago to earn his living turning out advertising copy while he tried to write fiction at night. Ben Hecht had interested Mencken in Anderson't first novel, *Windy McPherson's Son,* and a publisher accepted it on the condition that the author would agree to censor and revise it. In writing his second novel, Anderson had a breakdown and spent three months in a log cabin in the Ozarks. On the way back to Chicago, he threw the novel out of the train window and began to work on the stories that were to be published as *Winesburg, Ohio.* Mencken, involved in censorship troubles on *The Smart Set* at the time, had declined the stories, although after they appeared he praised them highly. Even so, Sara's admiration for them exceeded Henry's and strongly influenced her early work.

Mr. Anderson arrived for lunch wearing a baggy tweed suit and no hat. Although it had begun to turn warm, he had a plaid woolen muffler around his neck. He was a somber, middle-aged man, mellow and gentle, with fine, dark eyes that were at once thoughtful and penetrating, and an unruly forelock, which he kept brushing back from his eyes. His brother, he told us, was an artist, and he himself had done some painting in Fairhope, Alabama, and in New Orleans, where he had lived in an apartment on St. Peter Street in the Vieux Carré, near a temperamental young man from Mississippi named William Faulkner. When he found that Faulkner had turned from aviation to writing, he had agreed to recommend his novel to his publisher on condition that he would not make him read it. There were too many writers and too much talk about writing in New Orleans, he said; it was as bad as New York. Consequently, he was now on his way to Virginia to find a quiet place to write in the mountains there.

Edgar Lee Masters had none of Sherwood Anderson's good looks or charm. Masters had given up law for poetry long before we met him. Born in Kansas, he grew up in Illinois in the Spoon River country. After a year at Knox College, he began to read for the bar, and subsequently he practiced law in Chicago. He was a typical Midwestern attorney, flinty-eyed, gravel-voiced, pugnacious, with a hard, aggressive jawline that stamped itself indelibly on my memory as being incongruous with his sensitivity as a poet. Dreiser had called Mencken's attention to Masters some ten years before. By that time, most of the poems in *The Spoon River Anthology* had already appeared; but the Sage bought a number of his ballads for *The Smart Set* and, later, more of his poems and articles for the *Mercury*. When Mencken was in New York, he frequently went with Masters to drink beer at the Alt Heidelberg, whose brew, the poet declared, he preferred to Schellhase's. An argument between him and the Sage on the relative merits of the malt liquors ensued. Masters was a man full of crotchets and resentments, and it seemed to us that he was somewhat dull and long-winded in retailing them, but amusing enough when he talked of Mark Twain with a kind of pothouse humor or let the revered Abe Lincoln have the rough side of his tongue.

"The trouble about being an author," I said to Sara after his visit, "is that one lives surrounded by authors. They swarm together like so many bees from the same hive."

"Well, you seem to enjoy talking to them."

"Listening to them, to be more accurate." The problem of how to entertain writers and editors had been simply resolved by the discovery that they were more eager for appreciation than amusement, more delighted with an attentive audience than with a rival raconteur. In the course of the years of lunching and dining with Mencken and his friends, Sara and I became the marathon listeners of all time.

We were doing well in the art of audition, I thought, when Sara met me in the post office one morning with a note in her hand. "Mr. Mencken has asked us to lunch on Friday," she announced, "but I don't think you'd better go."

"Just as you say." Between literary parties, which always seemed to fall on Fridays or Saturdays, I had been hard pressed to find time to go dancing at Annapolis, sailing on the Eastern Shore, or riding in the Greenspring Valley, and the prospect of a free weekend was not unwelcome. "But why?" I asked, wondering if I had inadvertently committed a blunder or bared my ignorance before the cognoscenti in some unpardonable way.

"Well," Sara hesitated, as we walked on over to the Chelsea Pharmacy to get a Coca-Cola, "there's to be another guest—an author who's said to have had an affair with a tycoon—and I doubt that your mother would approve of my taking you along."

"A number of Mother's friends have had affairs of their own and it would never occur to her that such vagaries could put any ideas in my head or yours, either." After thinking it over, Sara decided that I should go. "There never would have been so much talk," she concluded, "if the lady in question had not contracted to write a preface to Defoe's *Roxana, the Fortunate Mistress.*"

If we expected Mr. Mencken's guest to look the part of a lost lady, we were certainly disappointed when we arrived to find her already seated beside him at the table. She wore a well-cut, expensively tailored suit and flat-heeled walking shoes. Her hair was simply parted in the middle and drawn back from a broad face, strongly-molded, placid, and unruffled. She had marvelous dark-blue eyes that were cool, appraising, and courageous.

All in all, she was as impressive as she was unpretentious, and she wrote with an artistry that no woman in America has ever matched. She had first attracted the Sage's attention by protesting at the way English was taught while she was at the University of Nebraska. When the Comstocks threatened to ban Dreiser's *The "Genius"* Mencken had written to her soliciting her signature on the petition drawn up to protest the impending court action. Several years later, on her way to Italy to work on a novel, she had dropped by the *Smart Set* office to see him, and he had bought a novelette from her. In the course of the conversation she had told him that she was leaving Houghton Mifflin for Knopf, a much better publisher for her, Mencken thought. In due course, she became Knopf's favorite author—and one of the few, he pointed out, who had never asked him for an advance.

Although the Sage had never seen her but once or twice, they had kept up an intermittent correspondence, and he found her "a very interesting woman—a much finer artist than she knew." In the course of soliciting contributions for the first issues of *The American Mercury*, he wrote to her, asking her to send him a story. She replied from Aix-les-Bains, where she was being treated for neuritis, that she was greatly excited about the new magazine, but because of her trouble with her right arm, she had hardly picked up a pen all summer. However, having great expectations as to his new review, if she missed putting in an appearance in the first number, she hoped to contribute to the later ones. On her return to New York, she wrote him to say that she had called him several times and had never been able to reach him. Thereupon he invited her to lunch. She was, he said, "the most wonderful woman in America." The year before she had won the Pulitzer Prize for *One of Ours*. Her name was Willa Sibert Cather.

Taken at their face value, Miss Cather's letters to Mencken appear to contravene Edgar Kemler, author of *The Irreverent Mr. Mencken*, who says that "Some of the Knopf authors, Willa Cather, for example, predicted that the *Mercury* would be bankrupt within a few months and advised Knopf to abandon the enterprise entirely." Miss Cather, as evidenced by the holograph letters, which the Sage carefully pasted in the front of his copies of her books, not only offered him one of her stories but sent him a contribution for the *Mercury*, which she declared to be better than anything that she could write. The contribution, clipped from a Paris paper, was a poem, *"Un Jeu International,"* which she advised him not to expurgate, in that few of his enlightened readers will remember the "Eclogues" sufficiently well to resent the French point of view:

> Un Anglais, c'est un imbecile,
> Deux Anglais, c'est un match,
> Trois Anglais, c'est une grande nation.
>
> Un Americain, c'est un buveur,
> Deux Americains, deux ivrognes,
> Trois Americains, c'est la prohibition.
>
> Un Allemand, c'est un pompe à bière,
> Deux Allemands . . . Alexis et Corydon,
> Trois Allemands, c'est le pas de l'oie.

In the second issue of the *Mercury*, Mencken reviewed Miss Cather's *A Lost Lady*, which he did not think as sound or as important a book as her *My Ántonia;* yet, he said, "The story has an arch and lyrical air; there is more genuine romance in it than in half a dozen romances in the grand manner, one gets the effect of a scarlet tanager invading a nest of sparrows—an effect not incomparable to that managed by Hergesheimer in *Java Head*." Thereafter, his admiration for Miss Cather's work began to wane. If he or Sara ever saw her in later years, I never heard of it. Despite the meticulous corrections that Mencken made on the manuscript of *The Irreverent Mr. Mencken*, he made no protest in regard to Kemler's statement about Miss Cather's attitude toward the *Mercury*, though the following paragraph, in which Kemler implies that Nathan, Dreiser, and Boyd were equally skeptical about the venture, was struck out in the manuscript and H.L. noted that they "simply hung back." In several of the transcripts of Mencken's letters in the Firestone Library at Princeton, references to Miss Cather have been deleted; and, in reply to Marquis Childs' query as to whether an article on her would appeal to him, Mencken declined to take the piece. For although he shared Childs' admiration of Miss Cather, there were reasons, he said, why he would hesitate to print anything about her in *The American Mercury*.

From Mr. Mencken's literary friends, I had learned at least one thing during my first year at Goucher: You can't judge a book by its cover nor the works of authors by their appearance. At the end of the term, I left immediately for home, but Sara stayed on in Baltimore for another month. She had introduced Miss Winslow to Mr. Mencken, and after I took off for the summer, Miss Winslow replaced me as chaperone at the literary parties at Marconi's.

When I next saw Sara in Montgomery, she told me casually that Mr. Mencken had written her, urging her to try her hand at a novel. She had so little to say about him that summer that it was obvious that something had happened, but it was not until she exploded over a note from him that I had any inkling of what it was. Earlier in the summer, on receipt of a letter from Mencken urging her to give him a contribution for his new magazine, Sara had sent him a story called "Miss Rebecca." In rejecting it, he said:

> Dear Miss Haardt:
> I have a feeling that the center of gravity of the story wobbles—that it is about the mother one minute and the daughter the next minute. Take a minute and prayerful look at it, and see if you can't pull it together better.
> Incidentally, get yourself cured of the quotation-marks disease; you have quoted every fourth phrase in some paragraphs. It is a clumsy device, and unnecessary. Ruth Suckow had it, and I had to use an axe on her to cure her.

Sara dutifully revised the story and sent it back to him. H.L., who was an inveterate tease, sent "Miss Rebecca" back again on the grounds that it was about an old maid, adding, "We are tired of the moonings of old maids."

When Sara read his note, she simmered, seethed, and boiled over. "Well, that's that! Deliver me from literary men and all their works. Their wives always have the devil of a time with them. Katherine Mansfield even had to support that tedious husband of hers. Every time Scott Fitzgerald writes a book, he performs a literary vivisection on poor Zelda. And there's Dorothy Hergesheimer, keeping the home fires burning at the Dower House while Joseph gallivants all over the country. I've seen enough of the literati to last a lifetime."

Sara promptly sent "Miss Rebecca," along with some poems of hers that Mencken had also rejected, to *The Reviewer*. Shortly before Emily Clark retired as its editor, she wrote her:

> We are keeping one of your poems the "On Reading Minor Poems," which we like tremendously. We are keeping the story, too, although it is not our policy to publish stories. I don't know yet which issue it will appear in. It is quite real, and Miss Rebecca is very Southern. I saw Mr. Mencken in September and he said extremely nice things about you.

A few days after Sara and I returned to Baltimore, in October 1923, she had a note from Mencken, telling her that his conscience troubled him about letting her carry the Alabama moonshine, which he'd asked her to import for him, through the streets of that great Christian city. He suggested that it would be safer for him to call for her and escort her and the moonshine to Dominique's restaurant. After he had sampled the white lightning, he reported that the medical examiners declared that he had suffered no permanent damage from it but that after the first swig of it his blood pressure had jumped to 170. A ringing in his ears was followed by flashes of orange light, a slight hemiplegia, with sensations of star shells exploding in his head. There ensued a gradual anesthesia, accompanied by a coma and Cheyne-Stokes breathing. It was, indeed, a potent refresher! After telling her what a pleasure it was to see her again and apologizing for having probably talked her deaf, he added, in one of the most self-revelatory phrases in all his letters to her, "What an audience!"

Just before he "assassinated" *The Smart Set,* Mencken had printed a story of Sara's, "Joe Moore and Callie Blasingame," in its October 1923, issue. The story contained the germ of her novel *The Making of a Lady.* Mencken was dubious about the first chapters of it, as well as about another story of hers, which revolved around the romance of a young doctor. "He falls altogether too quickly," the Sage said significantly. "Such a fellow, as a mere matter of routine, would at least make some effort to escape."

At the time, Sara was already discouraged about her writing and beginning to wonder if it would not be a good idea to marry one of her Montgomery suitors and forget it. All that fall while Mencken was busy, struggling to make up the first issue of *The American Mercury,* one of her Montgomery beaux had been ardently pressing his courtship, and Sara began to find his flattery and adulation soothing in contrast to H.L.'s frank editorial criticisms and avowed wariness with literary women.

On November 26, 1923, Mencken announced to Sara that the first number of the *Mercury* was ready to go to press. The last week of work on it had been so dreadful that his yells and curses could be heard a block, he said. It was such adventures that made a man crave "the civilized Influence of Woman." If she had any missionary zeal, she would join him at Marconi's on Saturday. As the winter wore on, however, Sara was increasingly casual about him. And when I spoke up for him, she pointed out brusquely that he had given all women fair warning and she had taken it. Literary men were not for her.

Despite her studied indifference, he continued his attentions and made life at Goucher interesting and exciting for us. There was a rainbow 'round our shoulders in 1923; but our days of grace ended abruptly with the year.

$\mathcal{F}$REELANCE DAYS

AFTER SARA DECIDED that literary men were not for her, she had resumed diplomatic relations with her Montgomery suitor, who promptly bought a ring and wired her that he was coming to marry her—whether or no! A mutual friend of ours put him on the train, bound for Baltimore. Before the Cannonball crossed the Alabama line, he was assailed by a great thirst. One drink called for another, and when he came to a week later in Charleston, South Carolina, he was legally married—but not to Sara Haardt.

Our mutual friend called me long distance from Montgomery to tell me about the marriage. But I declined to break the news to Sara or anyone else; let him explain his own misadventures. Sara had not been well, and the news would inevitably be a shock to her. But how could it be kept from her? She was expecting his arrival any day. One look at me would have told her that something drastic had happened, so I held my tongue and kept my distance until she sent for me. When I arrived at her room, I had a long face, and so did she. She knew before she handed me a letter from him that I was already only too well aware of its contents.

"I'm sorry, Sal," I said. "Yet, I can't help but feel that it's one of the luckiest things that ever happened to you." In the end, without doubt, it proved to be. At the time, however, she was understandably chagrined and hurt. If she ever told Mr. Mencken what had happened to her, he never mentioned it to me—nor I to him. But he evidently sensed that something was amiss with her. There was; Sara had not only been depressed but physically ill all winter.

H.L.'s detractors have frequently branded him as a hard-boiled critic, a ruthless iconoclast, a cynical misogynist. Where ideas were concerned, these labels, as he would have been the first to concede, admit of little argument. But Mencken the critic was as different from Mencken the man as his personal life was from public opinion of it. He was keenly perceptive, acutely sensitive to the sufferings of those close to him, and quick to respond by lending whatever aid or comfort he could. Being a poet, Robert Browning was certainly more sentimental, but it's doubtful that he was ever more understanding and compassionate with Elizabeth Barrett than Henry Mencken was with Sara Haardt.

Instead of attempting to probe the origins of her unhappiness, he wisely tried to divert her. In the midst of the constant crises that attended the birth of the *Mercury,* he took time out to drop her a note every few days and to lunch with her whenever possible between his trips to New York. In one of the notes, written after a meeting of the Saturday Night Club at 1524 Hollins Street, he revealed domestic virtues that she had never thought a literary man could possess. Mencken's mother and sister, whom he described as "virtual teetotalers," listened to the music for a few minutes and then politely retired upstairs, leaving the club members to their beer and Beethoven. Inasmuch as his mother was an immaculate housekeeper, Henry dutifully cleaned up the debris, emptied the ash trays, and rearranged the furniture before he went to bed—even while he was working night and day to get the *Mercury* out.

The first issue of *The American Mercury* appeared on the newsstands in January 1924. A number of the initial reactions to Mencken's requests for contributions to it had been tepid, even discouraging. Dreiser protested that the magazine sounded too respectable, too tame. Mencken warned him not to be deceived by the dignified green cover and elegant type. "What will go on inside the tent is another story," he added. "You will recall that the late P. T. Barnum got away with burlesque shows by calling them moral lectures." To Upton Sinclair's objection that the magazine lacked a constructive point of view, the Sage retorted that if it ever developed one, "it will be only over my mutilated and pathetic corpse. The uplift has damn nigh ruined the country. What we need is more sin."

However, the explosion that followed the inaugural number of the *Mercury* was touched off by satire, not sin; the bohemians, rather than the bluenoses and the booboisie, raised the hue and cry that met it. In one of its leading articles, "Aesthetes: Model 1924," Ernest Boyd attacked the Greenwich Villagers, the expatriates, and the literary fads imported by them. The news ran through Washington Square like wild-fire. By sundown, every newsstand below 20th Street had sold out its last *Mercury*. Next day, no one could obtain a copy anywhere in New York. The Villagers united and marched against Boyd's East 19th Street apartment, where they besieged him for three days, taunting him with bull horns, jamming his doorbell, throwing stink bombs through his windows, and bombarding him with ripe fruit and vegetables when he tried to escape.

The *Mercury* became an instantaneous success. Mencken was jubilant. On the strength of its sales, he said, Knopf had bought eight new chrome-yellow neckties and a carved weichselwood walking stick. The authors who had "hung back" buttonholed the editors in their new offices in the Heckscher Building, where Knopf had given them a suite, so somberly luxurious and subdued in contrast with their old *Smart Set* cubbyhole that Mencken called it "the undertaker's parlor." The post-man now poured out tons of manuscript on his desk there.

By the time H.L. returned to Baltimore, Sara felt well enough to help him celebrate his success; but by January 12, the date set for the party, she was too ill to go anywhere. He was gravely concerned about her, knowing as he did that she was alone and sick. On receipt of a note from him, asking me to let him know at once how she was, I called him. He urged me to take her to the hospital immediately. But there was a flu epidemic raging, and it was impossible to get a doctor or a nurse, much less a hospital room.

Sara's bronchitis soon developed into pleurisy and the pleurisy into tuberculosis. It was, of course, impossible for her to go back to teaching; and Goucher, with the magnanimity of such institutions, stopped her salary. Sara's friend, Dr. Marjorie Hope Nicolson, who was then teaching at Goucher, protested so vigorously to the president of Goucher that she incurred his displeasure. He remained unmoved and Sara unpaid.

Marjorie Nicolson was, as she used to say of Thomas Hobbes, a rare combination of wit and wisdom. She had taken her A.B. and M.A. at the University of Michigan, served as instructor there after teaching in Saginaw and Detroit, and taken her doctorate at Yale. In the autumn of 1923, she became a fellow of Johns Hopkins and assistant professor of English at Goucher. Her high coloring and cherubic expression gave her a youthful appearance that belied her scholarly attainments. Her hair was auburn brown, wavy, and worn in a coronet braid around her head in a way that lent dignity to her youth. She had a nobility, an unassailable intellectual integrity, a brilliant mind and a razor-sharp wit. Her field at the time was John Milton, but her Puritanical orientation ended with her research. She was equal to any diversions we could propose; she was an excellent raconteur and a delightful companion.

It sometimes required Marjorie and me both to make Sara stay in bed, eat, and take her medicine. When she threatened to get up and go out despite our objections, Marjorie took a firm line with her and Mr. Mencken wrote her.

> Zu befehl, Fraulein Oberst! I am at your orders Saturday. But I protest very violently, as a lay member of the faculty, against your leaving the house with a temperature still running. It is in such weather extremely dangerous. . . . . Stay in bed until you are back to normal.
>
> All I ask is that, when I come to judgment on the dreadful Resurrection morn, the fact be remembered that I sent you no flowers while you were ill.

But if Mencken, distrustful of his sentiment and always inclined to conceal it, avoided billets-doux and floral displays, he more than made up for it with books, wine, and cheerful notes. His attentions, Miss Winslow's constant encouragement, and Marjorie Nicolson's courage and selfless devotion sustained Sara during those dark days.

With the exception of Miss Winslow, there had never been anyone in the world like Marjorie to Sara or to me—and there never would be again. Nor were we alone in the feeling we had about her. In her autobiography, Mary Ellen Chase remembers that her early days as a lecturer were enlivened by "the good companionship" of Miss Nicolson, then a fellow instructor at the University of Minnesota. And again, when Miss Chase, who had had a long fight against tuberculosis, complicated by financial difficulties, learned from Marjorie that Sara now had similar difficulties, she wrote her a long reassuring letter, which she concluded by expressing what all those who were ever fortunate enough to have Dr. Nicolson for a friend have felt about her. "Give my love to Marjorie," she said. "I know what a bulwark she is to you. If I had to choose suddenly between the Lord and Marjorie, I'm awfully afraid I'd snatch for her. She's such an outward and visible sign, and I've always been eager for the tangible in times of need."

Without Marjorie's strength, loyalty, and care, I doubt that Sara would have survived that harrowing winter. Robust, tireless, endowed with intellectual vigor and a physical vitality such as few intellectuals have, Marjorie taught her classes at Goucher in the morning, did her work at Johns Hopkins in the afternoon, nursed Sara in the evenings, and then sat up half the night typing manuscript. On February 14, 1924, the *Goucher Weekly* reported: "Dr. Nicholson's [*sic*] edition of Shelley and Keats, published by Harper's, came out the week of January 28th, her edition of Tennyson, published by Houghton Mifflin, appeared a week later." How she did it all, and yet remained so calm, humorous, and amiable, neither Sara nor I ever knew.

In her own way, Sara was as remarkable as Marjorie. Day after day, ill, discouraged, alone, hard-pressed, and often cold in her bare little room, she sat up in bed, writing, rewriting, and revising with unfaltering pluck and determination. Despite her efforts to make light of her illness, it soon became evident that something had to be done for her. She was losing weight, and more than once I'd seen a streak of blood on the handkerchiefs that she tucked under her pillow when I brought over her meals. After a series of consultations with Miss Winslow, Miss Nicolson, and Mr. Mencken, we decided to put her in Maple Heights Sanitarium, at Sparks, Maryland.

While Sara was at Maple Heights, Mencken's constant solicitude and encouragement did more to speed her recovery there than anything in the materia medica. As soon as she was well enough to have company, every Friday afternoon at three o'clock a Yellow Cab ground to a stop in front of the dormitory; and Mencken, square-rigged and stocky, looking like a well-fed professor in his high collar and tightly buttoned blue suit, bounded out of it.

With a Victorian courtliness that was surprising, particularly from the literary lion of the moment toward a teen-ager, he bowed me into the waiting taxi, and we were off to visit Sara. On our arrival at the sanitarium, the doctors and nurses would crowd into her room to see the show that Mencken put on for her. He would pat down his cowlicks, settle his tie, whip a pious tract out of his pocket, and with a solemn face read an account of the Holy Rollers' antics or the evangelists' promises to the faithful of the golden streets and pearly gates awaiting them beyond this best of all possible worlds. Sara's doctor was a deeply religious man; but, shocked though he must have been, he never missed one of Mencken's performances. Whenever he saw the doctor blocking the doorway with half a dozen nurses and attendants behind him, craning their necks to catch the act, H.L. would shift from the fundamentalist pulpit to the medicine-show tent and lecture them on the virtues of Maryland madstones or Dr. Mencken's hay-fever cures, which had only one thing in common with those of the medical faculty: They invariably failed to work.

Mencken's first premise in regard to the human body was that it is a "horrible contraption," hence his delight in pointing out the defects and the ills to which it is heir. Preoccupied as he was with the weaknesses and diseases of the human organism, now that Sara had become a valetudinarian, his interest in her increased with each visit to the sanitarium. No father ever watched over a sick child more assiduously or more devotedly than H.L. did over Sara.

At the end of February, his visits to Maple Heights were temporarily interrupted by a series of emergencies in the *Mercury* office that required his presence in New York. Nathan was ill with the flu, the printer was drinking, and the stenographer had quit without notice. Her replacement, drawn from the intelligentsia, read Guillaume Appollinaire and Remy de Gourmont—with dire results to her transcription of editorial copy. Trouble, trouble! Mencken was up to his ears in it, he confessed. In reply to a note from Sara praising an editorial of his in *The American Mercury*, we have an inkling of what she meant to him

> You are right about the assault upon the poor peasants in the editorial; it was very fair invective. But how am I to write another unless I am refreshed? May I say with all respect that if you don't know the process of ideational genesis in an Artist then you are the hell of a psychologist. I have to talk the stuff out first, and you are the victim.

On learning from me that Sara had had a birthday on March 1, on St. Patrick's day Mencken notified her:

> I am sending you a modest bauble [a jeweled pendant, if I remember] bought in Berlin a year ago. I put it into cold storage, waiting for the appearance of a gal beautiful enough to wear it. Yesterday I unearthed it, and the fact dawned upon me that the hour had come. It is barbaric, to be sure, but you can manage it. It will make you look like the Empress Theodora.

Next time Mr. Mencken came to take me to see Sara, although he lacked the whiskers of the gray-bearded critic I'd envisioned before

I met him, he *was* walking with a cane. He had been lamed by a tumor on the ball of his foot, he explained, and he could hardly put his "hoof" to the ground. After I had expressed my sympathy, remembering his story of how G.B.S. had been captured by Mrs. Shaw after he was slowed down by a lame foot, I added, "Be careful, or that rich widow in Hoboken will overtake you."

"Deo volente!" he replied with a straight face. Although in reality, as he later pointed out, he had never been engaged to marry any one except Sara, he frequently invoked the mythical Mrs. Bertha Kupfernagle of Hoboken, New Jersey, as his fiancée. The widow of his dreams was, he declared, as handsome and well-padded as any soprano in a Wagnerian opera company; but more important to a practical man, her husband had left her $75,000 in Liberty Bonds, his jewelry, including a Masonic watch charm set with twelve diamonds, and a large library of pornographic books, most of them readily salable at tempting prices. Of such was the stuff from which the gossip columnists wove the inventions that periodically troubled Mencken's romance with Sara. Moreover, he was an inveterate tease, and being wide-eyed and credulous in those days, Sara was sometimes vexed by his reported betrothals and by the spoofing with which he camouflaged his affection for her.

Marriage, Mr. Mencken had frequently advised us, afforded a far more pleasant career for a woman than journalism. On receiving the announcement of my engagement, the Sage tendered his hearty and typically Menckenesque congratulations. His advice to ladies of letters, he said, never varied, it was always "Get married as fast as you can." It was a relief to know that I had chosen a businessman instead of a literary man. Women should avoid artists as they would the plague. A husband without money was worse than a husband with paralysis agitans. A wise girl's virgin fancy should be confined to rich Babbitts and prosperous Rotarians; in a word, to men engaged in a sound and lucrative business. Let her lead the goof to the altar and then lay in a stock of typewriter paper and begin her book. If it turned out to be a best seller, the Babbitt would be immensely proud of it; if not, he would give thanks to his Heavenly Father that she had been disembarrassed of her notions and returned to her household duties. Babbitts make the best husbands. Remember the sad lot of the wives of Shakespeare, Wagner, Ibsen, and in a later time, Sinclair Lewis and Theodore Dreiser.

The Sage spent a halcyon summer at his favorite pastime: covering the carnivals of buncombe at the national conventions. After the Republicans nominated Coolidge at Cleveland, Mencken reported to Sara that the performance there resulted in "the usual obscenity." But for the first time on record both the delegates and the alternates were sober—due, no doubt, to the refining influence of the unusually large number of women delegates present. After the passage of the Nineteenth Amendment four years before, Mencken had predicted that it would result in replacing alcoholism, the chief curse of American politics, with adultery. He later apologized for his prediction by pointing out that he had not then seen any great number of lady politicians. Now he found, taking them by and large, that they were more dissuasive than the Seventh Commandment. The average diameter of those that answered the Republican roll call he estimated at one meter.

The Democratic ladies at the Madison Square Garden Show a few weeks later he found slenderer and more sightly, but much less thrilling than the performance Governor Brandon put on with his unshakable "Alabama votes twenty-four votes for Oscar Underwood." But despite Brandon's efforts, the Democrats finally nominated "John W. Davis of Wall Street, West Virginia." To the argument that if Davis was a Wall Street lawyer he was also a gentleman, Mencken retorted that going into politics was as fatal to a gentleman as going into a bordello was to a virgin.

After the conventions, Mencken was hospitalized to have the tumor removed from his foot. Consequently, he saw little of Sara before she was released from Maple Heights. By November she was back in Montgomery. Since he had been exercising his talent as a brewer while he was lame, he offered to instruct her in the art and assemble the necessary equipment for her to take home with her. The introduction of sound beer, he stood convinced, would be the salvation of Alabama. At the end of January, H.L. wrote her that as a *coup de grâce* after an automobile trip through a blizzard with Paul de Kruif, he found himself involved in a gigantic literary lunch for Sherwood Anderson, at which "all the vermin of New York" were present. Anderson, he said, turned up in a yellow-and-brown tweed suit, a navy-blue shirt, and a flowing necktie with a ruby stickpin an inch in diameter—a remarkable get-up, due no doubt to the fact that Anderson had recently taken a new wife and was not yet himself. Dreiser, according to H.L., had been invited but declined and was thus spared the ordeal of a dry party, at which the ladies ran to adiposity and the only young and fetching ones were probably stenographers.

De Kruif gave the Sage all the details of his controversy with Sinclair Lewis over *Arrowsmith*. In forwarding a copy of the book to Sara, Mencken pointed out that it would probably not have the popular success of *Main Street* and *Babbitt* but that there was interesting material in it, "largely contributed by De Kruif, Lewis's collaborator." Henceforth, despite Lewis's dedication of *Elmer Gantry* to Mencken, their relations were never genuinely cordial again.

On March 4, 1925, H.L. wrote Sara:

> I have spent two whole days trying to discover and arrange the history of the Menckenii for Goldberg [Isaac Goldberg, who was working on a biography, subsequently published as *The Man Mencken*]. When that is finished I must go through all my early newspaper stuff, and make selections from it. Then I must try to remember the details of my spiritual history—how I became a Christian, etc. If I had plenty of time it would be amusing, but I have very little. Goldberg will give you a show, but he'll not make a book. That job is reserved for you. Title: "An American Patriot." I authorize you to publish it ten years after my exitus from these scenes.

Disgusted with fiction by the repeated rejections of her novel *The Making of a Lady*, Sara took his suggestion under advisement. At her instance, I brought my diaries over, and we wrote down all we remembered about Mr. Mencken. In the future, she decided, she and I were both to keep notes on the sayings and doings of that amazing gentleman. What happened to the data Sara collected, I have never discovered. There are a few of her rough notes on him in her scrapbook and a number of my jottings among my papers—all that came of that project.

All spring Mencken had been swamped by work, visitors, and correspondence. He once told me that while he edited the *Mercury*, he received between thirty and forty letters a day, which he meticulously answered, barring acts of God, by return mail. Although the circulation of the *Mercury* had soared to 77,921, editorial problems had begun to plague the Sage. After an article by Dr. Morris Fishbein appeared in the *Mercury*, the osteopaths demanded that its pages be thrown open to them and that they be given license to expound their gospel in it at length. Then an argument with Nathan arose over a play, *All God's Chillun Got Wings*, which Eugene O'Neill had written at Nathan's request for the first issue of the *Mercury* but did not finish in time to meet the deadline. The play dealt with miscegenation, and Mencken did not think it suitable for the *Mercury*, but Nathan insisted on publishing it in the February number.

When O'Neill was presented a gold medal for drama by the National Institute of Letters, the butt of many of Mencken's jokes, the Sage summoned O'Neill to the *Mercury* office and told him that he had received an insult, which he and Nathan proposed to erase by presenting him with a more suitable medal. The editors then produced a large horseblanket pin, to which was attached an immense pretzel, on which was pinned a piece of Westphalian ham, from which dangled a piece of bologna. After Nathan pinned the *Mercury* medal on O'Neill, Mencken steered the playwright toward a bottle of Napoleon brandy and invited him to have a drink. To his chagrin, O'Neill found the bottle and glasses cemented to the table. Finally, with harmony seemingly restored between them by their mutual delight in such horseplay, Mencken and Nathan took O'Neill out and bought him a drink.

But other disagreements on editorial policy followed. Getting the magazine going had been a much harder job than Mencken had anticipated. Thus far he had drawn no salary and had paid his own expenses. "I almost went crazy the first year," he confessed to Dreiser, "for reasons you may suspect." At the end of that time, in a polite, businesslike letter to Nathan, Mencken made him a give-or-take proposition:

> After a year's hard experience and due prayer, I come to the conclusion that the scheme of *The American Mercury*, as it stands is full of defects, and that to me, at least, it must eventually grow impossible.

He enumerated his conclusions as follows:

> 1. That the magazine is fast slipping into the formalism that ruined *The Smart Set*—in other words, that we are beginning to depend upon rubber stamps rather than ideas.
> 2. That this decay is due mainly to the need to stay within the narrow (and progressively narrowing circle of our common interests)—in brief to the duality of editorial control.
> 3. That no remedy is worth anything that doesn't strike at the root of the difficulty.
> Therefore, I propose the following alternatives:
> 1. I will, as of January 1st next [1925], take over complete control of the editorial department, put in a managing editor to run the maga-

zine and operate the magazine as Sedgwick operates the *Atlantic;* or
  2. I will retire from all editorial duties and responsibilities, and go
upon the same footing that other contributors are on.
  My inclination at the moment is to choose no. 2. I can see nothing
ahead, under the present scheme, save excessive and uninteresting
drudgery, and a magazine growing progressively feebler.
  In case no. 2 is adopted, . . . I am willing to cancel my stock or to
turn it into the treasury. I offer to write one article a month for the
magazine at the same rate paid the other contributors.

No proposal to dissolve an editorial partnership could have been
fairer or more calmly made. But Nathan was not pleased with it, nor
was he prepared to accept either one of Mencken's proposals, and he
delayed making a decision of any kind. Meanwhile, Knopf denied that
Nathan had any intention of withdrawing from the co-editorship of the
Mercury. On April 28, H.L. told Philip Goodman: "The Nathan divorce
proceedings are dragging horribly, but I expect to get rid of them very
shortly."

A visit from Dudley Field Malone on May 26 brought a diversion
from the *Mercury's* troubles. Malone and Clarence Darrow, both noted
trial lawyers, had appealed to their good friend Mencken to act as what
he termed "consulting Man of Vision" in the Tennessee evolutionist
trial in which they were to serve as attorneys for the defense. Mencken
advised them that the best way to handle the case was to convert it
into an all-out attack upon William Jennings Bryan, who headed the
prosecution of John Scopes, a rural schoolmaster charged by the fundamentalists with teaching the sacrilegious Darwinian theory in violation
of the enlightened laws of Tennessee. Bryan, the Sage pointed out, was
the central figure in the case, not the "poor worm" of a schoolmaster.
In Dayton, a typical small town in the hills of Tennessee, where the case
was to be tried, the local attorneys on both sides were candidates for
office and hoped to make political capital of the issue. The danger was,
Mencken thought, that the rural jury would quickly acquit Scopes and
so spoil the show at what promised to be the greatest trial since that
held before Pontius Pilate.

As the *Sunpapers* were preoccupied with the cultural lag in the
South, their editors took the Scopes trial seriously and prepared to cover
it elaborately. J. Fred Essary and Frank Kent, the political analyst, were
dispatched by the *Sun;* Henry M. Hyde and Mencken by the *Evening*

Sun. Edmund Duffy, whom Mencken had enticed to Baltimore as cartoonist for the *Sun,* went along to caricature the gyrations of William Jennings Bryan at first hand.

Christians of the Bryan sect break into a cold sweat when it is argued that they are descended from chimpanzees, Mencken said, and "Their grandchildren will sweat doubly, and their second reason will be better than their first." On May 26, 1925, he wrote Fitzgerald, who was then in Paris, "You are missing a superb show. In a few weeks I am going down to Tennessee to see a schoolteacher tried for teaching evolution. Match that in your decayed principalities if you can." In high glee over the prospect of witnessing such a circus as the "monkey trial"—with the Great Commoner denouncing the theory that man had evolved from a lower order of primates—Mencken announced to Tully on the eve of his departure, "I am off to Dayton, Tenn. to hear the trial of the accursed infidel who flouted Genesis. My pen is at the disposal of the sainted Bryan."

With the help of Edgar Lee Masters and several steins of Union Hill beer, the Sage composed a circular touting a mythical rival to Bryan, a fundamentalist, Elmer Chubb, LL.D., D.D., who promised to swallow massive doses of poison and allow himself to be bitten by poisonous snakes. Among the numerous testimonials offered was one by Mencken himself, saying, "Chubb is a fake." The Sage had a thousand of the handbills printed and hired a local boy to distribute them in Dayton. To his dismay, in the fundamentalist camp miracles such as Chubb promised to accomplish were taken so completely for granted that the circulars attracted not the slightest attention on the streets, or even in Robinson's Drug Store on the courthouse square, where the faithful gathered on sultry afternoons to refresh themselves with Coca-Cola spiked with mountain dew. From Chattanooga on July 8, 1925, H.L. told Sara:

> The show is five times better than I expected. That such a place as Dayton exists is really staggering, and a superb testimony to the virtuosity and the daring of God. I'll be writing about it for the next 10 years. Last night we were hauled to the top of Lookout Mountain for a bout with the Chattanooga noblesse. . . . The usual story in the Confederacy (and Nawth): the women are mainly very pretty and some of them were amusing, but the men were unspeakable. They are rich here, but money has done them no good. I have met a number of

charming young fellows, educated beyond the Jordan. Their fathers are all like Rotarians in Bethlehem, Pa.

The next day he informed her:

> I am moving out to Dayton today. It turns out to be impracticable to cover the story from here. Dayton is 40 miles away, over a hilly road, and it takes an hour and a half to get there even at high speed. The trip out and back yesterday gave me the worst scare I have had since the battle of Chancellorsville. There are five grade crossings, all magnificently concealed. At every one there is a big sign giving the number of a Chattanooga undertaker. The chauffeurs rush down the mountains at 40 miles an hour. Altogether, such riding is not for a man with a duty to Humanity. So the whole Baltimore *Sun* outfit moves to Dayton this morning. We have two rooms in the home of a Christian woman. We hope to come in every few days to change our collars. Temperature: 100 degrees.
>
> So no more this day from the eminent 100% American critic and publicist, Mencken, who kisses your hand.

On Bastille Day, from the home of the dentist where he had taken a room, he went on to say:

> The temperature here must be 120 at least. The peasants pack into the courtroom like sardines in a can, eager to see Darrow struck dead. Yesterday afternoon the whole assemblage began to steam. I have a window picked out, and shall jump forty feet when God begins to run amuck.

In the Dayton courtroom, what had promised to be an amusing farce soon deteriorated into theological controversy. The Great Commoner, gotten up to play the part in baggy trousers and short-sleeved shirt, without coat, collar, or tie, sat at the prosecution table, alternately catching at flies and waving them away with his tattered palm-leaf fan, looking "spavined, moth-eaten, and mangy" but still "full of Fundamentalist dynamite." Darrow, perspiring, red-faced, continually raking back the question mark of damp hair that fell into his eyes as he pounded away at the defender of Genesis, finally forced him to the wall. "The thing was downright fabulous," Mencken declared. "When Bryan began arguing that man was not a mammal I almost swooned."

Before it was all over, the Sage was more shocked than amused by what he saw and heard in Tennessee. He had never before rubbed shoulders with countrymen or been in daily contact with Christian fanatics, he said. About twenty-five miles back in the hills from Dayton there was a rather pretentious spiritualist camp, patronized in the winter by well-to-do converts from all over the country. When Mencken visited it in July, however, only "about thirty head of mediums were in residence," but still enough to give the old women who took part in the séances more information from their dead husbands than they had ever gotten out of them in life. One of the resident psychics, an English spiritualist, took the Sage aside to warn him that most of the American mediums at the camp were quacks. Even so, Mencken was less amazed by the antics of the mediums than by those of another local sect. One dull evening, after an equally dull day in the courtroom, he and Henry Hyde took off into the hills to investigate the theological orgies of a Holy Roller meeting. His caustic account of the safari in "The Hills of Zion" seared the eyeballs of all the fundamentalists who were literate enough to read it. On July 28, he wrote Gamaliel Bradford, "I set out laughing and returned shivering. The Fundamentalists are on us! They will sweep the South and Middle West, Bryan or no Bryan."

The death of the Great Commoner from apoplexy immediately after the trial provided a gruesome ending to his morbid forensics at Dayton. Bryan had won the battle against Scopes, only to lose his personal war with Malone and Darrow. "We killed the son-of-a-bitch," Mencken said, with the seeming callousness with which he so often camouflaged a painful emotion. His savage obituary, "In Memoriam: W.J.B." published in the *Evening Sun* on the heels of "The Hills of Zion," caused a furor in Baltimore. As the *Sunpapers* had not only provided Scopes's bond but, when he was found guilty, paid his one-hundred-dollar fine for him, there could be no doubt of their position in the controversy; but faced with a threatened boycott by the fundamentalists because of Mencken's assault on the stupidity, the ignorance, and the hypocrisy of the Bible Belt, the editors trimmed their sails and emasculated "In Memoriam: W.J.B." Irked by their action and jarred by a false report that he had been threatened by an armed mob in Dayton, the Sage wrote Sara on August 4:

> But life on this mud-pie is always a mess. I sweat all day, and still find it impossible to get to my book [*Notes on Democracy*].
> Judging by the clippings that continue to flood in, the Dayton bravos now let it be known that they actually ran me out of town. What a knightly outfit! They actually never even got up enough courage to call

me names (that is, openly) until after I had left. The reason was simple: there were 50 or 60 newspaper men in town. The business had the usual accursed effect: it brought me a ton of mail, mainly from idiots, Christian and infidel.

The canards that flew thick and fast after Mencken announced that Nathan had left his editorial bed and board, and withdrawn as co-editor of the *Mercury,* did nothing to sweeten the bitter aftertaste of the Dayton expedition. Rumor to the contrary, there had been no violent break between them; their dual control of the magazine had not worked, and Nathan had stepped down from co-editor to contributing editor. The *Mercury* had not run aground on the financial shoals that proved disastrous to so many new magazines. As Mencken told Dreiser in September, "There is now deeper water under the ship, and so it is possible to reward the virtuous. Don't blab this around. I don't want to be beset by the noble birds who, in the first days, refused to lend a hand. I have a list of them."

One of his loyal contributors, Ernest Boyd, had published *H. L. Mencken,* a short biography of the *Mercury's* editor, earlier in the summer. In commenting on it to Sara, the Sage said, "Boyd's book is certainly not bad. But he overlooked two things. First, that my whole body of doctrine rests upon a belief in liberty. Second, that I am far more an artist than a metaphysician." But of Isaac Goldberg's *The Man Mencken,* which appeared shortly afterward, the Sage said to Hergesheimer, "God help you if you try to read it. It is a shameless thing." The book somehow made him feel as if he should soon retire. On September 12, he would be forty-five, senility was toying with him and he contemplated applying for admission to a Trappist monastery. But perhaps he had served God enough. The Republic, he added, of course remained as ungrateful as it was to John Wilkes Booth. In sending Sara a copy of the Goldberg book, inscribed to "Sara Haardt, Ecce boobo! H.L. Mencken, 1925," he warned her:

> After reading it you will never speak to me again. Our beautiful idealistic friendship thus perishes. I shall, on receipt of your passports, marry the Hoboken widow and settle down in the Bismarck herring business. In years to come, when you loll at Palm Beach with your Babbitt, surrounded by your lovely children, Gustav, Calvin and Mignonette, give me a sad thought now and then. It is the correct thing to do.

In the September 1925 issue of the *Mercury*, Mencken had published Sara's article "Alabama." He had contracted also to take a story from her entitled "Mendelian Dominant," and she had sold another story, "All in the Family," to *The Century Magazine*. But worry and over-work during the heat of the summer had undermined her health, and in spite of her recent sales, she was in low spirits, and so was Mr. Mencken.

Before I went back to Baltimore that fall, Sara gave me instructions to make light of her relapse to Mr. Mencken and sent him a bottle of native bourbon, aged in the wood and recommended for mint juleps. He called for me in a cab "to make sure the paddy wagon does not overtake us on the way to the Marconi with the booze." He was, as Sara said of herself, "lower than a doodle," worried about her relapse, and depressed by his mother's illness.

Ever since his father's death, he told me, his mother had been the mainspring of the family. As the eldest son, he had been particularly close to her. Until arteriosclerosis incapacitated her, she had cleaned his office, straightened his books, kept his clothes in order, and seen to it that he looked presentable. After a slight stroke earlier in the autumn, she had been unable to pick up a book or hold a needle. Her malady, he knew, was incurable; all that could be done for her was to make her comfortable. That proved difficult because she was in constant pain and had to rely on drugs to sleep. He had been unable to get a nurse for her, and he was too concerned about her to concentrate on *Notes on Democracy*.

His explorations of the democratic processes at the political con-ventions in 1924 and at Dayton a year later, he said, had led him to conclude that democracy was based not so much on any rational theory as upon the organized hatred of the lower orders. This, as he intended to point out in his book, explained all its phenomena as no other theory did. Democracy, like puritanism, he maintained, was founded upon the hatred of yokels for those that were having, or seemed to be having, a better time of it. The puritan was a man who because of physical cow-ardice, lack of imagination, or religious superstition was unable to find any pleasure in the satisfaction of his natural appetites. If he took a drink, he saw himself headed for the gutter; grabbing a gal, the thought of hell staggered him. Such a pantaloon hated men who did such things joyously and innocently. The more innocent they were in their pleasure, the more the puritan hated them. And so with the democratic masses, envious of the gold and gear won by more intelligent men, they delighted in the subjection of their betters to the poltroons they put in office.

Mencken was part German, part Confederate, and like all the Southern gentry congenitally "agin the government"—religious or temporal, democratic or autocratic. With his Junker blood he had inherited not only a love of German music but an admiration for German scholarship and German philosophy. In his early polemics, he had been content to adopt the method he ascribed to G.B.S., that of making a dent in the cosmos with a slapstick. But as he matured, the influence of his "learned and bewigged ancestors" tended to lead him away from journalism toward more scholarly paths. Now he was planning a trilogy of books that would present his basic ideas on politics, religion, and morality in a more profound and philosophical vein than mere journalism would permit. He had high hopes for *Notes on Democracy*, the blast against universal suffrage that was to constitute the first volume of the trilogy. However, his attempt to put such a philosophical treatise on democracy down on paper—or asbestos, which he suggested might be more to the purpose—was impeded by his mother's illness and his editorial troubles.

Written during a period when Mencken was harassed and depressed, *Notes on Democracy* frequently bogged down in angry invective and gloomy diatribes, fell short of the goals that he had set for it, and added more clippings to the *Schimpflexicon* than kudos to his reputation. Nowhere in the book did he succeed in presenting his views of democracy as effectively as he did later in one succinct paragraph in a *Mercury* editorial:

> Now and then in a human body otherwise apparently healthy, certain lowly varieties of cells run amuck and begin assaulting their betters; their aim is to bring the whole body down to their own vulgar and incompetent level. The result is what is called a cancer. In social organisms the parallel phenomenon is called democracy. The aim of democracy is to destroy if possible, and if not, then to make ineffective the genetic differences between man and man.

To the Sage's chagrin, one of the most appreciative readers of *Notes on Democracy* was the German Kaiser, Wilhelm II, whom he had declined to visit while calling on the Crown Prince during a trip to Holland in 1922. After reading the book, the Kaiser sent its author two autographed photographs of himself, which Mencken discreetly hung in the back hall on the third floor of his house.

Early in December, in the midst of his travail with the book, the Sage arrived to meet me one evening at the Schellhase, looking careworn and distraught, with his jaw set in a stoical line and the ruddy coloring drained from his face. He was in a low frame of mind, he confessed. On top of her arterial troubles, his mother had developed tonsillitis, a streptococcal infection, which had attacked the glands in her throat and would necessitate a drainage operation. Undoubtedly she was gravely ill, and he and August were taking her to the hospital as soon as they could get a room for her.

In the midst of Mencken's distress, Dreiser blew into town on his way to Florida with Helen Richardson, his second cousin, whom he later married. Leaving her sitting out in the car in front of 1524 Hollins Street in a snowstorm, Dreiser went in to pour out his troubles to the Sage. Beset as he was by his own dreadful worries, Mencken listened patiently until he discovered that the Great American Primitive had left Helen to freeze outside. Brushing Dreiser's protests aside, he hastened to bring her in to thaw out before the fire and have a drink with them. By this time, he was thoroughly annoyed with Dreiser's callous indifference to everyone's problems but his own. He irked Mencken further by asking for a bottle of whiskey to take with him and by insisting on paying for it. Mencken retorted that he didn't go in for bootlegging, and they parted on a sour note. Dreiser, he told me later, did not even trouble to inquire about his mother or write him a note of condolence after her death.

On December 13, Mencken called me just before midnight to tell me that his mother had died at six o'clock that evening, quietly and mercifully; had she survived the operation, it would only have meant long years of suffering. When I asked if there was anything I could do, he said, "I've just dropped Sara a line. Write her more fully."

Before I could get a letter off to her, I was called back to Montgomery. There I found Sara downed again by a flare-up of the old infection in her right lung. The doctors recommended that she undergo an operation to collapse the lung and give it a chance to heal. They were sending her to a sanitarium in Saranac, New York.

On my return to Baltimore early in the spring, I found Mencken engaged in mixing mortar and laying bricks to build what he called "a wailing wall" in his garden—a diversion so unexpected I refused to believe it until I saw his handiwork. His mother, he explained, had wanted the house and garden kept up; he had no talent for such work, but he was trying to carry out her wishes. "I begin to realize how inextricably my life was interwoven with my mother's," he said. "A hundred times a day I find myself planning to tell this or that. It is a curious thing; the human incapacity to imagine finality. The house seems strange, as if the people in it were deaf and dumb." He had lost his jauntiness; at lunch, his heartiness was forced; for a man usually so full of laughter and mischief, he was subdued, almost solemn.

A few weeks later, I sailed for Europe. One spring afternoon in Paris, I ran into Scott Fitzgerald in the Ritz Bar. When he inquired about Mencken, I replied that I knew very little beyond what I read in the papers. Thereupon he launched into a garbled account of the Sage's fight against the Boston Comstocks.

I pointed out that what had really happened was briefly this: The September 1925 issue of the *Mercury* carried an article, "Keeping the Puritans Pure," in which the author, A. L. S. Wood, denounced the Reverend J. Frank Case of the Watch and Ward Society; in March, Case revenged himself by having the April 1926 issue of the *Mercury* barred from the newsstands in Boston. The excuse for the ban was that, in defiance of the wowsers, the Pecksniffs, and the bluenoses, in that number Mencken had published "Hatrack," a story about a prostitute by Herbert Asbury.

On the advice of Arthur Garfield Hays, who had been employed as counsel for the *Mercury,* Mencken decided to test the ban. Accompanied by Mr. Hays, he arrived in Boston and set out for Brimstone Corner to sell the issue of the *Mercury* that had offended the Watch and Ward Society. When at last one of the Watch and Warders managed to make his way through the crowds of cheering Harvard students around Mencken and approached him with an offer to buy the offending copy of the *Mercury,* Mencken took the fifty-cent piece that was given him for it and made history by biting it to assure himself that it would pass as coin of the realm. He was duly arrested for selling pornographic literature and booked for trial before a hostile judge. Through sheer luck, at the last moment the hearing was held before another judge and he escaped a two-year sentence.

Although Mencken was acquitted and his bail vacated, his dignity was offended by the clamor, and his reputation suffered from the vitriolic attacks of certain sections of the press. After the trial, at which the judge praised the *Mercury* and announced that he was one of the original subscribers, Case had the Greek owner of a newsstand on Harvard Square arrested for possessing copies of the magazine. When the Greek was convicted and fined a hundred dollars by the judge for disregarding Case's ban, Mencken and Knopf appealed the newsdealer's case. Mencken then entered suit in the federal court for fifty thousand dollars' damages and asked for a permanent injunction to prevent the Comstocks from molesting him further. As a test, the magazine was barred retroactively from the mails. The battle moved on from Boston to Washington, where the Coolidge bloc, the Methodist Board of Temperance, Prohibition, and Public Morals, joined the Comstocks in their fight against the *Mercury*.

In the midst of it, a racial incident in Baltimore brought the Ku Klux Klan into the opposition bloc. The Baltimore City Club invited Countee Cullen, a Negro poet, to a party at the Emerson Hotel and stood by without protest when Cullen was unceremoniously barred from speaking there. The incident, the Sage of Baltimore declared, would be hard to match in Mississippi and made the Maryland Free State ridiculous. The reaction from the Klan was immediate and vituperative and militated against Mencken's appeal for a permanent injunction.

Scott protested that his account of the "Hatrack" affair was more interesting than mine. "It should be," I retorted, "you have more talent for fiction than I have."

Undaunted, Scott went on to retail all the literary gossip of two continents and wound up by giving me a lurid account of Mencken's romance with the movie actress Aileen Pringle, a friend of Rudolph Valentino's and heroine of an Elinor Glyn film. "What do you suppose Sara Haardt thinks of that?" he demanded with a malicious grin.

"Nothing, probably. She's at Saranac and out of range of Hollywood fictions—or so I hope."

"It's not a fiction, it's a fact," he protested. Although it had not been long since he told Mencken, "I'd rather have you like a book of mine than anyone in America," Scott's stories of Mencken's adventures with the film star and the Comstocks were patently spiked with resentment and spiced with malice.

Whether despite or because of the Boston ban, the *Mercury* had been fabulously successful. Eighteen months after it appeared on the newsstands, its circulation was four times that of the initial issue. Knopf, Mencken reported, "had bought thirty new yellow neckties and taken a place in Westchester County to breed Assyrian wolfhounds." Back in Paris, I found that my French friends at the Sorbonne accorded Mencken a respect they had never shown for any American critic or editor except Edgar Allan Poe. Before I left for home, M. Régis Michaud, a noted scholar who was doing a study on Mencken, came to see me to talk over his plan for translating a selection of Mencken's *Prejudices* into French. At home and abroad, H.L.'s star was in the ascendant, and the influence of the *Mercury* continued to increase and its circulation to soar.

CHAPTER SIX

*R*OMANTIC DAYS

MENCKEN'S SAFARI into the plush jungles of Hollywood marked the pinnacle of his career as the *enfant terrible* of American letters. The best years of his life, he once said, were his forties. After fifty, a man begins to deteriorate; but in his forties, he is "at the maximum of his villainy." On his forty-sixth birthday, the Bad Boy of Baltimore was spoiling for mischief, looking for some diversion gaudy and hilarious enough to make him forget the griefs and frustrations of the past year. Despite his success with the *Mercury*, his reaction to his mother's death, Nathan's divorce from his editorial board, the sad spectacle of the Scopes trial, the long battle against the Comstocks, and Sara Haardt's relapse had left him so depleted and depressed that on September 12, 1926, he wrote her:

> I am 146 years old today, my typewriter is jammed and it is Sunday and I can't get a repairman, I have an infernal hay-fever cough and my eyes burn, and in an hour I must grab a Pennsylvania D-Zug and sweat and curse my way to New York. Three cheers for the Twelve Apostles! And a tiger! Knopf has the same birthday, but his hay-fever comes in the Spring. We shall celebrate tonight by devoting six hours to interrupted business, mainly legal and unpleasant.

After correcting the page proofs of *Notes on Democracy, Americana,* and *Prejudices V,* they seemed to him to be "dull as ditchwater" and likewise destined to be flops. To cheer him up, Joe Hergesheimer proposed that he join him on a trip to the West Coast. Mencken's interest in Hollywood had been aroused by two of its stars whom he had met during the summer. Early in August, he and Aileen Pringle had been guests of the Hergesheimers at the Dower House during a highly diverting weekend. Miss Pringle was not only beautiful and charming but amusing. Together he and she had written a one-act play, "very thrilling with a slight touch of the salacious," which they performed on the lawn and which Joe recorded with his movie camera. Mencken's appearance in the Dower House production and the publicity attend-ant upon it gave him a keen insight into the problems of Rudolph Valentino, to whom Miss Pringle introduced him shortly after-ward.

Valentino, who was suffering from a bad press and wanted the ad-vice of a sagacious journalist, asked Miss Pringle to invite the editor of the *Mercury* to dine with him at her hotel in New York. The night on which they met was so hot that it seemed to Mencken that the lid of hell was lifting. Miss Pringle, tactful as she was charming, retired in order to let the screen idol and the Sage take off their coats and discuss Valentino's troubles man to man. Mencken's first impression of the actor, whom he afterward described to Sara Haardt as "a great artist, unappreciated by the Philistine world," was the absurdity of such a formidable pair of suspenders on such a slender young man; his gal-luses were wide, thick, and strong enough to hold up the pantaloons of Chief Justice Taft.

On closer observation Mencken found Valentino attractive rather than handsome, a boyish fellow, curiously naïve and inexperienced, with an obvious fineness in him, which, for want of a better term, Mencken called the quality of a gentleman. The actor's difficulties, he sensed, arose from "the agony of a man of relatively civilized feelings thrown into a situation of intolerable vulgarity, destructive to his peace and dignity."

Valentino's request for Mencken's advice grew out of a tragicomic incident in Chicago. In the men's washroom of a hotel on Lake Shore Drive, an inquiring reporter found a vending machine that sold—of all things—pink talcum powder. His story of his discovery inspired an editorial writer of the Chicago *Tribune* to do a piece protesting against the effeminization of the American man, which he alleged to be due to the oriental splendors of Valentino in *The Sheik*. On the day that the article appeared, Valentino, on his way through the Windy City, ran into a battalion of newsmen, who demanded to know what he thought about it. The Italian's reaction was as fiery as an eruption of Vesuvius. To a Latin such an insult could only be answered in a duel. Valentino sent a challenge to the offending editor. When he ignored it, the actor demanded satisfaction with his fists—only to be met with laughter. Chicago laughed, New York laughed, even his Hollywood fans laughed. He had not only been dishonored and insulted but made ridiculous.

Dreadful as the screen idol's predicament was, Mencken advised him to ignore the ribald snickers and shrug off the jeers of the press. "Unluckily," he said, "all of this took place in the United States, where the word honor, save when it is applied to the structural integrity of women, has only a comic significance." Three weeks after they dined together, Valentino died. The tragedy of his life, pointed up by the irony of the postmortem tributes paid him by the press, touched Mencken deeply.

As he often did, Mencken masked his somber reflections with a jest. In accepting Hergesheimer's invitation to meet him in Hollywood—and thus "give the movie gals a double treat"—he announced, "Valentino has to have a successor, I might as well be it." To which he added in a letter to Ernest Boyd, "Valentino's death throws a heavy responsibility upon me. I am now the most powerful aphrodisiac in the Western World. I look to you to protect me."

After Paul Patterson, the publisher of the *Sun*, suggested taking H.L. on a tour of the South to make the acquaintance of some of the civilized newspaper editors of the Bible Belt, Mencken decided to proceed to the West Coast via the Sahara of the Bozart, accompanied by Patterson as far as New Orleans. The Sage's trip to Dayton the year before had aroused his curiosity about the Deep South, of which he had written so much and seen so little. While he was covering the Scopes trial, he had rubbed shoulders for the first time with the crackers of the fundamentalist bloc and the Ku Klux Klan. What the South was suffering from, he inferred after that illuminating experience, was not so much the Negro question as the rise to power of the poor white trash of an earlier time—in brief, the gradual solidification into custom and law of the mores "of a very low grade of Caucasian," led by ecclesiastical mountebanks. Convinced that the best way to break down the power of such charlatans was to describe them realistically, he wanted to study them further and discuss the threat they posed to the civilized minority of the South with some of the intelligent newsmen there. For publication, however, he conceded only that he was going to the Confederacy "to meet some people and have a good time" and, incidentally, induce as many white Southerners as possible to run for the presidential nomination.

On October 14, 1926, escorted by a convivial crew from the *Sunpapers,* he and Patterson boarded the train in Baltimore, bound for Richmond, where James Branch Cabell was giving a buffet supper for them that evening. Before the train pulled out of the station, they launched the first of their presidential booms by advocating Cabell's cousin, Governor Albert Cabell Ritchie of Maryland, as Democratic nominee in 1928—and thus touched off an avalanche of publicity. Much of it was as destructive to Mencken's peace and dignity as Valentino's press had been to his, and for a time it threatened to obscure Mencken's genius as a critic and philosopher by playing up his talent for making a dent in the cosmos with a slapstick.

The trip, which Heywood Broun described as Mencken's "vaudeville tour" and Arnold Bennett suggested proved him better fitted for the music hall than the editorial sanctum, began sedately enough with an elegant party at the Cabell's town house at 3201 Monument Avenue in Richmond. The next day, Mencken entertained Emily Clark, Ellen Glasgow, and his hosts of the evening before at a luncheon at the Jefferson Hotel. That night, the same party dined with Miss Clark at her stepmother's home. Between acts, Mencken took Patterson to visit the Richmond cigarette factories. "I grew up in this business," H.L. boasted, breathing in the familiar smell of Virginia leaf. "My father was a tobacco man, and I can still roll a cigar."

Before they said goodbye to the Old Dominion, they nominated its governor, Harry Flood Byrd, as Democratic candidate for President. Since Patterson was a Tar Heel, he insisted on showing Mencken what an enlightened institution the University of North Carolina had become; Gerald Johnson, formerly professor of journalism there, whom H.L. had lured away to the editorial staff of the Baltimore *Sunpapers,* also urged him to visit Chapel Hill, where he would find at least one oasis in the Sahara of the Bozart. On their way there, H.L. and Patterson stopped in Raleigh to call on another noted North Carolina newsman, Josephus Daniels, whose Prohibitionist edicts as Secretary of the Navy led Mencken to rate him as one of the hollowest and dumbest of Southern politicians, a grotesque relic of the professional spellbinders of the last generation who still clung to their black string ties and long-tailed coats. Daniels was not in, but Mencken reported, "We paid tribute to him by kissing his desk."

In Chapel Hill, the Baltimoreans put up at the Carolina Inn, where they were presented informally to the literati of the campus. Among those present at a dinner given for the visitors were the playwright Paul Green, the critic Howard Mumford Jones, and Dr. Fred Hanes of the University medical faculty, henceforth to be one of Mencken's closest friends. At the end of the evening, the Sage, who had left his brimstone at home and brought along a bucket of soft soap, pronounced Chapel Hill "one of the great intellectual centers of the country."

By the time they reached Atlanta, H.L.'s spirits had revived; once again he was full of sap and paprika and "at the maximum of his villainy." Under the headline MENCKEN, HORNS AND HOOFS HIDDEN UNDER GAY GUISE, SPENDS SUNDAY IN ATLANTA, the Atlanta *Journal* of October 19, 1926, described him as "L'Enfant Terrible of American Letters," a vitriolic editor who looked "like an ex-halfback" with "light blue eyes and a gusty Gargantuan humor." After a luncheon given him at the Piedmont Driving Club by Major John S. Cohen, editor of the *Journal*, the article continued, Frances Newman and Major Cohen took the visitors to see Stone Mountain. There, Mencken bought a memorial half dollar for his niece and posed with the author of *The Hardboiled Virgin* for a photograph, in which Miss Newman hoped that her friends would see how pleased he obviously was with Stone Mountain and how pleased she obviously was with him. His visit, according to Miss Newman, was "too julepy for conversation." But by the *Journal's* account there was conversation and a great deal of it—entirely too much for Sara Haardt, who turned her attention to writing "The Love Story of an Old Maid" and resolved to forget Mencken after the *Journal's* syndicated story appeared, in which he was quoted as saying:

> "Clever woman, Frances," Mr. Mencken told me privately. "She has an unusual mind."
>
> In the car, indeed, speaking of her new book, Mr. Mencken predicted great things for it and added selfishly that he proposed to make Miss Newman a rich woman and then marry her.
>
> "What do you think of that idea?" he asked Major Cohen.
>
> "Fine idea for you," he said. Mr. Mencken saw that the Major had him.
>
> Miss Newman was generous.

"It would be quite an achievement, marrying Mencken," she said. "Nobody has ever done it yet."

Having pronounced Atlanta "Perfect!" the editor of the *Mercury* made his obeisance to its financial titan, Asa Candler, by standing with his hat over his heart in front of the hospital where the Coca-Cola king lay ill. Then, after a tour of Emory University, he and Patterson entrained for Columbus to visit Mr. and Mrs. Julian L. Harris of the *Enquirer-Sun* there. Faced with the task of inducing another white Southerner to enter the presidential lists before they left, they passed over Georgia's governor and departed, tub-thumping for their host, Major John S. Cohen, as Democratic nominee.

In Columbus, they made a gallant gesture by presenting Mrs. Julian Harris with the flag of the Maryland Free State for her fight in behalf of religious freedom and racial tolerance. Her husband, Julian Harris, whose paper had won the Pulitzer Prize in Journalism in 1926, entertained them at lunch and took them on a tour of the city. Diplomatically brushing aside the news that *The American Mercury* had been barred from the shelves of the local public library, its editor's only comment was, "That is a matter for the people of Columbus to settle for themselves."

Another Pulitzer Prize winner, Sara Haardt's lifelong friend Grover Hall, editor of the Montgomery *Advertiser*, welcomed Mencken and Patterson to the Cradle of the Confederacy with a dinner party at the Exchange Hotel, where he had engaged the bridal suite for the occasion. The local florist sent up an enormous basket of roses, whereupon Mencken took one look at the floral tribute and exclaimed, "My Gawd! Who's dead?" Having broken the ice with that remark, he continued to keep his fellow guests laughing for the rest of the evening. Given a choice between Hugo Black, Cotton Tom Heflin, and Governor Bill Brandon as his latest Democratic candidate for President, he charmed his audience by nominating Plain Bill. Brandon, he said, had proved his mettle at the Democratic Convention two years before by stubbornly leading off every roll call with a stentorian "Alabama votes twenty-four votes for Oscar Underwood," thus creating seismic disturbances in the camp of the Hon. John W. Davis, whose stalwarts were bent on ramming the Wall Street minion down the throats of the Southern Democrats.

In New Orleans, Mencken ran into another bloodbath of publicity.

Before he left Baltimore, Upton Sinclair, the novelist and publicist, announced that the editor of the *Mercury* planned to visit him in Pasadena, where Sinclair proposed to convert that rock-ribbed Tory to socialism. Mencken retorted via the wire services that he would make a capitalist out of Sinclair when he arrived on the Coast—or else! One of the Pasadena papers picked up the story and suggested that Mencken should harangue the local Rotary Club. The Rotarians seized upon the idea of having a famous editor address them at their weekly luncheon, preferably with a stirring boost for California and Rotary. Their enthusiasm quickly faded, however, after one of their members, surprisingly literate, read them a broadside that Mencken had fired at the Rotary Clubs. Whereupon the editor of another local paper, alerted to the embarrassing situation with which the Rotarians were faced, protested in his columns at the unseemliness of inviting such a violent detractor of Rotary to address its members, denounced Mencken as a Bolshevik, and thus put a period to the episode—or so the Sage hoped.

Unfortunately, that was far from the end of it. The International Association of Fire Chiefs was holding a convention in New Orleans at the Roosevelt Hotel, where Mencken and Patterson were staying. H.L. and May McAvoy, the movie actress, who also happened to be in town, were promptly made honorary members of the fire chief's association. Mencken was photographed with her and with the chiefs, wearing one of their white fire helmets cocked over his ear. The pictures were broadcast from coast to coast in the rotogravure sections, accompanied by predictions that the Great Debunker himself would soon become a Rotarian.

After a tour of the restaurants in the French Quarter, he and Patterson spent a gay evening at John McClure's studio in Pirates' Alley. It was long past midnight before the painter took them back to the Roosevelt. Patterson turned in, exhausted from the festivities. But Mencken, the human dynamo, still going strong in the early hours of the morning, whipped out his pen and wrote a stack of thank-you notes so gracious and charming that they set his hostesses on the chicken-salad circuit aflutter.

Before Patterson left him in New Orleans to return to Baltimore, the two of them put their heads together and decided to overlook the Louisiana politicos in order to launch a serious campaign for Senator James A. Reed of Missouri, who for the moment seemed a more likely candidate for the Democratic nomination than either Ritchie or Al Smith.

Saying goodbye to Patterson, Mencken headed for El Paso alone. As he crossed the desolate bayou country west of New Orleans, the soft soap that he had had on tap so abundantly thus far began to run thin and he said nostalgically, "Better a doghouse in the Maryland Free State than a palazzo in New Iberia, Louisiana." He stirred up the Hollywood magnates by announcing that he had been offered two thousand dollars a week to star in the movies, but after extended consultations with his pastor, he had declined "because of false notes in the moral tone of the industry." His visit to the West Coast, he explained, was simply for the purpose of settling a question that had long nagged him as to which was the worse state, Georgia or California.

A brief stay in El Paso, plus a side trip to Juarez, where the free flow of vinous, spiritous, and malt liquors revived his somewhat desiccated talent for laying flattering unction to the souls of the local citizenry along his route. "If the East knew about Juarez," he told the press, "nobody would stay in the East except to do business."

By the time Mencken swung off the Southern Pacific in Los Angeles, he was hot, tired, worried over a piece of missing luggage, and in no humor to give any more fulsome interviews. He confined himself to telling the newsmen who swarmed around him, "I am in California for a few days' vacation. I am not going to write here, make speeches, or try to get in the movies. So far as I know, I'm the first writing man who ever came to Los Angeles without an ulterior motive as far as the films are concerned."

The beautiful actress who had met him at the station retrieved his missing suitcase, charmed the press into preserving her anonymity, and whisked him away to the Ambassador Hotel in her limousine. Installed on the upper floor of one of the Ambassador's bungalows, banked with fruit and flowers to greet him, Mencken surveyed the offerings and groaned that he had arrived stone cold sober and among the gifts there was not a drop to drink. It was a bad omen.

Within a few days he had broken out his typewriter and advised Raymond Pearl that Hollywood was at least nine times as bad as he had expected. He confessed that he had gone to hear Aimée Semple McPherson, the evangelist of the Four Square Temple, who had recently caused a sensation by disappearing on a morganatic honeymoon with her radio operator. Although Mencken admitted that he was not insensible to Aimée's charm, he cautioned his friends not to believe the liars who reported that he aspired to be her new radio operator. For, between the enervating climate and the general interest in the literati in Hollywood, he had troubles enough on his hands without asking for more.

Revivals had almost as much attraction for Mencken as political conventions and hangings. Although his reaction to Aimée was more carnal than spiritual, he confessed that it took all his fortitude to resist jumping in the baptismal tank. The evangelist, he said, was the most powerful preacher since apostolic times, and in addition very sightly. "Keep out of Los Angeles," he warned another agnostic in Baltimore, "or you will die a Christian." Aimée stretched a point and claimed him as a convert. He returned the courtesy by nominating her as Miss America and facetiously conceding her claim by wiring Philip Goodman:

WAS BAPTIZED BY AIMÉE LAST TUESDAY NIGHT YOU CAN HAVE NO IDEA OF THE PEACE IT HAS BROUGHT MY SOUL I CAN NOW EAT FIVE BISMARCK HERRINGS WITHOUT THE SLIGHTEST ACIDOSIS.

The flood of press notices that resulted from the exchanges between the evangelist of the Angelus Temple and the editor of the *Mercury* swelled under sudden freshets of copy from less benevolent sources. An inadvertent reference of Mencken's to O. Henry as a "jail bird" brought howls of rage from behind the bars from Alcatraz to Sing Sing. An even more virulent torrent of abuse poured over his head from the inkpots of the racist editors south of the Potomac after the Pittsburgh *Courier,* a Negro paper, quoted him as saying that he had gone to the West with a desire "to meet the intellectual Negro of Los Angeles, San Francisco, and the Pacific Coast."

Acting on the advice he'd given Valentino, Mencken turned a deaf ear to the blasts. Revived by the poteen supplied by Jim Tully, whom he had known ever since the Irishman began to write, and refreshed by a few good nights sleep, the Bad Boy of Baltimore was once more bouncy and out for sport. Joining forces with Anita Loos and Walter Wanger, production manager of Paramount, he helped them prepare an extravaganza to welcome Joe Hergesheimer, who was arriving to occupy the lower floor of the Ambassador bungalow.

When the *City of Angels* roared into the station with Hergesheimer aboard, Mencken met him with a battery of ten movie cameras. After he had embraced Joe, bussing him on both cheeks, Continental fashion, Aileen Pringle draped a garland of roses around the novelist's neck and presented him with an immense papier-maché domino as a souvenir of the games they'd played at the Dower House. The cameramen moved in as Mencken took a stance with an American flag in his hand and his foot on the domino. Then Aileen Pringle and Anita Loos linked arms with Hergesheimer and escorted him to a white Rolls-Royce, borrowed from Tom Mix for the occasion. Horns blared and sirens screamed as the party set off for the Ambassador, preceded by an escort of motorcycle police.

Mencken's Hollywood days were a strange interlude in his orderly, methodical life, and the accounts of them are many and varied. Jim Tully reported that Mencken stunned reporters there by his jocular announcement that since he was now in Movieland, Valentino would soon be forgotten. But Hergesheimer stole the role of Valentino from him by his oriental entertainments at the Ambassador. While Henry was bantering with newsmen and investigating the imbecilities of Los Angeles, Joe held court in his luxurious suite, surrounded by Anita Loos, Lillian Gish, Aileen Pringle, Norma Shearer, Betty Compson, and a dozen other film beauties.

According to Henry, Joe became one of Hollywood's most awesome figures after the story went round the studios that the novelist had put a very famous but boorish actor neatly in his place. "Of course I've heard of you," the Great Profile conceded, on being introduced to Hergesheimer, "but I've never read any of your damn books."

"And I've never seen any of your damn pictures," Joe retorted, "so that makes us both Elks."

Hergesheimer, on the other hand, credited the same riposte to Mencken in reply to a sally from Jim Cruze. There was also some diversity of opinion as to which one of them was boasting of his youthful adventures in a sporting house when a brash actress quipped, "I thought your face was familiar, Professor." Nor was the question ever definitely settled of exactly who borrowed Tom Mix's snow-white Rolls-Royce with the actor's initials on it in boxcar letters and parked it in front of a luxurious brothel. For the next ten years, the stories were told by Hergesheimer on Mencken, by Mencken on Hergesheimer, and by Tully on both of them. One fact, however, is indisputable: The

Sage had proved to himself that California was far worse than Georgia. Everything was looser on the Coast than in the South—clothes, manners, money, and morals—too loose for the Great Libertarian. He saw "nothing humorous in Hollywood save what is humorous. The place for all its petty strivings remains the complete *reductio ad absurdum* of civilization."

After being photographed with Louis B. Mayer, Irving Thalberg, and Paul Bern, who was to become Jean Harlow's husband, not to mention all the actresses of the Hergesheimer entourage, entertained lavishly by Aileen Pringle and Norma Talmadge, besieged by cameramen, starlets, and autograph hounds, Mencken was glad to board *The Lark* for a visit with the poet George Sterling on the Barbary Coast of California.

In San Francisco, Gobind Behari Lal, Hearst's science editor, met him and took him to the home of Idwal Jones, a *Mercury* author, for a Hindu dinner, featuring spiced duck cooked in coconut milk. Sterling, who was reported to have been rash in sampling the whiskey he had stocked in anticipation of Mencken's arrival, did not show up for the dinner. Later in the evening, H.L. went by to see the poet in his rooms at the Bohemian Club. At the time, Sterling seemed in good spirits. But when he did not put in an appearance at a luncheon given for Mencken at the St. Francis Hotel, H.L. became so uneasy that he returned to the Bohemian Club in search of Sterling and banged on the poet's door for a full ten minutes without being able to rouse him. His fears for his friend were confirmed next day when an AP man interrupted him at lunch to tell him that Sterling had been found dead in his room with a bottle of prussic acid beside him. He had left his swan song, a poem penciled on the back of a menu, an apologia for his untimely exit, with a notation below it, "Send this to Mencken."

Mencken was frankly "heartbroken" over Sterling's death. His trip West was ruined by the poet's suicide. Badly shaken and in a low frame of mind himself, Mencken left before the funeral to rejoin Hergesheimer in Hollywood. On November 22, aboard a private car hitched to *The Chief*, accompanied by, among others, John Gilbert, the Great Lover of the Screen, Walter Wanger, and his two wire-haired terriers, Henry and Joe departed for Albuquerque, New Mexico, in a final blaze of publicity.

On the way home Mencken stopped off briefly in Kansas City.

From Jim Reed's home there, he put in a plug for the senator as Democratic nominee before he returned to the Monumental City. His grand tour had left him with seven dollars in the bank, a sinus infection, and a heavy heart. Next day he wrote Hergesheimer that, although he'd had a gaudy time on the West Coast and believed that eventually the trip would do him good, he felt "unutterably miserable."

When he called Sara Haardt, who was now back in Baltimore, she was as distant as if she were still in the Adirondacks. She was living in a single room at 2309 North Charles Street, where he could not call upon her; whenever he invited her to meet him at the Schellhase, she pleaded another engagement.

When a woman lecturer at Columbia Teachers College alleged that Mencken and Shaw were attempting to overthrow monogamy, H.L. replied, in an effort to put a quietus on her accusation, that she "had the wrong sow by the ear" and proceeded to give an interview to Hannah Stein on "Why I Am Not Married," which almost chilled Sara's interest in him to the zero point. In the interview, copyrighted and syndicated by *The Philadelphia Public Ledger*:

> Mencken confessed that the fact that he was not married at 46 was a mere accident of fate, not due to any enterprise on his part.
>
> "If any woman of proper resolution had ever made up her mind to marry me," Mr. Mencken said, "I'd have succumbed like the rest of the poor dogs, and to the tune of pathetic hosannas. I have escaped so far because every woman who enjoys the honor of witnessing me sees at once that I'd make an impossible husband. I am too vain for the office. My interest in myself is so inordinate that it is obvious that nothing remains for a possible wife and children.
>
> "Here, of course, I do not refer to my literary work. That is not myself; it is simply my business. I refer to my rheumatism, my increasing baldness, my political and theological prejudices, my puerile snobberies, my Cro-Magnon table manners—in brief to all the things that constitute the essential man. They engross me, I regret to say. It would be impossible for me to give any seemly thought to a wife's hat, or even to the loftiest yearnings of her soul.
>
> "I am a firm believer in monogamy," H. L. Mencken said. "I have never heard any sound argument against it. It is comfortable, laudable, and sanitary. That I have escaped its benefits is not my fault; it is due to a mere act of God. I am no more responsible for it than I am for my remarkable talent as a pianist, my linguistic skill, or my dark, romantic, somewhat voluptuous beauty."
>
> But a twinkle of the eye betrayed the fact that he had given only

part of the reason why he is still unmarried. And in answer to the specific question, Mr. Mencken said that not many men, worthy of the name, gain anything of net value by marriage, at least as the institution is now met with in society.

"A man in full possession of the modest faculties that nature commonly apportions him, is at least far enough above idiocy to realize that marriage is a bargain in which he gets the worst of it, even when in some detail or other, he makes a visible gain.

"He never, I believe, wants all that marriage offers and implies. He wants no more than certain parts. He may desire, let us say, a housekeeper to protect his goods and to entertain his friends, but homecooking may be downright poisonous to him. He may yearn for a son to pray at his tomb, yet suffer acutely at the mere approach of relatives-in-law. He may want a cook or a partner in his business, or a partner in his business and not a cook.

"But in order to get the precise thing or things that he wants, he has to take a lot of things he doesn't want. So the moment his oafish smirks and eye rollings signify that he has achieved the intellectual disaster that is called falling in love, he and his life are hers to do with as she will."

It was open season for Henry among the ladies of the press. "If Mencken and Nathan would decide to take wives," declared a distaff columnist, "existence would be easier for the rest of us." The next lady to train her fire on him was the English novelist Rebecca West. Sinclair Lewis had given her an introduction to Mencken, to whom he hinted that Miss West would make an admirable wife. At a dinner at which H.L. sat beside her while she was in this country, he had said to her, "I hear you like lecturing, Miss West." Her British ear not being attuned to the American language, she misunderstood him and replied indignantly, "I don't engage in lechery, Mr. Mencken." In retaliation, she gave a spiteful interview to the press, saying that she found Mencken "perfectly charming but appallingly feminine. Feminine, that is, in the old abusive sense. He prefers to exploit his personality instead of doing the hard thinking he is capable of." Miss West added, "He is continually shaking his curls."

As Mencken's hair was straight as an Indian's, his mind the most virile since Rabelais, and his shoulders broad enough to shrug off such abuse, he refused to take offense at her remarks. Called upon for comment by the *Sun*, he replied blandly, "Whatever Miss West does or says is charming. But I refuse to accept her anarchistic definition of the word feminine. She herself is proof that the feminine can be witty and wise, and so I prefer to call it flattery and give three cheers."

Privately, he laughed to his friends about Miss West's "unmanly assault" upon him. He believed in free speech so thoroughly, he said, that he cheered for it even when it was against him. But let Miss West beware. His opponents always had bad luck; he predicted that she would marry a movie actor, the worst fate that could befall her.

Sara too laughed over Miss West's barbs. But she was far from amused a fortnight later when headlines in the New York *Morning Telegraph* announced that "Baltimore Thrills to Rumor H. L. Mencken and Screen Queen Are Engaged." Intrigued by the rumors, an enterprising reporter called 1524 Hollins Street. Mencken was not at home, but a member of his family laughed in reply to the reporter's questions and told him that Henry's engagement to Miss Pringle was old news and a joke. When the reporter asked whether the joke was on Henry or Aileen, his informant hung up the phone. Three days later, the *Telegraph* turned a double-barreled joke on both of them with a piece headed, "Mencken-Pringle Romance Strikes Snag." There was, indeed, the reporter had discovered, a serious obstacle to the match: Miss Pringle was already married to another man.

To add to Mencken's embarrassment, The Los Angeles *Herald* then put its oar into the troubled matrimonial waters that swirled about him by suggesting: "To heighten America's intellectual heritage, H. L. Mencken, a foremost author and critic, should marry a writer. Adherents of eugenics select Ellen Glasgow, considered as one of the greatest of modern novelists, as perhaps the most suitable wife for Mencken."

After my father's death, I reentered Goucher. One of the first questions I asked Sara on my arrival in Baltimore was, "How's Mr. Mencken?"

"His face is red, I imagine. Don't you read the papers?" She tossed a handful of clippings to me. "He's a closed chapter in my book."

Perhaps in Sara's book—for the time being—but not in mine. For Mencken stepped into my father's shoes and from that day forward stood *in loco parentis* to me. I continued to see him frequently; but Sara didn't want to discuss him, and I let it go at that until he asked me to lunch one Saturday and insisted that she come too. Sara, who had a touch of bronchitis, gave her illness as an excuse but urged me to go alone. "Get the lowdown for me," she instructed, "and don't bring it back decked with honeysuckle, either. I want it straight and unadorned."

On Saturday, when I met Mr. Mencken at Marconi's, he looked as if he'd been put through the mangle and all the bounce and gusto wrung out of him. He was, I gathered, even more unhappy about the turn matters had taken between him and Sara than she was. By the time he'd finished his brandy and cigar, his praises of her and her novel had become truly eloquent. "She's a wonderful girl," he said, giving me a bottle of his best Moselle to take her. "Try this soothing syrup on her and persuade her to continue to be polite to all Christian men, of which I have the honor to be one. Tell her I kiss her hand."

Between the wine and the messages—reported "straight and unadorned"—harmony might have been restored sooner had not Sara run into a head-on collision with "the half-baked virgin," as she called Frances Newman.

Toward the end of January, Joe Hergesheimer invited us up to a literary party that he was staging at the Algonquin, where he and Mencken were sharing a suite. Joe and Henry suffered more from the indignity of Prohibition than its drouth; the bar was well-stocked with rye, scotch, bourbon, and a monumental shaker of martinis. The guests gathered around the bar, exchanging pleasantries with us, and the party began pleasantly enough.

When Alfred Knopf and his wife Blanche arrived, Mencken presented Mrs. Knopf to us as "The Grand Duchess Cunegunde Wilhelmine Schwartz." How he derived the title, I never knew, but it fitted her. Small and slender though she was, she had great dignity and poise. Elegantly dressed by Chanel, she was cosmopolitan, sprightly, indefatigable—a dark-haired, green-eyed dynamo of energy and enthusiasm.

By contrast with her, Mr. Knopf seemed stern and remote. Although he was Mencken's junior by ten years, he had already acquired an Olympian manner, which with his erect carriage, bushy brows, and spiked mustache gave him the appearance of a colonel in the Prussian Hussars. Mencken claimed that Knopf had the most interesting wardrobe on the Atlantic Coast. His colorful jackets, handmade ties, and Sulka shirts of blue, black, and shocking pink impelled H.L. to observe, "He gets himself up to look like Abercrombie and Fitch. He's a fresh air maniac and his meals are gorges, but he has absolute integrity as a publisher. He's the least commercial man I ever had any business dealings with. Since I put on his silks, I have been completely free of all the concerns that other authors tell me of. I have never again given more than an idle thought to the design and printing of my books, nor to their merchandising, nor to matters of money."

Music was one of the great bonds between Mencken and his publisher. Every year he and Knopf attended the Bach festival together. Before Knopf went to work for Doubleday—at a salary of eight dollars a week—he had studied piano. He played so well that one evening while H.L. was visiting at "Borzoi Towers," as he called the Knopfs' place at Purchase, New York, he heard Chopin being played and on hastening to the music room to ask "Whose record is that?" found Knopf at the piano. Collecting phonograph records, stamps, and rare plants were among the publisher's many hobbies. Others were good food, rare wines, and a kennel of Russian wolfhounds, the inspiration of the borzoi used as the logo of the books published by his firm.

Born on Central Park West, Mr. Knopf was one of those rare specimens in Manhattan, a native of Gotham. Standing beside him was Carl Van Vechten, the most authentic New Yorker that ever came out of the Midwest—a tall, silver-haired critic, with eyes that could stare with a cold, blank look or scintillate with the kind of subtle humor that enlivened his *Blind Bow Boy*. He impressed us as hypercivilized and sophisticated, even a bit stuffy in his urbanity. Indeed, his wife, the actress Fania Marinoff, once said that he was allergic to fresh air and his only healthy habit was a daily bath.

After Joe presented him to me, he motioned me to a seat beside him. Ernest Boyd and Frances Newman brought their drinks over and sat down next to Carl. By her own description Miss Newman looked like "something between Katherine Mansfield and Jeanne d'Arc"—a flattering bit of self-appraisal from a novelist who looked no more like either one of them than she did like the glamorous heroines of her books. Nor did Ernest Boyd, dressed in somber brown from tie to shoes, look like the witty Irish critic he was. There was nothing gay or insouciant in his coffee-colored eyes. With his chestnut beard and melancholy smile, he appeared, as he said himself, "better fitted than Anton Lang for the chief role in the Passion Play at Oberammergau."

"Boyd's whiskers," H.L. alleged, "I suspect are a deliberate libel on our Redeemer."

Seeing that Miss Newman was eyeing Sara Haardt, who was bantering with Mencken and Nancy Hoyt, with a nod at Sara, Mr. Boyd asked Miss Newman, "How do you like the future Mrs. Mencken?"

"The future Miss Sara Haardt," she retorted acidly and emphatically.

A few minutes later, when Mencken brought Sara over to introduce her to Frances, Miss Newman appraised her at close range. "Miss Haardt?" The serpentine curve of Miss Newman's mouth slithered into an ophidian smile. "From all I've heard of you, I should not have thought you were so good-looking," she said in a tone that implied that she was disappointed not to find that Sara wore flat-heeled shoes and horn-rimmed glasses.

"And from all that I've heard of you, Miss Newman, I should have thought that you were," Sara replied suavely.

To her indignation, Mencken later reported to Cabell and Sinclair Lewis that she had "floored Frances with a dreadful clout."

Lewis, who had just read Miss Newman's *The Hardboiled Virgin*, groaned, "Jesus, such a woman! By God, if I spent a year on a desert island with Frances Newman, at the end of it she wouldn't be so hardboiled but she'd still be a virgin."

It was fascinating to watch the different facets of Mencken's personality catch the light. He was a delightful companion, jocular and easy with the gentlemen, gallant and sometimes coy with the ladies, kind and helpful to anyone who came within his orbit. The carapace of H. L. Mencken, the hardboiled critic, we soon discovered, had been developed as a defensive mechanism by an extremely sensitive man—and one with quick and keen responses not only to sense impressions, particularly aural impressions, but to the moods and feelings of others.

In February, when Knopf came to Baltimore to have his tonsils removed, Mencken hastened to the hospital to see him and assure Mrs. Knopf that her husband was recovering—and behaving. Knopf's fidelity to his marriage vows, he wrote her, amazed him and won his veneration; he had lined up five comely girls for Alfred's diversion, but he refused even to see them. For his own part, H.L. swore that all women had been safe with him since 1920.

However that may have been, they were far from safe with the press, and in order to protect Miss Pringle on her next visit to New York, he avoided subjecting her to further publicity by sidestepping the limelight of Gotham restaurants and taking her to dine in Union Hill, New Jersey. As he was constantly trailed by reporters at the Algonquin, he had already asked a friend of his to find a small bachelor apartment for him in New York. He planned to lead a very correct life, he was careful to explain; but, now and then, he'd like to invite some fair creature to dinner without having flashbulbs popping in her face.

While Henry was dining with Aileen in Union Hill and weekending with her at the Hergesheimers that spring, James M. Cain, a bold, handsome young writer on the staff of the *Sunpapers*, better known for his sartorial splendor than his novels in those days, was squiring Sara around Baltimore. Although she and Mencken still saw each other occasionally, they remained on distant terms.

At a party given for Emily Clark by Mr. and Mrs. Hamilton Owens, Sara had met their cousin John Owens of the *Sun* and R. P. Harriss, a young poet with fine eyes, dark curly hair, a romantic charm, and all the accomplishments of a man to the manor born. After his graduation from Duke University, R.P. began to contribute to the editorial pages of the Baltimore *Evening Sun*. At the age of twenty-three, he was promoted to its copy desk. Sara regarded him as "the white hope of the *Evening Sun*," enjoyed his attentions, and frequently went dancing with him in the evening.

Mutual friends on the *Sun*, meanwhile, reported that H.L. was busy tub-thumping for Ritchie as successor to Coolidge and more interested in presidential candidates than in ladies these days. He had given up trying to reform women, he said. Frances Newman had denounced him violently, but what her complaint against him was, he could not make out. Then Emily Clark, left rich and reckless with time on her hands after the death of her husband, began a book about which she wrote Mencken and the Knopfs so often that Henry finally served notice on her that if she mentioned it again in her letters he would drown her in a tub of malmsey. Her scathing reply, written by hand, covered four sheets of paper. He was in the bad graces of the Widow Balch, as he called her, as well as Frances Newman and Sara.

Another rough summer faced the Sage. The *Mercury* case ended in a stalemate when the U.S. Court of Appeals refused to sustain an injunction restraining the Post Office Department from refusing to carry the April 1926 issue in the mail. Mencken, who had hoped for a clear-cut victory over the Comstocks both in Boston and in Washington, contemplated an appeal to the U.S. Supreme Court. But the legal battles over the banning of the *Mercury* had already cost the magazine nearly $20,000, and the lawyers advised against making the appeal, which, in their opinion, due to legal technicalities inherent in the decision of the Court of Appeals, was unlikely to be granted.

In July, when a man in Missouri filed a libel suit against the *Mercury*, Mencken had to put aside *Prejudices: Sixth Series*, on which he was working, and go to St. Louis to settle the case. The first letter he opened on his return to Baltimore contained the notice of another libel suit. "What I can't understand," he said, "is why Sacco and Vanzetti objected to dying."

While Mencken was in Missouri, he had taken a seven-hundred-mile trip through the Ozarks, a dismal tour, for the rainy season had left roads slippery and the hairpin curves a constant hazard. With his spirit dampened by his gloomy vacation and by the new legal difficulties that faced him in Baltimore, he turned to Sara to be soothed and solaced. Always a man of original ideas, his next move in his courtship of her remains one of the most novel gambits in the history of romance. He gave her a job excerpting the scurrilous epithets that had been hurled at him from thirty fat clipping books for *Menckeniana: A Schimpflexicon*, a dictionary of abuse that he was compiling. Whether he intended to provide employment for her, or to test her affection for him, or to win her sympathy by giving her an insight into the stings and slanders that are the inevitable accompaniment of fame, he never disclosed. But whatever the intention behind it may have been, the method worked. Sara revised "The Love Story of an Old Maid." At the age of twenty-nine, its heroine discovers that:

> . . . a career is not something her fairy godmother hands out on a silver salver, all nicely tied up with blue ribbon and garnished around with banknotes; but that it is something a woman buys with her very heart's blood, with work and worry and loneliness—and never worth the price she pays for it.

"Come-to-realize" is the weakest of all plot types but the strongest of all human motivations. "The Love Story of an Old Maid," as published in the Blue Book series by Haldeman-Julius in 1927, ends, significantly enough, with wedding bells.

From Sara's letter to me of July 18, 1927, it was evident that there had been a rapprochement with Mencken, for in it she referred to him as "Henry" for the first time.

Mencken was soon writing Hergesheimer:

> I see Sara Haardt here very often; she is better looking than ever. I have a suspicion that you made a powerful impression on her. Aileen writes that she is working her head off, making movies that grow more and more idiotic. Just before Emily sailed for Europe she sent me a bitter note. I must have offended her in some way. Let God take the blame.

Miss Pringle came East again late in the summer, and Mencken spent another hilarious weekend with her at the Dower House, where she and the Hergesheimers welcomed him with a makeshift German band. Their evening concert reverberated in the press. The gossip columnists reported that Mencken had given Miss Pringle a shawl, variously valued at from fifteen to fifteen thousand dollars. Rumors of her impending divorce revived predictions that she was to marry the editor of the *Mercury*. The reports not only ended the *entente cordiale* of July between Sara and Henry but the *détente* in their romantic duel.

By fall, Sara had launched a counteroffensive, and she and Mencken had resumed their tilting match. She saw to it that I met R. P. Harriss, whom I found as attractive as she did. He and his friends escorted us to plays, concerts, and dinner dances. We had a gay time going about with them—not to mention running into them when Mr. Mencken took us out in the evenings. As of old, we still went frequently to the Schellhase or the Rennert for dinner with the Sage, but by prearrangement we invariably met some of our young men, who would insist that we all go to the Southern Roof to dance. By his own definition, Mencken waltzed "like an elephant doing the mazurka," so this riposte in the romantic duel not only left him without a parry but "sitting on the sidelines watching the intellectually underprivileged amuse themselves."

To pay him off for some of the practical jokes he played on us, we bought a large block of plasticine, modeled a variety of abstractions, to which we gave such irrelevant, high-sounding titles as "Metamorphosis of Melody" and "Pas de bourrée," set them up in my apartment, and invited Mr. Mencken to view the exhibition. He looked at our art, studied it, and passed his hand over his face a couple of times, as he always did when he was baffled. Then he gallantly dug down into his store of adjectives and came up with a few ambiguous encomiums: "Very striking," "Really extraordinary," and "Simply amazing." His words were one thing but the unholy light in his eyes was another. He was fond of saying that it was difficult to be a lady and a journalist; undoubtedly, at our exhibition, he found that it was all but impossible to be a gentleman and a critic.

Mencken regarded such countermeasures as a kind of *lèse majesté;* nevertheless, his reaction to them was amiable, even conciliatory. He curtailed his teasing, revised the tall tales of Hollywood, which he hung on Jim Tully, who was not there to protect himself, and omitted Emily Clark, Frances Newman, and Aileen Pringle from his conversation. During this temporary truce, R. P. Harriss was officially accredited to me by Sara. Jim Cain had gone to work in New York on the *World*. Thus Henry too was left with a clear field.

After his return from Hollywood, Mencken began to outgrow the Bad Boy of Baltimore role and settle down to his basically serious work as a social critic, philosopher, and philologist. He was graver, more sedate, less given to pranks and japes. Nor was that the only change in him; there were startling alterations in his haberdashery. He had shed his hightop shoes, stiff collars, and blue serge suits for black oxfords, Ivy League shirts, and Bond Street tailoring. To add the finishing touches to his 1927 edition of himself, he submitted to some extensive surgery. "I have had all my warts, moles, war scars, etc. cut off and I am full of plasters," he said. "But when they drop off I shall be one of the handsomest men of modern times." For her part, Sara bought a new wardrobe and laid in an extensive supply of cosmetics that she did not need.

In August, Sara went to New York to talk to the moguls of Famous Players about an offer they had made her to go to Hollywood. On Monday she was back in Baltimore with wonderful news. Famous Players had bought a scenario from her and given her a five-week contract, at $250 a week, to go to Hollywood, with all her expenses paid there and back. She was to get $3,500 for her first scenario and $5,000 for her second— more money than she'd ever had in her hands at once.

Before she left for the West Coast, Mencken took us to the Rennert to celebrate her success with Moselle and chicken à la Maryland. For this time her payment was not in fame but in specie. Henry had opened the doors of filmdom for her. New worlds and new adventures lay ahead of her. On September 29, she set out to have *her* fling in Hollywood, equipped with a choice selection from our combined wardrobe and a letter of introduction from Mencken to Jim Tully.

Henry had already written Tully, saying that Sara was "a special case" and asking him to find "a good quiet hotel" for her. "No gaudy bawdy house," he specified. Tully had recommended the Mark Twain Hotel, a conservative hostelry, where Sara made reservations.

Sara Haardt and Jim Tully were an oddly assorted pair for Mencken to have thrown together, even in Hollywood. Sara was essentially a Victorian—the polished product of a nineteenth-century Southern parlor—with all the graces, the delicate sensibilities, of the traditional ladies of the late Confederacy. Jim was an Irish emerald in the rough.

"Cincy Red," as Tully was called in the hobo jungles, where the knights of the road take their names from their places of origin, often said, "There's always a famine in Ireland, and when there's a dirty job like digging the Erie Canal, they send for hungry Irish ditchdiggers." Born June 3, 1891, as the son of one of these whiskey-loving, British-hating, fairy-haunted men of the bogs, he spent his first years in a shanty on the edge of a clearing near St. Mary's, Ohio. Into its scant space were crowded his father and mother; his brothers and sisters; his dog, Monk; and his grandfather, old Hughie, a fabulous teller of tales, who bartered wit for drinks. His uncle was a horsethief; his sister, a trollop; his father, a toper who deserted his mother. After her death, Tully, then a child of four years old, was put into an orphanage. There, he liked to remember, he won a rosary for memorizing the catechism. "But," he added wryly, "a more pious kid stole it."

At the age of twelve, he graduated from the orphanage to the streets. For the next ten years, he drifted from one flophouse to another, through corner saloons, cheap eating houses, friendly kitchens, and backyard woodpiles via the sidedoor Pullmans of the road. As a boy, he dreamed of becoming the world's greatest bank robber. But a railroad detective blasted his hopes for such a career by telling him that he'd be caught on his first holdup because he looked like nobody else on earth.

For Tully stood only five feet three inches in his shoes, though he weighed a hundred and sixty-five pounds—a square, stocky figure with heavy, powerful shoulders and the thighs of a burlesque queen. The roll and swagger of his walk would have identified him a block away. His face was sunburned almost to the color of his wiry, brick-red curls, which he boasted that he combed once a day, whether they needed it or not. A stubble of thick, rufous beard covered his heavy jowls. His eyes were a misty blue, sometimes sparkling with Irish humor, sometimes clouded with unshed tears. He talked out of the side of his mouth, frequently in such a low tone that it was difficult to hear what he said. His hands were small and square with pudgy fingers and nails bitten to the quick. When he was working, he wore a blue peasant's smock. For formal and informal occasions he preferred sport shirts. He ordered five-dollar ties and thirty-dollar tan shoes, custom-made for him in London.

His library contained the finest collection of books in Hollywood. He read everything he could lay his hands on. One winter he plowed straight through the *Encyclopedia Britannica* from A to Z. James Branch Cabell was his favorite author; Mencken and Nathan his closest friends. He was fond of saying that he had slept in Mencken's bed, on Nathan's couch, in the Algonquin's bridal suite, under a freight train, on the cold ground with nothing over him but the stars—and snored wherever he slept.

In his thirty-six years he had covered the country as a boxcar nomad, working his way as a circus roustabout, a stevedore, a chainmaker, a tree surgeon, and a prizefighter. After he was knocked unconscious for twenty-four hours in a California ring, he hung up his gloves, drifted to Hollywood, and became a writer of true confessions. He launched his literary career with a synthetic yarn on a subject about which, he confessed, he knew absolutely nothing, "The Memoirs of a Japanese Geisha Girl."

Tully's enemies said that he was the most feared—and hated—man in Hollywood; his friends maintained that he was the most lovable, loyal, devoted, and selfless fellow alive. He was temperamental and moody—a strange mixture of pride and humility, talk and silence, of a melancholy as black as a peat bog and a laughter as gay as the sun on the lakes of Killarney.

In his first book, *Emmett Lawler*, he wrote a hundred thousand words in one paragraph. He took it to Harold Bell Wright, who talked to him for five hours about his own work but never once mentioned Jim's manuscript. Tully then sent it to Upton Sinclair, who considered himself a friend of poor and lowly men. When Sinclair failed to return the manuscript or comment on it, Tully hired a boy to go get it. Sinclair, he claimed, set the dogs on his messenger. It was Rupert Hughes, the conservative, who finally helped Jim revise the manuscript.

By the time Tully finished his next book, *Beggars of Life,* he was so desperately hard up that he submitted it to four publishers at once. It was accepted by all four of the firms to which he had sent it. While he was writing it, he supported himself with potboilers and interviews, for which he took no notes but wrote from latent impressions after mulling over them for a week. Charlie Chaplin once tried to obtain an injunction to prevent the publication of an article that Tully had done about him. When he failed to do so, the comedian revenged himself on the Irishman by saying, "What Tully's forebears did with a shovel, Jim has tried to do with a pen."

On the other hand, Nathan and Ernest Boyd had high praise for Tully's work, to which Mencken added, "If Jim Tully were a Russian, read in translation, all the professors would be hymning him. He has all of Gorki's capacity for making vivid the miseries of poor and helpless men, and in addition, he has a humor that no Russian could conceivably have."

Mencken's attachment to the Irishman derived in part, I think, from transference of his youthful admiration of Mark Twain's Huck Finn to Tully, who shared so many of Huck's foibles and virtues. In literary circles, where envy, jealousy, and double-dealing were as ever present as pen and paper or the pronoun of the first person singular, Jim's devotion and loyalty to Henry were unique. Mencken not only had a deep affection for him but trusted him as he did few men. Therefore, convinced that Sara would be safer in the care of the stocky Irishman, with his tangled mop of red curls and his crooked smile, than in that of the handsome John Gilbert or some other Hollywood Romeo, Mencken selected Tully to act as her cicerone amid "the levantine debaucheries" of Hollywood. Perhaps another reason for his choice of Jim as Sara's defense against the wiles of its great lovers, particularly Gilbert, of whose fascination for women H.L. was admittedly wary, lay in the fact that Tully, a welterweight boxer in his salad days, had once polished off Gilbert in a round of fisticuffs with the polite explanation, "I just put him to sleep for his own protection."

However, in picking Tully as an escort in whom Sara was unlikely to take more than a passing interest, Mencken reckoned without her adaptability and breadth of sympathy and Jim's Irish charm. They were immediately and deeply attracted to each other, as opposites often are, and became devoted friends. When Mencken suggested that Sara do a piece on Tully for the *Mercury,* she wrote of him with such enthusiasm that he cocked an eyebrow as he read me her description of her first meeting with the Irishman:

> He got to his feet, and I saw that he was short and powerfully built; that he was heavy-jowled; that his chest was thrust out. Yet for all his bulk, I sensed a quickness, a kind of shrewdness in his movements. I could imagine his muscles springing into action so quickly that they almost thought for him, or tensing, with his teeth gritting together, into a stubborn unyielding wall of strength.

"The gal seems to have been more impressed with Tully's muscles than his books," Henry said with a wry grin. It would have been more accurate, however, to say that Sara was more impressed with Jim's writing and his personality than she was with the physical prowess of all the athletes on the studio lots. In Tully's humor and humility, she found a welcome antidote to the banalities and vanities of the film colony. Hollywood's "levantine debaucheries" left her convinced that the movie moguls were not only mad north-northwest but at all points of the compass. She listened amiably to their repetitions of the stories of Henry's invasion of filmdom the year before but declined to lend an ear to any criticism of him. After a party at Tully's house at which she was present, Tully wrote Nathan:

> Sara's poise has been bothering me. I had a young fellow begin on Eugene O'Neill then shift to you and Mencken. Her poise was 240 percent until he rapped you guys. Then you should have heard her say—Heah! Heah! Gawd, did she come to the rescue. I haven't told her she was framed yet.

By way of returning Mencken's faith in intrusting Sara to him, Tully confided his wife, Marna, then on a trip to the East, to Mencken's care in Baltimore. Meanwhile, Aileen Pringle was arriving in the East also, so Mencken hastened to New York to "extend her a civic welcome." He found her overjoyed at escaping Hollywood for long enough to spend a few days at the Dower House. In reply to Dorothy Hergesheimer's invitation to join in the reunion there, Henry wrote:

> I hope to surprise you by showing up cold sober, neatly shaved, and with my hat brushed. . . . But anything is possible to a really high-toned beau. Aileen will never believe it, even if she sees it. She reads Tully's accounts of me, and so sees only a longshoreman. But you know better.

On the contrary, Tully protested, he had dealt very kindly with "The Great Lover"—a title he borrowed from John Gilbert to bestow on Mencken—because when a man was as crazy about Miss Pringle as Henry was, he had enough to bear. The flare-up of Henry's infatuation with Aileen might have led him to the altar had not their idyll at the Dower House been cut short by Dorothy Hergesheimer's sudden illness. After Miss Pringle called from New York to say goodbye, knowing that he would not see her again until June, Mencken professed to having shed a tear into the telephone. Two days later he discovered that he was mourning for her like a cow taken from its calf.

The inevitable frustrations of a screenwriter's work frayed Sara's nerves. The crudity and inanity of the studio satraps affronted her. As none of her scenarios were ever filmed, the disappointment plus the incongruity of a piece of personal publicity provoked an explosion. Although it was her old friend Harry T. Baker who occasioned the outburst by inadvertently giving a release about her Hollywood triumphs to the Baltimore papers, Sara knew that his information too had come from Mencken. Next time I had lunch with him, I found his romance with her once more overcast with Hollywood smog. In an effort to dispel it, I wrote her how much Henry missed her and how fond of her he was, to which I added a few dithyrambs in praise of him. By return mail, she replied:

> I'm glad you enjoyed seeing Henry. I'm sure he enjoyed seeing you. He is all you say he is and a lot more. I'm devoted to him as you probably know.

Two days before Christmas in a wire to Philip Goodman's wife, Henry announced his approaching marriage to the Widow Golinghorst of East New Newark, New Jersey, to which he added, far less facetiously, I suspect, that he was tired of work and yearned for honest love. A week later when Sara arrived in Baltimore from the Coast to say that he was glad to see her—or she him—would be a grave understatement. Shortly afterward he summed up her Hollywood trip to Hergesheimer, saying:

Sara got back on Saturday, and is full of marvelous tales. [They] . . . as usual lied to her and kept her on the string, but in the end she got enough money out of them to keep her for a year or more, and a contract for enough to keep her five years.

Now that her financial difficulties had vanished, Sara decided to move into more comfortable quarters at 16 West Reed Street. On discovering that the apartment had a fireplace, Mencken offered to give Sara some logs from his famous woodpile. One piece, which he particularly fancied, a section of railroad tie, cut with his own hands, proved too long for the automobile. "Leave it," he said with a mischievous light in his eyes, "I'll get it to her." And, in due course, he covered it with postage stamps and had a groaning postman deliver it to 16 West Reed Street.

H.L. himself bought and lugged over a pair of brass andirons, a poker and shovel, and a fire screen. While we sat around Sara's hearth in the evenings, she regaled us with her tales of Hollywood. The most startling of the stories were those about the Fitzgeralds. About six months before Sara went to the West Coast, Scott had been summoned to Hollywood by United Artists to do a flapper story for Constance Talmadge. He and Zelda took an apartment in one of the luxurious bungalows of the Ambassador, where Carl Van Vechten and John Barrymore were also staying, and embarked upon a party that lasted three months. After United Artists rejected Scott's scenario, he and Zelda piled all the furniture of the bungalow into a pyramid in the middle of the floor, stuck their unpaid bills on top of it, and departed for Ellerslie, a neo-Colonial mansion they had leased near Wilmington, Delaware.

While Sara was in Hollywood, another scenario writer whom she met there criticized Scott's manners for insulting his hostess at a party and then sulking by lying face down on the floor. "But," Sara diplomatically protested, "Scott's basically a sweet, nice person."

"That may be true," his critic conceded, "but he behaves like a spoiled boy. Besides, he's a consummate snob. He may be as fine a writer as he says he is, but that doesn't entitle him to be so arrogant and so rude."

"His arrogance is a kind of defensive mechanism with him," Sara explained. "He's trying to cover up a feeling of social inferiority he's always had. Underneath it, he's really a generous, sensitive man, who wants people to like him."

"Underneath it," the scenario writer retorted, "as you and I both know, Scott's really a son of a bitch."

Mencken, however, inclined to be somewhat more charitable. "Scott," he said, "has gone Hollywood, which is to say, he's gone *mashuggah.*"

With that sapient comment, the Sage wrote off filmdom and turned his attention to the *Schimpflexicon,* to which his own Hollywood days had contributed more than their quota of abuse. When it appeared, he presented Sara a copy of it, on the flyleaf of which he wrote, "Dear Sara: This is far more your book than mine! HLM, 1928."

In *Pistols for Two,* Mencken explained that he and Nathan never quarreled over girls because George Jean fancied only very young ones, while he did not like women under thirty. His taste in female beauty ran to "a slim hussy, not too young, with dark eyes and a relish for wit," and sufficient intelligence to avoid sentimentality, "a masculine weakness, and unbecoming to the fair." Ten years after he laid down these specifications, he began to realize that Sara Haardt fulfilled them to the letter. In the spring of 1928, she reached the ideal age for women by his European standard; she was *une femme de trente ans*—slender, statuesque, with eyes like brown velvet, an appreciation of wit, and an astringent humor of her own that constantly mocked the sentimental Southerner masked by its sophistication.

The return of her health and the resolution of her financial difficulties brought a glow and a gaiety that enhanced her charm. Nearly half a century later, Marjorie Nicolson remembered Sara as the most glamorous of all her friends. Not only was she talented and amusing but ornamental; she appealed to Mencken's vanity as well as to his aesthetic sense. He liked to appear in public with her—even if it meant putting on a dinner coat and attending a formal party—and he delighted in showing her off to his friends.

He saw a great deal of her before he left on January 14 for Cuba, where the *Evening Sun* had sent him to cover the Sixth Pan-American Conference and present it with two Maryland Free State flags, sent by Hamilton Owens. The conference he described as "a kind of international Scopes trial"—at which nobody knew what was going on, if anything—"one of the most idiotic futilities ever heard of." The delegates, he complained, were all liars; those from the United States talked buncombe, and those from Latin America "talked buncombe doubly damned." If the meeting demonstrated anything, it demonstrated that the United States was cock of the walk from the Rio Grande to the Horn and would probably remain so for many years to come, due to the highly adept diplomacy of the Hon. Charles Evans Hughes. While Hughes was no Bismarck, he was a very competent lawyer. He met the Latin-American buncombe with more buncombe and used all the tricks and dodges of a ward politician to jockey them out of their plans to hamstring and denaturize the Colossus of the North.

Mencken had not been in Havana since he covered the revolution there eleven years before. It was now a very different place. The Cubans, he grumbled, had learned to imitate all "the ineffable flowers of American *Kultur*"—tough customs inspectors, traffic cops, realtors, Rotarians, press agents, and golf clubs. The bars were no longer like Spanish cafés. They had become American saloons with portraits of Coolidge, Lindbergh, Tom Mix, and Douglas Fairbanks, brass rails, and free lunches of olives, pickles, and rat-trap cheese. There were as many ladies as gentlemen among their customers. At Sloppy Joe's, the most popular bar in town, he was amazed to find so many American women who looked respectable, "even when they were awash with cocktails."

Next to the bars Havana's greatest attractions for his compatriots were the horse racing at Oriental Park and the gambling at the Casino. His aversion to horse lovers kept him away from the track, but he spent a couple of evenings at the Casino, where the same respectable ladies and gentlemen who frequented the bars made up family parties around the roulette tables—a far cry from Monte Carlo with its grand dukes, maharajahs, and glittering hetaerae. Although Mencken arrived at the Havana Casino in full evening dress, "wearing all his orders," he reported that not a single woman winked at him. He risked five dollars on a dice game and promptly rolled boxcars—the first time he'd gambled since he had lost ten dollars at Monte Carlo in 1908.

While Mencken was in Havana, Sara and I saw a great deal of the Cobbs and the Duffys, who had apartments in the same building with her. Margaret and William Cobb were both writing for the *Mercury*. Edmund Duffy was now cartoonist for the *Sunpapers*, and his wife, just a year younger than Sara, was an artist and a wit. The four of them made excellent company. Once or twice a week we spent the evening in the Cobb's apartment, where Gerald Johnson or R. P. Harriss frequently joined us; or on cold nights, we'd call them to come over for a hot buttered rum.

With H.L.'s return from Cuba, the visitors and parties increased, but he had begun to discover that the pleasures of the fireside at 16 West Reed Street outweighed those of the Schellhase, particularly since he could not easily be waylaid there and taken dancing. If he and Sara had no definite plans at the moment, at least the Hollywood smog had cleared away. They had had an understanding, as it were; in fact, they had become unabashed Victorian handholders.

Mencken's Rabelaisian blasts against puritanism and his ribald thrusts at the bluenoses were in odd contrast to the propriety of his personal life. He not only advocated decorum but practiced it. From the editorial rooms of *The Smart Set,* he once sent out facetious circulars announcing: "A woman Secretary is in attendance at all interviews between the Editors, or either of them, and lady authors. Hence, it will be unnecessary for such visitors to provide themselves either with duennas or police whistles." Nor was this merely an editorial precaution; he was all for chaperonage as a citizen in Baltimore as well as an editor in New York.

Since he had once violently attacked a proposed Maryland statute making any man found alone in a room with a woman, however innocent the meeting, liable to fine and imprisonment, he knew that it was even unwise to spend the evening in Sara's apartment without benefit of a chaperone. This meant that two or three nights out of the week for the last year I had had to take my books down to Sara's apartment and study in the kitchen while she and Mencken culled samples of choice invective from some thirty fat, dusty clipping books for the *Schimpflexicon* and refreshed themselves with gin and ginger beer, which Hergesheimer had gulled them into believing to be a more elegant drink than plain Pilsner or Berncastler.

My duties as duenna seriously interfered with my own romantic interests, and it was not long before I began to hint to Sara and Henry that a simpler solution to the chaperonage problem would be a nice, quiet wedding. In my efforts to catalyze their courtship, I had an astute and charming ally in Dorothy Hergesheimer. She pointed out to Henry that he had reached the age when the disabilities that he might suffer from marriage would be outweighed by the advantages he would incur and urged the publication of the banns. With a wistful grin, Mencken replied that it was a charming idea and would that it could be executed; but he had one foot in the crematory, and his spies reported that Sara was mashed on a rich Babbitt in Birmingham. To me, he would always reply mischievously, "If the benedicts knew as much about women as bachelors do, they wouldn't be married." On the other hand, he had at least given sufficient thought to matrimony to confess in print that he felt the need for "a marriage service for the damned"— one which would supply the humor that he felt to be as necessary to the nuptial rites as poetry to the burial service.

For her part, Sara merely laughed when I pointed out to her that every author should have at least one husband; she retorted that she was gathering source material for a book called *The Diary of an Old Maid*. All such evasions aside, it was evident to anyone who saw them together, day in and day out, that Sara and Henry were teetering on the brink of what he had once described as "that intellectual disaster known as falling in love."

$\mathcal{U}$HE DAYS OF DECISION

BETWEEN HIS CAMPAIGN TOURS with Al Smith, his articles for the *Evening Sun*, and his editorial work on the *Mercury*, the summer of 1928 had been a busy one for Mencken. Yet, with his incredible capacity for work, he found time to begin a new book, *Treatise on the Gods*. He did four or five hundred words a day on it, writing a thousand words one night and rewriting them the next. It was slow going, he complained, but then, "Shakespeare worked the same way."

The amount of copy that he turned out was but little less amazing than the range of interests that it covered. During that summer, for instance, he struck out from the pages of the *Mercury* at the dilution of democracy, the murrain of jazz and gin, the "rev. clergy," the lack of an unexpurgated history of the United States "from the rise of the munitions industry in 1915 to the infamies of the present date," and plugged for the addition of a course in honor to the curriculum of American universities—a vastly more important subject to his way of thinking than the courses they offered in Middle English, foreign exchange, Kantian epistemology, showcard writing, touch typing, and cornet playing.

The copies of *The American Mercury* that Sara had forwarded to me in London, where I was doing graduate work, were eagerly seized upon by my English friends there, who regarded its editor as an American phenomenon comparable only to Henry Ford or Will Rogers. If Mencken's influence in Germany and France was surprising, it was doubly astonishing in view of his anti-British bias to find how much interest and admiration he aroused in England, not only among the men of the elder literary generation such as Hugh Walpole, Arnold

131

Bennett, and Robert Bridges but among the young intelligentsia, particularly in the universities. As a friend at Oxford put it, "I'm dashed if Mencken doesn't edit the best magazine in America. And what a remarkable chap he is! He's never been to college, never belonged to a learned society nor accepted an honorary degree, never made a million dollars, never held a public office; and yet he's conceded to be the most influential private citizen in the United States." Indeed, he aroused more interest in England than Dorothy and Sinclair Lewis, who were then touring the British Isles.

On September 15th, Sara advised me:

> I think you would make a most competent foreign correspondent, as say Dorothy Thompson, Mrs. Sinclair Lewis. Her new book is *The New Russia*. These gals are treated with great respect and paid excellent salaries.

At the time, Sara had not met Dorothy Thompson but Henry had; and his first impression of her was "A bosky lass of considerable bulk." He found her a relief after Red's first wife, Grace Hegger, whom Lewis was satirizing in *Dodsworth*. After Grace left him, Lewis became something of a problem to his friends. Before he sailed for Bermuda, Phil Goodman had had what he described as "a hell of a time" with him. In fact he had to have the stewards carry Lewis aboard the boat on a stretcher. The stateroom door was too narrow to admit the stretcher, and as Red was unable to navigate under his own power, Goodman was forced to have him placed in a room five decks below, which had been used to house the passengers' pet animals until the port authorities put a stop to it because of the intense heat there next to the ship's engines. Lewis then turned up in France, where he was living at 24 rue de Varize in Auteuil with a woman who once played the Pantages circuit. He drifted to Germany, met Dorothy Thompson at a party in Berlin, and scandalized the diplomatic corps there by following her to Russia although Grace Hegger was still his wife. After Grace divorced him, he married Miss Thompson in London and took her on a wedding trip in a caravan—a honeymoon so unconventional that the English were still talking about it when I arrived in London.

Mencken's admiration for Dorothy Hergesheimer greatly exceeded his admiration for Dorothy Lewis. Mrs. Hergesheimer, he once said, is "one of the few females of this ghastly human race that I admire completely and unreservedly." In October, he urged her to come to Baltimore:

> Park Joe in his Riddle Street Bastille and I'll invite four of the handsomest men ever seen in the world. Down in these swamps, Ritchie is nothing; the girls class him with Coolidge, Hoover and Clarence Darrow. The really pretty fellows make even Jack Gilbert look like a retired police sergeant.

But Dorothy's visit had to be postponed because Sara, whom *The Bookman* had assigned to do an article on Ellen Glasgow, had to go to Richmond to interview her. Like Cabell, Miss Glasgow had been born and bred an aristocrat and never deviated from the pattern. She still lived in her ancestral home in Richmond, a lovely old gray house filled with Hepplewhite, Chippendale, and Sheraton heirlooms, and with her collection of dogs of Staffordshire and Chelsea china. To the physical attraction of her searching eyes, clear features, masses of bronze hair, and rich, autumnal coloring, not to mention the trim ankles that Hergesheimer called the best in American literature, there was added the inward beauty that comes from good manners, good breeding, and good taste. Mencken had omitted to mention her in "The Sahara of the Bozart" because he never believed that her novels were first-rate. Sara, however, had been strongly influenced by Miss Glasgow's work, particularly by her ironical, bittersweet tone and her pungent criticisms of the South. One of her wry aphorisms, which Sara often cited to Henry, was to the effect that religion was the only power on earth that could have made Southern women accept with meekness for so long the wing of the chicken and the double standard of morals—a remark that aroused no more appreciation from the Sage than did her novels.

After Sara's return from Richmond, in writing to thank me for a stiletto that had once belonged to the Corsican bandit Romanetti, which I had sent Henry for a letter-opener, H.L. advised me on October 10, 1928:

> The stiletto is magnificent. I shall carry it through the border states on the Al Smith tour, which begins at Richmond tomorrow. My very best thanks. . . .
> Sara is ill, and the quacks talk of surgery. I can't make out what it is. I hope and believe that it is not serious. . . . It is distressing to have to leave for two weeks while she is in the hands of the [medical] faculty.
> When are you coming home? Don't lurk in that awful England. They eat pie with a spoon and breed women to look like horses. I summons

you home in the name of the Flag. Al [Smith] is missing your vote, and needs it! The Christians are marching on Montgomery! My best thanks again. The stiletto may save my life.

Back in the States, the stars continued to be adverse. Tully was having marital troubles; Al Smith faced certain defeat; Mencken was housebound with flu. After Sara was rushed to the hospital, he said:

She has been ill, it appears, for a long time but let no one know of it. I then found it out by accident, and sent her to Dr. [Louis] Hamburger. I suppose that you have heard of Frances Newman's death.

The circumstances of Miss Newman's death were particularly distressing to Mencken, and he was keenly aware of the irony of her untimely end. In the November issue of *Vanity Fair* there appeared a parody of Miss Newman's novel *Dead Lovers Are Faithful Lovers*, called "Dead Novelists Are Good Novelists." Shortly before the magazine reached the stands, Miss Newman's publisher learned of the satire on her novel it carried and telephoned her, advising her to take it lightly. The next day she was found dead in her hotel suite—by one report from pneumonia, by another from an overdose of veronal. She was buried in West View Cemetery in Atlanta and fuchsias were planted around her grave.

Whenever it was possible, between his political safaris with Al Smith, Mencken spent the afternoon at Sara Haardt's bedside in the Union Memorial. On October 26, he reported:

Sara seems to be making very good progress. She has little pain and is beginning to eat. I took her some sherry and beer today and shall follow it with gin, scotch, rye, rum, Bourbon, vermouth, Swedish punch, Moselle, Chablis, Sauterne and Benedictine. This I hope will restore her to normalcy.

Three days later, I had a letter from one of Sara's former colleagues at Goucher, saying:

Sara asked me to write you, as she is low sick with the misery. She is in the hospital, in fact, recuperating from one of those "slight" operations most ladies have. Only it was not so slight as they expected, and after they got her down they apparently did a very thorough job of interior renovation, removing the appendix among other things. She was a badly broken blossom though at first—nothing but big black eyes. The editor [Mencken] of the *Amer. Merc.* had the flu and couldn't be present in person to see it done right, but he was out this afternoon with a suitcase full of beverages and a pack of Methodist and Baptist newspapers.

By the time Mencken recovered from his bout with flu, he had begun to get over the disappointment of the November elections. Al Smith's campaign had been too inept and *pianissimo* to please the Sage. Instead of tub-thumping openly for Repeal, the Happy Warrior had soft-pedaled the issue, even obscured it with speeches devoted to the tariff, conservation, and other safe and vapid issues, "written for him by a stable of intellectuals, corralled from the paddock of the *New Republic*." Although Mencken had long realized that Al Smith's defeat was inevitable, the results of the election had left him disgruntled.

Hoover, he announced, was just a "fatter and softer Coolidge." Not only Babbitt but Gantry had won the election; and Mencken predicted that "we are in for four (and maybe eight) years of high-pressure Christian endeavor, with a conservative Quaker plying the hose, and the sturdy Methodists and Baptists, all of them free from sin, manning the pump."

1928 had been a hard year for both Sara and Henry. Although the *Mercury* had paid off all the capital invested in it, had no debts, was showing a profit, an increase in circulation, "and every prospect of afflicting right-thinking people for sometime to come," its editor was in no holiday mood. On top of Sara's illness and Al Smith's disaster at the polls, one of Mencken's favorite projects, a translation of Ibsen's plays, had come to naught. In disgust, he had given his Ibsen collection to the University of Leipzig.

Shortly after the New Year began, R. P. Harriss reported from Baltimore:

> Of Sara Haardt I have seen little of late, although last time I chatted with her she was looking uncommonly fine. She appears to be thriving, having completely regained that charm of manner which, in a less prosaic age, inspired man to go out on the field of honor and shoot each other full of holes—(I hope I haven't said this before) I might add that one of her more mature boy-friends [Mencken] (you recall saying that he certainly is getting up in years?) dropped in today to say hello; and I thought the old Bottle of Vitriol looked younger than I had ever seen him look.

But Henry wrote me on April 6, 1929:

During the past two weeks Sara has been ill—apparently some remote effect of her venture into surgery. However, she seems to be making good progress and I expect her to come to dinner Sunday night. . . .

Hoover is turning out to be magnificent. He is already twice as bad as Coolidge. Thus I look forward to eight happy years.

Unfortunately, Mencken's hopes were soon blighted. The round of parties had exhausted Sara's slender store of strength; the doctors ordered her back to bed. On learning that she had had a relapse, I booked passage home on the *Leviathan*. A month later, I was back in the Maryland Free State.

Although Mencken detested the telephone, the invention of which he ascribed to the devil, he had a way of using it to locate me so infallibly that I was tempted to believe it was an occult art. When I landed in New York, a friend waylaid me and carried me off to the boat races at Yale with him. By one of his sleight-of-wire acts, Henry located me at the Taft Hotel in New Haven. He wanted me to come to Baltimore at once; the doctors were alarmed about Sara's condition.

Shortly after I arrived, Sara took a turn for the worse and fell into one of those inky moods into which her illness sometimes plunged her. Now that she felt that her death was close at hand, twice a day, morning and night, she made me promise to have her body cremated and her ashes interred in Maryland.

Proud and independent to a fault, Sara had struck out on her own, and she was determined to continue that way. Thus, when I returned to Alabama, she instructed me not to tell her family that she was ill; nor would she let Henry notify them. Consequently, they did not know that she was in the hospital.

On July 3, Mencken wired me from Baltimore:

EXAMINATIONS SO FAR COMPLETED INDICATE THAT OPERATION WILL BE NECESSARY SARA NOT YET INFORMED SHE FEELS BETTER AND IS IN GOOD SHAPE IF DIAGNOSIS IS CONFIRMED WILL PROBABLY OPERATE EARLY NEXT WEEK IF YOU CAN TRAVEL IT WOULD HELP HER A LOT TO HAVE YOU HERE AM WRITING

Mencken met me in Baltimore. It was a blistering July day. Heat waves danced over Charles Street as we came out of the station. Henry kept a handkerchief in hand to mop his dripping face; his seersucker suit, fresh from the laundry, was already sticking to his back, and his stiff collar was wilting. There was no humidity in Hell, he observed, with an effort at jocularity, but it was 95.5 per cent in the Free State.

At the hospital Sara was being prepared for the operation. She had frequently given me instructions as to her last rites. Now she repeated them. In lieu of the burial service, she requested that a verse from Swinburne be read at the grave:

> From too much love of living,
> From hope and fear set free,
> We thank with brief thanksgiving
> Whatever Gods may be
> That no life lives forever;
> That dead men rise up never;
> That even the weariest river
> Winds somewhere safe to sea.

Mencken turned away hastily to the window and whipped out his handkerchief. Two stiffly starched nurses rustled up and eased the stretcher out into the hall. As they pushed open the swinging doors of the operating room, I saw the surgeons already robed in their white caps and flowing gowns examining the shining instruments laid out for them. The door swung to as the nurses rolled the stretcher toward the operating table. Mencken's hand tightened around mine as we were left alone in the empty corridor.

As we waited outside the operating room, Mencken, between trumpetings into his handkerchief, told me that he and Sara had been planning to be married in the fall. Now, according to the medical faculty, even if the operation were successful, at best she would have but two or three years to live. "If she pulls through," he said, "I've promised myself that I'll make them the happiest years of her life."

When Sara finally began to emerge from the effects of the anesthetic, he posted me at the door to keep the doctors and the nurses out while he went in to tell her of his decision. "She's a wonderful girl!" he beamed, as he rejoined me. "You Confederates never forget anything. Her first word when she came out from under the ether was 'Gettysburg.'"

Sara survived the surgery, but due to the heat and the drastic nature of the operation, she made slow progress. Mencken was frankly frightened about her. He himself was so distraught between the combined effects of his long vigil at Sara's bedside and the humid, intolerable heat that for weeks he gave up work on *Treatise on the Gods,* confined his activities to going back and forth to the hospital, and, as he always did under emotional stress, to writing notes. On July 22, 1929, he wrote me in the morning, and again later in the day:

> I find that I'll be stuck all day tomorrow (Tuesday), until the eve-ning, too late to see Sara. If you see her tomorrow will you please tell her that I'll wait on her Wednesday? Why not together? I propose that we have lunch together, and then go to the hospital. That is, on Wednes-day. I'll call you up in the morning.

Mencken appeared for lunch with two unexpected guests. Admit-tedly, he was surprised when Sinclair Lewis called from Washington to say that he and his recent bride wanted to stop over in Baltimore to see him. For, on May 19, 1928, five days after Lewis' marriage to Dorothy Thompson, in reply to Mencken's suggestion that the newly-weds settle somewhere "in the Hergesheimers' country" near West Chester, Red wrote Mencken, "Dorothy married me only on my prom-ise that I avoid you and all your friends."

Lewis explained that his wife had absolved him of his promise in order to allow him to consult with the Rt. Rev. Dr. Mencken, who was reported to be authoring a *Treatise on the Gods*. The Deity, whom Lewis had dared to strike him from a Kansas City pulpit, had accom-modated him by striking the house that he'd recently bought at Twin Farms, Vermont, with a bolt of lightning. So Lewis had concluded that there was a God after all until he learned that the steeple of the Meth-odist Church in nearby Barnard had also been struck, a coincidence that inevitably aroused certain theological doubts, which he was sure that Mencken, his nominee for "Pope of America," could promptly dispel.

For all his facetiousness, Lewis was palpably shaken and nervous. He was so thin and cadaverous that he looked like a well-tailored scare-crow; his Savile Row clothes flapped about his lanky frame; his Adam's apple bobbed up and down like a fishing cork above a winged collar. A thin sprinkling of paprika-colored hair was slicked down over his balding head. His face was fiery red from an eczematous eruption; irri-tation had corrugated his forehead; his mouth was drawn together as if by an invisible pursestring.

Dressed in a flowing blue foulard, topped with a large winged hat—in a time when the fashionable silhouette was a severe straight-lined, long-waisted sheath and the chic headgear a close-fitting helmet—the second Mrs. Lewis looked more like the daughter of a Methodist minister from upstate New York, which she was, than a topflight European correspondent, which she also was. After her graduation from Syracuse University, she had been a paid worker for the Woman's Suffrage Party. There still was something of the Amazon, the Valkyrie, about her—something of a formidable Brünnhilde turned Cassandra. All the adjectives that applied to her seemed to begin with B—big, blond, brown-eyed, brilliant, brash, beguiling—but by that I do not mean to say that she was a seductive woman; had she been she would soon have talked her seductiveness to death, for no woman can be vociferous and charming too.

When I arrived, she and her husband were engaged in a vehement argument over a debate between them, which had appeared in the *Pictorial Review* the month before, in which Mr. Lewis took the affirmative, Mrs. Lewis the negative, entitled: "Is America a Paradise for Women?" When they both began to draw on their own marital experiences to illustrate their point, Mencken listened with one eyebrow lifted and an incredulous grin, an expression he reserved for occasions on which he was unable to believe his ears. The Lewises had been married only a little more than a year, and as the Sage had long since noted, "Whenever a husband and wife begin to discuss their marriage they are giving evidence at a coroner's inquest."

In an effort to restore harmony with a joke, Henry, who knew that I had recently stood in the receiving line beside President and Mrs. Coolidge at a reception given by the Chief of Staff, introduced me to Mrs. Lewis as "the girl who met Coolidge." Then turning to me, he said mischievously, "Sara, you've met Red, haven't you?"

Mr. Lewis, who was half seas over, took the bait, hook, line and sinker. "*Die Herzgeliebte?* Well, I'll be goddamned, Hank. Roping in a young filly at your age! How do you do it? Veeeery, veeeeery fine. Congratulations, brother. When's the great event to be?"

"Sorry, Mr. Lewis," I said, "but *the* Sara is in the hospital; I'm merely a temporary replacement."

"So I had the wrong filly by the bridle rein. Pardon the pun. So the girl who met Coolidge does not choose to run. That's a good one. Cal the Cool." Lewis, who was a superb mimic, launched into a lengthy monologue on Coolidge delivered in a nasal Vermont twang.

"Ladies, chentlemen, and Mr. Mencken, I muss sprechen a leetle speech in der defense of a solid Amurrican citizen, good old silent Cal."

"Speaking or silent, Mr. Coolidge says precisely nothing," Mencken put in. "There's nothing to be said against him, but then there's nothing to be said for him—except that he slept more soundly than any other President. Nero fiddled but Coolidge only snored."

"Coolidge is right about things," Lewis went on. "This country's hit the peak of prosperity. Now, watch for the big slide. The car's right at the summit of the rollercoaster. The hair-raising plunge is just ahead. I can see it, feel it, smell it in the air. I've just come back from North Carolina. Went down to see what was going on at Marion and Gastonia in the cotton strikes. Riots, bloodshed, evictions, police brutality. It was hell. I wanted to do a labor novel. But I'm bogged down on it. I hate to say it, but between the millowners and the strike leaders, the unions are being choked and the Bolsheviks are taking over."

All the while, Mrs. Lewis, who had been Berlin correspondent for the Philadelphia *Public Ledger* and the New York *Evening Post*, chief of the Central European Service in Germany, dean of the newswomen abroad, confidante of presidents and premiers, privy councilor without portfolio in half the chancelleries of Europe, was holding forth in competition with Mr. Lewis.

Both talking at once, Red and Dorothy alleged that Theodore Dreiser had plagiarized Miss Thompson's *The New Russia* in his book *Dreiser Looks at Russia,* which, she declared, should have been entitled *Dreiser Looks at the Evening Post.* Well, what was the matter with Dreiser, anyhow? He had been lukewarm about the committee for the defense of Tom Mooney, who had been imprisoned for life in San Quentin for a bombing of which they did not believe him guilty. And couldn't Dreiser see what Hitler's National Revolution meant on the Continent? Dreiser hadn't the faintest idea of how serious the situation was in Germany, Mrs. Lewis said.

"The situation? The situation? Goddamn the situation!" Lewis exploded. Mrs. Lewis retorted that no European man would make a remark like that to his wife. And another argument over Germany began between them. "If I ever have to divorce Dorothy," he was to say later, "I'll name Adolf Hitler as corespondent."

The common denominator of Mr. and Mrs. Lewis was a sharp intelligence, a veneer of extensive knowledge over a tough fiber, a colossal egotism better adapted to the dual stresses of push and pull than to the amenities of polite conversation. Caught between two conversational steamrollers, Mencken and I ate in enforced silence and excused ourselves as soon as possible on the plea that we were due at the hospital.

In Sara's room at the Union Memorial that afternoon, we rehearsed the sparring match that had gone on over the luncheon table for her benefit, with Henry imitating Sinclair Lewis and me imitating Dorothy Thompson, until we had to desist lest our laughter disturb the other patients. "What *will* happen to them, Henry?" Sara asked.

"No telling. Red will drink and Dorothy will talk until they both go *mashuggah*," he replied. "But you never know." And, certainly, after that lunch, he would never have guessed that within a year, Dorothy Thompson, the ardent feminist, would become the mother of a son, Michael Lewis; and within eighteen months, the author of *Babbitt*, current champion of the labor movement, would accept an award set up by a Swedish capitalist, Alfred Nobel.

Not even Mrs. Lewis, with her gift for political prediction, foresaw that. For it is said that when Lewis telephoned her to tell her that he had received the Nobel Prize, she retorted, "Oh, have you? How nice for you! And I've just been awarded the Order of the Garter."

When Dorothy and Joseph Hergesheimer drove down to see Sara, Henry told them of the Lewises' visit and, incidentally, of his suggestion that they settle "in the Hergesheimer country." Joseph bounced out of his chair. "For Christ's sake, Henry, what did I ever do to you? I don't know. But what I should do is to ask Knopf to make Irving Babbitt co-editor of the *Mercury*."

Irving Babbitt and Paul Elmer More, the prophets of the New Humanism, which Mencken described as "a religion without a God," had joined Stuart P. Sherman and Burton Rascoe as H.L.'s favorite whipping boys after they had belabored him in their anti-Mencken manifesto in the January 1928 issue of *The Forum*. The New Humanism, he retorted, was the blood brother of Rotarianism, a muddleheaded form of *Kultur* that served to convince its devotees that the evangelists of the Bible Belt were, after all, probably right in holding that the straw boss of a sashweight factory is really a better man than Cabell or Dreiser, that the United States sought no profit in the late war, that the editorials in *The Saturday Evening Post* are profound, that Sacco and Vanzetti, being wops, got what was coming to them.

The arguments with the visiting literati over the New Humanism that summer were briefly relieved by the arrival of Dr. R. J. Van de Graff, who stopped over on his way back from Oxford to his home in Tuscaloosa. Tee, as we called him, was, like Henry, a capacious beer drinker. Mencken found him "a swell guy and sound scientist," put him on the list of approved escorts for me, and invited him to go with us in the evenings to the Schellhase.

Although physiology and chemistry, not physics, were Mencken's chief spheres of interest in science, he was fascinated by the theological speculations of the English physicists. If the Sage had scant respect for the Yahweh of the Hebrews or the Jehovah of the Methodists, he had less for the deities of the scientists, which, he pointed out, followed the pattern of the men who originated them so closely that Sir James Jean's God was a mathematician, "by Euclid out of Genesis." "Granted that such a deity shows more plausibility than many of the others," Mencken said. "He lacks both the hearty, beefy bucolicity of Millikan's Middle Western corn-god and the sickly chlorosis of Eddington's gaseous Quaker, he neither belches nor swoons."

Mencken was also skeptical of the nuclear research then being done in England, where "The pursuit of the atom is embellished and made ridiculous by a parallel pursuit of the ectoplasm." He was, however, deeply intrigued by the practical possibility of the release of atomic energy and the chance of a resultant chain reaction then being discussed at Oxford. He questioned Tee closely about the work that he planned to do at the Palmer Physical Laboratory at Princeton the next fall.

Tee, a topflight physicist and an exceedingly cautious one, would go no further than to say that he had in mind a design for a high-potential generator, capable of producing the tremendous voltage necessary to bombard the atomic nuclei. If his design worked out, it might then be possible, on a very minuscule scale, to transform a common element into radium. That done, the road might possibly lead on to the release of atomic energy. In the summer of 1929, even as a remote possibility, it was an idea that staggered the imagination. If it could be done, in the layman's interpretation at the time, the energy in a glass of water would be sufficient to propel the *Leviathan* from New York to Southampton.

About this time, through Dr. Gustav Strube, a member of the Saturday Night Club, a violinist who taught at Peabody Conservatory and who organized and conducted the Baltimore Symphony Orchestra, Mencken met another violinist from the Peabody, a teacher and composer named Louis Cheslock. Cheslock was young and full of ideas, a charming companion with a profound knowledge of music and musical literature, who eventually became a member of the Saturday Night Club and one of Henry's closest friends. Many years later, after several of H.L.'s critics had questioned the Sage's musical knowledge and ability, I asked Mr. Cheslock to assess them for me from the point of view of a professional musician. Mencken's knowledge of music, he said, was amazing, "particularly the German Romantic School. Furthermore, he had very good taste. He was an excellent sight reader; and pianistically whatever deficiencies he had due to lack of professional training he made up in gusto." In his book *H. L. Mencken on Music*, Cheslock made a shrewd comparison between the Master of Bonn and the Sage of Baltimore:

> In the same sense that Beethoven was aware of the language of sound, Mencken was aware of the sound of language. In the same way that Beethoven would not and could not conform to the threadbare conventions of his art, neither could Mencken countenance the continuance of Victorianism in any of its forms. Both were disturbers of complacency. They were bold, forthright and strong personalities. Both gave battle— stormy, vigorous, and even brutal. Neither cared whether what he had to say was liked or not. Each, in his time, obeyed the inevitable compulsion to say what he believed, and what he had been born to say. There was no attempt to plushcover the hammer head. If a point had to be driven home, then the steel had to be hard. When each ended his encounter the old order was forever over, and a new sound had been heard in the land!

Hence, it is not difficult to understand why Henry felt the first movement of the *Eroica*, Beethoven's first formal defiance of the old symphonic music, remained unparalleled today. For the first movement of the Fifth, the third of the Ninth, and the sonatas, he cared less than I did, but on the Seventh and the quartettes we agreed. Magnificent! Of all old Ludwig's symphonies, H.L. preferred the Eighth. Yet, in his estimation none of its movements could compare with the first movement of the *Eroica*. Once, when he was asked what one piece of music he would choose to hear if he knew he had but a few hours left to live, he replied that his first choice would be the opening movement of the *Eroica*.

In the evenings at the Schellhase one or more of Henry's *Bierbrüder* from the Saturday Night Club usually joined us. Frequently it was Max Broedel, an artist and illustrator of anatomical texts, the club pianist, who for twenty years played *primo* to Mencken's *secundo* on Saturday evenings—a broad-shouldered, jovial man with a shock of grizzled hair and a dark mustache that skimmed the foam from his beer. Again, it might be Al Hildebrandt, the club's cellist, proprietor of a music shop in Saratoga Street, a maker of violins and owner of a Stradivarius cello, one of the few ever seen. He was tall, solid, balding, unpretentious and kindly in manner, best friend of the club members, and so benevolent that Mencken put him "very close to the Aristotelian ideal of the good citizen and the high-minded man." Now and then, Sam Hamburger, the first violinist and a charter member of the club, dropped in. Originally a pants salesman, Hamburger earned his living as an electrician and devoted his spare time to music. Once Mencken brought along a Hollins Street neighbor and friend of his youth, Dr. Franklin Hazlehurst, an ear-eye-nose-and-throat specialist, a big buttersoft man with a head as round and bare as a billiard ball, who played both the violin and the cello.

More often than not H.L. arrived with H. E. Buchholz. Heinie, as Mencken called him, had been financial editor of the old *Herald* in the days when H.L. was a cub reporter on the same paper. Later Buchholz became head of Warwick and York, a publishing firm that specialized in textbooks. He was a typical Baltimore German of the old school and a man of many idiosyncrasies, so methodical and punctual that his clerks set their watches by the time he arrived at his office. Every day at the same hour he strode down Charles Street to the same restaurant and took the same seat at the same table until he arrived one day to find it already occupied. He was so enraged that he never went back. With his hard hat, stiff collar, his gray hair roached back from his stern forehead, and his horn-rimmed glasses, he looked like a grave professor from the Fatherland—an appearance that belied his dry wit and convivial spirit. Although he had little talent for music, he was such good company that the club drafted him as its librarian.

Unlike most literary egoists, Henry was exceedingly modest in his private life. When his audience was confined to Sara and me, he would talk about himself, his theories, his work, and run on à la Polonius; but whenever one of his friends joined us at the *Biertisch*, he would promptly change the subject to some field in which the new arrival was interested—science, politics, or music, as the case might be. Usually it was music or musicians, since so many of the constant circle in Baltimore were fellow members of the Saturday Night Club.

Once H.L. got going on music, his verbal pyrotechnics were at their best. He was almost completely unmoved by painting and sculpture, and as a critic, he tried to view literature objectively and anatomically. Music was the only art that really stirred him. He had inherited his love of music from his father. Although August professed to be almost tone-deaf, he had some skill as a fiddler and owned two violins. H.L. used to complain that he too had such a poor ear that he could not tune a fiddle, but by the time he came of age, he had learned to know a good sonata from a bad one and had acquired an extensive knowledge of musical technique. He preferred chamber or symphonic music and abominated songfests, oratorios, and piano recitals. Piano music alone seemed to him to lack dignity, which may have explained his feeling that "Chopin is a sugar-teat." Huneker once said that "Mencken is too fond of roast beef to like Chopin." He never went to hear virtuosi, either of the piano or the violin, if he could avoid it. It offended him to see a performer getting the applause that belonged to the composer. As for opera, the Sage thought it was "to music what a bawdy house is to a cathedral." Jazz was the kind of music that people who went to the opera really liked to hear—a musical caricature, which might someday be embalmed in the scherzo of an ingenious symphonic composer, but that would be its only claim to musical immortality.

Being fond of experiments in the arts, Mencken took quite an interest in other kinds of modern music. However, the Russian school disappointed him. French music also left him cold; it was pretty, perhaps, but trashy, with the exception of César Franck. The English, Mencken observed, theoretically should have been good musicians; they had good ears, as their poetry demonstrated, and they excelled at teamwork. But, strangely enough, their output, with the exception of Sullivan, who was, after all, not English, was patently fourth-rate. "There are, indeed," he added, "only two kinds of music: German music and bad music."

For instance, he said, there was more music in Schubert's "Deutsche Tänze" than in all of Debussy's work. He rated Schubert as a genius of the first chop. "The fellow was scarcely human," H.L. said. "His merest belch was as lovely as the song of the sirens. He sweated beauty as naturally as a Christian sweats hate."

Like Schubert, Mencken felt that Mozart was beyond critical analysis. Too bad that the orchestras played only his *Jupiter* and G Minor symphonies and overlooked the smaller ones. Papa Haydn's string quartettes should be played once a year in every civilized city in the world. Schumann's First and Fourth symphonies appealed to him more than the Third. With the exception of the scherzo of the Scotch symphony, Mendelssohn was too sentimental for Mencken's robust taste. As a master of the larger forms, he put Brahms next to Beethoven.

In Germany, the Menckens had been closely associated with Johann Sebastian Bach and his son, Karl Philip Emanuel. Lüder Mencke, a royal councilor, rector of the University of Leipzig, and one of the directors of the Thomasschule, had brought Bach there to teach in the school and act as organist and choir director in the Thomaskirche. In the church, directly under Bach's choir loft, there was a splendid memorial window to the Leipzig Menckens. Johann Sebastian's son, Karl, had been court musician and accompanist to Frederick the Great, whom Anastasius Menckenius, Bismarck's grandfather, had served as private secretary. If Henry was a rebel where his family was concerned, he was also a traditionalist; he never missed a Bach festival if he could help it.

In a moment of enthusiasm, he once declared that "Wagner was probably the best musician who ever lived, as Schubert was the greatest genius that ever wrote music. His command of his materials was unmatched in his time, and never has been surpassed, save by Richard Strauss." On sober reflection, however, the Sage put Beethoven above them—even above Bach. Although neither Henry nor I ever knelt and prayed before a bust of the Master of Bonn, as H.L. claimed that Huneker did, the reverence we shared for Beethoven was close to worship. Instead of genuflecting to him, Henry poured out libations to his memory and concluded his hymns of praise by lifting his stein to "Old Ludwig, the Master of them all."

Between his daily visits to Sara and his sessions at the Schellhase, Henry spent the summer of 1929 laboring over his *Treatise on the Gods,* "a massive and high-toned work on religion," which he predicted would get him a LL.D. from Notre Dame—if it didn't get him hanged. In the course of his research for it, to the stock of reading with which he usually fed his omnivorous appetite for the printed word—novels, plays, biographies, histories, scientific and sociological treatises, newspapers, magazines, *The Congressional Record,* political broadsides, and patent-medicine advertisements—he had added a vast store of publications devoted to the theory and practice of soul-saving—Baptist sermons, Methodist hymnals, Presbyterian homilies, Catholic journals, Holy Roller tracts and so forth.

Complete agnostic though he was, H.L. prided himself on being "rather a subtle theologian" and often held forth on the doctrines and dogmas of ecclesiastics from St. Augustine to Bishop Cannon. Theology was anything but my forte, and I was not sorry when Henry's studies of religion led him into anthropology. He was planning to follow *Treatise on the Gods* with a book to be called *Homo Sapiens,* an extension of a section with the same title in *Notes on Democracy,* which he had long itched to rewrite. In *Homo Sapiens* he intended to describe man as he really is, from as scientific and impartial a standpoint as possible—to deal with *homo sapiens* as Fabre had with insects. There were to be chapters on human paleontology, the place of man in the scale of creation, the history of human creation, the mental processes of the species. While Sara was recuperating, he put her to helping him with the research for it, but if the book ever progressed beyond an outline, no part of the manuscript has ever been found.

Baltimore was like the inside of a steam kettle. In October the summer finally ended and with it a fabulous era. The Great Boom burst like a pricked balloon.

By the time Sara was released from the hospital, Henry was "damn nigh all in," exhausted from his titanic labor on the *Treatise* and the distressing circumstances under which he had worked on it. The life of an artist, as he reflected in his essay "An Appreciation of Schubert," is full of frustrations and disasters:

> Storms rage endlessly within his own soul. His quest is for the perfect beauty that is always illusive, always just beyond the sky-rim. He tries to contrive what the gods themselves have failed to contrive. When, in some moment of great illumination, he comes within reach of his heart's desire, his happiness is of a kind never experienced by ordinary men, nor even suspected, but that happens only seldom, more often he falls short, and in his falling short, there is an agony almost beyond endurance.

On Thanksgiving night, Mencken finished his *Treatise on the Gods*—and with loud hosannas. He said:

> By God's inscrutable will I have finished the book at last, and it is in the hands of the printer. Whether it is good or bad I don't know. I am sailing on December 27th, and shall not see any more of it until I return in March. . . .
>
> Sara seems to be doing better every day. . . .
>
> I have been up to my eyes in work ever since the book was finished. An immense amount of *American Mercury* work has accumulated.

With the book off his hands, before he left to cover the Naval Arms Conference in London, he had nothing to do, he complained, save to write three months' copy for the *Mercury* in two weeks, read and edit ten manuscripts, have his underwear patched, and beg his collars from the laundry. The business of getting off was enlivened for him, however, by the apocalyptic warnings of the Seventh Day Adventists, who scoffed at the all current diagnoses of the Depression—political, economic, and social—and announced that the end of the world was at hand. The signs and portents of Luke XXI, 25-2 had now been made manifest by the Adventists, Mencken declared, and "on some near tomorrow, maybe next Tuesday, possibly even Monday, the heavens will split wide open, there will be a roaring of mighty winds, a shock troop of angels will come fluttering down to earth, the righteous will be snatched up to bliss and the wicked will be thrust into Hell."

Although H.L. confessed to being of a skeptical, even agnostic turn of mind, as a prudent householder he was sufficiently impressed by the predictions of the Adventists to take certain precautions before he sailed, such as throwing out all his bawdy books and taking down the pictures of Ibsen, Nietzsche, and Darwin. If he still clung to a few jugs —well, the flesh was eternally weak.

In his facetious farewells before he sailed, Mencken solemnly promised to bring his friends a lock of Lloyd George's hair or a sample of excelsior from the beard of King George. Anticipating a dull voyage, H.L. announced that he expected to spend most of it sleeping, but he fell in with Dudley Field Malone and his bride, who were aboard, and promised to attend their wedding in London. He and Malone enjoyed swapping reminiscences of the Scopes trial; and as soon as the mocking Statue of Liberty was out of sight and the Münchener began to flow freely, Mencken found the crossing surprisingly pleasant.

Phil Goodman met Mencken at the dock in Cherbourg and acted as interpreter for him with the swarm of French reporters awaiting him at the Gare St. Nazaire in Paris. Mencken took the newsmen to task for allowing the beautiful countryside of Normandy to be obscured by billboards. After studying the journalists' gaudy raiment, he announced that he would have to go buy purple spats, a checked vest, and a bat-wing tie to be properly dressed in Paris. Goodman escorted him to the Hôtel La Tremoille, let him check in, and then set out to show him the town. At the Café de la Paix, he and Henry racked up such a stack of Pilsner saucers that it "had to be secured with guy ropes." Goodman reported that Mencken was more interested in the food and drink than in the girls. H.L. strode along the boulevards with his eyes on the handbills plastered on the kiosks, humming the waltz from *Eva*. Only once did he go over to the Left Bank. While he sat on the terrace of the Dôme, sipping his beer and watching the crowds swarm in and out of the bistros around the square, he worked out a formula that led him to declare that the cafés of Paris dangerously outnumbered its pissoirs.

Régis Michaud, who had translated Mencken's *Prejudices*, was also in Paris at the time. Henry looked him up, and Michaud, who had just published *L'Âme américain*, took him to see Ludwig Lewisohn, who was then living in an apartment on Montparnasse. A reporter from *Les Nouvelles Littéraires* met them there, and with Michaud as interpreter, did a double interview with Mencken and his host.

Lewisohn, author of *Up-Stream, Don Juan,* and *Mid-Channel,* for-merly an editor at Doubleday, Page and dramatic critic of *The Nation*, had been born a German Jew. In his childhood he had emigrated to the United States and settled in Charleston, South Carolina. "At the age of fifteen," he had boasted, "I was an American, a Southerner, and a Christian," but on discovering that religious tolerance in the Confed-eracy in the twentieth century was not what the Founding Fathers had intended that it should be, he had recanted, gone to Paris to make his home, and become an ardent Zionist. He and Mencken entertained their Gallic interviewer with an all-out attack on the inanities of American life, strafing the fundamentalists, pouring boiling oil on Comstockery, and firing broadsides at the puritans and the Prohibitionists. So virulent were their fusillades that a French critic feared that "If Mr. Grover Whelan, official greeter for the Mayor of New York, got hold of it, he would not commandeer his tug boat to meet Mr. Mencken at the Battery unless it be to hustle him all the faster to jail." Next day, Goodman took Mencken to see the anarchist Emma Goldman, who told him that she had just finished a 360,000-word autobiography. Knopf, she said, was to publish it in one volume. The Gideons themselves, H.L. assured her, could not do more than that.

From France, Henry proceeded to Germany, where to his unconcealed delight the *Berliner Tageblatt* welcomed him as a "humorous iconoclast, something like Heine or Voltaire except that his laughter is younger and more lusty and free from all poison and maliciousness."

Ten days later he reported from London that it seemed a shame to waste cable tolls on so dull a show as he'd been sent to cover:

> The Naval Conference turns out to be the usual tedious horror. The frauds meet all morning, and then issue idiotic statements, meaning nothing. The French always upset the apple-cart by telling the simple truth. It shocks the British beyond endurance. As for the Americans, they sit around vacantly, learning to drink tea.
> . . . Next week, I'll probably go to Oxford for a day to see Robert Bridges.

In 1924, when Dr. Bridges, the noted British philologist and Poet Laureate, landed in New York on his way to accept a chair at the University of Michigan as professor of English poetry, he had created a double furor—first by what he did not say, which inspired a poetically minded city editor to compose the famous headline "King's Canary Refuses to Chirp," and second by what he did say when he was met at the dock by a venerable embassy from the American Academy of Arts and Letters and asked if there were anyone else he would like to meet. "The only man I want to meet in America," he replied, "is H. L. Mencken." From the expression on the faces of his august hosts, to quote Burton Rascoe, Bridges might just as well have said, "I am badly in need of a whore. Will you please get me one for the night?"

After a pleasant day in Oxford with Dr. Bridges, H.L. returned to London. There he saw an English football match and attended Dudley Field Malone's marriage. The ceremony, which took place at the Mayfair Registry, was followed by a wedding breakfast at Claridge's, attended by a score of British earls, countesses, and viscounts, Lady Astor, Peggy Wood, Will Rogers, and the Sage of Baltimore.

While he was in London, H.L. investigated the regulation of the pubs and the closing hours of the bars. In Maryland, he gleefully pointed out to the English, there were no closing hours since the advent of Prohibition. In his pub crawling, he took along Ernest Boyd, who had turned up in London after an estrangement from Madeleine. Boyd returned to New York with Mencken on the S.S. *Bremen*. During the voyage, Henry used his talent for diplomacy in trying to effect a reconciliation between Ernest and Madeleine. He wrote Madeleine that, although his friendship for her could not be damaged by her differences with her husband, such differences made it difficult for their mutual friends, in that it was hard to see both sides without seeming to take one or the other. Ernest, he added, had cut down on his drinking, pulled himself together, and needed her very badly. Further, he believed that she would be far happier with him than without him. To facilitate the reunion, Mencken loaned Boyd some money. Shortly after he landed, Ernest went on a spree, disappeared for six days and six nights, and had the police dragging the rivers to find him.

When the *Bremen* docked in New York on February 18, 1930, Mencken predicted: "If anything is certain in this world it is that another war is coming." Otherwise, he was in fine fettle. He stole the show with the ship reporters from Richard Barthelmess, the movie actor, who was also on the *Bremen*, by producing the five-gallon beer glass he lugged back from Germany, having it filled with Pilsner, and passing around "the biggest beer mug in the world" as a loving cup to the thirsty newsmen who climbed aboard the ship. Despite the fears of the French critic, Mencken landed unmolested by Mr. Whelan. He stopped by the offices of *The American Mercury* for a few minutes and then hurried back to Baltimore and Sara.

When his *Treatise on the Gods* appeared in March, Henry wrote on the flyleaf of one of the first copies Knopf sent him, "Sara, this is as much yours as mine, H.L.M., 1930" and presented it to her. Taking a position of "amiable skepticism," in the second volume of the trilogy in which he proposed to discuss his basic ideas on politics, religion, and ethics, Mencken had attempted a rationale of man's faith in unseen powers and a survey of its manifold forms. All religions, he concluded, are pretty much alike. If one goes beneath the surface, "one finds invariably the same sense of helplessness before the cosmic mysteries, and the same pathetic attempt to resolve it by appealing to the higher powers." He considered *Treatise on the Gods* his best book so far; and his judgment was justified when it made the best-seller lists. Hitherto, his books had been more talked about than purchased. Now, it was encouraging to have written one that actually earned enough to pay his secretary. By the time he finished the third volume of the trilogy, the sales of *Treatise on the Gods* topped thirteen thousand and Knopf had issued a limited edition of it, priced at fifteen dollars a copy, and planned to reprint it in a cheaper edition.

On its first appearance, the book stirred up a hornets' nest. In the hostility that it aroused among the Jews and Catholics, not to mention the fundamentalists, Mencken's sound scholarship and brilliant insights into the varieties of religious experience were frequently overlooked by reviewers. One Jewish critic taxed him with having written "an encyclopedia of platitudes" to prove that "the Jews are the most unpleasant race ever heard of" and to show they lack many of the qualities of civilized men, such as courage, dignity, ease, and confidence. While some of Mencken's remarks on the Jews were no more flattering than those on the Methodists and Baptists, he certainly had no such intention. It is undeniably true that he frequently used the term "the Jews" as a pejorative for movie moguls, theatrical producers, and promoters of all kinds; but he intended to reflect upon their profession, not their religion. Basically, he had more admiration for the Old Testament than the New. Many of his close friends were Jewish—Nathan, Knopf, Goodman, De Casseres, Lewisohn, Untermeyer, Harry Rickel, Louis Cheslock, Marion Bloom, and Edna Ferber, to mention only a few. He often spoke Yiddish with them, celebrated their traditional holidays with them in their homes, and developed a taste for kosher food. Yet what he termed "a chance reference to them" in *Treatise on the Gods* brought down a storm of denunciations and an avalanche of mail demanding recantations.

After the Jewish Community Center of Des Moines, Iowa, published a scurrilous pamphlet entitled "H. L. Mencken—Analyzed–Dissected–X-Rayed–Discussed–Cussed–Praised and Exposed," his Jewish biographer Isaac Goldberg came out with a piece defending him against charges of being anti-Semitic. De Casseres, who was also Jewish, did an article supporting Mencken's position, which he submitted to the *Mercury,* but its editor declined it with the explanation that he hesitated "to tackle the Chosen." His reference to them in *Treatise on the Gods* had gotten his publisher in enough trouble to last a year, he added;

and Knopf had withstood the onslaught too nobly for the *Mercury* to publish an article that might prolong it.

The Catholic *Commonweal* also attacked Mencken and his book, though somewhat less virulently than the Jewish publications did. Mencken had always been curiously partial to the Holy Mother Church; Baltimore was a Catholic stronghold, and he had friends of the Roman persuasion from the cardinalate to the House of the Good Shepherd, a nunnery so close to his Hollins Street home that his windows overlooked its cloisters. Consequently, the disapproval of the Catholic critics was as painful as that of the Jews. But the Sage met their criticisms with silence and the vituperations of the fundamentalists with laughter.

Between inditing polite answers to the denunciations that flooded his mail and plowing through the alpine stack of manuscripts that had accumulated in the *Mercury* office while he was abroad, Mencken launched a book-selling venture. He and H. E. Buchholz, who not only published textbooks but learned journals, entered into partnership to form a firm, called Books-Baltimore, with the intention of going into the business of selling books by mail. Mencken compiled an elaborate catalogue, which Buchholz had printed through Warwick and York. But Buchholz's business had been so hard hit by the collapse of the boom that H.L. had to come to his rescue with a loan. With a financial crisis looming on the horizon, they decided that it was no time to start a new business, and the Books-Baltimore scheme ended with the printed catalogue. Henry now had more important matters on his mind.

$\mathcal{W}$EDDING DAYS

MENCKEN'S BETROTHAL to six imaginary fiancées had been reported since 1926. On August 2, 1930, Louis Azreal, in his column in the Baltimore *Post*, offered to bet, indeed, to give odds of 111 to 1 that the latest rumor of the Sage's impending marriage was merely another false alarm. Next morning, the official announcement of his engagement to Sara Haardt burst like a bombshell in the Baltimore pressrooms.

To a number of his friends, however, the only surprising thing about the announcement was that it had been delayed so long. For, behind a barrage of jocosity on both sides, Sara and Henry had been quietly discussing the pros and cons of such a step for over two years. Sara's long illness in 1928 and 1929 posed the major obstacle to the formulation of any definite wedding plans, but there were also minor impediments—domestic problems to be solved, difficult decisions to be made, many words in praise of single blessedness, by Sara as well as by Henry, to be privately eaten and publicly glossed.

Just before Sara's return from the West Coast, Henry had recanted to the extent of admitting:

> I believe in marriage, and have whooped it up for years. It is the best solution, not only of the sex question, but of the living question. I mean for the normal man. My own life has been too irregular for it. I have been too much engrossed in other things. But any plausible gal who really made up her mind to it could probably fetch me, even today. If I ever marry, it will be on a sudden impulse, as a man shoots himself.

That might have been a facile way out of his dilemma had he been able to maneuver Sara into a show of proper resolution or a precipitate commitment. But Sara was as well versed in the techniques of the romantic duel as he was and far more skillful in parrying the questions. Her fulminations against men and marriage in private were quite as perfervid and picturesque as Henry's public pronouncements on women and wedlock. Less than a year after she met him, she had become a valetudinarian, whose scant strength and vast tenacity were concentrated on writing, not on romance. As a result of her Hollywood contracts, she had achieved what Virginia Woolf held to be the two things most stimulating to creativity in women: financial security and a room of one's own. Hence she was as reluctant to surrender her freedom as Henry was.

There was not only the question of how two such confirmed and highly vocal celibates could make a dignified retreat from the cloister to the altar but of where they were to establish a home together. Mencken's house at 1524 Hollins Street was also the home of his sister Gertrude and his brother August, and both Sara and Henry were averse to disturbing them. Sara's apartment was too small for the prospective bride and groom to set up housekeeping there. Appalled by the disruption of their lives, and by the sheer physical effort that apartment hunting, moving, and a wedding would necessarily entail, Sara was, as Henry put it, "charmingly pessimistic as usual." Being congenitally more sanguine, he continued his eleventh-hour recantation in an article on Judge Ben Lindsey, written in 1928:

> The younger generation with its theories of companionate marriage is full of gas. A normal man does not marry a woman thinking of her as a possible enemy, as the companionate marriage experts seem to believe. He marries her thinking of her as a perpetual friend. He is willing to show her his secrets and the whole source of his delight in her is his trust in her. His hope, if he is normal, is for a complete merging of their interests.

In September of the same year, he conceded to an old friend in Chicago:

> The reports of my impending marriage are half true and half false. It is a fact that I am engaged. But the lady's mind has been poisoned against me by various enemies and so she hesitates to take me on. She is Mrs. Bertha Kupfernagle of Hoboken, New Jersey. I was well acquainted with her husband and have known her for many years. Before she began to put on weight she was one of the reigning beauties of Hoboken. I have seen the whole company at the Hofbrau House there jump up and cheer when she entered. Her husband died leaving her $17,000.

Henry continued to conceal his attachment to Sara behind such raffish evasions for another ten months. His decision to marry her crystallized, I think, while she was in the Union Memorial Hospital in the summer of 1929; rather, I should say, the first time that I ever heard him openly avow it was after Sara came out of the operating room there. It was another six months before any of their Baltimore friends suspected that they were engaged. A few weeks after Henry's return from London in the spring of 1930, Paul and Rhea de Kruif had dinner with him and Sara at the Schellhase. Rhea spotted Sara's ring that evening but discreetly kept her own counsel. In April, Sara went down to Montgomery to tell her family that she was to be married. On her arrival there, she called me in Tuscaloosa to say that her novel *The Making of a Lady* had been accepted for publication and to ask me to come to Montgomery at once; she had something to show me and something to tell me. When I told her that it was impossible for me to get away just then, I thought she seemed irked and said so; later in the day, she wrote me:

> It was nice to hear your voice today. How long I'll be here I can't say—probably not for long—whether I can leave or not is another question. Mama hasn't been well, and since it will probably be another decade before I get down [again], I have a feeling I ought to stick around. I wish you would come over. I'd love to see you.
>
> Don't tell anybody about the acceptance of my novel by Doubleday Doran, as they are supposed to announce it, so they allow. It's a relief to have it off. . . .
>
> Let me hear your plans. I am certainly not "mad" whatever you mean by that. Old loves, as my old friend Langdon used to say, are hard to down.

"Southern Credo," an article of Sara's in the May 1930 issue of the *Mercury,* in which she questioned General Pickett's conduct at Gettysburg, had "stirred up the animals" in the Confederacy to a pitch that Henry might well have envied, and she was eager to get back to the Maryland Free State and out of earshot of the ensuing pother over it in Montgomery.

When I did drive over to Montgomery, I discovered it was not "Southern Credo" that she had called me over to see or the babble about it that she proposed to discuss. It was her engagement ring that she wanted to show me and her future plans that she intended to tell me about. Although, as yet, no definite date for the wedding had been set, she and Henry had, at least, settled the question of where they were to live. They had found a seven-room apartment in a brownstone mansion near the Washington Monument, with deeply recessed windows, lofty ceilings, and marble mantles. Sara was pleased with it because it provided an elegant setting for her Victorian furniture. Henry took great delight in a stained-glass window over the stair landing, which he alleged had been taken from the smoking room of a North German Lloyd liner. The apartment was flanked on the south by the Christian Science Church and on the north by the Alcazar of the Knights of Columbus, a neighborhood so hallowed that her fiancé declared that he expected to look out of the window any night and see the Holy Ghost skipping about among the chimney pots.

Sara was interested in finding furniture and ornaments for her new apartment, so we spent our time looking for gold-leaf mirrors, lady chairs, tufted sofas, shellwork, wax flowers, china pin-boxes, and other such Victorian bric-a-brac in the antique shops of Montgomery. All the while, for the thousandth time, Sara was rehearsing the doubts about marriage that had beset her for the last seven years. Henry was eighteen years older than she and set in his ways. He had been so devoted to his mother and had so much admiration for her he would always be comparing his wife to her. Besides, he had had so much to say about love and marriage that his wife would never hear the end of it. And so on and so on.

"You've made quite a few derogatory remarks about marriage yourself," I reminded her, "but luckily for you, they weren't as widely publicized as Henry's."

"That's true. But what shall we say?"

"Say you've changed your minds."

"Well, we did. Still, what I don't know about housekeeping would fill a library. Besides, I'm ill. Suppose the TB flares up again?"

"It's a calculated risk—as Henry knows," I assured her. I did not say how well he knew it: Dr. Richardson and Dr. Walker had told us the summer before that she was doomed.

The skeptics who doubted the strength and depth of the love between Sara and Henry did not know either one of them very well. Year in and year out, they had endured the Baltimore summers, which are like nothing so much as three months in a Finnish sauna, rather than be separated. In order to marry Henry, Sara had to rise from a sickbed by an act of will, shake off the lethargy of her illness, and undertake domestic arrangements that were as foreign to her as wearing a bustle or eating with chopsticks. All of her life she had either lived at home, in a boardinghouse, or left the details of her slight housekeeping to me, Margaret Cobb, or Anne Duffy. In fact, she was so innocent of culinary matters that when she went to stock the pantry of her new apartment, she ordered fifty pounds of salt and ten pounds of cream of tartar, ten ounces of which would have lasted a lifetime.

On the other hand, to marry Sara, Henry not only had to do an about-face on his diatribes against women and wedlock—a great many of his most amusing and profitable epigrams among them—but he had to forsake the freedom of a bachelor's life to care for a semi-invalid wife. What was even more difficult for him, he had to move from his home at 1524 Hollins Street, which he had often said was as much a part of him as his two hands and feet. Having always lived with his family, he felt a wrench at parting from them. In a letter to Sara, telling her that her betrothal to Henry seemed the most wonderful thing that could happen, his sister confided that Henry seemed somewhat worried about leaving her alone; but, she protested, she did not want either of them to give it a thought. She could, she said, manage very well with August's help at 1524 Hollins Street; and being in the same town, she would see Sara and Henry very often.

As Emily Clark once noted after he gave her a valentine to mail to little Virginia Mencken from Richmond so as to conceal its origin, Henry was "crazy about his family." He was also exceedingly fond of children. During a visit from his niece, he had exclaimed, "What a father was spoiled when I dedicated my life to learning!" And again in later years, "I should have had not six children, but eight or ten. I am a natural born Polonius, and an audience that couldn't escape me would have been a considerable consolation in my old age." But, as he knew, because of the drastic surgery Sara had undergone, marriage to her meant surrendering any hope of an heir.

All these things were outweighed, however, by the simple fact that Sara and Henry were not happy without each other; even a brief separation became an ordeal to both of them. Consequently, Sara did not linger in Montgomery. On May 9, she told me:

> I enjoyed your visit so much, but you surely know this. I hope I'll be able to get around more the next time I come down.

> I'm leaving here the early part of the week. In a way I hate to go, I talked with Henry last night and he said it was 95 in the shade in Baltimore; so I am in for a siege before I clear out of there.

By "clearing out of there," she meant moving from her apartment to the one she and Henry were to occupy after their marriage. In order to conceal their wedding plans, Sara signed the lease on it. Thereafter, one of Henry's favorite ways of teasing her was to pretend that she was responsible for the rent and to have her billed for the $135 a month specified in the contract.

In July came a note from Sara:

> Dear Sari:
> My engagement to Henry will be announced in Montgomery on August the third but we wanted you to know it before then. I'm sure you won't mention it because it might get into the papers and I should be sorry of that. We are being married the latter part of August but we are not telling anybody, for it might prove a nuisance.

Meanwhile, Mencken had warned Dorothy Hergesheimer:

> If any scandal-mongers call you up and try to make you believe that Sara and I are to be joined in connubial bonds on August 27 don't deny it, for it's a fact. The solemn announcement will issue from Confederate GHQ. in Montgomery in about a week. Your congratulations I take for granted, for you know Sara, and you know what a lovely gal she is. If you write her please say nothing of my heavy drinking, or about the trouble with that girl from Red Lion, Pa., in 1917. I still maintain that I was innocent of any unlawful or immoral purpose.
> The wedding will be very pianissimo, in view of my great age and infirmities. We are taking a swell apartment in Baltimore overlooking Mt. Vernon Place and very close to Schellhase's kaif and several other excellent saloons. Wedding presents are absolutely forbidden under penalty of the bastinado.
> I shall continue my book-writing business as usual. Sara also purposes to engage in literary endeavor, but I suspect that cooking, washing and ironing will take up a lot of her time. Her novel "The Making of a Lady" has been taken by Doubleday, and will be published shortly. Thus in one year she gets launched as an author and marries the handsomest man east of Needles, Calif.

The wire that Joseph Hergesheimer sent Sara after Henry's letter arrived at the Dower House was an admirable expression of the feeling of all those who had been close to them during their long courtship:

DARLNG SARA YOU DO NOT NEED TO BE TOLD HOW HAPPY WE ARE THAT
FROM NOW ON OUR DEAREST FRIENDS WILL EXIST TOGETHER AND THAT
THERE IS NO LONGER NEED FOR US TO EVER SEE YOU SEPARATED OR SEPA-
RATE AGAIN.

To A. H. McDannald of the Baltimore *Sun*, who had long since married and settled down to the sober business of editing the *Encyclopedia
Americana,* Mencken said:

> Your congratulations had the authority of experience behind them!
> The case of the poor lady deserves your prayers. Enchanted by my
> beauty, she little recks what it means to marry a beer-drinker. I take her
> to Schellhase's saloon once a week to warn her gradually. She shows a
> Christian and indomitable spirit, and is giving me a 10-gallon brewing
> jar for a wedding present.

Further, he boasted, she had seen him "illumined by wine" and remained unshaken.

Like many another famous man, Mencken had learned the trick of
presenting himself to the public in the image in which they expected to
see him, i.e., the Bad Boy of Baltimore. In *Newspaper Days,* he came
nearer the truth about himself when he confessed, somewhat shame-
faced, "I am a cagey drinker." Indeed, he cared very little for strong
liquor—as long as it was not prohibited—and for all the beer and wine
I saw him consume during the thirty-three years I knew him, I never
once saw him even slightly drunk. He was a Dionysian—but a Dionysian
with an Apollonian sense of decorum, at least when there were ladies
present. And, since I never saw him in the company of any woman who
was not a lady, I incline to discount all reports of his Bacchic revels—
including his own. Bending over his arthritic Corona, he boisterously
ripped away the horsehair hypocrisies of the Victorians, needled the
Volsteads and Willebrandts, and gleefully plunged his pitchfork into
the well-padded posteriors of the Comstocks and Sumners. Sitting
quietly on the jade-green loveseat at 16 West Reed Street, which
Hergesheimer had contributed to the cause of romance, he drank
Pilsner and sedately held hands with Sara.

Despite the fact that they were constantly together, their secret was
so well kept in Baltimore that the day after their engagement was
headlined in the papers, Henry wrote Max Broedel:

> The news seems to have surprised the Saturday Night Club. Also
> the Sun brethren. All John Owens had to say was, "Well I'll be god-

dam!" But actually I have known Sara for ten years and if she hadn't been ill last year we'd be veterans by now.

But when Mencken cabled Nathan, who was aboard the *Aquitania*, on his way to meet Lillian Gish in Paris, "How about a doubleheader? My pastor offers inside summer rates?" his *Smart Set* comrade expressed no surprise. "I foresaw the marriage three years ago," he told reporters. "You must remember Henry is approaching 50, and age changes and mellows earlier opinions. Consistency is unimportant. Mencken and I both used to believe in Santa Claus and the wisdom of the President of the United States, but the passing years have changed all that." Henry, he explained, was basically a family man and a homebody, who "actually bellows with rage if he doesn't get his noodles by 6 P.M."

Although Nathan had severed all connection with the *Mercury* six months before, the banter between him and his former colleague over the latter's defection from the ranks of professional bachelors belied rumors of any personal estrangement between them. Nathan announced that he was returning immediately on the *Europa* because Mencken needed his advice more than ever before, since "love is an emotion halfway between idiocy and wisdom." On the eve of George's departure for France, Henry had sworn to him that nothing was further from his mind than marriage. Nevertheless, the only astonishing thing to Nathan about the news of Mencken's about-face was that he had won such a beautiful girl. Sara Haardt, he added, was the only person in the world he'd ever thought that Henry might marry.

With a wistful look over his shoulder at the days he and Mencken had spent together on *The Smart Set* and *The American Mercury*, Nathan later said that the four-handed scherzo they used to play together *vivacissimo* on the barroom piano of life had now become more suggestive of a Ländler waltz. The nostalgic tone of Nathan's remarks brought on speculation that he and Lillian Gish might be planning to follow Henry and Sara to the altar. Pleased with that idea, Mencken engaged to shave his head, to submit to immersion by the Hardshell Baptists, to run for Congress on the Socialist ticket, to go to ten movies on ten successive nights, and to read the complete works of Edgar Guest, E. Phillips Oppenheim, and Christopher Morley if Nathan had not become a benedict by 1932. He followed his cable to him with the admonition:

Resort to the jug at once. When you recover send me your blessing. This heroic act may be to your advantage. At intervals of six weeks, I shall tell you confidentially how the Noble experiment is proceeding. You may thus shape your own course.

A week later, just before leaving for North Carolina on his "last voyage as a free man," he continued to George Jean:

The newspapers on the whole were very decent. The gals of the tabloids now besiege the bride-elect, but so far she has managed to throw them off. My mail this morning was something appalling. I have been dictating for two solid hours, and the stenographer is at the point of collapse.

When the newshawks finally cornered Sara, she handled them skillfully. Reminded that Henry had often been quoted as saying, "Marriage is a great institution, but who the hell wants to live in an institution?" she replied with the consummate tact for which she was noted: "Mr. Mencken's present views on marriage will have to come from him. I agree with him on everything he has ever written about matrimony. You must remember, though, that he was writing in the abstract." Pressed to say what she thought of H.L.'s contention that marrying was like enlisting for a war or being sentenced to a form of penal servitude that made the average American husband into a slave, she maintained loyally, "I think Mr. Mencken's views are very well put, and he's absolutely right. They don't apply to every marriage, however."

Sara's mail was also mountain-high and fabulous in its content. One of the most amusing letters to her was from Grover Hall, saying, "that to bring down and tame the great rogue elephant of Mt. Celibate" would be an amazing achievement for most women, but for her it seemed a perfectly natural, even inevitable conquest. To this he appended a couple of pages of fatherly advice on the care and handling of husbands. After wishing her happiness, Tully said that he did not know a woman in the world who deserved more, nor of whom he was more fond. Jim Cain asked for a picture of her for the New York *World* to let the country see that intellect is not the main foundation of this marriage, and warned her that, inasmuch as she was getting the one model husband this land had produced, she should not try to break him of chewing tobacco.

Some months before, Mencken and Aileen Pringle had agreed to adjourn *sine die* and burn their letters to each other. Many years later, one of those twists of plot usually found only in fiction brought a happy ending all around. Henry's former girl, Aileen Pringle, eventually married Sara Haardt's long-time admirer, Jim Cain.

At a meeting of the Saturday Night Club soon after the announcement of his betrothal, Mencken confided that on her return from her honeymoon his bride-to-be would have charge of the beer crocks, siphons, and bottling machines in the brewery he planned to open at 704 Cathedral Street. When he had the heavy mahogany files that held his notes for *The American Language* sent over from Hollins Street, he advised them that he was moving half a dozen truckloads of bottles from his cellar to the guest room.

For a man so generous with advice, the Sage was strangely silent about the decoration of the apartment. Perhaps he realized the futility of a minority vote, since Sara had Anne Duffy and Anne's mother, a New York decorator, on hand to assist her. With their help, she chose green, rust, and gold brocade upholstery for the rosewood furniture to contrast and blend with the pale-gold walls and the green drapes and carpet. She arranged her glass bells, wax flowers, and china pinboxes on the marble-topped tables. The overflow of pinboxes she stowed away in cases on the walls with mirrors behind them. Opposite them, she hung a small gilt bracket, loaded with Dresden figurines.

To Henry's relief, the bracket finally fell and the dustcatchers were smashed beyond repair. He pleaded not guilty to being an accessory to the disaster. In addition, he denied all responsibility for anything that might happen to the collection of handmade valentines, covered with hearts, posies, and paper lace, with which Sara decorated the bathroom—"let the Freudian-minded think what they may." However, in the matter of a cast-iron plug hat, black on the outside and white on the inside, which Sara placed beside the fireplace to be used as an ash tray, he finally confessed, "I spit in it. But only once! The ensuing uproar dissuaded me thereafter."

Henry's chief contributions to the décor consisted of: files, cellar, and brewing equipment; his books and a large brass spittoon; a mechanical shadow box—a barnyard scene with a mechanism that set the cows to lowing and the chickens to pecking; a modernistic painting, taken from W. H. Wright as partial payment of a loan; a portrait of Kaiser Wilhelm for H.L.'s bedroom; an enormous chromo of the Pabst Breweries in full operation, their stacks belching clouds of smoke, for the dining room;

a large billboard to display a collection of Americana in the front hall; his collection of cuckoo clocks and radiometers; and his baby grand piano.

Sara, he announced, was to move the piano. It was a heavy job for a frail girl in such weather, and she had protested that Southern ladies were not expected to do that kind of hard manual labor, but he had told her that what went in one place didn't go in another. Contrary to her jocose fiancé, Sara did not move the piano on her back, although she addressed herself to tasks that were scarcely less arduous—and that during a heat wave. Besides the chore of moving, there were curtains to be hung, screens put in, carpets laid, and bookcases built. In the midst of it, an old friend of Sara's and Henry's, Anna, the senior waitress at Schellhase's, fell ill. They went to see her just before her death and were so appalled by her suffering that they were both "quite knocked out afterwards." Between Sara's distress over Anna, her hassles with the workmen, and her preparations for the wedding, she advised me from the vortex of confusion at 704 Cathedral Street on July 31 that she felt at the moment as if she had been slung off a flying Jinny. On the same day, Henry confessed to Joe Hergesheimer that he had begun to show the classical tremors but hoped to recover at the altar.

Since Mrs. Haardt was ill and not up to facing a wedding in Montgomery, Sara and Henry had decided to be married very quietly in Baltimore. On Sunday morning, August 3, 1930, the *Sun* came out with a four-column spread: H. L. MENCKEN TO BE MARRIED TO SARA HAARDT, NOVEL AND ENGAGEMENT ANNOUNCED SIMULTANEOUSLY, CRITIC'S WEDDING SCHEDULED TO TAKE PLACE SEPTEMBER 3RD. In a similar, if more restrained notice, *The New York Times* described Mencken as "almost a professional bachelor," but conceded that he had predicted his own ultimate marriage when he wrote *In Defense of Women*. Two days later, it headlined the discovery that "MENCKEN FINDS WISDOM," and "RECANTS JIBES AT TENDER PASSION." In the same article he was quoted as saying, "I formerly was not as wise as I am now." On one point, the *Times* continued, the Baltimore critic was consistent: After having gone on record as convinced that "being married with all your friends about you is as private and discriminating as eating in the window of a restaurant," he declared that his wedding would be very quiet. "It will be very refined," he said with a laugh. He added that plans for the ceremony were "very indefinite."

This gave rise to an unconfirmed suspicion in the newsrooms that he planned to give the press a runaround. Thereafter, the papers were not as polite as they had been. The headline writers had a field day: "WEDLOCK SCOFFLAW TO MARRY" and "ET TU, H.L.?" not to mention "BLACK BELT GIVES BRIDE TO MENCKEN" and "MENCKEN, ARCH-CYNIC, CAPITULATES TO CUPID" and many another such gaudy banner rolled off the presses. Editorial writers across the nation laughed up their sleeves. From Columbus, Mississippi, the *Commercial Dispatch* observed, "a southern girl as his wife should have some sort of refining influence in his life." The Fort Wayne *News Sentinel* imagined the shades of Schopenhauer and Nietzsche chuckling together. In Memphis, the *Commercial Appeal* predicted that Mencken might even "invite Paul Elmer More to dinner, hug a Methodist bishop and announce for Dr. Hoover in 1932." From Montgomery, "Old Grandma," as the *Advertiser* was called, pointed out that although:

> Mencken has not failed to mock many of the cherished illusions of Southerners . . . he is himself somewhat sentimental about the civilization of the old South, appearing to believe that it is the best civilization that Americans have yet produced. . . . Many thoughtful Southerners say Mencken has been the South's best friend.
>
> Be that as it may, he will now be the subject of raillery in the land. For, you see, the bachelor of bachelors, who has done a great deal of wise-cracking about marriage, is not only getting ready to marry in his fiftieth year, but is reaching into the "Cradle of the Confederacy" itself for his bride.
>
> But this will not surprise the judicious, for Miss Haardt is not only a young woman of unusual intellectual gifts and much charm, but she is also exceptionally beautiful.

The raillery redoubled when *Time* of August 18 appeared with:

> Elected: Henry Louis Mencken, babbitt-baiting editor of *The American Mercury,* to honorary membership in the Kiwanis Club of Montgomery, Ala., home town of Miss Sara Haardt who he last fortnight engaged to marry.

Forced into the defensive by the press in order to conceal the truth —i.e., that he had fallen in love with Sara, courted her seven years, and was marrying her, hoping to bring as much happiness as possible to her in the years that remained for him to share—Mencken laid down a barrage of buffoonery. Humor, he declared, was necessary to a marriage service, and he proceeded to supply it.

On July 8, he solemnly told reporters, "If I were marrying anyone, which heaven forbid, I should draw up a contract which would consist of two sentences: 'I hereby promise to do my damndest. You are hereby notified that I expect you to be polite.'" Now, he boasted, he was marrying one of the politest of women; and she was getting a husband whose politeness had the high polish of a mirror. Political differences between him and his fiancée, however, gave him pause; he was convinced that the Confederacy had violated the Treaty of Appomattox; its army still maneuvered in the swamps of Mississippi; in her native state of Alabama, more than a hundred thousand Negroes were still held in slavery. The resolution of his doubts about marriage he attributed to his having been informed and inspired by the Holy Ghost.

To his amazed friends, he quipped, "The bride is a lady from Alabama—(white)." He had promised to let her call him by his first name; and she had agreed to allow him five nights a week at the Schellhase, not counting the anniversaries of the great German victories. Would they kindly search their attics and find a Prince Albert coat with no moth holes in it for him? Had they, perchance, a frock coat that was not working? His brother's was somewhat too tight across the lower latitudes.

Such requests were followed by a series of farcical and extravagant bulletins on the progress of his lawyers' efforts to effect a settlement with the bride-elect. Sara offered to compromise for $350,000; he would have been willing to give her $5000, which it would cost him to get married; but she refused to hear of it. The chance to marry the handsomest man east of Needles, Calif., she said, comes but once in a lifetime. Her lawyer, Leon Greenbaum, was demanding a prenuptial settlement of 86 per cent of the entire Mencken fortune. His attorney, Otto Pagentecher, offered a compromise of 65 per cent, plus his pornographic books and personal jewelry.

When the press inquired where and how he intended to be married, he replied, "We shall follow the rite of the Church of England—after all, a very high-toned ecclesiastical organization, say what you will. I have rejected all evangelical bids." In a searching and accurate piece of self-appraisal, he declared:

> I have no objection to honeymoons, nor to church weddings, nor to wearing a plug hat. In all matters of manners I am, and have always been, a strict conformist. My dissents are from ideas, not from decorums,

and I do not favor wearing old clothes, or living in eccentric houses, or making odd noises.

The wedding obsequies, he suggested, might be less dreadful, however, if Sara would collaborate with him in composing a marriage ceremony for the admittedly damned. But neither of them had time for literary endeavors at the moment. Hence, since there is no such thing as civil marriage in Maryland, Mencken, who *in extremis* always showed a preference for the Episcopal clergy, asked Dr. Herbert L. Parrish, a contributor to the *Mercury* and author of an article advocating a more civilized God for America, to come down from New Brunswick, New Jersey, to perform the ceremony. Sara had unearthed a Victorian wedding certificate by Currier and Ives, which was readied for the occasion.

On August 21, Mencken applied for a marriage license. On the record book at the Court of Common Pleas Marriage License Bureau in Baltimore, a New York *Times* man found that a license had been granted to "H. L. Mencken, 49, 1524 Hollins Street, and Sara Powell Haardt, 32, 704 Cathedral Street." Unable to locate Henry, the reporter called Sara and asked why Mencken was getting the license so early since the wedding was not to take place until September 3. Sara laughingly replied, "I suppose he just wants to be sure to have it." Next morning the *New York Times* broke the story, "MENCKEN GETS LICENSE ACQUAINTANCES SUSPECT HE'LL WED MISS HAARDT BEFORE DATE SET."

Henry had deliberately given the date of the wedding as September 3 to avoid having newsmen and photographers bursting into the church and shooting off flashbulbs. But the announcements had already come from Tiffany with the correct date of their marriage, August 27, 1930, and were being mailed out. A new furor broke loose in the pressrooms after it was discovered that Mencken planned to steal a march on the newsmen by marrying before the date given them.

Between entertaining the family, handling the press, and making last-minute arrangements for their marriage, Sara and Henry both had their hands full. But somehow he found time for a session at 1524 Hollins Street with Raymond Pearl, and Heinie Buchholz, who had offered to instruct him in "The Facts of Life," a session which gave him some quiet chuckles in that they belonged to the early William Dean Howells school. On Saturday night, as usual, he attended the meeting of the club, the last before his marriage, at which he was given a dimestore wedding shower. Among the presents were a Benedict's medal, a gold purse, and a diamond-studded belt buckle.

On the eve of the ceremony, he reported that, curiously enough, he seemed to be holding up fairly well. "Perhaps I'll wobble a bit tomorrow when I see the actual sheriff," he said. "I'm taking him a couple of jugs this evening." In a valedictory letter to Nathan from "the brink of the precipice," he advised him:

> I spare you the horror of being a witness. It would unman you, and maybe kill you. My brother will hold me up.
>
> I should reach New York about the middle of September. Lillian has the right idea about wedding presents; groceries. Those two magnificent sausages are hanging in the pantry, awaiting my return. I shall fall upon them the day I get home. Give her my love when she arrives. And let us have a four-cornered session when we all meet in New York.

Shortly after four o'clock on the afternoon of the wedding, Mencken and his brother, August, who was to act as his best man, arrived at the side entrance of an unpretentious Episcopal church on North and Warwick Avenues in Baltimore. His other brother, Charlie, an engineer from Pittsburgh, Charlie's wife, and his daughter, Virginia, were waiting inside with the Menckens' younger sister, Gertrude. A few minutes later, the bride arrived with her mother, her nephew, her sister Ida, and her brother-in-law, Charles Wickliffe Stevenson, who was to give her away. With the exception of these nine relatives, the only other witnesses to sign the wedding book were Hamilton Owens and Paul Patterson from the *Sun*, whom Mencken had asked to handle the wedding publicity.

For the occasion, Henry was dressed in a pin-striped business suit, Sara in a tailored beige crepe ensemble. With it she wore a brown felt cloche and carried a spray of green orchids as a bridal bouquet. She came up the aisle on the arm of her brother-in-law. The groom met them in the chancel. Reverend Dr. Herbert Parrish read the Episcopal marriage service as they knelt there. Then Henry slipped the ring on Sara's finger and Dr. Parrish pronounced them man and wife.

Amid showers of rice thrown after them—a custom that Mencken called a barbaric relic of primitive tribal rites—they were driven to the Pennsylvania Station to board a train for Canada. At 9:08 P.M., they wired Nathan from New York:

PASSING THROUGH YOUR GREAT CITY WE SEND YOU THE BLESSING OF
OLD MARRIED FOLK ON OUR RETURN IN TWO WEEKS WE SHALL CONSIDER
YOUR SITUATION SERIOUSLY YOU GET THE TWO KISSES AND AN EXTRA ONE
FROM THE OLD MAN LOVE TO LILLIAN

SARA AND HEN

In thanking Paul Patterson for his good offices at the wedding, Sara
wrote him the next day, "It was a tedious business and you managed it
perfectly." To which Henry added, "It was a masterpiece. No publicity
has been better handled since the Snyder–Gray case." As Patterson had
predicted that Mencken would make her a good husband and a good
provider, Sara now assured him that he had been quite right; H.L. was
perfect in the role.

For all his jibes at the ancient estate of matrimony, in order to make
Sara's remaining years as happy and comfortable as possible, another
Henry had gone to Canossa. Like Galileo Galilei in the Holy Office,
Mencken had knelt and recanted; but by the time he reached Montreal,
he had risen from his knees to deliver his equivalent of *Eppure si
muove* to the newsmen who picketed the bridal suite. Irrepressible as
ever, he replied to the reporters' questions on his political views by
describing Ramsay MacDonald as a sort of Methodist evangelist, who
with his colleagues Lloyd George and Baldwin made "a trio of shabby
and preposterous politicians," who were "as little fit to save the world
as they were to square the circle." As for Dr. Hoover, he was "forever
leaping upon the stage in the shining armor of Galahad, and shuffling
off in the motley of Scaramouche." Having but little vested interest in
the stock market, H.L. could afford to dismiss Hoover's Depression
administration with the concession, "It's a comic government, but perhaps it's as good as any. When dreadful things happen, people laugh
and take the situation lightly."

Henry had favored spending his honeymoon at Max Broedel's place
in Ontario, but had yielded to Sara's desire to see the more historic
parts of Canada. They both enjoyed Montreal until hay fever attacked
Henry there. Then they moved on to Quebec, where the accommodations and the holiday pilgrims over Labor Day weekend made H.L.
swear. "Jesus, what a swell hotel! *Two Gideon Bibles*—and *one* towel,"
he exploded on a card to Goodman. "The weather is infernal due to
praying in 50 shrines. We are off for the Coast." After the St. Lawrence
Valley, where it was hotter than Arkansas, they were delighted by the

fresh sea breezes in Halifax. Reluctantly, they pushed on to Digby, crossed the Bay of Fundy by boat, and returned to the States via Boston. En route they stopped in Barnard, Vermont, for a brief visit with Sinclair and Dorothy Thompson Lewis at Twin Farms.

Henry's reunion with Red was strained by Lewis' facetious congratulations on his marriage to Sara:

> Don't let Phil Goodman persuade you that the lady will be able to tolerate you for more than seven weeks. Think! In over two years of marriage, Dorothy has left me forever not more than five times, and she is still with me—unless, possibly what she asserts to be a shopping trip to Woodstock shall prove to have been only a sly method of escaping. I believe then, that if the lady is a good cook and of remarkable patience, and if you will give up crème de menthe for breakfast, your union will endure.

Moreover, Mencken's japery at the time of Michael Lewis' birth earlier in the summer had not endeared him to Dorothy. H.L. had suggested that she name the boy Irving Babbitt Lewis. Worse, he had sent him Beethoven's Ninth Symphony and a platinum rattle, which he hinted Red would no doubt pawn for a drink; and he had also assisted Red in his boozy celebration of his son's advent. In a terse note of thanks for the presents, Dorothy wrote:

> The Michael whom you hail is red-headed, has a mighty nose, a prodigious frown, a tremendous yell, and a charming grin. There is no question of his legitimacy.

For her part, Sara was not amused by the *doubles entendres* of Red and Dorothy in the remarks they made on a pair of tomcats they had named Mencken and Nathan. Granted that Dorothy's talk about cats, babies, and rural life at Twin Farms and her analyses of cloakroom gossip in Washington or Hitler's rantings in a Munich beerhall were so far out of Sara's line that they all but put her in a coma, it is untrue that, as one of Mencken's biographers alleged, her lack of enthusiasm for Mrs. Lewis was responsible for Henry's alienation from Red. For Mencken's estrangement from Lewis began in 1925 after Lewis' differences with Paul de Kruif over the title page of *Arrowsmith* and was exacerbated by the charges of plagiarism that Red hurled against Dreiser; Mencken never felt the same toward Lewis again.

Shortly before Henry and Sara arrived in New York, I had driven up to talk to Maxwell Perkins of Scribner's about a manuscript, and had been introduced to Lillian Gish and George Jean Nathan at the opening night of a play. It was the first time I had ever met Mr. Nathan, and I found him quite as engaging as Sara and Zelda had some years before. At the time, Nathan was about forty-eight years old. But with his sleek head, his slender, lithe figure, and his debonair manner, he might have been taken for the juvenile lead in a romantic comedy had it not been for the brushing of silver at his temples. His features were as regular and clear-cut as a matinee idol's; his eyes were large, dark, and penetrating. His clothes, upon all occasions, were perfect examples of what the well-dressed man about town should wear, from his opera hat and cloak to his superbly tailored business suits—so much so that they gave the impression of being the costumes of an actor rather than the clothes of a critic.

Mr. Nathan was as amiable about Henry as Henry had been about him. Hence I inferred that the gossip columnists' reports about a feud between them had led to the dissolution of their editorial partnership were as farfetched as the canard that to Mencken's vast amusement, alleged that his "tiffs" with Nathan, Dreiser, and Lewis were due to the fact that he was passing through "the male climacteric." Moreover, when I saw Mencken and Nathan together in the middle of September, they were certainly on the best of terms.

A few days after I met Mr. Nathan, I had a note from Sara, asking me to call her at the Algonquin. When I telephoned her, she invited me to come over to the hotel for a late breakfast with her and Henry. I found Sara in a green velvet negligée and gold wave net, presiding over the coffeepot; and Henry, jocose and ebullient, still in his shirt sleeves, having left off his coat, he explained, to display a pair of bright-red galluses, a wedding present from the Baltimore fire chief.

We had breakfast in the suite. Mencken beamed, pleased with himself in his new role. As he drank his orange juice, he told me about some ash trees that Sara had bought in Canada. After he lugged them back to the States and paid fifty dollars duty on them, he'd found that they grew wild just across the border in Maine. Where would she ever find another husband to compare with him? Well, not this side of Tibet, where polyandry tended to teach men manners. Had I seen Sara's wedding pictures in the papers? She was still heaving with rage about them. Who wouldn't be? Sara protested; the pictures were libelous; they made her look like a Japanese pie woman. There was no need to worry about that, Henry consoled her; the next ones would probably be worse. These merely looked as if they'd been taken after her rural ordeal at Twin Farms instead of before.

"As you can see," Sara laughed, "marriage hasn't changed Henry a bit. He can't resist teasing me—and he still likes beer as much as ever."

"How are the Lewises?" I asked her. "And how did you like Dorothy Thompson?"

"Heavens, such a woman!" she replied, finessing the question.

As H.L. put on his coat and tie to go over to the *Mercury* office, he told us he'd be back for us around noon. Nathan had asked the Menckens to lunch; and, since Miss Gish had another engagement, he suggested that they bring me along.

We were interrupted by Hallie Pomeroy, a reporter from the NANA, who called up from the lobby. Sara bridled, made excuses, tried to plead off, and finally, rather than be rude, let her come up. "I suppose she has to make a living, too," Sara said.

When Miss Pomeroy arrived, Sara, her indestructible poise strained by having to face another interviewer, asked her to have a seat and played for time by ordering scotch and soda—an urbane gesture on her part, particularly since she had as little liking for scotch as she did for talking to reporters. While they waited, Miss Pomeroy took out her pencil and pad and began firing questions at her. "Ask Henry," Sara protested. "I haven't the knack for clever sayings that he has."

"Tell me about him," the interviewer prodded her. "Have you found out anything you didn't know about him before in the three weeks you've been married to him?"

Her question left Sara dumbfounded for a moment. Then her sense of humor came to the rescue. She threw back her head and laughed. "Indeed, I have! I've discovered that he's a Victorian at heart, though he probably won't admit it."

At this point Mencken returned and wanted to know why Sara thought he was Victorian. "Because I think a Victorian husband is ideal," she replied suavely. She brought out a copy of *The Lady's Toilet*, printed in 1848, and cited the author's ideas on the virtues a husband should have—piety, contentment, moderation.

"Even in drinking?" H.L. teased her.

"In everything, Henry." Sara read on with mischief in her eyes, enumerating the qualities desirable in a benedict in 1848: " 'Innocence, good humor, mildness, truth, compassion, fidelity, meekness, charity, and circumspection.'"

"Splendid!" Mencken applauded. "These are the ideals by which I live. That book should be republished immediately."

Sara skillfully deflected Miss Pomeroy's inquisition to Henry by suggesting that he explain to her his theories on what Colette so aptly called "conjugal courtesy." He pulled at his eyebrows for a moment as he did when he was engaged in unraveling a troublesome problem. "Politeness! That's the secret of every successful marriage," he declared. "And, in essence, politeness is the absence of the reformer complex, of any desire to improve other people. Leave them alone. They're doing the best they can, poor fishes. But then, of course, it's easy for Sara. She's married to a perfect specimen of German manhood with a good appetite, an educated thirst, and a generally serene and amiable attitude of mind." Sara gave him an indulgent smile. "She's not quite perfect," he continued, "but her defects are so small it would be pedantic to improve upon them." He cast an affectionate look at her. She laughed and excused herself to dress. "She doesn't know what to say to reporters," he chuckled. "She's gun shy."

Mencken escorted Miss Pomeroy down to the lobby, and when he returned, he took us across the street to Nathan's apartment in the Royalton for an apéritif. Nathan had lived in the same suite there since 1906. The décor appeared to have been contrived by Gordon Craig for a latter-day play of Oscar Wilde's. The walls were hung with tapestries and masks, the windows with brocaded drapes. All the lights were heavily shaded. In one corner was a bust of Nathan, in another a painted Indian head. Apparently, the butler, who must have been a stage manager at some time in his life, had carefully arranged the cushions on the divans, the ash trays, humidors, decanters, and seltzer bottles on the tables so that the setting gave the impression that the curtain was about to rise on a sophisticated drawing-room comedy. The only things to remind one that it was the apartment of a critic were a big workmanlike desk by the window and the quantity of books—books with gaudy dust jackets, books bound in red morocco, in yellowing vellum, and in blue and green buckram, jammed into the shelves and piled on the tables.

According to H.L., Nathan's wardrobe contained three top hats, three suits of evening clothes, forty sack suits, and thirty-eight overcoats, including one of Russian fur, one of Scotch homespun, and one with an alpine hood attached. He preferred to have his hats as well as his clothes made to order in England. The fundamental difference between the two men was highlighted by the contrast between Mencken's everyday seersucker suit and Nathan's Savile Row tropical worsted with knife-edged creases in its trousers. Although Hergesheimer and Nathan did not particularly care for each other, they shared a love of elegant clothes and fine textures, of smooth surfaces and muted colors; indeed, they had a great deal more in common with each other than with Mencken.

Henry plumped himself down on one of Nathan's incredible divans between Sara and me, proud, beaming, and cherubic as any paterfamilias in his ancestral Saxony. Nathan, the dapper bachelor, adept host, and skilled bartender, adroitly mixed a drink for us. After he served the martinis, he passed Mencken a Corona Corona and took one himself. H.L. bit the end off his; Nathan took a gold cutter from his vest pocket and snipped his with a gesture that was the Broadway equivalent of an Oxford man tamping the tobacco in his pipe. "His business is the theatre," *The Bookman* pointed out, "and his business is his pleasure, but of life itself he has made a play in which he is the leading character." Tully called him the First Apostle of the Self-Centered. "Nathan," said *The Bookman,* "is interested in Beauty, especially if it is small and blonde, while Mencken's mind ceaselessly revolves in the vortex of insoluble social problems, political chicaneries, and the endless circle of human folly. Ziegfeld's 'Follies' are a more engaging spectacle in the eyes of his colleague."

Nathan was essentially a critic of the drama; Mencken, with his broader range and deeper social consciousness, was a critic of ideas. In that dichotomy of interest between the drama and the human spectacle, between the stage and the arena of public life, between aesthetics and politics, between Broadway and the American scene, lay the explanation of the dissolution of their literary firm, I think, rather than in any personal animosity or critical vendetta.

When the question of where we were to lunch arose, Henry suggested the old Brevoort. At lunch Mencken, who ribbed "the local Laertes" as constantly as Nathan ribbed him, began to twit the drama critic about Miss Gish. No wonder George hadn't been able to put a halter on her. Hadn't he brashly declared that women at their best were mere playthings? Nonsense! Actually they were shrewder than men and frequently more intelligent. Nathan retorted that this was merely some hokum that Henry had cooked up to make himself popular with the women's clubs and induce the ladies to buy his books. What Mencken esteemed as woman's intuition was, in truth, nothing more than his own transparency. Henry, he said, was so ingenuous where women were concerned that he regarded any girl who smiled inscrutably and let him talk as a paragon of intelligence. Sara smiled inscrutably and let George Jean talk. Henry gave me a sly wink; we both began to laugh. For Sara's talent as a listener was patently working its spell on Nathan. On the other hand, his badinage, genial as it was cynical, amused her and attracted her; and when she told him goodbye, she issued him a most cordial invitation to come to Baltimore.

Before Sara left on her honeymoon, she had engaged a cook, with whom she had carefully left the menu of the dinner she was to prepare for the homecoming of the bride and groom. But at 704 Cathedral Street on the evening of Sara's and Henry's return, instead of a meal on the table, they found a telegram. In an encounter, supposedly with a toothpuller, Sara's cook had had her jaw broken and been invalided home to North Carolina. "Women," Henry conceded, "have their troubles, too."

As soon as Sara had installed another cook in the kitchen, she and Henry were constantly entertaining and being entertained—at lunches with visiting celebrities, at dinners with the Willy Woollcotts, the Hamilton Owens, and the Edmund Duffys. But they quickly discovered that the round of postnuptial parties was not only interfering with their work but taxing Sara's slender strength. Both she and Henry disliked formal affairs, and they soon came to limit their social activities. They preferred to spend their evenings quietly at home or have two or three friends in to dine with them.

Turning her scholarly training to the kitchen, Sara made out scores of menus, lists of different kinds and cuts of meat, catalogues of all the varieties of soups, vegetables, and entrées described in current magazines. She soon became an ardent collector of recipes and cookbooks as well as of shellwork and pinboxes and more interested in her home than her career.

The "Palazzo Mencken" was a spacious apartment, seven large rooms arranged as a duplex on the second and third floors of the building.

Sara and Henry had their separate living and working quarters on the lower level, while the upper was devoted to what H.L. called "the public rooms," adjoined by the pantry and kitchen. The furnishings were charming, reflecting as they did the divergent tastes of a couple both of whom were unique and discriminating. I was no less amazed than Henry at the efficiency of Sara's housekeeping; how she mastered the mysteries of the domestic arts so quickly, I do not know. But the apartment was spotless, the linens flawless, the crystal sparkling, the silver burnished. Fresh flowers were carefully arranged in the vases every morning; the cigarette and match boxes were filled.

Henry boasted that Sara had even turned out to be a fine bartender. She entertained easily and elegantly. Always prepared, she kept the table set for four. For Henry, she said, was apt as not to come home for lunch with a governor, a professor, a scientist, a journalist, a musician, or even a preacher of some esoteric denomination. Her cook and maid wore black uniforms with caps and aprons of crisp white lawn. The service at the table was faultless, the food and wine were delicious. Before his marriage, H.L. predicted that he would have to bear with gumbo in everything, including his coffee, and begged that a plate of cold roast beef be kept in the refrigerator for him and his friends, who were unaccustomed to the pungent viands of the Confederates. But now, he admitted, his fears had proved groundless; Sara quickly learned his tastes in victuals and catered to them, even to his preference for boiled turkey over the baked variety fancied in the South.

If I marveled at Sara's domestication, I was no less astonished at Henry's. He had always been exceedingly polite, thoughtful, and deferential with Sara; but after his marriage to her he was almost docile—and so intent upon pleasing her that he volunteered for household chores, emulated the husbandly virtues laid down in *The Lady's Toilet,* and studied the Confederate catechism. He professed to carry a copy of it with him wherever he went and read it as faithfully as a priest reads his breviary; he had already learned to admit that Jeff Davis was a handsomer man than Abe Lincoln. Mencken's transformation from one of the world's most obstreperous bachelors into one of its most devoted benedicts, which has frequently puzzled his critics, can best be understood in the light of his family history and its influence upon him.

"The mills of the gods grind slowly," as Sara once said. The Bad Boy of Baltimore was almost fifty years old before he began to revert to type and to the domestic mores of the Menckens. And not for seven long years after H. L. Mencken, professional misogynist and unreconstructed bachelor, delivered his fateful lecture at Goucher was he hoisted to the altar by his own petard on "How to Catch a Husband." His family motto was "Make Haste Slowly," and it was only after "much prayer and soul-searching" that he assumed the responsibilities of a benedict. But, thereafter, both by Sara's testimony and that of less biased witnesses, he made an incomparable husband.

$\mathcal{T}$HE DAYS OF THE BEAUTIFUL ADVENTURE

Now THAT THEIR HONEYMOON was officially over, Sara and Henry relaxed into their normal routines. Like Winston Churchill, Mencken believed that for husband and wife to breakfast together imposed an unnecessary hazard in marriage. He rose at eight o'clock as he always had, drank his orange juice and coffee alone, read the morning papers at the table, and was at his desk by the time Sara turned out at nine. She liked to have a leisurely breakfast in bed. "No one has anything of interest to say early in the morning," she claimed. "I want my papers and mail and Henry wants his."

Stopping only for lunch at noon and a short nap afterward, they worked on through until time for the "family hour." Having finished their afternoon stint, they met in the "public rooms" of the apartment for a drink and an interlude of "philosophical belching," as Mencken termed it. Usually they dined late and lingered at the table. Henry insisted that the tempo of a meal should be slow; the longer it lasted, the better the viscera could do their work. He had begun to wind up his day's labor at nine instead of ten P.M. so that he had more time with Sara in the evenings. If he and Sara were tired, they simply sat and talked; if not, they would call the Duffys, who lived nearby at 901 Cathedral Street, to come over for a nightcap or meet them, just around the corner on Charles Street, at the Longfellow, now the Park Plaza, where there was an orchestra of sorts.

Connubial bliss, Henry confessed, turned out to be a more pleasant state than he had expected; indeed, he was not only reconciled to it but planned to do a poem in praise of it before the end of the year. Marriage made little change in his habits and less in him. Beyond the

179

fact that he was healthier, happier, and more buoyant than ever, there was no great difference between Henry at home in his slippers and H.L. at the beer table with his coat unbuttoned. Only his working habits had altered; he had shortened his hours and jettisoned his antique portable. The high-backed, spidery little 1910 Corona on which he had pecked out all of his books and most of his articles for the last twenty years was still serviceable, but it made as much noise as a threshing machine, and in order not to wake Sara by hammering away on it early in the morning and late at night, he bought a Remington portable, which was said to be noiseless, but with hard-hitting Henry pounding on the keys, it was only relatively so.

Beyond Sara's sudden addiction to housekeeping, the only manifest change in her was a difficult one to understand. After her marriage, she never touched a guitar, never went to a concert if she could avoid it, and never joined in the musical talk that flowed as freely as Mencken's brewery at 704 Cathedral Street. The only explanation for it is probably that the musical knowledge of Henry and his friends awed her into silence. Admittedly, she didn't know Bach from Bartók and for some reason, peculiar in anyone with her intense intellectual curiosity, was disinclined to learn. Given the slightest encouragement, Henry would go to the piano and play for us for an hour before dinner or hold forth over his sherry on his idols, Johann and Richard Strauss, Wagner, and the three B's. But Sara, who had made a science of drawing him out, would divert him to belles-lettres, philosophy, or current events whenever she could. One of the few notes that remain from a vast collection that Sara made on the life and works of her famous husband is a brief, slightly wry one:

> Nov. 5, Sunday after dinner.
> Henry played Beethoven on the Victrola. He deplored my lack of knowledge of music and added that he would teach me someday. "I have always been an admirer of sheer technique," he said. "Old Ludwig was a master!" We are having supper at ten o'clock and he is brewing beer afterwards. It is dreadful work—scarcely the work, I firmly believe, for an artist.

The only musical things about Sara to survive her marriage were her laughter—bright and sparkling as a Mozart sonata—and her low, soft voice.

Conversation, Henry maintained, was vastly more important in marriage than sex. According to him, people, emotionally speaking, were divided into three main types: "homos, heteros, and nomos." In the last category, he placed not only nuns, priests, and other celibates, but those that the French call *cérébrales,* that is, those to whom love is more important as a psychic and intellectual bond than as a purely physical one. He and Sara were deeply in love, affectionate, and quietly demonstrative with each other; but during their long courtship, they had become mentally and emotionally so closely knit that their marriage merely set a physical seal on a romantic attraction. A slow fire, to quote an old English proverb, makes a sweet malt; and by the time they married, Henry and Sara were both emotionally mature and distinctly *cérébral;* consequently, their love for each other was more marked by the peace and harmony of an autumnal concord than by the violence of a vernal passion.

If they ever had a serious quarrel, I never heard of it. Between Henry's insistence on amiability and politeness in marriage and Sara's on conjugal courtesy, I doubt that they ever exchanged a cross word with each other. This is not to say that they didn't have their ups and downs—they did, before and after their marriage—but the end product of their disagreements was not a quarrel but an interlude of silence, occasionally so glacial on both sides that I shivered between them and dared not say a word to either.

Nor did they always agree on places, books, or people. Sara preferred the Schellhase to the Longfellow, where, as she tactfully put it, she could not hear Henry for the orchestra. When they were in New York, Henry liked to go to Lüchow's, where the *Lintensuppe* and sauerbraten were excellent, or to Hoboken, where the beer was even better. Sara frequently opted for Nick's or Moneta's, as she fancied spaghetti and red wine. Now and then she raised "frightful technical objections" to accompanying the Goodmans and H.L. on a malty expedition to Union Hill. "Well," he would say philosophically, "I believe in free speech and so I let her talk." But he retained the right to have his say-so, too. If, in the end, they followed Sara's ideas, then it was only because they were logically persuasive. "She never uses coercion on me," he added. "That is, never in an obnoxious manner."

Henry and August, who were amateur photographers, liked to photograph and be photographed, but Sara loathed cameras of all kinds and would rather have been shot with a rifle than a Kodak. Henry eventually persuaded her to let Carl Van Vechten photograph them together, and she professed to like the pictures. Although she made no comment one way or the other, she was less pleased, however, when at Carl's instance O. Richard Reid, a Negro painter, proposed to do an oil portrait of Mencken. For that matter, H.L., who gladly posed for the camera, was not enthusiastic about the long sittings required for sculpting a bust or painting a portrait. Nevertheless, since he not only fought for free speech but consistently opposed racial discrimination, he decided to give Reid a chance, although he warned him that he had no intention of buying the portrait. During one of the sittings, a reporter arrived to inquire why Mencken was having his portrait painted. Mencken carefully explained the situation and went on to say, tongue in cheek, "It's for posterity when my writings are forgotten."

Reid brusquely interrupted the conversation. "Try to keep the mouth still for a few minutes, Mr. Mencken," he snapped. "Remember I'm not doing a motion picture."

Mencken took the reprimand good-naturedly and continued to make trips to New York to sit for the portrait. He frequently brought Sara along with him, so that she saw a great deal of his friends in Manhattan that fall. One evening Henry took her to Lüchow's to sample a white fish in aspic that delighted him. Lily and Phil Goodman met them there and Ben De Casseres later joined them. De Casseres had recently published his book *Mencken and Shaw*. When he first proposed the idea, H.L. suggested that it would be better for him to write about Pontius Pilate, "the only intelligent man in the Bible." Nevertheless, De Casseres persisted in his original plan. He had wanted to dedicate the book to Mencken, but H.L. cited the criticism aroused by Lewis' dedication of *Elmer Gantry* to him and advised against it. So, instead, De Casseres dedicated it to the friend who had first suggested coupling Mencken, "the Fabre of the American insect," with Shaw, "the Irish disciple of the Uranian Venus." Henry winced and Sara lifted her brows when the book appeared. However, if Mencken was not carried away with De Casseres' interpretation of him in the book, he liked the vivid, aphoristic style of its author and proposed to him that he do an article on Lüchow's for the *Mercury*. De Casseres protested that since he had never known August Lüchow, it would be better to get Ernest Boyd or someone else to do it. Mencken refused to see why De Casseres should let that impede him. "After all," the Sage argued,

"I had no personal acquaintance with the twelve apostles, and yet I have been writing about them for many years."

On their trips to New York that winter, the Menckens saw more of Madeleine than of Ernest Boyd, who had compounded what was to H.L. one of the cardinal sins by failing to meet his obligations. Ernest had neither repaid the personal loans that Henry had made him nor turned up with the promised copy for the *Mercury*. After he came back from Europe, Ernest excused his conduct toward Madeleine by telling her, "I may be an S. O. B., but at least I've never bored you." This, she admitted, was true, and she took Ernest back. But their reconciliation was brief. Although Ernest and Madeleine never sought a divorce, they had now definitely separated. So Mencken gave up trying to straighten Ernest out and advised Madeleine to go in business for herself as a literary agent.

It was over one of Madeleine's clients that a major disagreement arose between Sara and Henry. The client, a young Harvard graduate, Thomas Wolfe, had met Aline Bernstein, a friend of the Knopfs and the Boyds, aboard the *Olympic* on his return from his first trip to Europe. Mrs. Bernstein, who was director and stage designer for the Neighborhood Players, became his dramatic patron and, eventually, his mistress. Wolfe took her the first draft of a Gargantuan novel that filled seventeen ledgers. Once he had a typescript of it, Mrs. Bernstein undertook to sell it for him. After Boni and Liveright turned down the manuscript, she asked Ernest Boyd, then a scout for Little, Brown, to read it. Novels did not interest Boyd, and he usually turned them over to his wife to read. Mrs. Boyd reported Ernest's reaction to Wolfe, who wrote a friend:

> Boyd said he thought the book could not be published in its present form because of "crudities." I don't know what that means—I'll have to see him. Perhaps his sensitive soul recoiled at some of the *langwidge*. He grew up in Dublin, you know, with James Joyce, but Mrs. B.—who is a big fat Frenchwoman (I hear)—did not agree with her gifted spouse. She translates French novels, and is a literary agent, and knows everyone. She seems to think there is a chance for it.

Madeleine and Ernest quarreled over Wolfe's novel; and, after Madeleine set up her own agency, she offered to handle the manuscript and announced, "I have discovered a genius!" But when her enthusiasm met with a series of rebuffs from publishers, Wolfe left for Europe with

Aline Bernstein, who had been sharing an apartment with him and contributing to his support.

As the result of a violent imbroglio with her, during which Wolfe not only threw her religion up to her but also struck her, he left her and took off alone for Munich, where he landed in the hospital as the result of a crack on the head in a brawl at the Oktoberfest there. When Madeleine finally persuaded Maxwell Perkins of Scribner's to talk over the publication of *Look Homeward, Angel* with Wolfe, she had to hire a detective agency to find him in Europe.

In January 1929, shortly after Scribner's announced that they would bring out Wolfe's novel, Madeleine wrote Mencken about it, and at his request sent him portions of it for possible publication in the *Mercury*. The Sage turned it down. He could not even read it, he said. On the other hand, Charles Angoff, his assistant on the *Mercury*, wanted to publish it. After Scribner's brought out the book, Sara read it, and waxed so enthusiastic that she and Henry had a vehement argument over it.

Although Mencken liked Wolfe personally and found him amiable, charmingly boyish, and one of the most modest authors he ever met, he never overcame his aversion to his work. Yet he spoke kindly of it in returning Wolfe's manuscripts to Mrs. Boyd. Wolfe, who held Mencken to be "the critic of the greatest range and power," wrote Madeleine, thanking her for the note from Mencken she had sent him and saying that although his praise was moderate, his belief in any author's work would be of tremendous value.

A few months later, however, Wolfe was less pleased with Mencken's criticism, and the editor of the *Mercury* with Wolfe's work. When Madeleine next sent a batch of Wolfe's short stories to the magazine's New York office, the Sage took one look at the dirty, dog-eared, greasy manuscripts, partially written on butcher's paper, turned to Angoff, and howled, "Take them out! They're not even sanitary."

Mencken's respect for Wolfe and his work deteriorated rapidly after Wolfe broke with Mrs. Boyd. Madeleine was volatile and high-spirited; Wolfe was quick-tempered and suspicious. Eventually, they clashed in a violent scene in Maxwell Perkins' office, in which Wolfe, incensed at her delay in sending him his advance on the German publication of his novel, accused her of irregularity in handling his money and discharged her. Madeleine retaliated by suing him for breach of contract. In the end, Wolfe was forced to pay her six hundred dollars.

Publicly, Mencken excused his distaste for Wolfe's work by saying that he found it as confused and verbose as Sherwood Anderson's later efforts. Privately, he found Wolfe's disorderly life, his treatment of Mrs. Bernstein, and his quarrel with Madeleine as distasteful as his unsanitary manuscripts. Henry and Sara differed in their views of rights and wrongs of the suit against Wolfe as well as in their opinion of his work, and from their vehement arguments pro and con, they came nearer domestic discord than ever before or after.

Some of Mencken's critics have taxed Sara with alienating him from his friends. Quite the reverse is true. She made a business of cultivating them and, being innately conciliatory, tried to repair his breaks with them, which in almost every case, in the last analysis, were due to the disorder of their lives and their failure to meet their obligations—matters in which Sara was inclined to be more tolerant than Henry.

The Menckens constantly had guests. Late in October, Henry induced Tully to come down for another meeting of the Saturday Night Club, luring him back not with a beer-drinking contest but with an invitation to blow the *Waldhorn* in competition with Raymond Pearl, the club's horn virtuoso. The A. H. McDannalds and the Clarence Darrows stopped over in Baltimore in November, and Sara invited them to lunch. At her instance, the Hergesheimers often drove down from West Chester. Since Joe had begun writing editorials for the *Satevepost*, Henry pointed out, he had become so prosperous that he had acquired a fleet of Lincolns and begun to burn ivory in his stoves. When he and Dorothy came to lunch, she and Sara adjourned to the "public rooms" afterward, leaving H.L. to ply Joe with liquor and "induce him to bubble," for he always arrived "full of interesting scandal, mainly about himself."

Unhappily, Sara and Henry also had a horde of less welcome visitors —not friends, but people they scarcely knew. They arrived in clumps, H.L. complained, and ought to be studied mathematically. They blew in at 11:50 A.M., expecting to be entertained royally at lunch, with the wine at just the right temperature. He had tried ground glass on them, he admitted, but they were tough. If such sudden invasions dismayed Sara, he boasted, she never failed to meet them competently and suavely.

On their trips to New York, she and Henry enlivened the Widow Balch's salon, had cocktails with the Van Vechtens, dined out with Lily and Phil Goodman, spent a couple of days with the Knopfs at "Borzoi Towers," and lunched with Nathan and Lillian Gish. Mencken's prediction that George Jean would be married by February 14, 1932, had been translated by the press into an announcement that Nathan was to wed Lillian Gish. H.L. assured her that he had not mentioned her name; he was "full of woe and lamentation" but he feared to do or say anything. If he issued a disclaimer, such were the wonders of journalism that it would be converted into an allegation that Nathan was married last Tuesday and not to Lillian but to a colored girl named Bertha Jackson of Knoxville, Tennessee. By way of making amends to Miss Gish, H.L. offered her a handsome apology and insisted that Nathan bring her to Baltimore for a visit. He had, he said, long promised the connoisseurs there a glimpse of her with George Jean in the full uniform of an Austrian dramatic critic, with a huge cape on his overcoat and a green feather in his hat.

H.L. secretly hoped that Nathan and Miss Gish would make a match; and when the holidays rolled around, Henry reminded George of the joys of family life by sending him a pair of carpet slippers and suggesting that Tully might speed him on his way to the altar with a gift of a pair of pulse warmers.

Despite the Depression, Sara always remembered the Christmas of 1930 as the happiest one of her life. Both she and Henry had an aversion to the holiday season, but this year they celebrated it with high hearts. They decorated the apartment with holly and mistletoe, hung the ornaments on the Christmas tree, and piled the presents at its base. Mencken strung his Christmas cards about the room. After the holidays he wrapped them up and sent them to the historical section of the New York Public Library to show future generations how "a typical American family" celebrated Christmas in the year of our Lord 1930.

Their happiness remained unclouded until Sara fell ill again. After a visit from Nathan and Lillian Gish in January 1931, Sara contracted influenza, ran a high temperature, and had to be hospitalized. Henry too was somewhat under the weather as the result of a sinus infection. By the end of January, however, it subsided and he began to feel brisk and sinful again. But he was lonely at 704 Cathedral Street while Sara was in the Union Memorial. Less than five months married, he moaned, and he had come to such a point that he was miserable without his wife.

Sara suggested a stag party to lift his spirits. So he invited half a dozen friends to dinner at the apartment and regaled them with stories, invented for the occasion, bemoaning the reforms that Sara was effecting—in his clothes, his table manners, and his tobacco chewing—begging them not to relay any unfavorable reports of his backsliding to her. He swore that not a wench had entered the door since he began keeping bachelor's hall. However, he confessed that he had been tight two and a half times. In such periods of stress a grass widower needed strong drink to sustain him. Besides, cold as it was, alcohol was not only necessary to human beings but to automobiles. Why didn't some genius invent a way of alcoholizing the atmosphere to a slight extent so that by merely breathing it in men might be heartened and stimulated to greater achievement?

In his efforts to build up Sara's strength, he urged her to drink sherry, slightly diluted with milk. She drank the wine gladly, but protested that the milk would make her fat. "Obesity," he argued, "is preferable to pleurisy." As she could not gainsay that, she drank milk and put on weight until he said, "She begins to look like a German soprano." But the gain in weight did not prevent her from developing pleurisy. On Valentine's Day, Henry reported that she was dreadfully ill with a racking cough and a temperature of 103°. On March 1, she celebrated her thirty-third birthday in the Union Memorial.

The reviews of Sara's novel, which she had rewritten seven times under Mencken's instruction, did little to cheer either one of them. Henry had already warned her that some of his more virulent critics would "fall upon her with tons of bricks." But, he reminded her, she had written plenty of bad reviews of books in doing the checklist for the *Mercury*, and so she shouldn't complain now when criticism came home to roost. However, the reviews were more encouraging than the sales of the novel, for it was no time to publish a book.

Prosperity, Hoover promised, was just around the corner. But with the army of the unemployed rapidly increasing, the queues in front of the soup kitchens lengthening, and the veterans selling apples on the streets growing leaner, the President's establishment of the Reconstruction Finance Corporation to aid the bankers, brokers, and life-insurance companies was greeted with jeers and his optimistic predictions with the catchphrase of the Depression: "Oh, yeah?"

The times were too uncertain for Henry and Sara to take the extended trip they had planned, and even the little visit they had intended to make the Hergesheimers had to be postponed when Dorothy developed typhoid fever. On May 30, 1931, Henry wrote her:

> For six weeks I have had Mme. Beulah Jackson, the best colored sorceress in these parts, laboring in your behalf. She has used up a ton of chicken feathers and rabbit's feet. Now I am discharging her with a kiss. She is black but beautiful. (Say nothing to Sara.)

In July, however, Sara and Henry did go to Twin Farms. In 1927, Lewis had created a sensation by refusing the Pulitzer Prize; in November 1930, he had created another by accepting the Nobel. In his address in Stockholm, he had lauded Mencken as the critical genius of the age. The following March, Franklin Pierce Adams noted in his column that he had spent the evening with Mencken at Philip Goodman's, where in a discussion of who would have won the Nobel Prize for Literature if there had been a popular vote in this country, some said Edith Wharton, some said Cabell, some said Dreiser, but only F.P.A. and Mencken thought that Lewis would have won it—and that by a landslide. Yet, only four days before the gathering at the Goodmans', when Alfred Knopf told Mencken that after leaving Harcourt Brace, Lewis had "made violent love" to him in London with an eye to securing a large advance on his next book, Mencken had replied brusquely, "The more you give him, the more he will drink and loaf, and the less likely you'll be to get a good book out of him."

Mencken's admiration for Lewis had been slowly eroded by Lewis' protracted sprees and bibulous high jinks rather than by his acceptance of the Nobel Prize or Sara's lack of enthusiasm for Dorothy, as one of H.L.'s biographers intimated. Early in March, at a dinner at the Metropolitan Club, when Dreiser attempted to congratulate Red on having received the Nobel Prize, Lewis threatened to break a bottle over his head and declined to speak "in the presence of a man who had stolen three thousand words" from his wife's book. After Lewis refused to retract his charge, Dreiser slapped him twice in the face. "The slap heard round the world" was still reverberating in Baltimore when Lewis and his English publisher, both boisterous and reeling, barged in at three o'clock in the morning to pay their respects to the Menckens.

Red's nose had been bashed in and there was blood all over his over-coat. He explained that he had tripped and fallen in Washington. Mencken laughed it off by saying that he suspected that Dreiser had been following Lewis around the country and beating him up once a week. As Sara was still too ill to be disturbed at that hour of the night, Lewis' welcome at 704 Cathedral Street was tepid, if not frigid.

Nor did the Menckens' and the Goodmans' Fourth of July visit to the Lewises at Twin Farms tend to restore a warmer relationship. By her own admission, Dorothy Thompson's affections sometimes veered to the distaff side; and if Henry had an aversion to such aberrations, Sara, if possible, had a more intense one. Lewis insisted on taking them for long walks through the fields, from which they returned covered with chiggers. Phil Goodman slipped on a piece of *Blutwurst* on the steps and sprained his ankle. Before their arrival, Dorothy had rustled some Malson ale from across the Canadian border, which, according to Henry, produced "a very artistic belch." But it soon ran out, and the heat and the tension were exacerbated by the drouth. On his return to Baltimore, H.L. sent the Lewises a large package containing malt, hops, corn, sugar, a bag of caps, a capping machine, a siphon, and elab-orate instructions for making home brew to remedy the dearth of malt beverages at Twin Farms.

The following month, on the first anniversary of his marriage, Mencken hinted to Phil Goodman that when a man wedded late in life, he should speed up the usual anniversaries, celebrating the silver anni-versary at the end of the first year, the golden at the end of the second. Of course, it was customary for friends to send suitable remembrances on such occasions, but he adjured Goodman not to succumb to such nonsense. Frankly, he said:

> I expected to make rather heavy weather of the first year. I feared I'd be homesick for Hollins Street, and that it would be more difficult to work in new surroundings, eating purely Southern cooking—hams and greens, corn-pone, hot biscuits, etc. Nothing of the sort ensued. I am far more comfortable than I was in Hollins Street. Sara takes all tele-phone calls. The bills leave me $1.50 for Uncle Willies. Such is life with a really Good Woman.

In *Sententiae* Mencken maintained that "Husbands never become good; they merely become proficient." However that may be, he had certainly become adept in the benedict's virtues. He seldom appeared in the "public rooms" in the afternoons without a surprise for Sara—a china pinbox, a jar of Jordan almonds, a bottle of wine.

One of the few times that I ever saw tears in Sara's eyes was when she told me that a friend of hers, who brought her little girl to see Mencken, had somehow given the child the impression that she was going to see Mickey Mouse. When the Sage appeared instead of Mickey Mouse, the little girl burst into tears. Greatly distressed to find his small guest crying, Henry discovered the cause of her sorrow, hurried into his coat, and set off to find her a toy mouse. When he returned with a mechanical Mickey Mouse, he got down on his hands and knees to demonstrate the acrobatic tricks it could be made to do. Before she left, the little girl pleased him immensely by confiding to her mother that she would rather play with Mencken than with Mickey Mouse.

During the Christmas holidays of 1932, both Sara and Henry were felled by a siege of flu. Henry was still suffering from the aftereffects of his illness when they boarded the North German Lloyd liner *Columbus* for an eighteen-day cruise in the Caribbean. One of the news photographers, seeing that H.L. looked a bit shaky, hastened to offer him a chair. Mencken protested that he was not quite old or feeble enough to require such septuagenarian attentions, but implored the cameramen to see that their pictures of him were captioned, "This man is sick—not drunk."

Warmed by the tropical sun and heartened by the ample beer and wine list of the *Columbus,* Mencken soon took on new life and emerged from the shelter of his deck chair to play poker dice in the bar and shuffleboard on deck. However, he opined that "shuffle Pilsner" was a better game, provided that the barroom steward was lively. As it was Sara's first sea voyage, she was, for all the Coca-Colas, apples, and other nostrums she had laid in, somewhat slower in getting her sea legs and looked forward with undisguised eagerness to the stops at Puerto Rico, Jamaica, Havana, San Juan, La Guaira, Curaçao, and Panama.

By the time they reached Cuba, Mencken had regained his high spirits. He fascinated his fellow passengers by showing them how to down a liter of draught beer at one gulp. Then, inspired by his malty feats, he assumed the editorship of the *Columbus*'s paper, the *Caribbean Caravel*. Under the headline "Confidential Information," he revealed that the North German Lloyd was about to launch a 1,500-foot super-luxury liner:

This Doppelschraubenpostexpressluxuskolossairiesendampfer will have a half mile cinder track, a stadium seating 2,000 and a fourth class for professors. In the first class accommodations, there will be no cabins but only apartments. There will also be twenty penthouses. The ship's doctor will have twenty assistants and there will be a hospital equipped to extract fifty appendices and 500 tonsils a day. There will be Catholic and Protestant churches on the top deck, and space for communists, single-taxers, birth controllers and other reformers will be provided on the boat decks, with free soap boxes. There will also be half a dozen speakeasies.

"Henry," Sara said on her return, "was not only sober during the entire voyage, but he was also in good humor." He was full of a new venture and eager to get back to his desk at 704 Cathedral Street. He proposed to write a third volume to complete the trilogy that included *Notes on Democracy* and *Treatise on the Gods*. In it he intended to adopt a scientific rather than a metaphysical approach in discussing ethics and morality. All during the cruise, he had been debating appropriate titles for it. Eventually, he settled on *Treatise on Right and Wrong*—a bad title, he admitted, but neither he nor Sara had been able to dig up a better one.

He also had a book of reminiscences on the fire, he announced, a delicate little treatise on the literati in which he would prove that two-thirds of them were insane and nine-tenths of them were cads and lushes. He was tired of fooling with them, and glad to turn his attention to the politicians. However, the charm of politics, he conceded, was simply the charm of fraud. In no other craft were so many thumping quacks to be found in such high places. Thus, for him, the best of all sideshows was a convention, the best circus an election that gave the boobs a chance to decide between two gangs of mountebanks and pantaloons, both with india-rubber principles and backbones of butter.

In high glee over the spectacle in prospect, in June of 1932 the Sage oiled his typewriter, packed his bags, and set out for Chicago to cover the Republican Convention. Mencken's candidate for the Republican nomination was Hoover's sole opponent, Senator J. E. France. Although France lost, Mencken made so stout an advocate for him that Will Rogers cracked that had the Senator been elected, *"The American Mercury* would have replaced the *Congressional Record."*

The Democratic contest promised to provide Mencken with a more interesting time, involving as it did both the political fortunes of Maryland's Governor Ritchie and the fate of Prohibition. Mencken voiced the hope that National Museum would be able to forego the addition of his "stuffed carcass" long enough for him to witness the orgies. Nothing short of an earthquake could have prevented him from being on hand when the Democratic Convention convened on June 27. He plugged hard for Ritchie, but to his disappointment F.D.R. won the nomination by a landslide. Afterward, Mencken said of Franklin D.:

> In him, alas, there are many imperfections, some congenital, some acquired. He shares the common Roosevelt quality of being somewhat theatrical: he is only too often far more an actor than he is a statesman. His mind, secondly, performs its operations in a sort of pink and perfumed fog, and what he has to say has usually been said before, and far better said. He is, thirdly, loaded with enlightened self-interest, and may be trusted, even in the gravest emergency, to remember assiduously that there is such a fellow in the world as Franklin Delano Roosevelt. And, fourthly, he is in intimate communion with a number of extremely suspicious characters, including that most dismal old plug, John Nance Garner of Texas.

When I had lunch with Henry in New York later on that summer, I found him unimpressed by Hoover's warning that if F.D.R.'s New Deal went into power in November, the grass would grow in the streets of a hundred cities. He was fed up with the Hoover nostrums. Yet, upon one point, he inclined to agree with President Hoover, "Prosperity is just around the corner." Mencken refused to believe that the crash of 1929 had dealt a fatal blow to our economy. He reflected wryly that the Depression would be well worth its cost if it brought the American people to their senses and to the rediscovery of the massive fact that hard thrift and not gambler's luck was the only basis of national wealth. In the end, we'd probably all be poor, but we'd all be happier when we finally sobered up after the grandest jag in the history of the modern world.

Although H.L. admitted that he had been having a little labor trouble at the *Mercury* and that subscriptions had fallen off, the Depression, he declared, was nothing more than a hangover after the financial binge of 1929. Yet one had to face the fact that industry was limping along at less than fifty per cent of its capacity; wages and dividends had been halved; stocks were worth only a fraction of their former value.

Faith in private enterprise had collapsed with the crash of the stock market. More and more intellectuals began to advocate radical changes in the social and economic order. Quite a few openly adhered to the Communist party line; others rallied under the banners of Thorstein Veblen. To Mencken, Veblen's institutional economics smacked of "Socialism and water." A libertarian, first and last, Mencken, like his preceptor Herbert Spencer, sensed that all Socialism involves slavery and inveighed against the growing academic craze for collectivism. If he had little faith in democracy and capitalism, he had none whatsoever in Fascism and Communism. "Communism," he said, "is a show that quickly wears out; it is clowning by undernourished clowns." A staunch believer in laissez-faire economics, H.L. was also opposed to F.D.R.'s plans for government controls.

For all his battles with the Bible Belt, Mencken's political beliefs reflected his Southern heritage and strongly resembled those that the Confederate gentry cherished. Like them, he was congenitally "agin" the government. Moreover, he was convinced that the problems of government were "inherently and incurably insoluble"; and any man who claimed to be able to solve them, he suspected, could *ipso facto* be convicted of quackery. Like the Jeffersonian Democrats, Mencken believed that the best government is that which governs least. Being honest, decent, upright, and master of himself, he was capable of self-government and wished all other men were, although he was entirely too realistic about *homo boobiens* to believe that law and order could be maintained without a police force. The least objectionable form of government to him was the rule of an intellectual and ethical elite; and, as Guy Forgue has pointed out, he sometimes looked back nostalgically for guidance "to an idealized vision of antebellum life in the aristocratic South."

After the conventions, Knopf had urged Mencken to turn his coverage of them into a book. Eventually, in a matter of thirty-six hours, he whipped his reports of the Democratic and Republican orgies into *Making a President*. The October issue of *The Bookman* announced that "It is something less than an immortal masterpiece, but it is worth a dozen such fiascos as *A Treatise on the Gods* and *Book of Prefaces*." The Marxists and the fellow travelers denounced it roundly. The New Dealers promptly labeled him a reactionary and pronounced his boisterous tub-thumping old hat. The circulation of the *Mercury* had slipped from 67,000 in 1929 to 42,000 in 1932. In an effort to bolster its subscription list, in the October 1932 issue, Mencken inaugurated a section called "The Soap Box," which offered its pages as a rostrum to anyone about anything that appeared in the magazine, anyone with novel and persuasive schemes for getting rid of war, sin, or the Depression, or anyone with schemes to sell something who was clever enough to get his propaganda past the alert editors. But the circulation continued to sag.

Between his editorial difficulties and a recurrence of Sara's illness that necessitated hospitalization, the brightest spot on Mencken's horizon was the coming election. To him politics was the greatest of all spectator sports and the antics of the politicos an inexhaustible source of fun. "Has the art of politics no apparent utility?" he demanded. "Does it appear to be unqualifiedly ratty, raffish, sordid, obscene, and low down, and its salient virtuosi a gang of unmitigated scoundrels? Then let us not forget its high capacity to soothe and tickle the midriff, its incomparable services as a maker of entertainment." The collapse of the Republican campaign after the GOP leaders tried to straddle the Prohibition issue provided Mencken with belly laughs all fall; and in the defeat of that "pathetic mud-turtle, Lord Hoover" on November 8, he found cause for rejoicing, even during the height of the Depression.

$\mathcal{J}$HE DAYS OF DISASTER

MENCKEN WAS ONE of the earliest champions of civil rights for black and white alike; and he began to turn his skill as a demolition expert on the segregationists in earnest after Richard Reid, the Negro artist who had painted his portrait, was arrested in a New York cafeteria for attempting to have a meal there with a white friend. Mencken declared that the whole thing sounded as if it had happened in Mississippi. The Mississippi editors riposted so violently that in rebuttal, after debating the question of which was "the worst American State" in the *Mercury*, Mencken awarded the dubious palm, not to Georgia or California, hitherto strong contenders, but to Mississippi. "Altogether," he decided, "it seems to be without a serious rival to the lamentable preeminence of the worst American state."

Before the furor over his exchange with Mississippi died down, a diatribe of Mencken's on Arkansas, called "Famine," in which he alleged that the state was the capital of Moronia, whose inhabitants were starving to death through congenital stupidity, provoked a resolution of censure from the state legislature in Little Rock. When asked to comment on it, Mencken said, "My only defense is that I didn't make Arkansas the butt of ridicule. God did it." The Arkansas house of representatives stood and offered prayers for the soul of H. L. Mencken. Asked for a statement on the subject by the Associated Press, Mencken replied, "I felt a great uplift, shooting sensations in my nerves, and the sound of many things in my ears and I knew the house of representatives of Arkansas was praying for me again."

The Sage had once again joined battle with the scribes and Pharisees in the Sahara of the Bozart, who bombarded him with enough scurrilous epithets to fill another *Schimpflexicon.* "By cutting through six inches of fat and drilling through four inches of bone," one irate Confederate declared, "one might possibly find Mencken's brain cavity— but he would not find any gray matter there." Another ranted at him as "This modern Attila! This brachycephalous Caliban! The Black Knight of Slander! And intellectual Houyhnhnm!" Mencken gleefully clipped the choicest samples for his scrapbook and replied with a counterblast of invective at the Bible Belt, "the bunghole of the United States, a cesspool of Baptists, a miasma of Methodism, snake-charmers, real-estate operators and syphilitic evangelists."

Years before, as a specific against lynching, Mencken had proposed introducing bullfighting into Georgia, Alabama, and Mississippi. "It was my contention," he explained, "that every bull that was killed would save a Christian Ethiop." When a series of lynchings on the Eastern Shore of his native Maryland erupted, he proposed to detach it from the Free State, amalgamate it with Delaware, drive the combination out to sea and sink it. In "The Eastern Shore Kultur," printed in the *Evening Sun,* he subsequently castigated its citizens for "obscenities worthy of cannibals." The newspapers on the Eastern Shore hit back by charging that Mencken was affiliated with "anarchist and communist groups, composed for the most part of men and women from the lowest strata of the mongrel breeds of European gutters." Local firms on the Eastern Shore threatened to boycott Baltimore businessmen unless Mencken and the *Sun* apologized. The *Sun's* paper trucks were ambushed, their drivers beaten up, and their papers dumped into the bay. Telegrams poured into Hamilton Owens' office, threatening to lynch any *Sun* reporter who set foot on the Eastern Shore.

There and elsewhere Mencken was attacked as anti-Semitic and pro-Nazi. Both allegations appeared to him too ridiculous to be taken seriously. He declared that his old belief in the inspiration of the Talmud was being shaken, and it was entirely possible that he might even turn Christian. Further, he had had a postcard from Hitler, saying that he was not really anti-Semitic at all; some of his best friends were Jews. Although Mencken himself had been blacklisted by the Nazis, his refusal to take the Führer seriously seemed to some of his Jewish friends to lend color to the charges that he was pro-Nazi; nor were they amused by the jokes with which he laughed them off. But De Casseres, Angoff, and even Goodman refused to see that, as Mencken had long argued, one horselaugh was worth a thousand syllogisms—or denials. The trouble with both him and Goodman, he pointed out, was that they were never serious. They made a joke about everything. Surely, he added, Goodman many times also must have had the experience of having people swallow in all seriousness what he had said in jest.

A further strain on Mencken's friendship with Goodman resulted from a curious incident that also involved Nathan and Sinclair Lewis. Mencken, who had seen Lewis occasionally in New York during the past winter, concluded that Lewis had "completely blown up." The change in Red's attitude toward him Mencken had at first attributed to Dorothy Thompson. For, in his euphemism, she was not one of his customers. However, when Lewis and Goodman sailed for Europe together aboard the S.S. *Dresden* in April 1932, H.L. was infuriated by the criticisms that Lewis leveled at him in an interview that Mencken believed Nathan had instigated. "Lewis," one ship reporter announced in headlines, "Sees Marriage Ruining Mencken." In an effort to protect Sara from "the wonders of modern journalism," Henry had been on the defensive about his marriage from the beginning. He resented his friends' levity about it; consequently, Lewis' interview left him too angry for once to make a joke of a criticism, and his letters to Goodman on the subject are among the bitterest he ever wrote.

Lewis, he said, must have been somewhat upset by stimulants to make such a statement. It was, he assumed, inspired by Nathan and attributed to Red while he was under the influence of alcohol. Ultimately, he promised to revenge himself on George in a way that would delight a malicious mind. In the light of a memorandum from Lewis to Nathan written six months before, there appears to be some ground for Mencken's suspicions. In it Lewis advised Nathan to tone down a chapter in a manuscript of Nathan's so as to keep it from indicating so clearly that Henry was no longer the same old Mencken and to end the account of the Sage more affectionately and favorably, no matter how much he had to lie.

As for Lewis, Mencken declared that it was highly improbable that he would ever see him again; for once a man became acutely disgusting, it was hard to be polite to him. It took more than one generation to breed out the stigmata of Sauk Center. Lewis was simply a peasant and must be dealt with as such. How many speeches did Red make in the smoking room? H.L. inquired. How soon did he slap the captain on the back and begin to call the stewards by their first names? After Goodman reported that Lewis had delivered a monologue on ordure in four-letter words aboard the *Dresden,* Mencken said that while Grace Hegger might have been a "bogus duchess," she, at least, kept Red headed away from the dunghill; but, evidently, his present consort had gotten him back on the ancestral track.

In July, when H.L. received a post card from "our lamented friend George," he wrote Goodman, somewhat testily, that why Nathan should be sending him greetings, he could not make out. A few days later, on learning that Goodman's daughter, Ruth, and her husband contemplated a visit to Dorothy and Red at Twin Farms, Mencken exploded. He could not imagine anyone spending a week there with Lewis. The parts of Lewis' new novel, *Ann Vickers,* that had appeared in the *Red Book,* he continued sarcastically, were almost as good as one of Mary Roberts Rinehart's; Red was beginning to see life clearly and see it as a whole—the result, doubtless, of living with a good woman and one who takes an intelligent interest in public affairs. Grace Hegger, Mencken added, tongue in cheek, had almost ruined Red by making him write *Main Street* and *Babbitt;* but now he is on the the right track at last.

Later in the summer, Lewis joined with Nathan, Boyd, Dreiser, and Eugene O'Neill to publish the *American Spectator.* Mencken viewed the combine as another affront from his former friends. When Goodman protested to Ernest Boyd that H.L.'s feeling was not unwarranted, the Sage was sorry that he had done so, for he said that nothing would please that outfit better than the notion that he resented its operations. The *American Spectator* struck Mencken as a poor thing, puerile in content, badly printed in a newspaper format, and almost unreadable. Nathan, he told Raymond Pearl, had been playing about with some such idea ever since he was relieved of his duties on *The American Mercury.* Apparently, he had found an angel willing to stake a few numbers; but Mencken predicted that the *Spectator* would die very quickly. Actually, it lingered on for five years. In 1935, Charles Angoff, Mencken's former assistant, joined the dissidents to become its editor. Two years later, the *American Spectator* folded, leaving little except a history of editorial quarrels and bitterness behind it.

When the first number of the *Spectator* appeared in November 1932, it sharpened Mencken's distaste for the New York literati. While he venerated some of the brethren, he said tartly, he preferred the society of the host at the Schellhase, who not only was a more agreeable fellow but also knew much more than they did.

Buchholz, he grumbled, was the only really healthy member of the Saturday Night Club; most of its members were ailing. Al Hildebrandt, who had long suffered from dropsy, died just before Thanksgiving, leaving a lot of worthless oil stock, five hundred fiddles, and his Stradivarius cello. Henry spent two dismal days helping to give him Christian burial and settle his estate. A new member of the club, its young fiddler, Louis Cheslock, "a quiet lad and a very useful addition," since he played the viola as well as the first violin, helped to fill the void in the constant circle left by Al Hildebrandt's death.

Mencken, whose mind brimmed with musical ideas, suggested to Cheslock that he set to music Vachel Lindsay's "The Congo," one of the few modern poems that both Sara and Henry admired. Cheslock's score for the the poem eventually won a prize for him. Mencken was delighted with it, especially because the piano part was not too difficult to be beyond "the technique of a true patriot." But, alas, the vocal parts were out of the range of the club's "croaking voices."

The approach of the holidays brought another ebb in Mencken's usual gusto. Dorothy and Joe Hergesheimer were under the weather and in low spirits too. In an effort to encourage Joe, who had written himself out, Henry noted to Dorothy that in his omnivorous reading, he had discovered via the annual report of the Librarian of Congress that two of Hergy's books had been done in Braille for the use of the blind. Next, he supposed, there would be an expurgated edition of Joe's books for the use of the Methodists.

On December 23, prompted by a gift of partridges from Fred Hanes, Sara and Henry gave a small dinner party, at which a rare combination of cocktails, claret, brandy, and beer left the host to reflect next morning that the passage of the years corroded the noblest constitutions; once upon a time, he could have downed four times as much and never felt it. Next night, the gallon of eggnog with which he and Sara celebrated the Yule made them sleep well, but brought them up on Christmas morning with "a certain gloom in their hearts." Both of them had been plagued with colds all winter; and as the damp bone-chilling cold of Baltimore made them long for the sun, they decided to take a short vacation at Sea Island, Georgia.

To add to Mencken's pleasure in the sunlight and sea air in Georgia, he had been forewarned of the moratorium and he had taken along a large supply of cash in the form of gold notes. When the banks closed on March 4, 1933—the very day on which F.D.R. took office—Mencken found himself a moneyed man among the penniless millionaires of Sea Island. The year before, although convinced of the knavery and stupidity of politicians, H.L. had announced that he was very reluctant to believe that bankers were idiots; now he was forced into a more skeptical position.

So far, the panic had affected Sara and Henry only mildly. Sara, H.L. told me, had sold more stories in a month than she had sold in any year before. He added complacently that, despite the Depression, by the next year he expected her to be earning enough to support him far more comfortably than he was now supporting her. But, always a prudent man, he had hit upon a novel method of safeguarding himself from financial difficulties in his old age. He had printed and distributed to his friends a "Form of Bequest," legally approved by a firm of his own invention, Messrs. Goldfarb, Feinberg, Spritzwasser, and O'Shaunessey. By merely filling in the amount of the bequest and signing the form, the testator could will a portion of his fortune to Henry Louis Mencken in appreciation of his services to his country as a patriot and a Christian and in consideration of his probable bodily and spiritual needs in his declining years.

The "Form of Bequest" elicited a truly Irish response from Tully, who willed all the royalties on his unwritten books to the Sage. In October, Tully was astonished to hear that Mencken planned to relinquish the editorship of *The American Mercury* to Henry Hazlitt. In writing Tully shortly afterward, Sara told him that while she was sorry in a way to have H.L. resign his editorial chair, in a number of other ways she was glad he had decided to do it. The work had become purely routine and very bad for him, especially since it left him little time to work on his books.

Mencken was tired of newspaper work, tired of book reviewing, and tired of the *Mercury*. Fiction appealed to him less and less. For over a year, he had not reviewed a single play, poem, or novel in the "Library" section of the *Mercury*. Then, when Sinclair Lewis' *Ann Vickers* appeared, he let it have both barrels. It was, he said, simply a bad novel with a few bright spots. Like Tully, he was struck by the fact that its heroine talked very much like Dorothy Thompson. Under the influence of his wife, H.L. feared that Lewis would soon go the way of Dreiser, whose *An American Tragedy* Mencken found vastly inferior to his early novels, especially *Jennie Gerhardt*.

Cabell had turned essayist. Although Mencken had published Fitzgerald's story "Crazy Sunday" in the October 1932 issue of the *Mercury*, he felt that Scott's work had fallen off of late. On the other hand, he continued to admire Ring Lardner's "incomparable studies of the lowdown American" and the novels of James Farrell and H. L. Davis. John Dos Passos had once appealed to him as a promising youngster, but now he found his novels dull, incoherent, and unreadable. Ben Hecht, said Mencken, was "probably the nearest approach to Rabelais that this Great Christian Republic has yet produced." Ford Madox Ford, being half German and half English, appeared to Mencken as "a sort of walking civil war—too much engrossed by the bombs going off in his own ego—to make much of an impression on the rest of the human race."

The great literary renaissance of the twenties, the Sage believed, had ended with the decade. He had little praise for the writers of the thirties. Much has been made of his lack of appreciation for the work of Hemingway and Faulkner. Hemingway had satirized Mencken and the *Mercury* in the *Torrents of Spring,* and Mencken had criticized his *In Our Time* as having been "written in the bold bad manner of the Café Dôme." However, in his review of *A Farewell to Arms,* while he lamented Hemingway's handling of his protagonists and his sometimes faulty English, he praised the book highly for "its brilliant evocation of the horrible squalor and confusion of war." Mencken pronounced Hemingway's *Death in the Afternoon* an extraordinarily fine piece of expository writing, but then he qualified his tribute by reflecting that although Hemingway had been praised very lavishly, he had somehow failed to make his way into the first rank of American authors. In a frequently quoted passage, H.L. added, "Only too often he turns aside from his theme to prove fatuously that he is a naughty fellow, and when he does so he almost invariably falls into banality and worse." He felt that Hemingway also dragged in ancient four-letter words to shock the Ladies Aid Societies; and, he concluded, "They will give the Oak Park W.C.T.U. another conniption fit. The Hemingway boy is really a case."

William Faulkner, Mencken believed, was a much better novelist than Hemingway. He had first met the Mississippi writer at a party given by the Knopfs in their New York apartment, at which Faulkner and Dashiell Hammett turned up three sheets to the wind. His appreciation of Faulkner has doubtless been obscured by his reports of that incident and a story about the novelist that Mencken was fond of repeating. Frank Case, the host of the Algonquin, he said, met Faulkner in the lobby one morning looking somewhat the worse for the night before and asked, "What's the matter, Mr. Faulkner?"

"I feel like the devil," Faulkner replied. "My stomach's upset."

"Too bad," Case said. "Something you wrote, no doubt."

But, for all that, as a matter of record, Mencken was one of the first editors to encourage Faulkner. Between July 1930 and his retirement he published four of Faulkner's short stories in the *Mercury,* and in the February 1934 issue there appeared a fifth, which he probably contracted for before he retired.

Although Mencken continued on as a director of Alfred A. Knopf, Inc., he edited his last issue of the *Mercury* in December 1933. Among the farewell presents he received were two cases of beer. On learning of Mencken's resignation, Grover Hall observed in an editorial in the Montgomery *Advertiser* that apparently the Depression had not wiped out the resources of the Baltimore writer, for he had forsaken a profitable connection with *The American Mercury* to devote his talents to the writing of two books, one on morals, and the other on advice to young men.

On December 17, Mencken, Alfred Knopf, Raymond Pearl, Gustave Strube, and Buchholz went to Schellhase's new place on Howard Street to celebrate Mencken's release from the *Mercury* at a session of the Saturday Night Club, which had met in a back room there ever since Repeal. Two men distributing a pamphlet, "War and Fascism," tried to force their way into the meeting. "Heinie" Buchholz, the club's sergeant-at-arms, barred their way. One of the men clipped him on the ear. When Mencken saw Buchholz' ear bleeding, he gave chase to the intruders and overhauled and subdued them. To his great amusement, he and his friends were hailed into police court the next day to tell the magistrate how they had defeated the pamphleteers. With great gusto, H.L. wrote Hergesheimer:

> You should see Buchholz! He has a magnificent cauliflower ear, and there is evidence that his brains have been shaken and precipitated

beyond repair. The battle while it lasted was very amusing. For the first time in thirty years I found myself engaged in actual fisticuffs. When Pearl began to thrust himself into the air the enemy surrendered at once, and what followed was rather banal. In the morning both criminals, after spending the night in the society of colored felons, were full of remorse and their lawyer was eager only to get them out. The Club is suing Schellhase for $200,000, and hopes to take his kaif in compromise.

I approach the holidays with my usual sour stomach. In all probability I'll get down no more than ten or twelve drinks on Christmas Eve.

The Baltimore winter once more proved too severe for Sara. Therefore, Mencken decided to take her on a Mediterranean cruise. On February 10, they embarked on his favorite ship, the *Columbus*. The voyage was enlivened by three Catholic bishops, whom Mencken found excellent company after his work on *Treatise on the Gods* and *Treatise on Right and Wrong*. The life aboard ship, he opined, suited him exactly; it was the existence of a vegetable, and a canned vegetable at that. There was even a machine to blow the foam off his beer. Long before the ship docked at Naples, he had begun "to bulge and grow matronly."

Mussolini, he reflected, had repealed the whole of Italy and reenacted it. The trains now ran on time, the roads were superb; even in the back streets of Naples, there were no children wallowing in the gutters, no spaghetti drying on the rocks, no stench of garbage, and no chamberpots emptied out of the upper windows. The chauffeur he and Sara hired to drive them to Pompeii, Amalfi, and Sorrento was as careful as a hearse driver and so courteous that he had to be run down the next day to be paid. If a shill for a brothel importuned a tourist too vigorously, the visitor had only to call the nearest Black Shirt, who dragged the offender off to jail.

In Algiers, the Sage was flung out of a taxi on a hairpin curve. Luckily, he landed on the cobbles on his derrière instead of his head and thus sustained only a few minor bruises. The scenes on the docks in Cairo and Port Said reminded him of those in pre-Mussolini Naples. Porters threatened to beat up Americans for insufficient tips; police captains thwacked the porters across the face with their whips. Between the Continental Savoy and Shepheard's Hotel in Cairo, Mencken reported that there were at least two hundred dragomen offering to show all comers to brothels where sex was purveyed in all of its oriental variations.

In Egypt, land of wonders, Henry persuaded Sara to mount a camel and have her picture taken, perched precariously on its hump. He had post cards made from it, one of which he sent me, inscribed with a promise of a bottle of holy water from the River Jordan. The research that Mencken had done for *Treatise on the Gods* made him look forward eagerly to visiting the Holy Land. As he approached G.H.Q., he observed that "the wonders of Yahweh increase in ingenuity." In Jerusalem, he picked up a souvenir for Ernest Boyd, which he claimed to be a gallstone passed by Abraham 1700 B.C., a cherished heirloom handed down by succeeding generations of the Margolis family. In view of his veneration for Pontius Pilate, H.L. planned to visit his tomb and drop a tear there. The Sage also hoped to visit Gomorrah, his favorite town of antiquity. But, to his great disappointment, since the archaeologists could neither agree on its location nor that of Sodom, he gave up the search and went to Magdala instead to lay a wreath on the tomb of its greatest daughter at the behest of the Association of American Chorus Girls.

Having procured a bottle of water from the Jordan, Henry and Sara proceeded to Constantinople, which they found more interesting than Athens, where they had only enough time to see the Acropolis and try the resinous wine. Henry declined to visit Socrates' prison because he had always been of the opinion that Plato's mentor deserved to die, if not as a traitor and an atheist, then as one of the worst lawyers ever known. Someday, Mencken said, he hoped to do a critical analysis of Socrates' defense of himself as reported by Plato.

As the Menckens had very little time in Paris, Sara decided to spend it in shopping and Henry in eating. Consequently, on his return voyage, for the first time in thirty years, he suffered from seasickness. By the time he landed in Manhattan from the S.S. *Europa,* he was in a gloomy mood. He foresaw that Europe would undergo a tremendous upheaval in the next twenty years and predicted that its peoples as well as those of the United States would fall under the sway of a man on horseback.

> "I am convinced," he declared, "that the majority of people don't want liberty. I am still a libertarian and believe in it but I think most people would prefer to be ruled, governed, and directed. It may be that the ordinary man doesn't have to worry about so many things when he has no liberty."

On his return, with the Depression at its worst, Mencken "walked down the gangplank and into a sea of troubles." His *Treatise on Right and Wrong*, over which he had labored two years and a half, met with what he described to Scott Fitzgerald as "the usual violent denunciations" from the critics. In forwarding a copy of it to Hergesheimer, H.L. said that if Joe read it he would be very ill advised; it was solemn stuff. During the "Mencken Twilight," his great trilogy was relegated to obscurity, and twenty years were to pass before the magnitude of his accomplishment began to be appreciated.

The best that he and Sara could say for their trip was that they had had a fair time and had come home hardly more exhausted than when they sailed. He had lost five pounds, Sara fifteen. The cruise had not benefited her as he had hoped it would. She arrived in Baltimore running a temperature from a mysterious infection that she had picked up in Algiers, and wound up in the hospital.

While Sara was in the Union Memorial, Mencken saw Fitzgerald frequently, for Zelda had been hospitalized after a nervous breakdown. Scott's luck had run out; calamity pursued him like a jealous mistress. In June 1933, while on a visit home, Zelda tried to burn some old clothes in an upstairs fireplace and set the house on fire. The blaze had been quickly extinguished, but not before they had lost many of their personal belongings, which they could ill afford to lose, for they were already in financial straits. Among Sara Haardt's papers, there appears a receipt, dating from this time, from which it is evident that Scott either sold or pawned to her two of Zelda's pictures: "Received $100 for painting 'Morning' and one other by Zelda Fitzgerald—with stipulations in my possession—by F. Scott Fitzgerald for Zelda Fitzgerald."

As Fitzgerald's debts piled up, his drinking increased, and he had to be hospitalized for alcoholism. The final revisions of *Tender Is the Night*, as he afterward said regretfully, were made on the bottle. In January 1934, while he was correcting the page proofs of his novel, Zelda broke down again. He had her committed to the Sheppard-Pratt Hospital and tried to resign himself to the belief that she would never be well again. "I left my capacity for hoping," he said, "on the little roads that led to Zelda's sanitariums."

Although he refused to let us see her while she was at Sheppard-

Pratt, by April she had sufficiently recovered to go to New York to arrange for an exhibition of her paintings there. In the little catalogue of them there appeared the poignant inscription, *Parfois le folie est la sagesse.* On April 14, 1934, *The New Yorker* announced the opening of a show of "Paintings by the almost mythical Zelda Sayre Fitzgerald; with whatever emotional overtones or associations may remain from the so-called Jazz Age." In the same issue, *The New Yorker* panned *Tender Is the Night,* which had been published two days before. "In Mr. Fitzgerald's case," the reviewer declared, "money is the root of all novels. The latter part of the book, in which Dr. Dick Diver, having cured his schizophrenic wife only to have her fall in love with a Gallic adventurer, goes ingloriously to seed, and becomes merely an anatomy of moral disintegration." To add to the bitter rivalry that Zelda's successes aroused in Scott, *Time* reported: "There was a time when Mrs. Frances Scott Key Fitzgerald was a more fabulous character than her novel-writing husband. That was when she was Zelda Sayre, a Montgomery, Ala. girl."

Before Judge Sayre's death, he had frankly advised Zelda to divorce Scott. Neither he nor his family had ever wholeheartedly approved of Zelda's choice of a husband. Nor did they think that a young girl of Scottie's age should be left alone in his care and subjected to the inevitable unpleasantness created by Fitzgerald's brawls with his drinking companions. In the event that either Scott or Zelda ever made good their threats to file divorce proceedings, there was certain to be a contest over the custody of Scottie. In view of these things, it is impossible to know whether Fitzgerald deliberately wrote certain portions of *Tender Is the Night* in retaliation for the parts of Zelda's *Save Me the Waltz,* which he and Perkins forced her to cut, whether he was unconsciously preparing a psychological defense against a court fight, or whether, equally unconsciously, he was simply slipping into one of the paranoid projections to which he was increasingly given as he approached a crackup. Whatever his motive, in the sketch for Nicole in his notes for *Tender Is the Night,* he says of its heroine:

> At fifteen she was raped by her own father under peculiar circumstances—work out. She collapses, goes to the clinic and there at sixteen meets the young doctor hero who is ten years older. Only her transference to him saves her—when it is not working she reverts to homicidal mania and tries to kill men. She is an innocent, widely read but with no

experience and no orientation except that he supplies her. Portrait of Zelda—that is, a part of Zelda.

Further along, under the heading "Classification of the Material on Sickness," he lists:

A. Accounts

B. Baltimore

C. Clinics and clipping

D. Dancing and 1st Diagnoses

E. Early Prangins—to February 1931

F. From Forel (include Eleuler Consultation)

G. Hollywood

L. Late Prangins

M. My own letters and comments

Even without the evidence of the notes, by implication *Tender Is the Night* did as gross an injustice to Zelda and the Sayres as any author ever had done to his wife and her family—even in a time when novelists frequently ran through with three or four wives in the course of writing as many books and coldbloodedly vivisected them, one to a volume.

After Hemingway accused Fitzgerald of having turned out in *Tender Is the Night* not an account of people but a series of "beautifully faked case histories," Sara and Gerald Murphy, to whom the book was dedicated, voiced the same objection. Scott attempted to excuse himself by a strange explanation. "The book," he said to Gerald Murphy, "was inspired by Sara and you, and the way I feel about you both and the way you live, and the last part of it is Zelda and me because you and Sara are the same people as Zelda and me." Despite this curious attempt of Scott's to mend matters, the Murphys were offended by *Tender Is the Night*, the Sayres were affronted, and the Menckens felt that Scott had shown bad judgment and worse taste in not deleting its slanderous innuendoes.

William Manchester, one of the best of Mencken's biographers, reports finding in the Sage's library "an author's copy of *Tender Is the Night* with a pathetic note from Fitzgerald, begging him to read it and support him against the herding critics. The pages are still uncut." Whether Mencken ever actually read the book or not, no one knows—for, in the copy of the novel with Scott's note pasted in the front of it, now in the H. L. Mencken Room at the Enoch Pratt Free Library, all the leaves have been cut, presumably, if it is the same copy, after Manchester saw it, but whether by H.L. or another reader remains uncertain. At all events, when Scott, in desperate need of encouragement after the unfavorable reviews of his book, complained to Mencken in a letter of April 23, 1934, that the critics had misunderstood his intentions in writing it, Mencken replied with his usual kindness on April 26, 1934:

> I hope you don't let yourself be upset by a few silly notices. The quality of book reviewing in the American newspapers is really appalling. Reviews are printed by imbeciles who know nothing whatever about the process of writing, and hence miss the author's intentions completely. I think your scheme is a capital one, and that you have carried it out very effectively in this book.

In December 1933, four months before the publication of his novel, Scott had moved into more modest quarters in Baltimore at 1307 Park Avenue, one block over and six short blocks north of the Menckens' apartment, where he often arrived unannounced at odd hours, often with strange companions picked up on the streets. In May, Zelda was brought back from a sanitarium in New York in a catatonic state. Scott rewrote three of her articles, sold them to *Esquire,* and, in June, left her in Baltimore to go on an extended bender in New York. He had been drinking heavily all summer and engaging in one trivial, sordid affair and then another, which he was fond of discussing in mixed company.

Mencken's own domestic life was well-ordered, happy, and decorous; his financial affairs were always carefully regulated, and his love of wine, women, and song was tempered with moderation and good taste. Consequently, he had little patience with the chronic disorder in the life of Fitzgerald, or, for that matter in the lives of Hemingway, Wolfe, Faulkner, Lewis, Dreiser, or Ernest Boyd. Further, Scott's accounts of his infidelities offended Mencken, who regarded adultery as "hitting below the belt," and he was now inclined to write Fitzgerald off as hopeless.

In November, Mencken, who had been a member of the *Sunpapers'* staff since 1906, was elected a director. In reply to a congratulatory note and a contribution to his cellar, he wrote me on December 6, 1934:

> You are storing up a rich reward in heaven. I tapped one of the bottles the instant they came in, and so got aboard the train in an extremely

friendly and optimistic frame of mind. The stuff is excellent indeed, and I haven't the slightest doubt that it will help me to get through a hard Winter safely.

Sara is writing to you. She is in excellent shape physically, and in good humor mentally. The chiropractors want her to remain at rest as long as she can stand it in order that there may be no chance of a return of the pleurisy. My own belief is that they should liberate her at once, but I never argue with such fellows.

My best thanks again. I kiss both your hands.

When the Gridiron Club, organized by the elite of the Washington Press Corps, met at the Willard Hotel on December 8, the guests included the President, the Chief of Staff, a number of cabinet members, senators, governors, lords of the press and radio, and the Sage of Baltimore. As he and F.D.R. were to be the only speakers of the evening, the occasion called for a tail coat, white tie, and boiled shirt. On his arrival in Washington, he found that Sara had sent him off with nothing but soft shirts. Fortunately, Paul Patterson, with whom he had driven over from Baltimore, had brought along an extra evening shirt. Mencken tried it on, dressed hurriedly, and shaved. When he reappeared, Patterson's eyes bulged. The white expanse of Mencken's boiled shirt was stippled with large red polka dots. He had cut himself in shaving and failed to notice the disastrous bloodstains. Patterson's chauffeur had to comb the town until he found a haberdashery open and supplied Mencken with another shirt.

The evening was ill-starred for the Sage from beginning to end. He had recently suggested that F.D.R. might be made king by a slight change in the Constitution. Roosevelt would make, to be sure, a fourth-rater. "But even a fourth-rate king is better," he added, "it seems to me than a fourth-rate President with his eyes on 1936." When the long Gridiron Club dinner was over and Mencken rose to speak, he compounded his *lèse-majesté*. Turning to Roosevelt, he began another lampoon of the New Deal. "Mr. President, Mr. Wright," he bowed to the presiding officer of the Gridiron Club, "and Fellow Subjects of the Reich." He was, he continued, more hopeful of the future since he had discovered that the New Deal had left one article of the Bill of Rights inviolate. So far no soldiers had been quartered in any man's house without the consent of the owner. After he finished, Roosevelt grinned and began his speech with an amiable reference to "my old friend, Henry Mencken." F.D.R. then launched into a denunciation of the American press for its "stupidity, cowardice, and Philistinism." He went on to say, "There are managing editors in the United States, and scores of them, who have never heard of Kant or Johannes Müller and never read the Constitution of the United States; there are city editors who do not know what a symphony is or a streptococcus, or the Statute of Frauds; there are reporters by the thousands who could not pass the entrance examination for Harvard and Tuskegee, or even Yale. It is this vast and militant ignorance, this widespread and fathomless prejudice against intelligence, that makes American journalism so pathetically feeble and vulgar, and so generally disreputable."

Roosevelt's speech ended in an excruciating silence. Mencken's face was the color of oxblood porcelain. For a number of fourth-estate bigwigs present were sufficiently literate to recognize that the President's castigation of the press was quoted verbatim from Mencken's *Prejudices: Sixth Series.* It was a blow below the belt, which both *The New York Times* and *Time* magazine found too offensive to include in their report of the Gridiron Club. Inasmuch as Mencken's remarks about the New Deal had been checked beforehand by Roosevelt's secretaries while the Sage was kept in ignorance of the vindictive rebuttal until F.D.R. exploded his bombshell at the press dinner, Roosevelt's performance was unsportsmanlike, if not ungentlemanly. Mencken was, understandably, embarrassed and indignant, and he began at once to whet his ax for use against Roosevelt in 1936.

Three days later, Henry wrote me about it—his only reference to the Gridiron Club speech then or thereafter:

> I got in a bout with a High Personage at the dinner and was put to death with great barbarity. Fortunately, I revived immediately, and am still full of sin.
>
> Sara is in an excellent state. Unluckily, her mother has just had a stroke of apoplexy, and is seriously ill—in fact, there is some chance that she may die.

Henry's mother had died on December 13 and his father on January 13. One of his most cherished superstitions was that thirteen was an unlucky number for him; another was that Christmas always brought a time of woe, a death, or an illness to someone near him. In 1934, his belief was fully justified. Sara Haardt's mother died early on the morning of December 24 and was buried on Christmas Day.

Sara was too ill to go to Montgomery for the funeral. Her sadness over her mother's death, added to the depression that always overtook her during the Christmas holidays, had sent her spirits and her vitality spiraling to their lowest ebb. Dr. Baker was alarmed about her. Mencken, who had been trying to get to work on *The American Language,* was so dejected himself that he let his research go and tried to mitigate the horror of the holidays by reading detective stories. To Hergesheimer's Christmas greetings, he replied that it was the second reminder of the season to reach him. The first came from a gentleman who was serving a life sentence for murder in the Trenton hoosegow. In lieu of Yule logs, H.L. promised to send Joe by ox wagon fifty Gideon Bibles stolen from as many hotels. They make excellent firewood, he explained. He saw the old year out with the mordant reflection: "Let us give the Holy Ghost credit, He has got off some masterpieces in 1934."

By February, Henry was glad to hear from Knopf that he had sold the *Mercury* to a young man named Paul Palmer, who had plenty of money. Thus the future of the magazine seemed to be assured. But Charles Angoff had succeeded Henry Hazlitt as editor, and by March the new owner and editor were involved in labor troubles with the staff of the magazine. Mencken arrived to find that the labor trouble at the *Mercury* had developed into what its present publisher, Lawrence E. Spivak, called the "soviet rule of employees." The hired help were demanding a twenty-one-dollar-a-week minimum and two weeks' vacation a year. In a humorous manifesto, Mencken pooh-poohed the "world revolution" in the *Mercury* office, the influence of "Moscow and Fourteenth Street," and the inadequate ability of the shop committee. Hereinafter, he announced, all manuscripts addressed to the *Mercury* would be searched for bombs. The employees, who were in no mood to appreciate the Sage's humor, carried out their threat to strike.

Once again the literary gossips were in full cry over a feud between Henry and George Jean, which Mencken pronounced "wholly imaginary" and Nathan never mentioned. Early in April, Mencken was, as Sara put it, "so low he'd have to jump up to touch bottom," but his dejection was not the result of labor troubles or literary quarrels. He had undertaken to revise *The American Language,* and the slow, tedious work involved by that "dull and dusty labor" wearied him deeply. He was forced to seek refreshment so often that he grumbled, "Before this thing is over, Schellhase will make more out of the book than I do."

Further, the Fitzgeralds' plight preyed on Mencken's mind. Sara's recurrent illnesses had given him a deeper insight into the effect of Zelda's collapses on Scott and created a new sympathy for him. Threatened with cirrhosis of the liver, Fitzgerald had gone on the wagon. By making a severe overdraft on his strength, he turned out a book of short stories and went to Hendersonville, North Carolina, to recuperate. His life there in a drab hotel, where he did his own laundry and lived off potted meat, oranges, and Uneeda biscuit, added up to a "bankrupt's comedy," as he termed it. He was still so ill when he returned to Baltimore that Dr. Baker insisted on having X rays of his chest taken. He had suffered from mild tubercular lesions in 1919 and 1929. Now the X rays showed a serious cavity in one lung. Dr. Baker quietly packed him off and put him under the care of a lung specialist in Asheville.

Scott's relapse depressed Henry and frightened Sara. On May 23, 1935, Mencken wrote Fitzgerald that, since Sara had contracted what appeared to be another mild case of flu, he planned to take her to the Adirondacks. But that afternoon Sara was stricken with a splitting headache. The trip to the mountains had to be postponed, and she was taken back to Johns Hopkins Hospital. From there on Sunday night she wrote me a note, in which she enclosed a tract entitled, ironically enough, "The Last Prayer Meeting."

It was the last letter Sara ever wrote. Like John Keats, she was "half in love with easeful death." Monday she was so ill that Mencken canceled his trip to stay beside her. On Wednesday a spinal tap revealed that she had tubercule bacilli in the spinal fluid. On Friday, May 31, 1935, at six o'clock in the evening, Sara died of tubercular meningitis.

Henry was so dazed with grief that he seemed incapable of deciding on the funeral arrangements. The only thing that he was certain of was that he did not want to go to the mortuary; he wanted to remember Sara as he had known her in life rather than in death. He had her body cremated in accordance with her wishes. Her ashes, however, were interred in Mencken's family plot in Loudon Park Cemetery—not cast into the Alabama river, to be borne out where even the weariest river winds somewhere safe to sea, as she had requested in her romantic youth.

In an interview, quoted in her obituary in *The New York Times*, Sara had revealed that America's most confirmed bachelor had proved a model husband:

"It stands to reason that a bachelor would make a good husband. A bachelor is likely to be much more interesting because he has had a more varied life. Then, he is set in his ways. I think it is pleasant to live with someone who knows what he wants. Last, and I guess most important to a woman, I think a bachelor is apt to be more thoughtful of his companion. He is more conscious of her. He never just accepts his wife as part of the household.

"Marriage hasn't changed Henry a bit," she added. "He still likes to drink beer even more than ever. He never was a real cynic about marriage. He just held some views about life and matrimony and was frank in discussing them. I never think of Henry as radical. He always seemed conservative and very conventional."

Whatever he may have had to say about matrimony in print before he became a benedict, in practice thereafter Mencken was as faithful, devoted, and "incomparable" a husband as he was a son, a brother, and a friend. His marriage, he said, had been a "beautiful adventure" while it lasted. Despite illness and misfortune, he had known a few years of requited love of a rare kind with Sara; and Joe Hergesheimer came very close to the essential truth in saying that those years had fulfilled Mencken's youthful dream of what love should be. "Henry's right-mindedness," Joe added, "was inherent; at 23 in *Ventures into Verse* he asserted, 'Dilettante love will fail.' It was a simplicity of the heart that kept his *Defense of Women* to the shabbiness of men. He escaped insensate nature by an ideal of constancy repaid in idyllic marriage."

CHAPTER ELEVEN

𝒯HE DAYS OF THE MORE ABUNDANT LIFE

AFTER SARA'S DEATH, Henry stayed on at 704 Cathedral Street, unable to tear himself away from the memories it held for him. His brother August, who was just out of the hospital, where he had undergone a sinus operation, moved into Sara's rooms to be near him. Still shocked and numbed, the Sage wrote me on June 8, 1935:

> My brother and I are planning to clear out on the Bremen next Friday, but if we do so we'll barely make the boat. Sara's small estate has to be administered, and that means visits to the lawyers and the courthouse, and submitting constantly to the convenience of other people. . . .
>
> A man named Bodine on the staff of the *Sun* made the best portrait of Sara that she ever had. It really was excellent, and I assume that he still has the plate. . . . It shows her almost full length and the expression is natural and charming. Most of her photographs as you know were terrible. The moment she got before the camera she would screw up her face and the result was usually a horrible caricature. The pictures printed in the papers were all newsprints made at the time of our marriage. Without exception they were libelous.

On June 12, he added from the Savoy Hotel in London:

> The temperature here is 83, and the English are dropping like flies. But they stick to their door-mat tweeds, and most of them still wear underwear 1 inch thick. They will learn how to dress in Summer after millions of them have perished. The weather seems very comfortable to Baltimoreans.
>
> My brother and I begin to feel pretty well. We are doing intensive loafing. Yesterday we went up the river. We are booked to return by the 15th. My office at home will be piled mountain high.

215

The trip up the Thames with Paul Patterson, enlivened by a picnic and a punt race with Mencken wearing a straw boater and acting as coxswain, helped him to recover something of his old zest for life. With James Bone of the Manchester *Guardian* and his other English friends, Mencken put up a brave face and kept them amused by his remarks on the histrionics of Anthony Eden, which he had witnessed in the House of Commons, and a barrage of quips leveled at Hitler, "an idiot followed by idiots."

By the time Mencken landed in New York on July 12, he had at least recovered his energy and planned to plunge into his research:

> I begin to feel fit for work again. But you can imagine that the house is full of ghosts. It will take me a long time to adjust myself.
> . . . That infernal "American Language" book is riding me. During the last year Sara's frequent illnesses interrupted it and kept me in a state unfit for steady work. Thus a great deal remains to be done and I must tackle it at once, for Knopf wants to publish the book early next year. I'll probably be blazing away twelve hours a day by next week.

Mencken doubtless knew that *The American Language* was to be the pinnacle of his scholarly achievements and a philological masterpiece. But he was also well aware that it was a gigantic task—and one he approached with humility and humor. Much of Mencken's wit depended upon exaggeration, incongruity of simile and metaphor, irreverence, and self-deprecation. One of his most endearing characteristics, and one which was never more apparent or more exaggerated than in his reflections on his *magnum opus*, was what in the Orient is called self-naughting. When the book was finished, he predicted that it would be denounced by the young Communists and patronized by the pedagogues, who, even as they mined it for material in the years to come, would sneer at it as an amateurish and ineffective effort. Experts like Dr. Kemp Malone, the noted philologist at Hopkins, would have no interest in it, he declared, and they are right; it is just journalism. If it earned him over three thousand dollars at most, it would be a miracle, he added; and he had a great mind to take to drink or become a romantic actor in the movies.

Through a mutual friend of ours in Baltimore I learned that although Mencken seemed to have taken Sara's death "like a soldier," he was "pretty miserable." So on my way back to Fort Monroe, I stopped over in Baltimore to see him before returning to Alabama. Happy as he and I were to see each other again, the memories dredged up by the rust, gold, and green brocade, the Victorian pinboxes, the shell pictures, the hand-painted valentines, and the yellowed *Godey's Lady's Books* in the Cathedral Street apartment lay heavy on our hearts.

"As you know," he said at lunch, "when Sara and I were married, the doctors had said that she had only two or three years to live at best. But we had almost five years together—two more years of happiness than the quacks allowed me."

As we lingered over our coffee and liqueurs, I asked about Scott and Zelda. There was an uncomfortable silence. Scott, it appeared, was on the ragged edge. He had just moved to lodgings, which he described as "the attic," in the Cambridge Arms Apartments near Johns Hopkins. Zelda was in a sanitarium in North Carolina, and on her brief visits to Baltimore she and Scott would invariably quarrel and he would begin to drink. She frequently complained that he was dangerous and should be watched. Scott's stories were being steadily rejected. The self-revelatory portions of *The Crack-Up*, which had begun to appear in *Esquire,* impeded his attempts to get another contract in Hollywood to bolster his shattered finances. In his despair, a glimmer of the truth began to haunt him. His success as a writer dated from the time Zelda had shown him the diary and letters that he used in *This Side of Paradise* and *The Beautiful and Damned.* By his treatment of her and his merciless psychological vivisections of her, on which his novels and many of his stories were based, he had not only killed the thing he loved but also dried up the wellsprings of his literary success. And under the stress and guilt of this realization, Scott himself was slowly cracking up in a Greek tragedy that would have required a Jazz Age Sophocles to write.

After lunch, Mencken pulled himself up by the arms of his chair, buttoned his coat, slicked down his cowlicks, and anchored them with his straw boater. "I'll call a taxi and we'll go to the cemetery," he said.

We stopped at a florist shop to get a sheaf of the copper roses that Sara Haardt had loved, then we drove on to the Loudon Park Cemetery. Mencken looked out of the window, his cigar clenched between his teeth, his face set in an expression that would have served for the mask of a Stoic philosopher. We left the roses on Sara's grave and stood there in the autumn sunshine, desolate and silent. Finally, with the effort of a man attempting to throw off a burden too heavy for his shoulders, Mencken tried to shake off the weight of his grief. "Come on," he said huskily. "Let's go. I think a libation is in order."

After he had drained a seidel of Würzburger, he said, "Sara, didn't you tell me you'd done a scenario on old Ludwig? Send it to me."

When I realized that he was speaking to me, I was too startled for a moment to thank him for his kindness. Hitherto, he had usually called me "Mayfield" or "The Duchess of Idlewyld" or *"Die Jungfrau"*; thereafter he addressed me as "Sara"—as if there were, at least, a remnant of consolation in having someone to answer to the name. For "H. L. Pygmalion" seemed to find solace of a sort in the thought that he still had one of his Galateas left, and I was fortunate enough to inherit a lion's share of the advice and guidance he had formerly bestowed upon the other.

The best English ever written, he frequently reminded me, was to be found in the King James Bible; the worst, in Dr. Johnson's ornate and involved sentences, Walter Pater's rounded periods and sugared phrases, and Dreiser's labyrinthine paragraphs. The chief aim of every tyro, in fact, of every conscious artist in the English language, should be to write simply. Prefer the short word to the long; the Anglo-Saxon to the Latin; the verb to the adjective. Make the verbs do the work. As Huneker used to say, far better an honest staccato phrase than a wilderness of sostenutos. The English language, particularly its American variety, teemed in rich and pungent phrases. Use them—and a pox on the pedagogues, their usage, and their rules. Was there any ironclad ukase of the grammarians that could not be broken? No, not one! A good writer put down what he had to say in his own words and his own constructions. Take Mark Twain or Carlyle, for example. What they did to the pedants' rules remains to delight us. Style? Nothing, according to Mencken, ever came out of an artist that was not in the man. Buffon laid down the rule, *"Le style c'est de l'homme."*

Although critics most often praise Mencken's own famous prose style for its vigor, vividness, surprising similes, and rollicking humor, he himself maintained that its chief virtue was its clarity. Once when I asked how he had acqured his style, he replied that he was born with it; it was as natural to him as his breathing. Learning to get it down effectively on paper, however, had been another matter. He had studied the prose of Thomas Henry Huxley, Addison, Swift, and the aphoristic style of Nietzsche and Bierce. As a young reporter, he had grasped the importance of the lead sentence, of the who, where, when, what, and why, and of telling a story clearly, simply, quickly.

Yet he sometimes regretted the long years and thousands of reams of paper he had spent, working as a journalist, torn between the urge to say what he had to say and get it over with and the desire to write something worthy of being handed down to posterity. As long as a man was actively engaged on a newspaper, it was almost impossible for him to get any connected outside writing done. Journalism was the most dismal trade ever known to man; it meant cruel labor, night and day, and its only visible reward was public infamy. Huneker had warned him against it long years ago, as well as against the danger of criticism to a creative writer. "Criticism," like journalism, Huneker had pointed out, "is the worst possible school for dramatic writing. Criticism freezes the emotions, kills the creative instinct when it exists."

Mencken admitted that he had been too young to listen to Huneker, just as I was too young to listen now. If I wanted to write a good play or a good book, he said, leave the theater and the newspapers alone and get down to the business in hand. Granted that journalism came easily —too easily for him—the material was there before him, and all he had to do was to put it down on paper. But the next day saw it wrapping fish in the Lexington market or replacing the Sears and Roebuck catalogue in an outhouse. On the other hand, it took time, sweat, and blood to turn out a book or a play, which might or might not endure. Get it down on paper, write, rewrite, revise, correct, rewrite, revise, correct *ad nauseum*. Hard writing, Mencken said, quoting Chester A. Arthur, makes good reading.

In sorting Sara's papers, he said, he had been impressed by the excellence she had achieved by long labor on some of her short stories, and he had signed a contract with Doubleday to publish a volume of them, to be called *Southern Album*. Alexander Woollcott once remarked that, after plowing through five hundred pages of *The Education of Henry Adams*, he had been shocked not to find a mention of Adams' married life. Critics have noted the same curious omission in Mencken's auto-biographical *Days* books, but his silence in regard to his married life is not difficult to understand in the light of the fact that he once told me that the hardest thing he ever tried to write was the poignant, tactful account of Sara with which he prefaced *Southern Album*. In it, he said, he ran the risk of offending half a dozen people, some of whom he would not want to wound "for all the diamonds in Hollywood."

Shortly afterward, Mencken gave the Goucher College library a set of scrapbooks bound in blue morocco, in which he had arranged clippings of Sara's published stories and articles, notes and typescripts, as well as rough drafts of articles she planned to write, and names of persons and places she intended to use, noted down on the backs of envelopes and advertisements. "Sara," he explained, "wrote her stories in longhand in pencil, then typed the manuscript herself and seldom, if ever, made a carbon." To Goucher he also gave Sara's library, which included autographed copies of the books of James Branch Cabell, Sinclair Lewis, Jim Tully, Emily Clark, Ellen Glasgow, Joe Hergesheimer, Robert Frost, and Vachel Lindsay, not to mention an almost complete set of her husband's works and a large collection of tomes on the Civil War and the Victorian Era.

Ellen Glasgow—who was to lament in her autobiography, "Another dear friend, lost to me now, was Sara Haardt, the wife of Henry Mencken. I loved her, and I like and enjoy him"—added her recently published *Vein of Iron* to the collection. On the flyleaf she wrote, "To Goucher College Library, in memory of my beloved friend, Sara Haardt Mencken, a loyal, lovely, and gallant spirit." At the presentation, Miss Winslow made an address on "The Meaning of Books to Mrs. Mencken and to Goucher." Joe Hergesheimer had come down for the ceremony. As they were leaving, Mencken remarked to Hergesheimer that Sara would have "larfed" to have seen them together in the Groves of Academe. And doubtless Marjorie Hope Nicolson also "larfed" in remembering the long, bitter argument she had waged in vain with Goucher College when Sara Haardt's salary was stopped after she was stricken with tuberculosis in 1923.

When the focus of public attention shifted in the early thirties from social and intellectual rebellion to political and economic revolt, both Mencken and Fitzgerald, the idols of the twenties, found themselves relegated from the spotlight to the penumbra and forced to turn to potboilers. In the autumn of 1935, both Scott and Henry had reached the nadir of their literary fortunes.

It was not a change in the Sage's thinking that resulted in "The Mencken Twilight," but a drastic alteration in the ideas and ideals of the United States. From first to last, the Old Defender fought for the principles set forth in the Constitution and the Bill of Rights. In his eyes, no political or financial crisis warranted the New Deal's tampering with them. Still a staunch advocate of laissez-faire economics, the Brain Trusters' financial juggling and drastic federal controls baffled and enraged him. The ancient truth that all that goes up is bound to come down, he grumbled, had been expunged from the books in Washington and the immutable law of supply and demand repealed by executive order.

The economic materialism of the twenties—the worship of prosperity, the belief in mass production, standardization, high-pressure salesmanship, bigger and better Babbitts—and the Philistinism and intolerance that were its end products and the butts of so many of Mencken's iconoclastic barbs had been laid low by the Depression. The advent of Repeal in 1933 had deprived him of another favorite target. By 1935, not only Prohibition but also Puritanism, Comstockery, Daytonism, the Klan, and the Red scare had drooped and died as timely issues, thereby diminishing the importance of Mencken, their most valiant opponent, as a social critic. The postwar disillusion of the intellectuals that stemmed from the failure of the crusade to make the world safe for democracy and a consequent loss of faith in the infallibility of the majority, which had contributed greatly to Mencken's following, ended in a left turn of the intelligentsia toward Socialism, Communism, or technocracy, leaving him to defend capitalism in the role of another Horatio at the bridge.

Howard Scott's technocracy, like Leninism or Marxism, seemed to him an economic panacea that cured nothing, not even a headache. The thirties provided a fertile soil for all such quacks. Brain Trust wizards, New Deal messiahs, faith healers, astrologists, numerologists, and tea-leaf readers were all in the same category as far as H.L. was concerned. He lashed out at F.D.R. and his New Dealers with the same swashbuckling humor and mordant wit with which he attacked the fellow travelers and parlor pinks. Nevertheless, Elizabeth Dilling "exposed" him as an agent of Moscow in her book *The Red Network*. A libel suit against her, he averred, promised to give him a great deal of fun; but, unfortunately, it would cost more than it was worth.

His intransigency toward the radicals and the do-gooders cost him a considerable part of his audience and several of his best forums.

Because the *Sunpapers* persisted in a pro-Roosevelt policy, he had to trim his sails in writing for them. After Charles Angoff took over the editorial chair of the *Mercury,* he followed the New Deal party line, and the pages of the magazine no longer afforded Mencken a vent for his polemics against F.D.R. and his Brain Trusters. And, after Oswald Garrison Villard left *The Nation,* Mencken's name, which had been on its masthead for eight years, was removed by the radical brethren who took over as its editors.

What the country needed, Mencken declared, was the leavening humor of a lively Tory magazine. But, he added, he wouldn't take the *Mercury* back "for a bonus of two million baloney dollars." He swore that he was done forever with editing magazines. In fact, at present, he did very little writing for them—now and then, an article for *Liberty* or a review for *Books* at Irita Van Doren's request. In one of the latter, he pronounced H. L. Davis' *Honey in the Horn,* which won the Pulitzer the next year, the best novel since *Babbitt.* In another, he lamented the tragic decline of Sinclair Lewis, whose "political monkeyshines" in *It Can't Happen Here* he attributed to Dorothy Thompson's furious denunciations of the Germans. His batting average as a literary critic, however, never fell below .300, despite the attempts of the New Deal pundits to inter him with the twenties.

Indeed, he was more amused than worried by the efforts of the critics who insisted on celebrating his literary funeral. But to judge from his mail, even at the height of the clamor intended to relegate him to the limbo of forgotten men, the influence of the Lion of the Twenties, his detractors and their gratuitous obituaries to the contrary, was still respected by the Silent Generation. Although he groaned under the labor required by the work on *The American Language,* he realized that he was laying the cornerstone of his reputation with a scholarly work that would give him a surer title to enduring fame than any of his articles or books—"an anchor against oblivion," he frequently called it.

On November 23, 1935, he said in a letter:

> I have been working twelve hours a day on that infernal book. It is now so close to the finish that I begin to feel optimistic at last—indeed, if all goes well I'll have the manuscript off my hands by the end of next week. The proof-reading and the preparation of the index, of course, will have to follow, and both promise to be formidable. But they'll be child's play compared to the actual writing of the text.

On December 6, 1935, he continued:

> I turned the manuscript over to Knopf last Monday. It runs into 325,000 words without indexes, and will make a truly formidable book. Whether we'll be able to sell it remains to be seen. . . .
>
> I am now plunging into a long series of magazine articles to boil the pot. For six months past I have done nothing but work on the book.

Ten days later he announced:

> "The American Language" is now in the hands of Knopf, and he shivers every time he looks at the manuscript. But however he shivers, he will never suffer as much as I did with the writing of it.

Earlier in 1936 he had told Dorothy Hergesheimer that he had taken oath on the family Bible to avoid all serious writing for the rest of his life. Hereafter, he planned to be "a carefree butterfly" with no more sense of responsibility than a glamour girl in Hollywood or the President of the United States. Instead, he came down with bronchitis. As the medical faculty had no remedy for it, he was thrown back on prayer, which he found a very slender reed. "Show me a wart actually cured by prayer," he said, "and I'll apologize profusely."

In March 1936, the collection of Sara's stories, *Southern Album,* appeared. In April, Knopf published Mencken's fourth monumental revision of *The American Language.* In it Mencken had retained little more than the title of the three earlier editions. He had reinforced his original thesis with masses of new evidence, collected during the thirteen years that had intervened since publication of the third edition, and added an extensive compilation of word lists. Tracing the development of the American language from the King's English of the earliest Colonial days to the present, he predicted that it would eventually supplant English and, after undergoing a radical transformation, be accepted as a universal language.

The reviews of *The American Language* were excellent on the whole. Mencken especially delighted in one by a Catholic priest in Oklahoma with whom he had corresponded for many years. Better still, *The American Language* made the nonfiction best-seller lists. The Book-of-the-Month Club chose it as a dividend to its subscribers and took over a hundred thousand copies.

After he finished *The American Language,* Henry found living at 704 Cathedral Street unendurable. It seemed too empty, too lonely, too full of reminders. So he and August decided to give up the Cathedral

Street apartment and move back to their old home at 1524 Hollins Street.

August was taken ill again as he and Henry were in the midst of moving back to Hollins Street, and Mencken was left among "piles of redundant and supernumerary chinaware" and mountains of furniture. Shoving heavy pieces around was beyond the strength of an elderly literary man, he protested. He needed the better muscles of an engineer and would have to wait until August was released to straighten out the house. Fortunately, Joe Hergesheimer and H. L. Davis were in town to keep him company. Joe, who was suffering from glycosuria, came down frequently to consult Dr. Benjamin Baker. His visits were good for Mencken's morale, if not for the progress of his new book.

Shortly afterward in a letter he said:

> I am hoping to tackle "Advice to Young Men" in the Autumn. It will be a relatively short book, and I have an enormous pile of notes for it. Unfortunately, I must first clear off the *Sun* history and then tackle the two conventions. The *Sun* wants me to go abroad after the conventions, and I may do so, but it will only be for a short while. I begin to hate travelling. My old joints now creak, and I can't drink more than thirty per cent of what I used to get down.

Mencken had been mulling over a book to be called *Advice to Young Men* ever since I had known him. In it he intended to sum up his theories on life, love, and the romantic comedy in an expansion of Section XVIII of *Prejudices: Third Series*. The end and aim of the book was to supply young men with better instruction in the strategy and tactics of the immemorial duel of the sexes. What he referred to was not sex hygiene, as he pointed out to the editor of a college magazine; in that sphere, there was more than ample instruction, most of it indignant and inaccurate. But, as far as he knew, there was not a single book devoted to teaching the technique of defense in the barbaric war in which the females of the species tried to get themselves husbands while the males attempted to put off their capture as long as possible. Boys graduated from college completely ignorant of the deceits and stratagems they faced. Consequently, all too many of them found themselves married before they made any headway professionally; and, as a result, the country overflowed with worried and incompetent men. Further, as the Sage had subsequently observed in the *Mercury*, there had long been a great need among young men, troubled between the promptings of their hormones and the questionings of their consciences, for a handbook setting down precisely under appropriate rubrics, not what their elders say, but what they actually do.

As he pondered *Advice to Young Men,* H.L. quizzed me so frequently as to what virtues women admire in men, what tactics were most effective with them, that I sent the Sage the outline for a fictitious work that afforded us both a bit of amusement:

FOR WOMEN ONLY
A GUIDEBOOK FOR YOUNG GIRLS
DEDICATED TO
THE GENTLEMAN WITH THE QUESTIONS
IN THAT:
Greater love hath no woman than that she tell a man
anything faintly resembling the truth.

In the middle of April, Mencken took a trip to New York, where he made an address at the annual luncheon of the Associated Press at the Waldorf Astoria. There he was introduced by Frank B. Noyes, publisher of the *Washington Star* and president of the AP, as an "extraordinary combination of a great journalist, a great radical and a great conservative."

On his return to Baltimore, H.L. settled into his old workroom on the third floor at 1524 Hollins Street; he enjoyed being back in its familiar surroundings. Three of his windows looked out over the green oasis of Union Square. It was pleasant to watch the nuns in their cloistered garden in the next block, practicing golf strokes and playing badminton. When the wind blew from the west, it wafted a delightful odor, which he attributed to an emanation from their brewery and found "highly conducive to literary composition." So stimulated, he wrote from his desk there on May 12, 1936:

> Now that "The American Language" is off my hands, I am devoting myself to a history of the *Sun.* The work turns out to be very tedious. It involves plowing through old files, and many of them are filthy and falling to pieces. One of the things that interests me is that all of the office legends, on investigation, turn out to be false. There are dozens of them, and it amuses me to look them up in the records. In every case so far I have discovered that what is generally believed never really happened.

Even more interesting to Mencken than the old files of the *Sun* were the current Washington newspapers, filled as they were with the tricks and turns of the "reigning clowns" and the gallimaufry of platitudes cooked up daily by the Brain Trust. Although he professed to be gravely concerned over the antics of the "jitney messiahs," he derived vast amusement from the rash of economic panaceas that became epidemic after the Depression. The More Abundant Life was now just around the corner, according to the New Dealers; but the impatient prophets of the Lunatic Fringe, as the Grass Roots Utopians were called in Washington, had blueprints of their own for bringing about the millennium.

The most aggressive of them was Senator Huey P. Long, a demagogue whose "Share the Wealth" program helped to establish a dictatorship in Louisiana so absolute and so corrupt that it prefigured the state of the nation in the Sick, Sick Sixties and moved Mencken to predict a dark future for American politics. "The booboisie are for anything that promises loot," he said. "They don't want honest government and able men; they want a bigger slice of pie and quacks who will promise it to them."

F.D.R. countered Long's proposal to make "Every Man a King" by leveling increased income, inheritance, and corporation taxes against the "Economic Royalists," and the rivalry between F.D.R. and Huey P. persisted until Long was shot by a man whose relative the Kingfish was said to be holding as hostage in the State Hospital. By that time, Howard Scott's modest plan for revamping the democracy into a technocracy had gone the way of the all crackpot credos and fly-by-night fads. But Upton Sinclair's EPIC plan for ending poverty in California was creating such a furor it moved the Sage to suspect that there were "more lunatics at large in America than in lunatic asylums." When "the saviour and boss" of California ran for governor, Mencken wrote him brusquely that he appeared to him to be merely "a professional messiah like any other" and one who would not be too polite to the "money-mad widows and orphans" whose stocks and bonds he coveted once he was in power.

Mencken was more lenient with Father Coughlin, the radio prophet from the Shrine of the Little Flower and his National Union for Social Justice, and Dr. Francis E. Townsend of Long Beach, California, author of the Townsend Old Age Revolving Pensions Plan. Coughlin and Townsend were "glorious idiots," he said. He refused to go to Boston— "the anus of America" to him ever since the Hatrack trial—to cover the antics at the Harvard tercentenary; instead he attended the Townsend rallies and the Coughlin orgies. "I like politicoes much better than I like professors. They sweat more freely," he claimed, "and are much more amusing." The Townsend show, he confided, was really colossal. "Imagine 20,000 morons penned in a hall, and belabored for eight hours a day by the most magnificent rabble rousers on earth." The nights were devoted to all sorts of "deviltries" that kept Mencken up until three A.M.; but that, he felt, was a small sacrifice to lay on the altar of God and country.

After Charles Angoff relinquished the editorship of the *Mercury*, Mencken was once more free to use its pages to assail the More Abundant Life as unmitigated quackery. In the March 1936 issue, he attacked Roosevelt and all his works so vehemently that *The New York Times* took him to task for treating the Presidency with "gross disrespect." Mr. Roosevelt's brain trust he dismissed as a "mob of mountebanks" who were unable to agree on anything except that a man who worked hard and saved his money was a "low and unmitigated scoundrel." H.L. concluded that the jig was now nearly up, and if Roosevelt could be beaten in the election next November, he could be beaten with a Chinaman or even a Republican. When the Republicans convened in Cleveland and nominated Alfred M. Landon, the Kansas Coolidge, Mencken began to campaign for him before he left the smoke-filled rooms of the convention, although he privately thought that "Poor Alf's" chances of election were nil.

On Mencken's return to Baltimore from Philadelphia, where he not only witnessed the "orgies of the Democrats" but, worse in his eyes, the nomination of Franklin D. Roosevelt and John Nance Garner, he exploded:

> What a God-awful world it is! I hear of nothing but death and disaster. The only man who continues lucky seems to be Franklin Delano Roosevelt, and I am in hopes that God will turn upon him anon.

In August, Mencken left for Cleveland to cover the convention of Father Coughlin's National Union for Social Justice. The Sage's personal amiability and rare charm gave him the ability to make warm friends among his political adversaries. Just as he had emerged from his fight against the Prohibitionists during the Volstead era on a Damon and Pythias basis with the Dry Messiah, Bishop James M. Cannon, so he returned from a verbal Donnybrook with the NUSJ in Cleveland with Dr. Francis Townsend and the Reverend Gerald L. K. Smith as his enthusiastic press agents. In fact, they offered him the editorship of the *Townsend Weekly*—an honor he was hard put to find some tactful means of declining. Back in Baltimore, on August 19 he groaned:

> I begin to feel as old as Methuselah. When I got in from the Coughlin orgies at Cleveland the other day I was half dead. . . .
>
> I have been so busy with the campaign and with the history of the *Sun* that I have done no writing of any consequence. However, I am hoping to get to work on "Advice to Young Men" by the end of the year.
>
> I am off tomorrow to join Landon. I begin to believe he is the greatest man in American history since John Wilkes Booth.

Privately the Sage reflected that we would have four more years of F.D.R. and his "quacks," in which if he survived, he would do some loud "larfing." In an article in *The American Mercury*, "The Case for Dr. Landon," he gave his unqualified endorsement to "Poor Alf," saying:

> He would cut a poor figure in opera but he looks to me to be a pretty good hand with a shovel. He probably knows a good deal less than the Hon. Mr. Roosevelt, but much more of what he knows is true. And when he promises to do this or that, laying his hand on his heart and rolling his eyes toward the Throne of God, there is at least a reasonable possibility that he will make an honest effort to keep his word.

When the issue of the *Mercury* containing the article appeared on the stands, *The New York Times* suggested in an editorial that since Geraldine Farrar was to sing and Mencken to write in behalf of Landon, the Sage should compose a Landon song and play the accompaniment for Miss Farrar to sing it at the next meeting of the Saturday Night Club.

Mencken's growing preoccupation with politics temporarily eclipsed all his other interests, and his letters were full of the campaign. On September 24, 1936, he wrote:

> I had hoped that one of the other of the candidates would make a tour through the South, but neither seems to have thought it worth while. The reports from all the Southern States are that the Confederates are preparing to vote for Roosevelt almost unanimously. This unanimity has its penalties. One of them is that they will miss seeing two of the greatest men in human history. Roosevelt, I believe, will be put by historians far above Abraham Lincoln, and even above John Wilkes Booth.

On October 1, 1936, there was another note from him:

> Politically speaking, I give the South up as hopeless. It is engaged at this minute in a sword-swallowing act of unparalleled magnitude, and what is worse, it is not aware of what it is doing. Ah, that the carcass of Thomas Jefferson could arise from the grave and make a stumping tour! What a grand show he would give!

In his next letter, he said:

> The *Sun* wants me to travel with poor Alf on his last campaign tour. It will begin in about ten days. He is now sunk so deeply that the largest steam dredge in the world could not bring him to the surface. Nevertheless, he remains a true patriot and a sincere Christian, and I shall vote for him until the last sad scene on the gallows.

On October 31, Mencken wrote:

> I find your note on my return from the last Landon tour that this world will ever see. My parting with him in New York the night before last almost brought me to tears. I think he knows he is licked, but all the same he keeps up his spirits, and in general shows a very gallant air.

On November 6, 1936, he added:

> You will recall the proclamation that General Lee issued to his army after the Battle of Gettysburg, beginning, "Soldiers, we have sinned." I am suggesting to Alf that he lift it. His colossal defeat can be accounted for only on the ground of Divine intervention, based upon Divine wrath. It may be that my own boozing had something to do with it. If so, I stand ready to sign the pledge.
>
> I am looking forward to four gaudy years. The circus will begin as soon as Congress meets, and thereafter it will go on in ten rings day and night. The chances are very good that Franklin will blow up after the mid-term elections, and that he'll go out of office in 1940 in the character of Public Enemy No. 1. The mob always crucifies its messiahs in the long run. I can find no exception in the whole course of history.

By way of a holiday celebration, on December 20 Mencken gave a historic dinner for "Poor Alf," who stopped off in Baltimore en route to a Gridiron Club dinner in Washington. It was, Mencken said, "Just a private affair at which the guests include a few Maryland Democrats who have forgotten politics and want to give Landon a square meal." The bill of fare, which Mencken had served up to his guests in a private dining room of the Southern Hotel, consisted of cocktails, Chesapeake Bay oysters, terrapin à la Maryland, cream sauce, grilled bacon, corn fritters, potato croquettes, Bordeaux wine, Maryland ham, Maryland hearts of lettuce, Maryland water ice, and champagne.

Between hosting the dinner and assisting at the funeral of an old friend, Mencken was exhausted before the holidays rolled around. On the day after Christmas, he said from Johns Hopkins Hospital:

> Just a line to report that I am still alive. I came down last Monday with a severe infection of the trachea, and the brethren clapped me into the hospital. Christmas here turned out to be most comfortable. With no telephone calls, no mail, and no obligation to eat or drink anything I didn't really crave, I put in a rather comfortable day. I am hoping to be liberated early next week.
>
> Here's hoping we are all lucky in 1937.

Unfortunately, the cure proved to be of short duration, for on February 19 he said:

> Two weeks ago I landed back in hospital, this time for some minor surgery. What appeared to be an abscess developed during my illness at Christmas, and when it refused to go away the doctors decided to explore it. It turned out to be a harmless cyst. They took it out and threw it into Chesapeake Bay, and I am now in pristine and magnificent condition.
>
> I seized the opportunity while I was in hospital to have three small wens removed from my scalp. I'll thus present a lovely contour when I grow bald at last.

However the Freudians and post-Freudians may explain Mencken's affection for his ailments, they will doubtless overlook the fact that he derived constant amusement and an unfailing source of sardonic humor from them. As he grew older, he inclined more and more to find relief from overwork and boredom in frequent trips to Johns Hopkins, where he relished discussing new diseases, new cures, and new operative techniques with the medical faculty.

After a trip to Florida to recuperate, Mencken wound up *The Sun-papers of Baltimore,* which he, Gerald Johnson, Frank Kent, and Hamilton Owens had been set to write. He next turned his attention to drafting a new constitution for the State of Maryland, which provided among other things for abolishing the bicameral legislature, excluding from the law-making body ministers, bankrupts, lunatics, and lobbyists, allowing unrestricted divorce after the third year of marriage, raising the voting age to twenty-five, and sterilizing criminals. After his unique constitution ceased to divert him, he began tub-thumping for the sterilization of the indigent and insane by bribery. When I reminded him that the plan would doubtless bring howls of protest from the electorate and its representatives, particularly Alabama's Congressman Frank Boykin, whose perennial campaign slogan was "Everything's made for love," H.L. said on September 6:

> The Hon. Frank Boykin is a new one to me. Please give him my kindest personal regards the next time you encounter him. His platform seems magnificent. If he'd let the whole country hear of it he'd be well on his way to the White House. The late Woodrow Wilson, I'm informed, entertained the same principles, only *in petto*. The Hon. Mr. Boykin is the first to bellow them from the house-tops.

In October, Mencken addressed a writer's symposium at Columbia University, at which he led off with a blast at F.D.R.'s fireside chats. "He is not a stylist," the Sage declared. "He just sits down and puts briefs together. And his voice doesn't sound very musical. It sounds too tenorish to me." He pronounced Gertrude Stein "a quack" who "has no ideas and can't express 'em." Then, once more, prophecy proved irresistible. Sinclair Lewis, he predicted, "would die in the bosom of the church" and Middle Western speech would prevail because it was clear, distinct, and not unmusical.

As the year drew to a close, ignoring the Japanese attack on China, the aid given by Hitler and Mussolini to Franco in the Spanish Civil war, even the uproar of the isolationists at home, Mencken concentrated his fire on the Roosevelt administration and its emphasis on "social significance." His aversion to the New Deal, however, was not premised entirely upon his personal antipathy to F.D.R., for he remained profoundly skeptical of all reformers, do-gooders, and adventures in uplift. To him the More Abundant Life was "just another political swindle, simply a scheme of robbing A to buy the vote of B," and therefore a target worthy of the most potent blockbusters in his arsenal.

$\mathcal{N}$EW DEAL DAYS

AFTER JOHN OWENS was promoted from editor of the Baltimore *Sun* to editor-in-chief, Hamilton Owens, editor of *The Evening Sun,* replaced him. Paul Patterson then asked Mencken to take over Hamilton Owens' former job. In explaining the changes that were taking place, R. P. Harriss has said that it was not the happiest time around the *Sunpapers*:

> John Owens was made editor-in-chief of the morning *Sun*—a post created at the time to keep the *Sun* and *The Evening Sun* in line editorially. They had been veering apart, *The Evening Sun* being more liberal, the morning *Sun* increasingly anti-New Deal. We had a big editorial powwow, following a joint staff luncheon in the boardroom, at which we were all invited to speak our pieces before Paul Patterson laid down the law. The only one to speak up in opposition was Gerald Johnson, who was soon to resign. Later on . . . I also resigned.

R.P. did not leave the *Sunpapers,* however, until after "the Mencken interregnum," which he found "exhilarating." The Sage had agreed that upon his return from a Caribbean trip in January he would act as temporary editor of the *Evening Sun* for three months. Invigorated by the sun and salt air, he returned from his cruise eager to assume his editorial duties. During Hamilton Owens' absence, R.P. had been acting editor, but now that Mencken was editor and R.P., whom he had long since instructed to call him "Henry," was his associate editor, R.P. addressed him formally in the *Sunpapers* office as "Mr. Mencken." But when they went down to the composing room to make up the editorial page together, R.P. was amused to find that the printers, who had known the Sage in his early days, completely oblivious of his fame and title, still called him "Henry."

Even so, the eyes of his old friends in the pressroom bulged as Mencken's maiden issue of *The Evening Sun* rolled off the press. Five-sevenths of the editorial page was covered with black dots, printed through what is known to the trade as a Ben Day screen at the rate of thirty-five hundred to the square inch. There were 1,000,075 dots in all—one, he explained in a column headed "Object Lesson," for each person in the federal government's "immense corps of jobholders. . . . The dots unfortunately had to be made very small. . . . Even so the chart is too large for the taxpayer to paste in his hat. Let him hang it, instead, on his parlor wall, between the 'American's Creed' and the portrait of Mr. Roosevelt. . . . If there were no jobholders at all every taxpayer's income would be increased twenty-seven percent. Such is the bill for being saved from revolution and ruin by wonder men."

For the March 4 issue of *The Evening Sun* Mencken had Philip M. Wagner and Gerald Johnson fill seven columns with "Five Years of the New Deal"—one of the longest editorials on record—to which the Sage added a mordant introduction and conclusion. R. P. Harriss noted in his diary:

> Life with Mencken continues to be full of zowie. Phil Wagner and I have frequent loud but good-humored arguments with him over the make-up of the editorial page. We had a really violent row today. He began waving his arms and bellowed: "No, *no, NO!* You two are ganging up on me and by God I won't *let* you put that katzenjammer over on me!"

No doubt, H.L. "stirred up the animals" while he was "serving his term" as editor of *The Evening Sun*; but before it elapsed, the constant uproar proved too much for him. He complained that he was beginning to oxidize around the edges; and on April 12, 1938, he suffered a slight coronary thrombosis. But by April 21, he was once more full of gusto and looking forward to a vacation:

> My tour of duty [at *The Evening Sun*] will end here on May 7th and I'll probably put in the next month trying to clear up my accumulated private business. If all goes well I hope to sail for Germany about the middle of June. I have not been there for ten years and I am eager to find out what is really going on. My guess is that the news dispatches are full of hooey.

Politically speaking, the Sage acted as a prosecuting attorney rather than an impartial judge. On everything from aviation to xylophone playing, he said, he had fixed and invariable ideas, which had not changed since he was four or five years old. He was too honest to pretend to be unbiased; he had never claimed to be a fair man, nor one who wished to hear both sides—an absurd contention on the part of the author of six volumes of *Prejudices*. He had almost as deep an aversion to the Fighters for Freedom as to the Nazis; to him Roosevelt was a Führer in embryo, hoping for a war that would keep him in power, and Hitler was merely a renegade German Ku Kluxer. Nor did Mencken ever change his mind sufficiently to take either Roosevelt or Hitler seriously.

It was incredible to the Sage that the German people, particularly the Junkers, could be led, much less misled, by an Austrian housepainter, a blatant mountebank. However, the New Dealers, whom Mencken had antagonized, and even some of his biographers chose to misinterpret the levity with which he treated the Führer. For instance, in *The Irreverent Mr. Mencken,* Edgar Kemler says that when "it was reported that Mencken was sailing for Hitler's Germany on the *Europa,* the inference was that he had become a Nazi." If so, the inference was drawn from fantasy, not fact. In an interview given to *The New York Times* just before he sailed on June 11, 1938, he confined himself to the announcement that he had completed an eight-volume work on the banning of Herbert Asbury's "Hatrack," which he had published in *The American Mercury* in 1926. He added that he had willed the manuscript to the New York Public Library, as he did not want it published until after his death. "There are," he said, "many personal letters and references to living people in the book. I consider it the first complete record of the fight against Comstockery." To infer any Nazi sympathy from Mencken's statements is as erroneous as to report that he was sailing on the *Europa.* In point of fact, he crossed on an old favorite, the *Columbus.*

August Mencken, who had planned to accompany H.L. on his trip to Germany, backed out at the last moment; the Sage was forced to make his six-week tour alone. He hired a car and motored through East Prussia. It was during the early harvest time, and he noted that there actually seemed to be a shortage of labor there. The farmers worked from five A.M. to ten P.M. with their women beside them. The hours were long, but the work was not hard; and it kept the yokels from thinking about politics and theology. Men and women alike seemed singularly contented. The peasants of Europe, he observed, had a talent for turning the harvest into a holiday, and after it was over they always had a party. In the evenings, they held a parade or two, with the bands blaring and the tuba players worked to death.

In Bonn, Mencken bought a life mask of Beethoven to bring home with him. After a look at the tomb of Eilhart Mencken in Marienwerder, he went on to see the University of Leipzig, and then paid a visit to Hindenburg's tomb on the Tannenburg battlefield. In an attempt to appraise Hitler's military might, whenever he met a German staff officer he stopped to talk to him. Otherwise, he kept away from officials and newspapermen and tried to learn what the plain German citizens were thinking. He reported that the situation of the Jews was dreadful and the pressure on them terrific. All decent Germans, he noted, seemed ashamed of the business; with the exception of a few idiots, he found them opposed to the Nazis. He was outraged by the pogroms. But neither the grim terrors of Nazi Germany nor Mencken's personal tragedies drowned out the sardonic humor—derived, as of old, from laughing to keep from crying, a humor that seldom failed to bring down criticisms that were as unjust as they were vitriolic.

Unable to resist a jibe at Roosevelt, invoking his talent for making overstatements that highlighted their kernel of wit, he opined that Hitler's New Deal seemed to be working better than Franklin's. And again, opposed to psychoanalysis as Mencken was, he predicted that history would accord the Nazis at least one white mark for having thrown Freud out of Vienna. He collected Nazi postcards, Kemler noted, and mailed them out, sarcastically inscribed "Behold the Superman" and "This proves that *Der Führer* loves children." Kemler should have added that H.L. also had pictures of the Emperor Franz Joseph's palace at Schönbrunn printed with the caption "Mr. H. L. Mencken's Summer Estates on the Chesapeake," wrote cordial invitations to a weekend there on the back of them, and broadcast them to his friends. It would be as humorless to assume that the Schönbrunn postcards indicate delusions of grandeur as it would be to infer that Mencken's japes at the expense of Roosevelt and Hitler are signs of Nazi sympathies. H.L. still believed one horselaugh to be worth ten thousand syllogisms; but understandably, his Jewish friends were in no laughing mood. De Casseres and Goodman resented Mencken's jests, Kemler misinterpreted them, and Angoff has made capital of them ever since in his attempts to stigmatize Mencken as pro-Nazi and anti-Semitic.

After Mencken's return from Germany, he reported on July 27, 1938, that he found traveling by himself so lonely that he would never cross the ocean again unless he found someone to go with him. From Baltimore on September 12, he said:

> I am putting in my birthday, as usual, in prayer and meditation. The [senatorial] campaign here in Maryland has been extraordinarily vicious. I am hoping that [Millard] Tydings will win but I am not too sure. The New Deal goons have been pouring millions into the state. If Roosevelt loses both Maryland today and Georgia on Wednesday, the time will be on us to begin considering his political funeral. Soon or late, he is bound to bust, but my guess is that he'll hang on a couple of years longer, and maybe even have a third term.
>
> My trip abroad was a success, but I am still somewhat rocky, and certainly do not feel like work.

On Halloween, the Sage listened with eyes popping to Orson Welles' Martian broadcast simulating an invasion from the skies and issued a typical Menckenesque communiqué to the effect that the broadcast "darn nigh wrecked Baltimore." Over two hundred patients in Johns Hopkins hospital leapt out the windows, he said, followed by sixty per cent of the medical and nursing staffs; the Maryland Club was emptied in twenty-two seconds. The week after Welles' broadcast, Mencken was again astounded by the radio news. "The Holy Ghost," he announced after he heard the election returns, "came down into Maryland last Tuesday and did a swell job. Millard Tydings was re-elected to the United States Senate by the largest majority ever heard of."

But on the literary front the news was depressing. Tom Wolfe had been brought back from Seattle, where one incompetent doctor after another had attempted to treat him, to Johns Hopkins Hospital. He arrived there in a state beyond remedy. Although Mencken had never been a Wolfe enthusiast, upon learning that the novelist had been taken to Johns Hopkins, he immediately called Dr. Walter E. Dandy, who was Wolfe's physician. Dr. Dandy told him that Wolfe's condition was completely hopeless. Wolfe died so quickly that Mencken did not get a chance to see him. His relatives "rushed" the remains back to Asheville, where, according to H.L., Wolfe was given a magnificent Christian funeral, "with music by the choir and very instructive remarks by the pastor."

At the end of October, Henry spent a weekend at the Dower House and returned, cheered to think that the Hergesheimers had not noticed that his new—and imaginary—toupée had been glued on with Duco. He went back to work in high spirits, once more bubbling over with jests, japes, and good humor. But the renewal of the hostility directed against him from a certain sector of the New York literati brought a somber reaction to prepare him for the invariable gloom that overtook him during the holidays. The offenders were Burton Rascoe, Nathan, and Charles Angoff.

Burton Rascoe was at the time drama critic and editorial writer for the New York *World-Telegram*. In his salad days, on the Chicago *Tribune*, Rascoe, who often bent an elbow with Mencken, Nathan, Ernest Boyd and Alfred Knopf, in New York, had written for the *Tribune* a eulogistic sketch of Mencken, called *Fanfare*, which was later published by Knopf. On his part, Mencken had considered Rascoe a young critic of great promise. They had corresponded frequently and collaborated in championing Dreiser and Cabell. In 1934, however, after Mencken declined to write an introduction to *The Smart Set Anthology* being compiled by Rascoe and Groff Conklin, or to allow them to mine his files, Rascoe took a schoolboy revenge.

In Rascoe's preface Mencken was taken aback to find himself pictured as "a peasant standing in the aloof aristocracy of George Nathan." As the Sage had once pointed out, "There are more Ph.D.'s on my family tree than even a Boston bluestocking can boast; there was a whole century where even the most ignorant of my house was at least Juris Utriusque Doctor." Rascoe's preface he dismissed as sheer nonsense. He laughed for two days over it. The material, he told Tully, obviously came from Nathan. It amused him greatly to discover that George probably thought he envied him his great prowess as a fencer, when so far as he knew, Nathan's fencing was confined to a few bouts as a college student. As for Rascoe, he was merely "a tremendous ass." Mencken was disgusted not so much by the attack on him as by Rascoe's gross libel of Alfred Knopf, which he was forced to withdraw from the original version. Knopf was not only one of Mencken's staunchest friends, but his publisher, and Mencken declared him to be the squarest man in money matters that he had ever known. Mencken, always personally averse to noticing vituperation of that kind, advised Knopf to take action in that Rascoe's libels injured his business.

In *The Smart Set Anthology,* Rascoe had alleged that Dreiser, for whom Mencken had tub-thumped the length and breadth of the land, had refused to help Mencken by sending him contributions for the magazine. Dreiser wrote Mencken at once to clear himself of the charge, and he and Mencken resumed their correspondence. The Sage eventually learned that the "blather" about himself in *The Smart Set Anthology* originated with Willard Huntington Wright, not Nathan, as Rascoe insinuated. Nathan and Mencken cleared the matter up between themselves and continued their friendship, strengthened by their mutual contempt for Rascoe.

Once more Mencken met with Tully and Nathan at Nathan's old apartment in the Royalton. George Jean's hair was brushed with silver at the temples and his face lined; he had the air of man born tired and growing world-weary at an accelerated pace, but he was still dapper, witty, sartorially impeccable. Although Mencken's hair was fast graying, he was round, cherubic, hearty as ever, and but little heavier. Swinging down 44th Street with his rolling walk, Tully looked exactly as he did twenty years before but for a few strands of gray in his mop of red curls. From the Algonquin Hotel, after a session with Nathan and Mencken, Tully said: "Well, at any rate, yesterday was different—it was really a golden coin in the ragged garment of life."

The pleasant interlude ended just before Christmas with the appearance of a vicious article by Charles Angoff entitled "Mencken Twilight: Another Forgotten Man—That Enfant Terrible of Our Era of Nonsense." Mencken's friends were incensed by Angoff's treachery. Tully vented his indignation in a note written two days after Christmas "Angoff has a terrible article on Mencken in *The North American Review Quarterly,*" Jim said, after reading the piece in the December 1938 issue of the magazine; "he was his assistant—and I feel that he has turned state's evidence on him . . . a lousy trick." With his habitual *sang-froid* in the face of such attacks, Mencken brushed it off lightly. A subsequent letter to me revealed, however, a poignant reaction:

> I continue to disintegrate gradually and politely. Towards the close of foggy afternoons, I can hear the rustle of angels' wings, and even smell the angels. It may interest you to know that their aroma is not unlike that of turkeys. I suppose that they are edible, though I can't

recall finding any account in the literature of any Christian venturing to try them.

In February, Harry T. Baker invited Mencken and Hergesheimer to make another joint appearance before his students at Goucher. The date of the address agreed upon was April 4. But early in March, Mr. Baker fell ill, and died on the 17th, sixteen years almost to the day after he had introduced Sara and me to the Bad Boy of Baltimore. Mencken was deeply distressed by Mr. Baker's death. "Yahweh," he said, "had fired the opening guns of his Spring offensive."

On April 19, 1939, he complained:

> I am going to Washington tomorrow to harangue a meeting of newspaper editors. I always dislike such jobs. The brethren will listen politely, but there is not much likelihood that they'll be impressed.

The following day Mencken addressed a meeting of the American society of newspaper editors in the capital. The Old Defender frequently described himself as a "libertarian"; and as such the Bill of Rights was to him what the Gospels are to the Christians and the Torah to the Jews. Of the fundamental freedoms guaranteed by it, freedom of the press was to him one of the most vital. Two years before, Mencken had warned the same association of editors that "They will not be printing true news until they show what is behind every effort to corrupt it." Now he cautioned them that in case of war the freedom of the press would be gravely endangered, particularly in that "the head of the state will be running for re-election and itching to heat up his partisans and confound his opponents." The Sage was already sharpening his ax in preparation for the election of 1940. His opponents of the New Deal retaliated by clumsy attempts to consign him to oblivion. Harold Ickes, F.D.R.'s Secretary of the Interior, took to the air to tell the New York Newspaper Guild and a radio audience what he thought of the Fourth Estate "calumnists." "By the way," he cracked, "whatever became of Henry L. Mencken?"

In Baltimore, when the Sage was not laughing at the antics of the Brain Trusters, he was busy working on his robust and hilarious autobiography, *Happy Days.* Eighty percent of it was true, he announced, the rest was icing on the cake. In an autobiography, he explained, "the author almost invariably lies"; but when his false pretenses are detected, "they do not spoil the interest of his story; on the contrary, they add to that interest. Every autobiography thus becomes an absorbing work of fiction, with something of the charm of a cryptogram." On May 1, 1939, he reported:

> My new book is going slowly, but I am having a lot of fun doing it. Some extracts from the early chapters will probably begin to come out in the *New Yorker* within the next few weeks. I assume that you read that great moral journal.
>
> God knows when I'll get to New York. In addition to all my other reasons for avoiding the town, there is now the massive reason that it is nabbing boobs with a so-called World's Fair.

On June 8, he groaned:

> I have just finished the better part of a week with the Worker's Alliance at Washington. The spectacle was really appalling. Next week I am going to Indianapolis to attend the orgies of the Townsendites.

The following week, when Mencken arrived in Indianapolis, he asserted that he believed that Dr. Townsend was an honest man, and he would like to see his plan tried. But then, he added, he would also like to see a volcano erupt or to watch New York bombed from the air. Before the meeting was over, he declared that the New Deal was a "dead horse" and startled the press by announcing, "I'm for the re-election of Roosevelt for a third term. He ought to be made to bury his own dead horse. It would be a cruel or unusual punishment to permit anyone else to take over the autopsy."

Selections from Mencken's boyhood reminiscences in *Happy Days*, which had begun to appear in *The New Yorker*, had met with an enthusiastic reception. Alfred Knopf wanted him to continue his memoirs, decade by decade. Henry had his doubts about so extensive a project, but he was contemplating a series of sketches on the lush and gaudy episodes of his days on the old Baltimore *Herald*. First, however, he had to finish *Happy Days*. The heat in Baltimore was so terrific that he planned to go down to North Carolina, where he could work in comfort. But he had a spell of vertigo; his blood pressure began to shoot up, and he had to be hospitalized. Convinced that he had had a mild stroke, he began to put his affairs in order. After he had settled his financial matters, he had his literary papers bound in blue leather and willed them to the Enoch Pratt Library and the New York Public Library.

To the Sage, death was preferable to decay, and he faced it with a stoical indifference. If he could be said to have any religious belief, it was a firm conviction that men created their gods in their own image. All piety, he contended, was rooted in fear; he could no more understand a man praying than he could his carrying a rabbit's foot to bring him luck. As an agnostic, he neither believed nor disbelieved in a life after death. But against the possibility of awakening on Judgment Day to stand before the throne of Heaven, surrounded by the Twelve Apostles, he had readied his apologia. "Gentlemen, I was wrong," he would say.

Back home after a ten days' stay in Johns Hopkins and a short visit to Dr. and Mrs. Fred Hanes, he wrote me on August 23, 1939:

> After I got out of hospital, I went down to North Carolina for a little rest, and have just returned. I feel a great deal better, but work is still somewhat difficult. Inasmuch as I have promised to deliver the book [*Happy Days*] by October 1st, I begin to feel jumpy. However, I am still hoping to do it.

At the end of August, he was startled from his labors by Hitler's announcement that he intended to seize the Free City of Danzig. In commenting on it, he said:

> I incline to believe that despite all the uproar now going on there will be no war, at least for the present. Soon or late it is bound to come. I take no stock in the notion that it will ruin Civilization. Civilization may get a considerable wallop, but it will nevertheless survive.

After Hitler invaded Poland, Mencken made clear what his position would be in the event that the United States became involved in it:

> I am naturally against the dialectic on tap in Washington, and have been denouncing it in the Baltimore *Sun*. If the United States actually horns into the war, of course, it will be impossible to write any more on the subject.

While the time allowed, however, H.L. pulled no punches. When the news of the Russo-Nazi pact broke, he gleefully reminded the New Deal parlor pinkos: "The will to believe is not cured by a single sell-out or even by a dozen on end. It is a chronic affliction, and as intractable as gout, the liquor habit, or following the horses. The American pinks have had it for a long time and they will carry it to the grave and, even, let us hope, beyond."

He predicted that if the United States entered the war, this country would be put under a military dictatorship and the Schellhase closed by the police. Christmas found him full of a human sorrow that was difficult to distinguish from "a gastric pain." He spent a dreadful day, he said, trying to accumulate a fair brannigan.

Having the foresight to see that the day was not far off when he would be forced to clamp down his self-imposed censorship, he began to cast about for noncontroversial projects with which to occupy himself. In addition to writing the sketches for *Newspaper Days* and correcting the proofs of *Happy Days,* he began to sort some thirty thousand aphorisms, proverbs, and saws from which he planned to complete a new dictionary of quotations to replace the out-of-date Bartlett's.

When *Happy Days* appeared in January 1940, Mencken, as usual, spoke lightly of his work. But never yet had a book of his met with such praise from the critics. It was compared to the best of Mark Twain and said to be worthy to stand on the shelf beside *Huckleberry Finn.* Edward Weeks, the ultraconservative editor of *The Atlantic Monthly,* declared in the March 1940 issue that it was "A book to be read twice a year by young and old, as long as life lasts." Knopf pressed Mencken to finish *Newspaper Days.* Once more, he was a campus idol, with invitations to speak at Harvard, Columbia, and Chicago. In February, he went to Boston to "harangue" the postgraduates in the Harvard School of Journalism, and then on to Chicago.

After his trips, he turned his attention from journalism to F.D.R.'s campaign oratory. Since all the President's radio time was devoted to "the intoning of mellifluous dithyrambs, with music by dulcimers and accordions," the Sage announced:

> My guess is that Roosevelt will be renominated and re-elected. The returns from Wisconsin in the papers this morning certainly indicate that much. There is no way to beat a man who has all of the boobs behind him. As for me I don't care. If Roosevelt is renominated he will undoubtedly take the country into the war, but again I don't care.

Still strongly isolationist and convinced that "The Hon. Mr. Roosevelt and his associated wizards are itching to horn into the great crusade to save humanity," Mencken tried to resign from the interventionist *Sunpapers.* Paul Patterson, however, insisted that he remain on as news consultant at half his former salary; but H.L. did not continue the Sunday columns he had been writing for the *Sun* and tendered his resignation as adviser to the news and editorial departments because he felt that his ideas clashed too strongly with the paper's policy.

Now, Mencken's New Deal opponents hoped that his guns had been spiked and his bombardment of Capitol Hill had been silenced for the duration.

$\mathcal{T}$HE DAYS OF THE
FATE MOTIF

NOT ALL MENCKEN'S OPPOSITION IN 1940 came from the New Dealers. He coined a new term for stripteasers, "ecdysiasts," from a Greek
word meaning "a getting out"; and his philological invention led him
into a verbal sparring match with Gypsy Rose Lee. When the news
reached the queen of the stripteasers, she exploded: "Ecdysiast he
calls me! Why the man's an intellectual snob. He has been reading
books."

Not only had the Sage been reading books, he had been addressing
the annual convention of the American Booksellers Association in New
York on "The Future of Publishing." "Such questions," he said, dis-
claiming any talent as a prophet, "are vast, incomprehensible, un-
solvable. Why authors write I do not know. As well ask why a hen
lays an egg or why a cow stands patiently while an underprivileged
farmer burglarizes her."

After he returned from the Democratic Convention at Chicago in
July, he was, if possible, more pessimistic about the future of the
country than about the future of publishing. The show in Chicago,
he reported, was so incomparably obscene that he began to believe
that the end of the Republic was in sight. Nor had he seen any encouraging signs in the Republican Convention at Philadelphia, which
he had covered earlier in the summer. He arrived there, carrying his
seersucker coat over his arm, snapping his red galluses, and rooting
loudly for Willkie, though privately he considered him a "weak sister"
and his candidacy a lost cause. Willkie's youthful adversary, Governor
Harold Stassen of Minnesota, Mencken dismissed as a juvenile con-

tender who age he estimated at "somewhere between thirty-three and seventeen." H.L.'s friend Alfred M. Landon was chairman of the subcommittee charged with writing a foreign-policy plank. When poor Alf's effort was handed to Mencken, his brows shot up and his horn-rim glasses slid down his nose. "It is so written," he chortled, "that it will fit both the triumph of democracy and the collapse of democracy, and approve both sending arms to England or only sending flowers." After Willkie's nomination was accomplished, "through the aid of the Holy Ghost," Mencken reported that the event bore evidence of a miracle. At one time, he declared, he had actually seen an angel in the gallery— an angel in a Palm Beach suit but, nevertheless, clearly an angel.

There was no such miraculous intervention at the Democratic Convention. The odds against beating Mr. Roosevelt, Mencken said, "are something less than 10,000 to 1." By way of a campaign slogan for the New Dealers, he suggested: "It is an act of lunacy, and not only an act of lunacy but also immoral and against God, to change barrels going over Niagara." In his eyes, Roosevelt had committed an act of war in sending planes to Great Britain, even as German troops were poised on the English Channel preparing to invade the island. For all that, to Mencken's disgust, the Democrats nominated F.D.R. for a third term by a landslide. Snapping his portable shut, Mencken buttoned up his seersucker coat, clapped his straw boater on with an air of finality, and shook hands all around the press box, saying, "Goodbye, goodbye. I'm afraid we won't see each other again in 1944. This is the last political convention that will ever be held in this country." Before he left, he gave instructions that if he should perish in the public service while covering the campaign, his "carcass" was to be stuffed and given to the National Museum.

In November, to Mencken's chagrin, F.D.R. defeated Willkie by a thumping majority. Before H.L. could recover his usual high spirits, Charlie Mencken's wife died in Pittsburgh. Later in the month, however, the bleak, wintry days were enlivened by Mrs. Alfred Du Pont's visits to Baltimore. Henry and Sara had met Alfred and Marcella Du Pont on a Caribbean cruise. Later, the Menckens had introduced the Du Ponts to the Hergesheimers, and the two couples frequently met in Baltimore or in West Chester. Marcella was young and gay, chic and charming, with a warmth of manner and a soft voice that endeared her to the Sage, who was, as ever, extremely sensitive to women's voices. She was now under the care of Henry's friend Dr. Benjamin Baker, and when Dr. Baker hospitalized her at Johns Hopkins for some serious surgery, Henry waited upon her faithfully, always equipped, as when he used to visit Sara there, with a suitcase full of wines, magazines, and tracts.

Occasionally, on his trips to New York, he took Anita Loos to dinner at Lüchow's to renew old memories and escape from the "glittering swinishness" of midtown Manhattan. He had known Miss Loos ever since his *Smart Set* days. In her autobiography, *A Girl Like I*, she credits Mencken with the responsibility for her point of view in her *Gentlemen Prefer Blondes*, which was derived from his "just as a gadget can be produced by the important theory of a scientist." In those days, she later confessed, she was more than half in love with Menck, as she called him. One evening, George Jean Nathan brought a naïve blonde along on a party with H.L. and Miss Loos. The blonde was ingenuous, even stupid, and Mencken was so intrigued by her simple-minded chatter that he egged her on in a way that made Miss Loos jealous. In trying to puzzle out why the "golden-haired birdbrain" had such an attraction for men, particularly for men of the intellectual stature of Mencken and Nathan, Miss Loos picked up her pen and did a character sketch of Lorelei Lee, the heroine of *Gentlemen Prefer Blondes*, a book which eventually earned millions of dollars.

Miss Loos, who oscillated between New York and Hollywood, always had news of Mencken's friends on the West Coast. Both Jim Tully and Scott Fitzgerald were now writing for the movies. Of late years, Mencken had had little contact with the Fitzgeralds, for before Scott left for Hollywood he had spent most of his time in Asheville, where he had placed Zelda in a sanitarium.

In the latter part of his life, as Joe Hergesheimer pointed out, Scott could write but didn't; did drink but couldn't. He had left Zelda for his fourth-estate prima donna Sheilah Graham, and abandoned the Garden of Allah for a place rented by her from an actor, who had named it Belly Acres. Fitzgerald and his "paramour," as he called her, led a cat-and-dog life there, where she was matriculating, to use her own euphemism, in "the F. Scott Fitzgerald College of One." After Scott was stricken with a heart attack in November, she moved him into her apartment in Hollywood, where he was weaving the story of their liaison into *The Last Tycoon*. He stopped drinking, stayed in bed, and worked on, hoping to finish the first draft of the novel and send it to Maxwell Perkins by the middle of January. But on December 21, 1940, he suffered a second and fatal heart attack.

In his will he had ordered: "Part of my estate is first to provide for a funeral and burial in keeping with my station in life." Later he wrote over "for a funeral" in pencil "the cheapest funeral" and added, "the same to be without undue ostentation or unnecessary expense." His body was taken to an undertaking parlor on the other side of the tracks in downtown Los Angeles and laid out in the William Wordsworth room, which apparently seemed to the morticians to be the most suitable place for the last rites of a literary man. Lying there he was said to look "like a cross between a floor-walker and a wax dummy in the window of a two-pants tailor." His hair was neatly parted on one side. None of it was gray and no lines showed in his face; but his hands were wrinkled and thin—the hands of an old man.

Fitzgerald's body was shipped East for burial in the family plot of the Catholic cemetery in Rockville, Maryland; but the bishop refused to allow Scott, who was a relapsed Catholic, to be buried in hallowed ground. So the funeral was held in a mortuary chapel in Bethesda, and he was interred in the Rockville Union Cemetery, a small Protestant burying ground across from the Catholic one. By request of his daughter, Miss Graham was not present. There were not more than thirty people at the graveside: Scotty, his cousins, Rosalind Sayre's husband, Newman Smith, Max Perkins, Harold Ober, his agent, and a number of friends from Baltimore. But Mencken did not come with them.

Among the letters in my papers chronicling the Fitzgeralds' decline and fall, destroyed out of deference to their families, before Sheilah Graham elected to vivisect Scott as thoroughly in *The Beloved Infidel* as he had vivisected her in *The Last Tycoon* and Zelda in his more successful novels, there was a note from Mencken. In it he gave as incisive an appraisal of Fitzgerald's life and works as has ever been made. In effect, Mencken said, Scott was the incarnation of his heroes; Zelda, of his heroines; and his significance lay, not so much in what he wrote, but in what he was—the eponymous figure of a fabulous age, the image of the easy, overnight success and the sudden collapse, the bursting of that bright bubble, the American Dream.

Early in January, Mencken predicted from Baltimore that 1941 would be the happiest year since the Black Death. Although his position as news consultant on the *Sunpapers* yielded only half his former salary, it gave him more time to spend with his friends. He went for a visit to the Dower House in December and again after the first of the year. At the end of January, Henry and Joe set off to Princeton. Julian P. Boyd, then librarian of the Firestone Library there, had been a classmate of R. P. Harriss' at Duke University; and later on, R.P. had been best man at his wedding. Through R.P.'s matchless stories of Mencken, Boyd had become interested in the Sage and now proposed to edit a volume of his letters. Boyd persuaded Mencken to change his mind and withdraw his objections to having any of his correspondence published while he was still alive. Indeed, Boyd charmed Mencken into collecting some twelve thousand letters from his friends, which were transcribed and microfilmed before return to their owners and which now form part of the remarkable collection of Menckeniana in the Firestone Library.

The first week in May there was a card from Mencken from Havana. After another siege with "the resurrection men" who once more had him in their "animal house" at Johns Hopkins Hospital, he and August had decided to take a trip to the Caribbean. Laid low with an attack of laryngitis, August could not go. Leaving him speechless but able to navigate, Mencken sailed alone on a United Fruit steamer. In Havana he amused himself by haranguing the bartender at Sloppy Joe's, attending the Havana Philharmonic, watching the overstuffed divas in a performance of *Carmen* "throwing their ramparts all over the stage," and gloating over a bull fight in which the killing of the bulls was forbidden by municipal edict, which made no such provision for protecting the matadors. When these diversions palled, he decided that he might as well see Miami. But Florida struck him as such a dreadful place that when Hitler took over the country he intended to propose to him that he detach it from the mainland and set it afloat. He returned to Baltimore, red and peeling like an onion. "My sunburn is wearing off," he announced, "though several hard patches of skin are still hanging loose. I hope to have them glued back with Duco, and in a week or two I should be restored to my usual loveliness."

When the Sage turned up in New York later in the summer, he

looked heavier and sterner. Opposed to our entry into the war, he had no desire to try to operate under the so-called voluntary censorship, so he had simply "shut down the plant" as he had done in 1917 and 1918 and refrained from discussing the current news. He would wait until the fever died down; then his chance would come again.

As usual, he spent his birthday nursing hay fever and cursing all the nostrums that had failed to cure it. After wrestling with the proofs of his book of quotations, he grumbled that he would have been happier had he applied himself to rolling cigars and never learned to read and write. Nevertheless, his *Newspaper Days,* portions of which were appearing in *The New Yorker,* had met with applause from his fellow journalists and acclaim from the literary critics. "If Mr. Mencken doesn't continue with vols. III, IV, V, and so on of his memoirs," the New York *Times* announced, "he will be guilty of a major crime."

Even before the Japs struck at Hawaii, Mencken, faced with the bleak prospect of the holidays, threatened to escape their gloom by taking to the road under an assumed name. After the attack on Pearl Harbor, however, he announced from Hollins Street that he was looking forward to the New Year with great interest. Probably, he said, it will drive us all crazy; but, nevertheless, it might have its moments. But by the time another January rolled around, he was groaning, "God help us one and all! It must be plain even to a blind man that Our Heavenly Father has washed his hands of the human race."

Since once more the American people had set out "to save the world," as Mencken put it, he held his fire against the New Deal crusaders and devoted himself to his philological research and his dictionary of quotations, which he derided as "the result of twenty-five years of literary scavenging."

In writing *Happy Days,* Mencken had frequently refreshed his memory by reading over his early correspondence with Phil Goodman, which they at one time had considered publishing. But before they got around to it, they broke off relations with each other. Out of courtesy, Mencken publicly laid the termination of his friendship with Goodman to Hitler; privately, he admitted that there were other reasons for the breach. After the Nazis promulgated the first laws against the Jews, Goodman began to bombard Henry with letters denouncing all Germans "as fiends in human form and going back in history for evidence of it." Subsequently, during the Depression, Goodman suffered heavy financial reverses. In 1933, after a series of crushing losses in the theater, he cabled Mencken from Paris, asking for a loan of a thousand dollars. Hard-pressed though Henry himself was at the time, he sent him five hundred, which Phil never repaid. To top it all off, Goodman announced that he had become a Communist. That was too much for Henry; he abandoned the idea of publishing the letters and ceased to see Goodman. But after Goodman's death in 1940, when his daughter, Ruth Goodman Doetz, told Mencken that her father had also completed a book of reminiscences in the last years of his life, for which she had not been able to find a publisher, Henry asked her to send him the manuscript. Now that the war had given him time to tackle it, he whipped Goodman's *Franklin Street* into shape and persuaded Knopf to publish it. Thus, after so many years, he noted, two books instead of one had been derived from their letters—of which three bound typescript volumes, containing some of the most gorgeous Rabelaisian humor since Gargantua and Pantagruel, remain unpublished in the Enoch Pratt Free Library.

In the spring of 1942, Mencken finally published his book of quotations, which he had been accumulating ever since his early days on the *Sun*—a collection that filled 1,347 closely printed double-column pages and moved a number of critics to pronounce it better and more useful than Bartlett's famous compendium. Between his titanic labors on it and his household chores, he still found leisure enough to bounce around the country. After attending a labor hearing in Washington, he and Hergesheimer made another trip to Princeton to see Julian Boyd. En route, he stopped over for a farewell visit to the Dower House. Dorothy and Joe were moving into a cottage at Stone Harbor, New Jersey, since running so large an establishment under wartime strictures was too great a strain on them, physically and financially. Mencken returned to Washington for a funeral there. Next day, he arrived in New York, where he and Carl Van Doren were to be among the speakers at a dinner in honor of Oswald Garrison Villard. After sitting through nine speeches, H.L. and Van Doren ducked out to the Ritz bar to relieve the aridity with steins of Pilsner. But even malt liquor was no specific for the overdraft on Mencken's strength. He caught cold and contracted a throat infection that sent him to Johns Hopkins for two weeks at the end of April. A course of sulfonal drugs cured the infection, but left him so depleted and edgy that he postponed the surgery that the doctors advised. Always acutely sensitive to sound, he threatened to drive nails into his radio, pour melted wax over his victrola, and take out the telephone, "the greatest boon to bores ever invented. It has set their ancient art upon a new level of efficiency and enabled them to penetrate the last strongholds to privacy—the most infernal invention of the twentieth century."

On finding that time now hung heavy on his hands, H.L. rolled up his sleeves and finished *Heathen Days*, the third volume of his auto-biography. He rose at eight o'clock, had a light breakfast, plowed through his daily stack of mail, read the papers, and lunched at home. Afterward, he would walk down to the *Sun* to chat with Paul Patterson and Hamilton Owens. Then he would set to work in his front office, leaving Herr August to labor in his shop on the magnificent ship models and beautiful inlaid chests he made in his spare time. At nine o'clock in the evening, they would meet to amuse each other with their inimitable tall tales and pungent views on the state of the world.

With the publication of *Heathen Days* in March 1943, Mencken's popularity soared. Even *The Nation*, which during the thirties had been inclined to belabor the Sage for his "Toryism" and his ridicule of the New Deal's social-welfare programs, received the third volume of his memoirs enthusiastically with a review in which Joseph Wood Krutch said:

> Mr. Mencken is certainly one of the most accomplished and most delightful writers our country has ever produced. This third installment of his own remembrance of things past is a sheer joy to read if only for the pleasure one gets from observing how successfully he has created an instrument for communicating the flavor of his particular and peculiar zest for life. Time has served only to perfect a style which was always robust and exuberant, but which has grown with the years better balanced and better integrated until it has achieved now an almost classical perfection without losing its individuality.

Malcolm Cowley, writing in *The New Republic*, again compared Mencken to Mark Twain. By way of criticism, he added that what he called H.L.'s "bourgeois traits" limited his imagination and restricted his sympathies to the middle classes, which vastly amused the gadfly of the booboisie. Concurrently, Henry also "larfed" when the magazine *PM* appeared with a photograph of Hergesheimer taken with a formidable, well-padded lady, and he hastened to issue "a feeble and belated warning" that muscular women were extremely dangerous "to us oxidizing men." But when the Sage was felled shortly afterward, it was not by a formidable lady but by a persistent allergy.

Schubert once wrote in his diary, "My compositions spring from my sorrow." During the dark days in which Mencken was forced to retire into the silences, he did some of his best work, despite his reports that he contemplated retiring to a monastery and devoting himself to engraving the Lord's Prayer on the heads of pins. Left without targets for his lance, he resurrected the ghost of Prohibition. "Here in Maryland, where anything and everything has been allowed," he howled, "it is now proposed to stop the sale of beer on Sunday. This will certainly throw me into a decline. Where am I to spend Sunday evening, after prayer meeting is over?" Then he demanded, "What is to be done about the plague of venery in poor old Baltimore? The police report that 1,765 girls under 16 were put to the torture between January 1st and January 15th. Of these fully 80% liked it so well that they are now leading lives of shame."

Having exhausted all the fun in that idea, H.L. wrote to Tully, who being of Irish extraction was no Anglophile either, telling him that he had a dream the night before in which he saw an army of 100,000 angels descending upon England. Some of the angels, he claimed, were colored, but the majority were white. Subsequently, opposed as Mencken was to all minority crusades, he advised Walter R. White, a Negro author, against taking part in them, despite the dream of the flights of colored angels flying to aid the Anglo-Americans. Moreover, the Sage expressed doubt that the pledges that the New Deal had made to the Negroes would be fulfilled:

> You have all of them [i.e. the pledges that White wanted from political candidates] from Roosevelt, but how many are being carried out? All the frauds will promise you everything you ask for, and all the honest men, if any, will be daunted by the visible impossibility of doing anything effectual. Race relations never improve in war time; they always worsen. And it is when the boys come home that Ku Klux Klans are organized.

Although Mencken forebore to make destructive comments on New Deal policies during the war, he kept so well abreast of the world situation that the chief of one division of our intelligence in Washington was so struck by the accuracy of H.L.'s appraisals of world events that he was convinced that the Sage had better sources of information than most of the United States agents at home or abroad. When the chief went to Baltimore to discover what Mencken's sources were, he was astonished to find that Henry derived his information from diligent reading of domestic and foreign papers and interpreting the news they recorded from his own perspective.

For all that, he was now spending more time on philology than journalism. Early in 1944 he announced that he hoped to complete a supplement to *The American Language* before the year was out. To his amazement, many of the additions and observations that he was preparing to incorporate in the supplement had come to him from the blind readers of the original Braille edition. Toward the end of March he confessed to Joe Hergesheimer:

> In these closing agonies of a long and misspent life, I conclude somewhat dismally that the pleasantest occupation I have ever encountered is work. I am putting in eight or ten hours a day on the supplement to "The American Language." It is at bottom dull pedantry, but nevertheless I somehow enjoy it.

During the conventions and the campaigns of 1944, Mencken maintained an admirable restraint in regard to F.D.R., the Brain Trust, and the New Deal. On November 14, 1944, he went so far as to admit to me:

> I voted for Roosevelt, and with the greatest pleasure. The country richly deserves him, and during the next four years I hope and pray it will get a sufficient dose of him. . . .
>
> I hope you are in good health and spirits. As for me I continue to deteriorate, but am still able to eat three meals a day and to handle a reasonable amount of ethyl alcohol. I have had to give up opium, cocaine and prussic acid, but no doubt I am better off without them.

The New Year found Henry tackling a chapter on *The American Language* that he had been asked to contribute to the *Literary History of the United States,* which was to be issued by Macmillan. By the end of January, he had finished the page proofs and index for *Supplement I, The American Language.* He got through that tremendous patriotic labor, he said, only by the aid of the Holy Spirit. He felt himself inspired by it all that spring.

On April 12, 1945, Franklin Delano Roosevelt died. Harry Truman, who was sworn in as his successor, found little more favor than his predecessor in the eyes of the Sage, to judge from his letter of May 1 to James Branch Cabell:

> I protested bitterly to the new Führer against the paper shortage, but in vain. His reply was: "Go to hell. I have plenty of troubles of my own. How would you like to be the successor to one of the Twelve Apostles?" I don't know what the reaction was of the patriotic people below the Potomac, but in these nefarious wilds the late catastrophe [F.D.R.'s death] apparently produced a great deal more joy than grief—in fact, it seemed to be difficult for a great many Baltimoreans to conceal their relief. A few flags are still at half mast, but in general the people seem to have put the whole business out of their mind.

In writing me while I was in San Francisco covering the formation of United Nations, Mencken omitted all mention of the war or the German surrender. Nor did he refer to it in writing to Cabell on May 15, 1945; instead, he confined himself to purely literary matters, concluding with an amusing sidelight on the author of *Babbitt*.

> I note that Red Lewis has turned literary critic, and has written for *Esquire*. His first article leaves me unconvinced that his talents lie in that direction. As you probably know, he has moved to Duluth, Minnesota. When I asked him why he picked out so remote a place, he told me that it was near his home town. On subsequent cross-examination, however, it turned out that it was two hundred miles away. I suspect that there is a female in the case.

The female in question was Marcella Powers, a young actress whom Lewis had met in Provincetown, where he was playing the role of Nat Miller in Eugene O'Neill's *Ah, Wilderness*. Miss Powers subsequently became Lewis' protégée and was introduced by him to his friends as his "niece." Mencken had met her when Jack T. Levine's *The Good Neighbor* was tried out at Ford's Theatre in Baltimore. After Red was divorced in 1942 by Dorothy Thompson Lewis, "The Talking Woman," as he now called her, he moved to Duluth, where he was joined by Miss Powers and her mother. Although Mencken did not allude directly either to Dorothy or Miss Powers, in writing to Lewis, he said:

> I am, God knows, no gynephobe, but I like women who appreciate their men. We bucks do a great deal for them. We defend them, support them, soothe their frenzies, and even admire them. I think they deserve that admiration—but not when they try to make slaves of men who are their betters. In any combat between superior and inferior I am for No. 1. So is our Heavenly Father.

Yet the atomic bombs that fell on Hiroshima aroused a completely contradictory reaction in the Sage. "The atom bomb," as he later wrote Dr. Julian Boyd, "is the greatest invention that Yahweh has made since leprosy. Certainly it has given great glory to the Christian physicists of this country. Try to imagine a decent cannibal throwing it on a town full of women and children."

That fall in Baltimore, I found H.L. rotund, bouncy, full of steam and "malicious magnetism." He was just back from a weekend with Dorothy and Joe at Stone Harbor, where he had acquired a violent sunburn. His face was fiery red and several people, he announced, had already mistaken him for Sinclair Lewis. Over a lunch of softshell crabs, washed down with the Schellhase's best Löwenbrau, he said that World War II had been covered wordily rather than well. The war correspondents, he grumbled, were "a sorry lot, either typewriter statesmen turning out dull stuff, or sentimental human-interest scribblers, turning out maudlin pieces about the common soldier."

Afterward, Mencken quizzed me about the United Nations Conference and the diplomats who participated in it. In all creation, he claimed, there were no stupider men than diplomats, nor any more antisocial. Their dishonesty, he added, was so deep-seated that most of them were quite as unconscious of it as a Georgia Cracker is unconscious of his hookworms and his fleas. The United Nations, he predicted, had no more chance to survive in the face of Communist pressure than the Ku Klux Klan would have in the Vatican. Now that we had pulled Great Britain's chestnuts out of the fire again, he hoped that the English would no longer be worshiped as "great moral engines." Naturally, however, he was jubilant that the war was over. His "whole vocabulary" was no longer forbidden, and he was once more free to turn his verbal blowtorch on politics without bringing the wrath of the professional patriots down on his head. All the returning veterans he had talked to were more disillusioned, if possible, than their fathers had been after World War I. It was hard to know whether the politicians who made the war or the brass hats who fought it would be more unpopular, now that their days of saving the world were over—another war had passed into history and taxes.

$\mathscr{A}$UTUMNAL DAYS

SUPPLEMENT I to *The American Language* brought acclaim both to its publisher and author. On January 24, 1946, Alfred A. Knopf received the Carey Thomas Award for publishing and handling the book. Although Mencken warned Hergesheimer that if he read it seriatim, he deserved his sufferings, since it was a book designed for bedside dipping, Edmund Wilson, whom the Sage regarded as one of the ablest American critics, in reviewing it for *The New Yorker,* declared it to be "perhaps the most readable of all the various installments of the book. For anyone with an interest in words, the new volume is absolutely fascinating."

Mencken's mind teemed with other books that he hoped to do. He toyed with the idea of compiling a really first-rate dictionary of American slang, but decided that such an ambitious enterprise should be left to a younger man. The idea of chronicling his adventures as an editor also appealed to him. In fact, he already had put a substantial part of it on paper; and, doubtless, the manuscript and that of *Advice to Young Men* are buried somewhere in his papers. In the end, however, he settled upon writing a second supplement to *The American Language.*

When he went to New York to discuss the prospect with Alfred Knopf, he happened to see the novelist John O'Hara and his wife sitting across from his table at Twenty-One. He sent them a bottle of champagne with the explanation that it was his birthday, and he didn't like to celebrate alone. Touched by his gesture, O'Hara slipped out and bought him a thirty-five-dollar box of cigars. "You musn't do this for me," the Sage protested. "I couldn't let you do it. I really couldn't." He made O'Hara take the cigars back.

It was a trivial incident, but one that highlighted several traits of Mencken's that frequently pass unremarked. For one thing, he found it more blessed to give than to receive. He liked to present gifts, particularly to women and children. But with the exception of food and wine, it embarrassed him to receive them, and he never accepted them if he could avoid it. Many an aspiring lady lost her chances with him by giving him a handsome gift. He disliked being made much of—a thing which, he said, only pleased people who are unsure of their position, and he had been certain of his ever since he was a boy. Further, as O'Hara noted, he was an extremely sensitive man and, under his carapace, a deeply emotional and keenly perceptive one.

For a man of his robust physique, Mencken's senses were acute and delicately attuned. He himself often noted that the world presented itself to him as a complex of aural, rather than visual, sensations. Consequently, when one of his neighbors acquired "a large powerful male dog of breed or breeds unknown to your orator," whose nightly barking, to quote Mencken again, was "abnormally loud, harsh, penetrating, violent, and disturbing," he appealed to the courts to restore his domestic tranquillity, nocturnal rest, and peace of mind. He had filed the suit, expecting to have some fun, but the dog was sent away twenty-four hours after Mencken's bill of complaint was presented. He also hoped to recover two or three million dollars in damages, he announced; but needless to say, he realized more fun—and more publicity—than money from the farcical suit.

Admittedly, Henry was hard put to find diversion in those days. All too many friends of his earlier years had passed away or become immobilized by illness. Ellen Glasgow died in Richmond on November 21, 1945. Three weeks later, Theodore Dreiser suffered a fatal heart attack in Hollywood, a few months before his novel *The Bulwark* was published. According to the Sage, it was the best novel Dreiser ever wrote. In the introduction that Mencken did for *The Bulwark,* he demonstrated his genius for drawing in a few bright strokes a character sketch of a man whom he had served for more than forty years as hack writer, critic, adviser, editor, promoter, agent, champion, and trouble-shooter-in-chief. Although Mencken confessed that he had spent the better part of that time in trying to induce Dreiser to reform his style and electrify his turgid, brackish paragraphs, he had had no more success than if he had attempted to dissuade him from his belief in non-

Euclidian arcana or to induce him to take up golf. On the other hand, he conceded that the defects of Dreiser's style had been exaggerated "by a long line of literary popinjays, including myself"; Dreiser, he added, was capable at times of writing simply, even gracefully.

Jim Tully, who had recovered from his initial heart attack, had been silenced by a relapse that confined him to a wheel chair. Because of his failing health, Joe Hergesheimer had published little since *The Foolscap Rose* appeared in 1934. He was ill, discouraged, and afflicted by a literary paralysis. In "The Divine Afflatus" Mencken had diagnosed the cause of such an impediment as what he delicately termed "stenosis." The remedy that he now prescribed for Joe's creative block is as unique in the history of pharmacology as in the annals of literature. He had been in the same state a couple of years before, he admitted, and found the cure for it in a course of sulphur and molasses.

Joe came to Baltimore frequently for treatment, and he and Henry hobnobbed with a few of their old cronies who could navigate under their own power. Mencken still kept in touch with his younger friends in other places. Jim Cain had become an editor of *The New Yorker.* Marcella Du Pont, who was living at Calmar, her "palace" in Greenville, Delaware, drove Henry and Joe to Stone Harbor—and that at such a speed Mencken threatened to jump out and start shooting at the tires. R. P. Harriss had gone to work for the New York *Herald Tribune* in Paris. But he continued to write for the Baltimore *Evening Sun*, contributing to it first a Paris column and later a series of editorial-page pieces. In addition, he wrote for the Manchester *Guardian* under a pen name and published a number of essays, poems, and short stories in the United States.

The year after R.P.'s novel *The Foxes* appeared, he married Margery Willis, a family friend of the Menckens and a great favorite with Henry. During World War II, R.P. was away from Baltimore for long periods of time, flying about the West Indies and Central and South America under the aegis of the State Department, acting as United States observer at the Anglo-American Caribbean Conference, and doing diplomatic coverage for the *Sunpapers*. After his resignation from the *Sunpapers*, R.P. joined the editorial staff of the Baltimore *News-American*. He also joined the Maryland Club, where he frequently met Mencken in the evenings and recalled the good old days when they worked together on *The Evening Sun*.

In his autumnal years, Mencken also saw a great deal of another family friend, Richard Hart, whose mother had been a friend of Mencken's mother and sister. Hart, a poet, a Poe specialist, and author of several opera librettos, became head of what was then the Literature Department of the Enoch Pratt Free Library and did much to make the Enoch Pratt the great cultural center that it is. Through his influence, Mencken was persuaded to address the library's staff meetings, to speak before its Writer's Forum, and to endow it with one of the most remarkable collections in America.

The Enoch Pratt had been a favorite haunt of Mencken's ever since he first stumbled into it as a young newspaperman, bent on doing "a little precautionary reading" before setting out to cover a performance of Mendelssohn's *Elijah.* He had a deep affection for the library; and as its director, Edwin Castagna, recently pointed out, the "long, warm friendship" between the Sage and the Enoch Pratt was far from being a one-way affair. Mr. Castagna said:

> When I speak to members of the staff about Mencken their eyes light up. They warmly reciprocated his attitude towards them and the Library. He is remembered as a perfect patron, one who would not make unreasonable demands. If a book couldn't be found for him at the moment, he would wait until it could be located. He is remembered for his manners, which were those of a Southern gentleman. When there were others waiting, he hung back. He insisted that even young people should be served in turn, although the librarians were always eager to show deference to a friend who was also one of the great writers of his time.

Not only was Mencken given a cordial welcome at the Enoch Pratt but also at the offices of the *Sun.* Hamilton Owens and Paul Patterson were still on hand there to chat with him when he stopped by on his daily walks. Both of them were suave, amiable, and well informed and made the editorial rooms a pleasant place to linger. But Mencken doubtless missed Gerald Johnson's genial presence there. In 1945, Gerald had retired from the staff of the *Sunpapers* to become a radio commentator, a job which gave him more time to devote to his historical research.

Although Mencken continued to attend the annual sessions of the Gridiron Club with Paul Patterson and the Bach Festival with Alfred Knopf, he no longer toured the country as he once did. On his now

Infrequent trips to New York, he lunched with Nathan at Lüchow's, looked up the Carl Van Vechtens, dined with the Knopfs, and conferred with Julian P. Boyd on Boyd's proposal to edit a volume of Mencken's letters while he was still alive—a scheme that, unfortunately, Dr. Boyd later abandoned to engage in his monumental work on the papers of Thomas Jefferson.

In the summer of 1946, Mencken was cornered in New York at the Stork Club by Roger Butterfield of *Life*. While the Lord High Lambaster of Baltimore regaled himself with boiled beef, cabbage, and butterscotch pie, he held forth on World War II, the atomic bomb, the New Deal, the American penchant for pulling British chestnuts out of the fire, Communism, and the labor racketeers. In conclusion, when his interrogator inquired whether Mencken had rather be called the Sage of Baltimore or the Man Who Hates Everything, he replied:

> I don't give a damn what you or anyone else calls me just so long as you don't call me an old dodo sneaked out of the dissecting room. I'm 66 years old, I work hard all the time, and while it is perfectly true that I may be snatched into heaven tomorrow, I am still going strong today. I have written five books since I was 60, and all of them sold better than my previous books.
>
> In the present case it is a little inaccurate to say that I hate everything. I am strongly in favor of common sense, common honesty and common decency. This makes me forever ineligible to any public office of trust or profit in the Republic. But I do not repine, for I am a subject of it only by force of arms. By birth and of free choice I am a citizen of the Maryland Free State.

Mencken tossed his napkin aside and rose, adding:

> I have to go back to the Public Library. And after that I am meeting George Jean Nathan. I first met George 40 years ago, and he's lasted surprisingly well for a man who violates the laws of God and man. He smokes all the time and drinks too much, and his taste in girls is remarkable—he likes them very tiny. I don't agree.
>
> We may go to Lüchow's tonight, on 14th Street. It's the only place in New York that hasn't changed since I first went into it in 1901—good food, good beer and wonderful waltzes. The musicians always play the Brahms waltz in A flat when I come in; somebody told them it was my favorite. It isn't, but it is still very lovely.
>
> But tomorrow I want to be back in Baltimore.

The interview appeared in *Life* on August 5, 1946. In the course of it, Mencken had noted:

I have always been a fan for theology and the present religious churches are in an advanced state of decomposition and, save in the moron South, no one takes them seriously.

When an irate Confederate who had seen the article asked me what Mencken meant by the "moron South," I referred the question to Mencken. In a letter to me of August 24, 1946, he explained:

If any professional patriot ever asks you what I mean by the moron South, tell him I mean those Southerners who ask what I mean by the moron South. This will give him something to ponder on and keep him from suffering too much. That interview in *Life* in its first form was much longer. Unhappily, it had to be cut at the last moment because of the crowding of space.

Schellhase's is far gone along the road to Hell. The place opens every day at 11 o'clock and closes at 9 p.m. Worse, it has no good draft beer. I am thus reduced to boozing with my brother at home.

The "cagey" drinker's boasts of his Dionysian feats had not diminished with the increase in his age. Many years before when Dreiser quoted George Sterling as saying that he doubted whether he would let Mencken live in San Francisco because he was unworthy of its bohemian resources, selecting "impregnable virgins" and clinging to water as if it were his "heart's blood," the Bad Boy of Baltimore let out a howl of protest more heartrending than his plaint that Schellhase's new hours restricted his boozing.

Nathan once analyzed H.L.'s character in terms of such contradictions:

He is a champion of the Nietzschean doctrine, and spends considerable time each year in toy stores picking out doll babies and choo-choo cars for the youngsters of his married acquaintances. He has above the writing table a large framed photograph of the Iron Chancellor, and on his writing table a small framed photograph of a very pretty girl. He chews tobacco and his favorite musical compositions are the waltzes of Johann Strauss.

He is a foe of democracy and politely sees every person, however asinine, who comes to call on him. He believes and stoutly maintains that one strong enemy is more valuable than two mediocre friends, and then makes friends with the strong enemy soon after he shows up. He is in favor of a merciless autocracy and collects stamps for his brother's little child. He is a rabid anti-prohibitionist and gets a violent attack of heartburn and a sour middle whenever he drinks two cocktails.

He scorns society, but has his evening clothes made by one of the best and most expensive of Fifth Avenue tailors. He lustily derides golf players and amuses himself every afternoon playing with some pet turtles in his backyard. He writes vehemently against quack doctors and has tried ten of them in an attempt to get rid of his hay fever. He insists that he likes only the company of middle-aged women, and associates solely with young ones. He ridicules any man who is vain in the matter of personal appearance, and goes out and buys a new necktie if the one he is wearing does not match his shirt. He is an exponent of the "Be hard" doctrine, is in favor of killing off the weak, and sends milk twice a month to the starving babies of the war-ridden European countries. He is a fatalist and doses himself daily with a half dozen various philtres.

Jim Tully, who knew the Sage almost equally as well as Nathan did, once said that in the vernacular of the ring, Henry would be known as Baby Face Mencken. Round, innocent, unlined, his face was no index to the depth or incisiveness of his mind; nor his bland smile, to his trenchant wit. His eyes were always wide; nothing escaped their cold clear vision; at times they were filled with sentiment or laughter, with pity or contempt. A born Aristotelian, he was master of the Socratic method and Socratic irony as well as of prose satire.

Just before Christmas in 1946, Alfred Knopf published a satirical little sketch of Mencken's—a moral tale that, perhaps, represented his most pious effort: *The Christmas Story.* In Mencken's coruscating prose, it recounted the story of a local freethinker and scofflaw, Fred Ammermeyer, who made up his mind to outdo the missions by giving a Christmas feast for the Skid Row derelicts. At the blowout, there were to be bountiful viands and abundant spiritous, vinous, and malt beverages, but no hymns, no prayers, no preaching to embarrass the outcasts. It was to be "a dinner that went on in rhythmic waves, all day and all night until the hungriest and hollowest bum was reduced to breathing with not more than one cylinder of one lung." However, as soon as Fred Ammermeyer's guests began to feel the effects of his Christmas cheer, they completely confounded him by automatically doing what they thought was expected of them. In beery voices they raised the tune of "Are You Ready for the Judgment Day." One Salvation Army hymn followed another. When at last silence fell over the group, a bleary-eyed sinner rose and began to confess in a quavering voice. Frustrated and defeated as a do-gooder, the freethinking host fled the festivities.

Ironically enough, Mencken's *Christmas Story* brought on trouble with the pious Britishers across the border. Early in the new year, his Canadian publishers decided to withdraw it on the plea that it was sacrilege.

On January 13, 1947, Mencken was again in the news when *Time* and *Newsweek* played up his extraordinary contract with a Canadian cinema company. In exchange for the rights to Mencken's *A Neglected Anniversary,* a deadpan hoax on the origin of the bathtub, written for the New York *Evening Mail* some thirty years before, the Canadian producer agreed to furnish Mencken with two cases of Labatt's ale a month for the rest of his life. Mencken stipulated that he was not to be required to return the bottles or cartons in which the ale was shipped. The contract provided for a board of arbiters. The cinema company was to be represented by a Canadian committee; Mencken, by the Governor of Maryland. In the event that this worthy should be "inebriated or otherwise incapacitated," the Chief Justice of the United States was to serve in his place.

On Tuesday, February 18, 1947, the Sage went to the Enoch Pratt Library to meet Edgar Kemler, a Washington newspaperman who proposed to do a biography on "The Irreverent Mr. Mencken." He proved to be, as Kemler notes, a most cooperative subject, placing his papers at the biographer's disposal, entertaining him weekly at luncheon in Baltimore, writing long autobiographical accounts for him, withholding no information, and making no suggestions as to how the data was to be handled. And Kemler's mother, who outlived him, still remembers Mencken's kindness. His attitude towards his biographer was both generous and courageous, although he was skeptical of the project from its inception.

Kemler quotes Mencken as saying of the favorable passages, "This is sweet stuff and far more accurate than Harvard." Of the unfavorable passages, he adds, H.L. said nothing directly. Why should he? He had already said, "A biographer is an unjust god." He was, however, highly pleased with "The Old Humbug," the portion of Hergesheimer's abortive autobiography, dealing with his friendship with Mencken:

> An intimacy serene after four decades almost, based on common sense and a mutually contentious humor. Except for an opening blast, Henry's letters throughout all that time recalled the fantods of artwork and eternity. A gravity of the comic genius kept him from literary effects and metaphysical sky writing. His high spirits, his response of

courage to a profound sense of life's dark underside, his regard for human dignity were inflexible; his high sense of honor, his uncurable virtue, no less fixed than Thomas Huxley's closed universe.

Mencken gave Joe *carte blanche* to say what he pleased; he asked only one thing: "make it clear that I am a baptized man and a fanatical lover of the flag." When Joe bogged down on his book, Henry tried to comfort him by telling him that all of his own books had been written in spurts. Mencken had not written a line, he said, since he finished *Supplement II*, and he was stymied by the thought of tackling the revisions. "This lying fallow," he concluded, "is probably a good thing." As time passed, however, Henry began to suspect that Joe had abandoned the book and threatened to have him penned up in the Baltimore jail until he put a hundred thousand words on paper.

After lying fallow himself for a brief period, Mencken was once more full of steam. During the first week in July, he exploded to the New York *Post's* Earl Wilson, "I'm in favor of war and I hope it starts soon!" Jimmy Cannon, an ex-GI, then columnist on the *Post*, attempted to pin H.L.'s ears back with a Menckenesque tirade:

> It could be that the liverwurst sage intended his little talk to be comical in the old tradition of the professional cynic. But I can locate no fun in Mr. Mencken's cemetery wheezes and there can be no little pity in anyone if this crusader for tolerance has been transformed by the years into a macabre clown—Mr. Mencken sounds like the voice of doom playing a kazoo.

Mencken was fond of quoting Nietzsche's contention that "The free man is a warrior"; and being as doughty a freelance as ever took up arms against an assailant, the Sage delighted in exchanging thrusts with his critics. He refrained, however, from replying to Cannon, for Dr. Benjamin Baker had already warned him that his circulation had been impaired and that any explosive outburst might have disastrous consequences. On the morning of August 6, 1947, he was more sternly cautioned. He awoke with a dull headache. He felt confused and his speech was thick. His right hand was so numb that he could not use the typewriter. Realizing that he must have had a slight stroke, he remained at home and rested for a few days. As soon as the numbness passed, he went back to work. Dr. Baker, who examined him the next week, found nothing alarming in his condition. But the shadows that were to darken his last years had begun to fall.

For some years Mencken had been playing with the idea of "a funeral service for the admittedly damned." He and Sara Haardt had actually begun to draft an outline of such a rite. Yet, when she died, "in order to avoid scandalizing her Alabama relatives beyond endurance," he had asked a High Church Episcopal rector to read the burial service at her funeral. For his own part, however, he made his brother, August, whom he had named as his executor, swear to have his body taken to the "undertaker's studio" and cremated promptly without rites, mourners, or flowers.

He announced publicly that he was to be "stuffed post mortem, and offered to the National Museum at Washington." He added regretfully that he feared that the science of taxidermy was not sufficiently advanced for the job; and even were that not true, the medieval laws of Maryland would, no doubt, prohibit such a plan. In his *Minority Report,* he admitted:

> It is a folly to try to beat death. One second after my heart stops thumping I shall not know or care what becomes of all my books and articles. Why, then, do I try to keep my records in order, and make plans for their preservation after I am an angel in Heaven? I suppose the real reason is that a man so generally diligent and energetic as I have been finds it psychologically impossible to resign the game altogether. I know very well that oblivion will engulf me soon or late and probably very soon, but I can't resist trying to push it back a few inches. Civilized man, indeed, is essentially indomitable. He refuses to yield to the natural laws that have him in their grip. His life is always a struggle against the inevitable—in Christian terms, a rebellion against God. I'll know nothing of it when it happens, but it caresses my ego today to think of men reading me half a century after I am gone. This seems, superficially, to be mere vanity, but it is probably something more. That something is a sound impulse—the moving force behind all cultural progress—to take an active hand in the unfolding of human life on this sorry ball. Every man above the level of a clod is impelled to that participation, and every such man desires his contribution to last as long as possible.

It had been a year to turn Mencken's thoughts to somber matters: Ernest Boyd died on December 30, 1946, Willa Cather on April 24, 1947. A still heavier loss awaited Mencken. Jim Tully, whose unwavering loyalty and devotion had inspired a deep affection in Mencken, suffered a final heart attack on June 22 and was buried in Forest Lawn Memorial Park at Glendale, California.

In the fall, when the editorial writers held their first national conference in Washington to discuss the decline of the editorial page, Mencken was invited to administer "a kind of shock treatment." The trouble with editorials, he maintained, is that editorial writers write too many. They should hold their fire unless they have something to say. Besides, most of them have no business writing editorials. "We are recruiting editorial writers . . . from reporters who have trouble with their legs, and from desk men who have trouble with their spelling." Editorial writers should do their share of pavement pounding. "No editorial writer," he contended, "ought to be allowed to sit in his office year after year contemplating his umbilicus. On the big city paper, an editorial writer doesn't know anybody. . . . Let him cover the police court or a good national story. Don't let him become a professor." He found the attempt to shift the blame for the decline of the editorial page onto the publishers' shoulders farfetched. Publishers, he pointed out, are people of backward mentality, who sop up their opinions from the men around them. American journalism, he was convinced, suffered from too few street-walking reporters and too many golf players; they, not their bosses, were responsible for most of the imbecilities of the press.

Toward the end of the year, on reading in the Baltimore papers that no local museum had a painting by Thomas Hart Benton, the Sage volunteered that he had one himself, which was in his cellar at the moment, gathering dust. The painting, which Willard Huntington Wright had passed on to him as part payment of a debt, was an abstraction done in Benton's "earlier and more foolish days." The Baltimore Museum of Art bid for it, and Mencken delivered it to them, free of all cost and expense, asking nothing in return except to have the gift deducted from his income tax.

Early in the spring of 1948, Knopf published *Supplement II to The American Language*. Heartened by its reception, Mencken set to work on a long-cherished project. He had always enjoyed putting together scissors-and-paste jobs, and he particularly relished the idea of culling a Mencken anthology from his vast accumulation of articles, essays, and epigrams. As a title for it, he proposed *A Mencken Chrestomathy*. Knopf protested that the title would baffle the average reader. Mencken, who shied away from "anthology," "treasury," "miscellany," and "omnibus," stuck to his guns, supported by George Jean Nathan. Knopf,

Nathan reminded him, had turned thumbs down on the *Autobiography of an Attitude* as a title for Nathan's highly successful volume of that name.

When the political pot began to boil that summer, Mencken was too engrossed in digging out the juiciest excerpts of his work for the *Chrestomathy* to watch it with his usual interest. A good politician, he had long since decided, was as unthinkable as an honest burglar. The fundamental error of the electorate lay in making the false assumption that some politicians are better than others. Most of them entertained F.D.R.'s concept of government, which was that of "a milch cow with 125,000,000 teats."

After the campaign swung into high gear, H.L. turned thumbs down on Dewey, even though he admired the way in which he used the American language in his oratory. Stassen, the Sage declared, was "just another quack—A Republican Henry Wallace." The Revolt of the States' Righters against Truman promised to be as good a show as Wallace's Progressive Convention. Nevertheless, Mencken declined Paul Patterson's invitation to cover the 1948 "political, homilectical, and patro-inspirational orgies" for the *Sunpapers.* Twice he had been forced to retire into the silences when the *Sun* had given its support to those who claimed to be making the world safe for democracy; he flatly declined to go back again. Besides, against his advice the *Sun* had set up a television station, and he was also irked about that. "I quit writing for the *Sun* in January 1941," he wrote McLean Patterson, "and it is highly improbable that I'll resume for the two conventions. Thus you had better chalk me off. I'm beginning to yearn for television. In a little while you'll hear and see me crooning."

But eventually, as everyone who knew him well could have predicted, the lure of the summer campaigns proved irresistible to Mencken. The gaudy show of the political conventions was too great a temptation. He dropped into the *Sun* office wearing a button as big as a pie pan, reminding the public to "Vote for Taft," which on close inspection proved to be of the vintage of 1908. However, when Paul Patterson again importuned him to cover the conventions, he shook his head. "Alas and goddam, but I fear that one all night session—and the Democrats always have them—would deliver me to the Pathology Department. Better not count on me." But to a New York columnist who raised the issue, he added, "I'll probably end by going and blowing up and coming home on a shutter. Oh, well. It's a heroic death." At length, when the Pattersons renewed their request, he agreed to go if Paul accompanied him to the conventions, saying that either they would restore him, or they would kill him.

When summer came, he bought a new seersucker suit, slicked down his cowlicks, clamped on his straw boater, and, portable in hand, set out for the nominating conventions in Philadelphia. As usual he was on hand in time to watch the set-up of the circus, glad-handing his old friends, quizzing porters, policemen, and doormen, ear-biting with cronies in the press box, and goggling at the preparations to televise the convention. He sat with the young fry, high up on the wooden press benches, simmering and half-blinded by the blue-white arc lights. Unperturbed by the glare or the bawling loudspeakers, he snapped open his portable and set to work, hitting the keys with his forefingers and spacing with his elbows. Constant shifting from the terrific heat of the glaring arcs to the air-conditioned comfort of the *Sun's* hotel suite gave him a violent cold. His old enemy tracheitis flared up, and he was forced to retreat temporarily to Baltimore.

Indomitable as ever, he returned to Philadelphia like a reactivated volcano to cover the Democratic "orgies." The walkout of the Alabamians in protest against Truman's renomination delighted him. He was even more intrigued by a young Alabamian who was secretary of the Democratic National Committee. "Women politicians," Mencken had once remarked, always reminded him of "a battered, old British tramp steamer, all decked out for the coronation," but Dorothy Vredenburg completely upset his theories. She was "slim, pretty, and smartly clad," and the Sage paid due homage to her as "the Democrats' secret weapon."

Mencken could not have asked for a better show than the Democratic split in Philadelphia in 1948, but the antics of Henry Wallace's third-party convention there in August reduced the walkout of the States' Rights Democrats the month before to a one-ring circus in comparison. Before the Progressives converged on the City of Brotherly Love, the pro-Communists managed to secure control of the convention machinery. Wallace, under pressure, followed the Communist party line. It was as if Wallace, Dorothy Thompson said, "being an absent-minded man, had started sabotaging himself." To increase his discomfort, Mencken joined forces with Westbrook Pegler to make "Old Bubble-head Wallace" admit that he had written some weirdly mystical notes —known as the Guru Letters—to a grass-roots occultist named Nicolas Roerich. After Wallace had sourly declined to talk "to Pegler or any Pegler stooge," Mencken rose and pointed out with an ironic grin that, although he could hardly be considered a Pegler stooge, he thought the matter of the Guru Letters had gone so far that it should be cleared up by Wallace. Still declining to answer the questions, Wallace strode out in high dudgeon. The Wallace orgies, Mencken said, were really frightening; he began to believe that all was lost in this great country, including honor. The Sage's coverage of the "Wallace obscenity" was trenchant and highly flavored, and it ranks with the best of his political reporting. Under the overline "Mencken and the Swami," his July 22 report of the attempt "to heave Henry [Wallace] into the presidency of this great Republic" bore the headline MARX, LENIN, UNCLE JOE MISSING AT CONVENTION.

The Progressive Party of Maryland was not pleased. Its leaders denounced Mencken in fantastic terms of Red-baiting, Jew-baiting, and Negro-baiting and drafted a resolution to be presented to the convention: "Therefore be it resolved by the delegates here assembled, that this convention severely censures H. L. Mencken and his contemptible rantings which pass for newspaper reporting." To Mencken's immense disappointment, the chairman threw out the resolution. So he drowned his grief at a post-mortem party in the *Sun* suite, drinking beer with some of Wallace's henchmen who stumbled in by mistake, joining them in singing their campaign songs, and adding his basso profundo to the chorus of "Henry Wallace, Friend-ly Hen-ry Wallace," and then into a malty "Maryland, My Maryland"—a grand finale to his last barnstorming tour and to forty-nine years of covering political conventions.

Although the convention coverage left him somewhat depleted, by the time Mencken returned to Hollins Street he had recovered enough steam to raise the question in the *Sun* of whether the current investigations of Communist activities were a violation of civil liberties. He blistered Truman for blocking the admission of a mass of evidence assiduously collected by the Army, the Navy, and the F.B.I., and declined to sympathize with the innocents gored by the inquiries of the Un-American Activities Committee. In defense of his position he noted the absurd fact that although he had once been cited by Elizabeth Dilling in *The Red Network* as an agent of Moscow, no one had ever seriously believed that he was guilty of "guzzling the Marxist hooch." On the contrary, he was attacked by Ilya Ehrenburg, the Russian foreign expert, for saying "sooner or later—probably, very soon—we will engage in mortal combat with the Russian barbarians." Writing in *Pravda*, Ehrenburg said, "If Mencken were only an eccentric or a psychopathological case, I would pay no attention to his remarks. Unfortunately this aesthete reflects the thought of various businessmen, military men, and politicians."

Concurrently, through a typical act of simple kindness, the Sage found himself the target of equally preposterous criticism in the Un-American Activities controversy. In the early days of *The Smart Set* Mencken had published some of Ezra Pound's verse and thereafter carried on a desultory, often highly critical and even acrimonious correspondence with him after the poet became a voluntary exile in Europe. When Italy fell in World War II, Pound was arrested in Pisa by the United States because of his radio broadcasts from Europe in support of Fascism and in condemnation of the war efforts of the Allies. He was flown to Washington to stand trial for treason. After being examined by four alienists, he was declared to be of unsound mind and committed to St. Elizabeth's Hospital, where Mencken, as was his custom in similar misfortunes, paid him a brief courtesy call. Mencken found him more distraught than his *Pisan Cantos* might have indicated. Subsequently, in *The Irreverent Mr. Mencken,* Edgar Kemler notes in the last chapter with no documentation and no corroboration that Mencken and Pound "had been joined again in the intellectual precincts of Fascism; and but for the grace of God, he too [i.e., Mencken] might have ended in some such hideous predicament." R. P. Harriss, who had published small parts of Kemler's as well as Manchester's biographies of the Sage in *Gardens, Houses and People,* protested Kemler's charge, and Kemler tried to withdraw it. But it was too late; the book had already gone to press.

Once more Mencken was being denounced by both the Fascists and the Communists, for his star was again in the ascendant. His new wave of popularity in 1948 crested little short of the high-water mark of the twenties. *The New Yorker,* to which H.L. transferred his allegiance after the decline of *The American Mercury,* had published his sketch called "Love Story" in January and his account of Dreiser's adventures in the Village, "That Was New York," in April. On his occasional trips to New York the one person he wanted most to see was *The New Yorker's* editor, Harold Ross.

In May, *The Saturday Review of Literature* carried an article on H.L.'s current reading, in which the Sage confessed, "I read a great deal of trash and find some of it edifying." The list included a dozen or more true-detective magazines, the *Supreme Court Reporter, The Pittsburgh Courier,* autobiographies, letters and private papers, *The Kinsey Report,* and books on linguistics and etymology. Strange to say, he omitted from the list a favorite item in his intellectual diet, the *Congressional Record.* His account of his omnivorous reading was followed the next month by an interview recorded for the Library of Congress on two long-playing records in which he gave an account of his career as a newspaperman and his rules for drinking. "I am omnibibulous," he declared. "I drink every known alcoholic drink and enjoy them all. I learned early in life how to handle alcohol and never had any trouble with it. The rules are as simple as mud. First, never drink if you have work to do. Never, secondly, never drink alone. That's the way to become a drunkard. Thirdly, even if you haven't got any work to do never drink while the sun is shining. Wait until it is dark."

In "Sabbath Meditation," included in *A Mencken Chrestomathy,* which was ready for the printer, Mencken continued to mine the same vein of self-analysis. His essential trouble, he reflected, was that he was wholly lacking in spiritual gifts. He had inherited his agnosticism from his father; and being, therefore, congenitally irreverent, he had always been incapable of religious experience. He disliked any man who was pious; and all pious men, he claimed, disliked him.

The literary output of Mencken's autumnal days, however, was far from being confined to introspection and reminiscence. *Science Digest* for July carried an article of his that inquired into the most popular names for boys and girls in America. In the September 25 issue of *The New Yorker,* he unraveled "The Mystery of Podunk," which, he had discovered, was not a hypothetical entity "like the square root of zero, an honest congressman or one drink," but an actual place name of a village near Worcester, Massachusetts. In "Hell and Its Outskirts," he unearthed the ancient and honorable lineage of the expletive. His "The Vocabulary of the Drinking Chamber" and his "Video Verbiage" also appeared in *The New Yorker* during the fall of 1948. A current issue of the *Quarterly Journal of Speech* quoted him as opposing G. B.

Shaw's proposal that the twenty-six letters of the alphabet should be increased to forty and consigned his former idol to the limbo of all spelling reformers, who were in Mencken's estimation "very impudent and even foolish fellows." Shaw, he added, "like all reformers is too eager for quick results."

In addition to these diverse activities, Mencken followed Truman's campaign with interest and amusement. On the night of the election, he hurried to the *Sun* office to watch the results chalked up on the great bulletin board there. When he left, Dewey was believed to be an easy winner. Truman's astonishing victory, which did not manifest itself until after Hamilton Owens had sent a masterly analysis of the Republican victory down to the printer, appeared to Mencken to be a mathematical impossibility. Yet, there it was. The sudden demise of Dewey's hopes, he thought, demanded a coroner's inquiry.

A fortnight later, the English novelist Evelyn Waugh, who had long been anxious to meet Mencken, had arranged to have lunch with him at the Maryland Club. The day before they were to meet, on the evening of November 23, 1948, Mencken took a manuscript to his secretary, Rosalind Lohrfinck. As it was damp and chilly, she fixed a cocktail for him, and they sat chatting over it in her sitting room. Manchester records that Mrs. Lohrfinck noticed that Mencken was behaving rather oddly:

> Suddenly in the midst of a perfectly lucid sentence, he began to babble incoherently. She, alarmed, called Dr. Baker immediately. When Baker arrived, fifteen minutes later, Mencken was greatly agitated; he referred to the doctor as Stalin and talked wildly of Roosevelt. Baker decided not to call an ambulance, since he would have objected to that. After a time they quieted him down and helped him down the elevator to the doctor's car. Lingerers in the lobby of the building thought they were merely taking a liquefied old gentleman home. They wished it were that simple.

Mencken was carried to Johns Hopkins Hospital and admitted there. It was announced to the press that he had suffered a small stroke, but his condition was satisfactory and his outlook for recovery improving. Actually, Dr. Baker realized that his life was hanging in the balance. For Mencken had been stricken with a massive cerebral thrombosis, which had left his speech centers and his right side paralyzed. The paralysis spread, and for a week he hovered between life and death.

He could neither read nor write, nor remember names, dates, or specific events. When he tried to speak, he would begin coherently enough, only to find himself floundering in a morass of words.

As Dr. Baker wrote Hergesheimer, it was a great tragedy, too great indeed to be measured. Henry was alive and promised to continue to be; but just how much return to his former self there would be, it was impossible to tell. Unfortunately, he was fully conscious and aware of the magnitude of the blow Fate had dealt him. Words and the meaning of words, the expression of his thoughts in words, and their use in the analysis of the thoughts of others had been Mencken's whole life, the end and aim of all his effort since he discovered Mark Twain's *Huckleberry Finn* in his father's old-fashioned secretary the year after he learned to read. "There is no irony like God's irony," Heine once said. The blow that Mencken had suffered was as heavy and as terrible, as precise and ironic, as that with which Beethoven was stricken when he became deaf.

Slowly, Mencken's physical health began to improve. After six weeks of intensive treatment, the paralysis of his right side gradually passed off and he was able to use his arm and leg again. With a fraternal devotion unparalleled even by Edmond de Goncourt's care for his brother Jules, August spent as much time with Henry as possible, faithfully and attentively attempting to divine what Henry intended to say and endeavoring to carry out his wishes. Although his speech centers remained afflicted and the resultant semantic aphasia robbed life of all the meaning it had had for him, by Christmastime Mencken's physical condition was sufficiently satisfactory to permit August to move him back to 1524 Hollins Street.

He was made comfortable in his old quarters on the third floor. August built a little gate in his workshop to close the stairway and prevent Henry from falling down it, if he should wander about at night. Mrs. Lohrfinck came every day to handle his mail. Sometimes in the evening, she and August would take him to one of the neighborhood movies. Occasionally, he went by the Peabody Book Shop to chat with Siegfried Weisburger, who was making a collection of Menckeniana. Afterward they would adjourn to the Park Plaza for beer. But Mencken now inclined to avoid public places. His difficulty in carrying on a conversation embarrassed him, and when Hergesheimer came down to see him shortly after the New Year, he suggested that Joe have lunch with him at home, as his speech was so bad he did not want to meet anyone at the Maryland Club.

By February, he was well enough to go with August to Daytona Beach for a few days' vacation. A month later, he spent a weekend with his sister on her farm, digging in her garden and working on her woodpile. But he no longer stopped by the editorial offices every afternoon to joke with Hamilton Owens and Paul Patterson, though he did put in an appearance when a committee from the Gridiron Club was entertained by the staff of the *Sun*.

One evening when Paul Patterson dropped in at 1524 Hollins Street to see him, Mencken tried to tell him of Mrs. Lohrfinck's unfailing kindness. Finally, he threw up his hands with a despairing gesture. "She's been my secretary for twenty years," he groaned, "and I can't remember her name." Patterson tactfully reassured him by saying, "I've known her almost as long as you have and I can't remember it either."

Louis Cheslock often came in the evenings to listen to music with him. R.P. and Margery Harriss stopped by now and then to cheer him. They found him in surprisingly good spirits, particularly when he told them with something of his old gusto of the efforts of the nuns of Bon Secours Hospital, where he went for treatment of his speech impediment, to convert "The Irreverent Mr. Mencken" to Catholicism.

Whenever he could, Alfred Knopf made a trip from New York to see him. Nathan came down to see him twice. Between trips, he helped to wind up Mencken's affairs in Manhattan. He also corrected the proofs of "Postscripts to the American Language," which included H.L.'s "Scented Words," urging used-car dealers to find a two-dollar word to designate their profession comparable to realtor, mixocologist, and commissionaire; and "The Life and Times of O.K.," tracing the origin of the expression to a campaign slogan of Martin Van Buren. Nathan also helped with the corrections of *A Mencken Chrestomathy*, which appeared in June 1949, and joined in the general acclamation with which it was received. Even *The Saturday Evening Post*, never given to praising the Sage, carried an editorial on December 17, 1949, "The American Scene Owes Much to Mencken's Labors."

Now that the dust of Henry's forays against the jingoists, the demagogues and the *führers* of the Right and commissars of the Left began to settle, the press and the papers slowly realized that for all the epithets hurled at him by the extremists on both sides Mencken was as

American as apple pie, the Bill of Rights, or *The Saturday Evening Post*. Indeed, Burton Rascoe spoke of him as being "the one true American."

Despite the kindness of his old friends and the constant solicitude of August, who had retired in order to be with Henry at all hours, the days dragged for Mencken as he sat dumbly beside the radio and made an effort to listen to "the torrent of imbecilities" that poured from it. August tried obtaining recorded books for him from the Congressional Library, but they proved unsatisfactory. An ophthalmologist from Johns Hopkins made up a special pair of spectacles for him, but he was unable to use them. Eventually, the *Sun* arranged to give William Manchester, a member of its staff, time off to read to Mencken for a few hours every day.

Manchester's interest in Mencken dated from his college days. While he was a student at Amherst's Massachusetts State College, a denunciation of H.L. by one of his professors had sent him to the library to dig into Mencken's *Prejudices* for himself. After he had seen service with the Marines during World War II and had been wounded on Okinawa, Manchester entered the graduate school of the University of Missouri, where he could have access to a complete file of *The Smart Set*, and continued his research on H.L.M. On his graduation in 1947, he presented as his thesis *A Critical Study of the Work of H. L. Mencken as Literary Critic for the Smart Set Magazine, 1908–1914*. When he sent a copy of the thesis to Mencken, the Sage replied with an invitation to visit Baltimore and the suggestion that there might be a berth for him on the *Sun*. During the time that he acted as reader for Mencken, Manchester utilized the opportunity to collect data for a book on him.

Meanwhile, in April 1950, Edgar Kemler's book, *The Irreverent Mr. Mencken*, appeared, prefaced with a backhand compliment, which proved to be a misapprehension: "As I see him, Mr. Mencken is a sceptic of the first rank—an American Rabelais, Swift or Shaw—who has somehow abused his gifts. As an artist, he might have written a *Gargantua* or a *Gulliver's Travels*. Instead he devoted himself almost wholly to the passing scene, and except for *The American Language*, the *Days* books and a few selections from the others, has produced no works likely to endure."

Consequently, Manchester was faced with the task of correcting egregious errors of interpretation as well as of fact. Nevertheless, his excellent *Disturber of the Peace,* published in 1951 by Harper and Brothers, is the most accurate and complete biography of Mencken to appear to date.

As far back as 1935, Mencken and Dreiser had discussed the ultimate disposal of their manuscripts. Mencken, at that time, was thinking of giving most of his collection to the Library of Congress in Washington. He evidently reconsidered, for on his seventieth birthday, September 12, 1950, he gave the bulk of half a century's literary accretions to the Enoch Pratt Free Library. Emerson Greenway, then director of the library, called it the outstanding gift of the year. The volumes filled nine tiers of seven shelves and consisted of books, manuscripts, and thousands of items, ranging from the notes for his 1919 edition of *The American Language* to his bound scrapbooks. By way of an additional celebration, Manchester records that Mencken had a quiet luncheon with a few old friends in the board room of the *Sun.* Paul Patterson lit the seven candles on Mencken's birthday cake. As he blew them out, the Sage chuckled, "Well, I'm ready for the angels."

A month later, on October 12, 1950, Mencken suffered a heart attack. He was removed to Johns Hopkins Hospital and remained there in a critical condition. Dr. Philip Wagley, to whom Mencken had been dictating the medical history of his life, reported on October 23 that Henry showed a tremendous improvement. He was removed from the oxygen tent, took nourishment, and was much more alert than he had been for some time. He slept most of the day; but when he awakened periodically, he still showed flashes of the quick wit and humor for which he had been famed for fifty years.

On March 20, 1951, Mencken was finally allowed to return to his home. He was in an unusually cheerful mood as he was wheeled from his room to the main entrance of the hospital. He walked unassisted from there to Dr. Wagley's car. A registered nurse accompanied him and remained with him at 1524 Hollins Street until he readjusted himself to the new routine, which limited his activity to a little light work in his backyard garden.

Despite his courage and outward cheerfulness, the loneliness and inactivity weighed upon his spirits. When the chill and damp kept Henry indoors, he would sit by the window overlooking Union Square and think about the books he would liked to have written: a book on new types of quackery; a tome on music; a study of his German ancestors, for which he had long been accumuluating material; and *Advice to Young Men,* parts of which Betty Adler, his bibliographer, thinks he incorporated later in *Minority Report.*

Often his reveries would be interrupted by a small voice from below. Seeing him sitting at the window, his chief playmates, the little boys next door, would call up from the sidewalk, "Come here," and the Sage would obediently put on his coat and trot out to see the youngsters' latest treasures in the way of a frog, a turtle, a new agate, or a BB gun. When Christmas came, he turned up with gifts for all the children in the neighborhood, despite the fact that, like G.B.S., nothing in the way of a present could have pleased him better than the head of Father Christmas on a charger.

In the evenings, he worked on his correspondence. His failing eyesight did not deter him in sorting a lifetime's accumulation of letters. For his sense of touch had become so acute that he could feel the differences in stationery and identify the letters in that way.

During Mencken's illness Alistair Cooke, Washington Correspondent of the Manchester *Guardian* and emcee of the TV *Omnibus* programs, dropped in one chill, wintry evening. Cooke found Mencken drawn up close to the fire in his Hollins Street sitting room, feeding the blaze with pieces of boxes, chair legs, and broken branches from the famous woodpile in the backyard, which he and August amused themselves in accumulating and chopping up into firewood—an inventory of the kinds and sources of which fills several pages of Mencken's unpublished "Autobiographical Notes" in the Enoch Pratt Library.

On the evening of Cooke's visit, Mencken was wearing a green eyeshade and an old herringbone jacket that boasted three large Baltimore Police Department buttons, whose origin he proudly pointed out. He pulled up a chair for his visitor, and in reply to an inquiry as to his health, he drew a long face. "Imagine my day!" He waved toward the shelves of books that lined the room. "I can't read any of them. I wish it were all over." He had been a conscientious student at the Johns Hopkins' Speech and Hearing Center and had spent futile hours at home trying to relearn words that were built with his lettered blocks. His speech had improved; but the ability to read and write, the mainspring of his existence for fifty years, could not be retrieved.

August brought in foaming steins of the Canadian ale still sent to Mencken in return for the rights to the story of the bathtub hoax. With a long Havana cigar in one hand and a tall drink in the other, the Maestro's spirits began to revive and his wit flashed as of old. Then the visitor asked about Edgar Lee Masters: "I believe he died in 1948, didn't he?"

"Yeah." Mencken's grin faded. "I believe he died the same year I did."

On the days that the weather permitted, H.L. sat in the warm afternoon sunshine in the garden. When he felt up to it, he weeded the flower beds, chopped wood, and stacked it neatly near the kitchen door. In cleaning their paint brushes, he and August painted the woodpile in a gay red and yellow pattern and gave the inside of the pony's stall a coat of bright blue. "Very high-toned," Mencken observed. But a doctor to whom he and August were showing their handiwork told them that if he ever wanted to have either one of them committed, all he'd have to do would be to show this woodpile to a psychiatrist.

In 1951, the American Academy of Arts and Letters, long the butt of many of Mencken's jokes, presented him with its gold medal. Angoff and W. A. Swanberg say that he accepted it. But Mrs. Lohrfinck explained that this was untrue. For when the medal arrived, Mencken was too ill to be told about it. Rather than return it and create a controversy that might upset him, Mrs. Lohrfinck simply put it away and dropped a note to the Academy by way of explanation.

Despite his disability, Mencken continued to be quoted and reprinted. *The American Mercury* attempted to scotch its decline by republishing some of his old pieces; in January 1952, it carried "Mencken on the Military" from its September 1929 issue. By and large, he took a dim view of the military. He found that Douglas MacArthur, General of the Army, was "a dreadful fraud who seems to be fading satisfactorily." But he protested that he "did not dislike Ike," adding that he thought that Eisenhower was "a better than the average president" and "doing very well for a general." In December 1952, the *Mercury* again carried the Sage's famous piece from its maiden issue of January 1924:

> The pedant and the priest have always been the most expert of logicians—and the most diligent disseminators of nonsense and worse. The liberation of the human mind has never been furthered by such learned dunderheads; it has been furthered by gay fellows who heaved dead cats into sanctuaries and then went roistering down the highways of the world, proving to all men that doubt after all was safe—that the

God in the sanctuary was finite in his power and hence a fraud. One horse-laugh is worth ten thousand syllogisms. It is not only more effective, it is vastly more intelligent.

On Mencken's birthday in 1953, *The Nation,* to which Mencken had served as contributing editor from 1921 to 1932, took time out from analyzing the morbid state of world affairs to prepare a bouquet of tributes from authors who had known him for the issue that appeared on his anniversary. Thyra Samter Winslow's appreciation was poignant and evocative:

> As H. L. Mencken has always been just one step—and not a very deep step—below God for me, it is pretty hard for me to get any opinion of him down in a limited number of words.

In his tribute, Gerald Johnson pointed out that "H. L. Mencken would be a rich man today if he had worked for himself half as hard as he worked for countless young hopefuls." To which James Branch Cabell added, "There in brief has been, and I think there can be, but one Mencken." The Sage, Mr. Cabell continued, had no predecessor and would have no successor in American letters "as monarch of a literary era."

Dr. Carl Dolmetsch visited Mencken in the summer of 1955. Dr. Dolmetsch, who was then writing his dissertation on the history of *The Smart Set,* had expected to find Mencken "a statuesque, sharp-featured man with a flinty countenance or someone with piercing eyes like Carl Van Vechten's." Instead, he found himself shaking hands with "a mild-looking man in shirt sleeves and suspenders, tie somewhat askew, of medium height, round face with thick steel-rimmed glasses—neither lean nor fat, but pudgy—with iron-gray hair parted in the center, slightly stooped and quite visibly aged." Mencken, he added, "seemed a bit nervous and shy," but not at all ill at ease, although he moved slowly and spoke a bit thickly. After August had introduced Dr. Dolmetsch, Mencken's first words were "What do you want to drink, boy? August and I are just having some cocktails. Do you want a Manhattan, boy, or would you like something else? We have every drink here known to man."

"Every drink, Mr. Mencken?" Dr. Dolmetsch was incredulous.

"Well, by God, you try to name one we don't have. August, take him down and show him our cellar. My father built that cellar in the 1880's and we have stuff in there still from Prohibition days."

The Sage himself showed Dr. Dolmetsch his files, which contained some 500,000 letters. "There is enough there," Dr. Dolmetsch estimated, "for entirely new biographies of almost every leading American writer in the period up to 1930—Dreiser, Lewis, Fitzgerald, Cabell, Hergesheimer, *et al.*"

Exhausted after seventy-four years and twenty books, Joseph Hergesheimer died on April 25, 1954, and was buried, not far from his beloved Dower House, in Oakhill Cemetery, West Chester, Pennsylvania. Hergesheimer's death was, as Mencken said in the letter of condolence to Dorothy, which Mrs. Lohrfinck wrote for him, "a tremendous blow to him." Mrs. Lohrfinck continued:

> As you know, he can't write to you, but he wants you to know how much he has loved you for so many years. He recalls that you, your husband and he became friends exactly forty years ago and how many pleasant times you spent together. He says that in all that time there was never any disagreement between you. He knows what a wonderful wife you were and he believes you were the finest wife that ever lived.

A week afterward, she wrote Dorothy another letter for him, saying, "He sends you his best love and the hope that you are feeling fairly well. As you know, your husband was his closest friend and his death was a great shock to him." Six months later, in a letter to Dorothy initialed by Mencken, he was still grieving for Joe. "What a friend he was for so many years," he said, "and what a genius he was!"

In May 1955, William Manchester introduced to the Menckens a young student from Johns Hopkins, Robert Allen Durr, who was engaged to come every weekday morning for two hours to read and talk to H.L.M. Young Durr proved to be an acute observer. In describing Mencken in the *Yale Review*, he said:

> He was older than the pictures I had seen, and his hair was grey; but the same antique center part surmounted the same large face and intense eyes. His oval torso and thin, slightly bowed legs and arms still wore the neat close-fitting clothes of the twenties. When we shook hands his look was direct and interested. I addressed him as "sir" and thereafter it did not occur to me to use any other form than that and "Mr. Mencken." The instant's impression of the man himself overcame the years' idea of "H. L. Mencken—the beer-swigging blasphemer of bouboise beatitudes, the liberated man for whom anything goes." For clearly this was a man of dignity and principle.

Durr's impression of the Menckens at 1524 Hollins Street was equally perceptive:

> As they talked with Mr. Manchester I took in the room more fully. It was old, Victorian, with a high ceiling. The furniture was dark, rose-wood with fine tapestry upholstery on the arm-chairs. A woodframed, straight-lined settee stood against a glass-doored book-case on one wall, and next to the fireplace in the nook for which it was built was August Mencken Sr.'s tall, plain secretary, now filled with old vellum and new blue morocco books. The room was solid and rich; it was established and quiet. Especially it was unselfconscious. Things had come to be what and where they were as a consequence of a family's having lived with them so long. One sensed no striving after effect. The conventional, though fine and masculine Victorian contents of the room and, as I learned, of the whole house, had come to express, in no definable way and as a result of no conscious endeavor, the character of the Mencken family.
>
> The way to entertain company, both brothers later assured me, was to greet them with a drink—a strong drink—in your hand. We had not been seated long after introductions before August Mencken supposed it might in fact be a good idea if we had something to drink. Mr. Manchester preferred a special beer the Menckens had on hand, but the rest of us shared a decanter of very dry martinis. When we were settled Mr. Mencken got up for a cigar and asked me if I would join him. He and his brother were vigilantly yet unobtrusively solicitous of our ease and comfort. My glass was never allowed to remain empty of martini nor my fist of a Havana cigar.

On September 12, 1955, Mencken celebrated his seventy-fifth birthday by breaking into print again when Knopf published a new anthology of his work, *The Vintage Mencken,* edited by Alistair Cooke. At eight A.M. on the morning of his birthday, Mencken's colored valet, Rancho Brown, arrived as usual to bathe, dress, and shave him—to "prettify" him in his phrase. After August had fixed him a light breakfast of orange juice, toast, two soft-boiled eggs, and coffee, and brought it up to his office, Mencken was joined there by Mrs. Lohrfinck. Together they sorted through some thirty or forty pieces of birthday mail. Then Mrs. Lohrfinck brought out the files that told the story of H.L.M.'s friendships with the great writers of his time. Since it was the height of the hay-fever season, he sat with his handkerchief to his nose, while Mrs. Lohrfinck read the letters to him. Finally, to get away from the pollen, they put aside the files and took refuge in an air-conditioned movie. Late in the evening, August and Henry were sitting out in the garden, enclosed by the ivy-covered wall, built with the Sage's own hands and studded with family coats of arms, Beethoven's mask, the opening bars of the Fifth Symphony, and the stone cupid that served as a fountainhead, when the doorbell rang. It was an old friend, John E. Semmes, a Baltimore attorney and a descendant of Admiral Raphael Semmes of the famous Confederate raider the *Alabama,* who had dropped in to wish Mencken a happy birthday—his only birthday visitor.

On Wednesday, January 25, 1956, R. P. McHugh of the Associated Press stopped by 1524 Hollins Street. He found Mencken rather subdued, but looking forward to the publication of *Minority Report,* which he had written before he was taken ill in 1948, had put in an envelope and had forgotten until Mrs. Lohrfinck unearthed it. "It will be nice to be denounced again," he chuckled. But the next day he wrote Nathan, whom he had not seen since George Jean came to Baltimore to see him nine months before, that he was feeling very badly and was in despair.

On Saturday evening, he and August entertained Louis Cheslock at a little dinner, prefaced with cocktails and fresh shrimp. About nine P.M., Mencken retired to his room on the third floor and turned on a program of symphony music. Two hours later, as August passed his door on his way to bed, he noticed that his brother was breathing as if he were asleep.

Early on Sunday morning, January 29, 1956, when Rancho Brown arrived, he found Mencken dead in bed. August called the family physician, Dr. Joseph Muse. His examination revealed that H. L. Mencken's death was due to a coronary occlusion, a closing of an artery near the heart. Apparently he had died in his sleep without suffering or struggle. Thus ended seven years of what to Mencken was the most terrible of afflictions, yet the valiant old warrior had fought against his infirmity with the same courage and gallantry with which he had combatted the evils of a lifetime.

In accordance with his request, Mencken's brain was given to Johns Hopkins Hospital for study. His remains were taken there for an autopsy, which showed that he had suffered two coronaries and a stroke at some earlier time. After the autopsy his remains were released to the undertaker and cremated.

The burial service in the Book of Common Prayer, Mencken once confessed, sometimes aroused in him a sneaking wish "that the departed could actually be imagined as leaping out of the grave on the last morn, his split colloids all restored to their pristine complexity, his clothes neatly scoured and pressed and every molecule of him thrilling with a wild surmise"; but, as he regarded funeral services as barbaric rites and doubly offensive in that they were distressing to the survivors, he was buried without benefit of clergy. As he had wished, a few close friends gathered at the funeral parlor shortly after noon on February 1. Acting as spokesman for the group, Hamilton Owens said, "August wanted me to tell you what most of you already know. Henry didn't want any funeral services. All he wanted was a few friends to see him off on his last journey." His ashes were interred in the Loudon Park Cemetery beside Sara Haardt's.

Mencken had coined an epitaph for himself: "If after I depart this vale, you ever remember me and have thought to please my ghost, forgive some sinner and wink your eye at some homely girl." To this, R. P. McHugh appended a classic one of his own: "As I watched I couldn't help but think what an unlikely vehicle a hearse was for a doughty old warrior like Mencken. In my view, they ought to have carried him away on a shield."

*A*NCHOR DAYS

THE SAGE OF BALTIMORE had neither hope for nor faith in a life after death. Yet, despite his aversion to the idea of personal immortality, reincarnation, or an everlasting survival beyond this best of all possible worlds, he spent a large part of his autumnal years in sorting, classifying, and embalming his contributions to American life and letters, in forging "anchors against oblivion" to secure them as best he could against the winds of chance and the piracy of time.

Under the terms of his will, the income from his estate, valued at approximately three hundred thousand dollars, was to be divided between his brother, August, and his sister, Gertrude. After the death of his immediate survivors, one-fourth of his estate was to go to Johns Hopkins Hospital and three-fourths to the Enoch Pratt Free Library. To the Enoch Pratt he also left all the books, pamphlets, and notes made in anticipation of a third supplement to *The American Language*. To Louis Cheslock of the Peabody Conservatory he willed all his sheet music, records, and books on music; to August all his wines, liquors, cigars, and personal effects; to his brother, Charles, five thousand dollars; to Virginia Mencken Morrison, his niece, five thousand dollars; to Rosalind Lohrfinck, his secretary, ten thousand dollars; to Emma V. Bail, his servant, five hundred dollars and fifty dollars a month for the rest of her life; half of his stock in Alfred A. Knopf, Inc., to August and half to Alfred Knopf. August and the Mercantile-Safe Deposit and Trust Company of Baltimore were named as his executors. After his brother's death, the Mercantile-Safe Deposit and Trust Company was to act as sole executor.

The bulk of Mencken's vast literary and editorial correspondence was bequeathed to the New York Public Library. Under the terms of the will, the majority of these letters are restricted and will not be available until 1971.

In July 1957, the Enoch Pratt Free Library announced that, under newly disclosed terms of Mencken's will, it had received sixteen volumes of the unpublished work of H.L.M.; a five-volume diary and four volumes, titled, "Letters and Documents Relating to the Baltimore *Sunpapers*," which are not to be opened until 1981; and other unspecified volumes, restricted for another ten years. The following September, it was learned that he had bequeathed duplicate copies of the seven unpublished works, the originals of which had already been deposited in the Enoch Pratt, where they were nailed in wooden boxes in a fireproof vault, to Dartmouth College Library. Yet another duplicate set of the seven works, which consisted of four volumes of "My Life as Author and Editor" and three volumes of "Thirty-five Years of Newspaper Work," were given to the New York Public Library. With the manuscripts went instructions that they were not to be released until 1991 and were to be opened "for examination only to graduate students or those of higher grade engaged in serious critical or historical work."

The Yale, Princeton, and Harvard libraries have also accumulated impressive stocks of Mencken's manuscripts, typescripts and letters. The Library of Congress Collection includes a recording made by H.L.M. before his death. Among the Hergesheimer papers, recently acquired by the University of Texas, there is a great deal of very valuable Mencken material. Many Mencken letters have been deposited in the Theodore Dreiser, the James T. Farrell, and the Burton Rascoe Collections at the University of Pennsylvania Library. The Mencken-Cabell correspondence is now in the hands of Mrs. James Branch Cabell. The Walter Prichard Eaton, the James Southall Wilson, and the Emily Clark Balch Collection at the University of Virginia contain a number of items of Menckeniana. A large portion of the Mencken-Nathan correspondence now reposes in the Cornell University Library. The Newberry Library in Chicago houses many of the letters between H.L.M. and Sherwood Anderson. Mencken's letters to Edna Kenton are now in Columbia University Library. His correspondence with James B. Pinker and Lew R. Sarett is in the Northwestern University Library; with Horace Meyer Kallen, in the Jewish Research Library; and with Bishop James Cannon, in the Duke University Library. The Amelia

Gayle Gorgas Library at the University of Alabama Library has a collection of letters from Sara, Henry, and August Mencken and contemporary diaries, journals, and clippings relative to them, covering the years from 1918 to 1967. In addition there are a number of Mencken letters, autographed books and pamphlets in the hands of private collectors. One of the most extensive of these is that of Elizabeth M. Taylor of Kansas City, Missouri, which is to be willed to the University of Kansas.

The H. L. Mencken Room in the Enoch Pratt Free Library in Baltimore, which Bissell Brooke called "the Cradle of Twentieth Century Literature," was established on April 17, 1956, not quite three months after the Sage's death. The room was formally opened by two of Mencken's friends, Hamilton Owens and Alistair Cooke, the British author who edited *The Vintage Mencken,* published the year before.

The Mencken Room, which was made possible through the generosity of August Mencken, the Deiches Fund, and voluntary contributions by the Sage's friends, was designated by Mr. Cooke as existing "for the comfort of sinners and the astonishment of the virtuous." To which it should be added, "and to the eternal gratitude of all Mencken scholars." Located in a large, rectangular, air-conditioned room in a quiet section on the third floor of the Enoch Pratt Library, "the Cradle of Twentieth Century Literature" is doubtless as near paradise as any student of contemporary letters will ever get on what "The Irreverent Mr. Mencken" called "this sorry ball."

Its walls are lined with long rows of walnut bookshelves filled with richly bound tomes and elegant blue morocco scrapbooks. On a large oriental rug of harmonious colors rests an immense fourteen-foot reading table, flanked by high-backed chairs of carved walnut, upholstered in rose-rust. In the far corners are two individual study tables with convenient lamps and comfortable chairs.

Over the door hangs the heraldic shield of the Saturday Night Club. Quartered by fat link sausages, the arms of the club display a boiled lobster couchant, a garland of onions and pretzels, a fiddle, and a beer stein rampant. On each side of it are Jack Engeman's colored photographs of Mencken at the club and with R. P. Harriss. Near them are the last unposed photographs of Mencken, made on his seventy-fifth birthday by his favorite photographer, A. Aubrey Bodine of the Baltimore *Sun.*

From the end wall, the portrait of "The Lion of the Twenties" by

Nikol Schattenstein looks amiably down on the mellow warmth and quiet dignity of the room. The portrait was painted when Mencken was forty-seven and at the height of his career. He is seated with his head resting on one hand and, characteristically, a half-smoked Uncle Willy in the other, as if he were relaxing for a moment from his labors. He is wearing his working clothes: a white shirt, open at the neck, and a pair of old trousers, held up by the red and blue suspenders given him by Rudolph Valentino, once the idol of Hollywood. From his vantage point at the far end of the room, the genial Sage of Nikol Schattenstein appears to survey his work and find it good. And well he might.

Ranged around the walls are the published copies of all Mencken's works. Beside them, bound in dark-blue morocco, are volumes of Mencken's original manuscripts, notes, working drafts, galley proofs, letters, and records, including eight fat tomes devoted to "The Hatrack Case" and a score or more filled with his contributions to newspapers and periodicals. Further, there are a hundred and six black buckram scrapbooks, stamped in gold, and filled with the clippings, from which Sara Haardt long ago culled the diatribes, denunciations, and tongue-lashings directed against the Palm of Learning, who to her, at least, was a *chevalier sans peur and sans reproche*—choice samples of invective which the Sage published as *Menckeniana: A Schimpflexicon.*

In addition, the H. L. Mencken Room houses Mencken's personal library. Among his books are some twenty-five hundred presentation copies, among them fifty-one by Theodore Dreiser, thirty-four by Joseph Hergesheimer, and a copy of *Elmer Gantry*, dedicated to Mencken and enclosing an informal letter to him from Sinclair Lewis. Many of the books are autographed; in them are found the signatures of and letters from James Branch Cabell, William Saroyan, Carl Sandburg, Edgar Lee Masters, Willa Cather, Scott Fitzgerald, James T. Farrell, Aldous Huxley, and Leon Trotsky, who inscribed a copy of his *Geschichte der Russischen Revolution* to the Sage in French with this remark: "my English is very pitiful."

The task of cataloguing and indexing the collection, a truly formidable one, was entrusted to the capable hands of Mrs. Lohrfinck, the gracious, gray-haired lady who had served Mencken as secretary ever since he began to dictate the notes for his *Treatise on the Gods* to her. During the years that Mrs. Lohrfinck worked for Mencken, she had become thoroughly familiar with the collection, which the director of the Enoch Pratt believed to be "unprecedented in size, content, and completeness for the period it covers. And relative to Mencken himself, it surpasses the outstanding Mencken collections at Harvard and Dartmouth." Through the efforts of August Mencken and those of Richard Hart and of William Forshaw, both of the Enoch Pratt's Humanities Division, and of Edwin Castagna, the present director of the library, additions to the collection are constantly being made. Among them are a number of very important contributions, the genealogical papers that Mencken had unearthed with the intention of writing a history of his family, as well as what Betty Adler, who completed cataloguing the collection, describes as "almost a mountain" of photographs.

In his article "Forging the Mencken Myth," Dr. Carl Dolmetsch of the Department of English at the College of William and Mary, whose doctoral dissertation at the University of Chicago was *A History of the Smart Set Magazine, 1914–1923,* points out: "Of the making of many books about Henry Louis Mencken, late Sage of Baltimore, there is no end. In the seven years since his death, at least one volume a year, on an average, has been issued to swell the H. L. M. Legend." The first of these, Charles Angoff's *H. L. Mencken: A Portrait from Memory,* which appeared in 1956, shortly after the Sage's death, Dr. Dolmetsch called "a vindictive failure."

The most important of the recent Mencken books in the estimation of his bibliographer, Betty Adler, is *The Letters of H. L. Mencken,* a selection from the literary correspondence made by Guy Forgue, a Parisian, who is now writing a critical biography of Mencken as his doctoral dissertation at the Sorbonne. By far the most scholarly and useful work on Mencken yet to appear is *H. L. M.: The Mencken Bibliography,* compiled by Betty Adler with the assistance of Jane Wilhelm and published in 1961 by the Johns Hopkins Press.

After Miss Adler completed the Mencken bibliography, she suggested supplementing it with a quarterly magazine, which would not only contain a bibliographical check list of current Mencken items, but contributions from "Menckenthusiasts" and unpublished material by H. L. Mencken. Her suggestion was adopted by the Enoch Pratt Free Library, and she became editor of *Menckeniana,* as the new quarterly was called, with Richard Hart acting as liaison with the library. The first issue of the magazine appeared in April 1962. The response to it was overwhelming. Subscriptions poured in from thirty states, from Canada, and from France. *Menckeniana* is said to have brought a greater response in a shorter time than any other Pratt Library publication. Under Miss Adler's able guidance the magazine has become one of the most successful periodicals of its kind and has been widely acclaimed and quoted by the press.

In the same year, Knopf brought out one of the most delightful of the post-mortem books about the Sage, *H. L. Mencken on Music,* edited by his friend the Baltimore composer Louis Cheslock, who announced on H. L. Mencken's birthday in 1962 that he had completed an opera using Mencken's play *The Artist* as a libretto. The opera was dedicated to August Mencken and reviewed in R. P. Harriss' column, "The Lively Arts," in the Baltimore *News-American,* October 21, 1962.

Earlier in the summer, the Duke University Press had issued Dr. M. K. Singleton's controversial study *H. L. Mencken and The American Mercury Adventure.* August Mencken, who had seen the book in manuscript, found that the first eight chapters were not too bad, but protested at the ninth. Dr. Dolmetsch concedes that in Singleton's study there is to be found "a glimpse—but only a glimpse—of the real Mencken. . . . If Dr. Singleton sometimes quotes out of context to bolster his arguments and if his judgment may occasionally be faulty, he has at least compiled a readable and at times diverting chronicle of a once-bright journal that survives today only in name." Soon afterward came an updated one-volume edition of Mencken's *The American Language.* In 1965 appeared one of the best of the Mencken anthologies, *H. L. Mencken: The American Scene,* edited with a preface by Huntington Cairns and published by Knopf. Alfred Knopf has announced that he will soon publish a biography of Mencken by Dr. Carl Bode of the Department of English at the University of Maryland. The most recent and one of the most significant contributions to the Mencken saga is Dr. Carl Dolmetsch's fine book *The Smart Set,* published by Dial late in 1966.

Most of the writers of Mencken's day were freelancers or journalists. In the search for security born of the Depression and intensified by the hazards of nuclear warfare, social revolution, and spiraling inflation, more and more authors found shelter in colleges and universities. The resultant tendency of American writing to become increasingly academic, which would have aroused volcanic protests from the Sage, has, nevertheless, redounded to his glory. *H. L. M.: The Mencken Bibli-*

ography lists four master's theses and six doctoral dissertations that have been done on Mencken; one of the latter is in German, another in Hungarian. Moreover, at the University of Wisconsin and the University of Maryland, seminar courses on Mencken are to be conducted during the coming academic year.

Another recent phenomenon that has contributed to the Sage's posthumous fame is the popularity of paperback books, particularly those devoted to reprinting American classics. *In Defense of Women, Treatise on the Gods,* and *H. L. Mencken on Politics: A Carnival of Buncombe* have already appeared in paperback editions, and reprints of more of his works are under consideration.

In Betty Adler's monumental *H. L. M.: The Mencken Bibliography,* which August Mencken commended as an astounding piece of work in which nothing was overlooked, the author lists nine books with sections devoted to H.L.M. and a selected list of sixty-nine articles, including obituaries, that appeared between his death and the time the bibliography went to press. After its appearance, a check of the *Reader's Guide to Periodical Literature* reveals that almost a score of articles have been added to that amazing total.

The majority of these literary post-mortems are eulogistic. In regard to a few that are hostile, Guy Forgue has made a shrewd observation in his "Myths About Mencken," in which he says that, unfortunately, in a number of the articles that appeared after the Sage's death, "the public was offered what purported to be reminiscences about him, but were in fact belated expressions of private grudges suppressed while he was alive." Such posthumous attacks are too spiteful to warrant noting them; for most of them can be conveniently subsumed under a single title as "The Officeboy's Revenge." Fortunately for Mencken's personal and literary reputation, such detractions have provoked double their number of contradictions. The preposterous charges that Mencken was a racist, pro-Nazi, and anti-Semitic have been ably dispelled by less biased critics.

R. P. Harriss, as well as Guy Forgue, has effectively answered one of these far-fetched allegations in an article entitled, "Was Mencken Anti-Semitic?—No." In his witty review "No Editor Is a Hero," Jim Cain, who was Mencken's colleague on the *Sun* for many years before becoming an editor of *The New Yorker,* demolished Charles Angoff's malicious charge that Mencken's scholarship was bogus by reminding

Mr. Angoff of the thousands of four-by-six cards that still exist in the Enoch Pratt Free Library in a locked room next to the Mencken collection as mute but incontestible evidence of H.L.M.'s minute and painstaking research. Further, he implies that Mr. Angoff's own scholarship in his *H. L. Mencken: A Portrait From Memory* is by no means impeccable. Mr. Cain cites the omission from Angoff's bibliography of *Men Versus the Man* written by H. L. Mencken and Robert Rives La Monte. He also points out to Mr. Angoff that Sara Haardt came from Montgomery, not Birmingham, Alabama.

One of the most trenchant appraisals of the Sage after his death comes from Joseph Wood Krutch, who ventured to predict that in time to come it would be generally recognized that "Mencken's was the best prose written in America during the Twentieth Century. Those who deny the fact had better confine themselves to direct attack. They will be hard put to find a rival claimant." Henry Hazlitt, who succeeded Mencken as editor of *The American Mercury,* paid tribute to his predecessor as "the outstanding American literary critic of his generation, its most influential stylist, its most prominent iconoclast, the chief scourge of the genteel tradition and a great liberating force."

If anyone inclines to regard these panegyrics as post-obit eulogies, let it be remembered that back in 1926, no lesser pundit than Walter Lippmann declared in a review of *Notes on Democracy* that Mencken was "the most powerful personal influence on this whole generation of educated people."

Henry Mencken, as he was known to his close associates in Baltimore, is admirably revealed in numerous articles by R. P. Harriss and Louis Cheslock in the columns of the *American* and the *Sun* and in Hamilton Owens' introductory note to Guy Forgue's edition of the *Letters of H. L. Mencken.* Three articles of Gerald Johnson's, "H. L. Mencken, 1880–1956," "Henry L. Mencken, 1880–1956," and "Oh, for Mencken Now," taken together, constitute not only one of the most accurate estimates of the Old Defender's greatness and influence but also an intimate and endearing portrait of the man himself as he was known and beloved by a small circle of friends in his native city and by an even smaller circle elsewhere. An excellent picture of this same Henry Mencken is to be found in Alfred Knopf's warm-hearted and endearing "For Henry With Love." And shortly before her death, Rosalind Lohrfinck, who succeeded her sister as secretary to H.L.M., noted: "He was soft-spoken, always considerate of others and the very personification of politeness."

The year after Mencken's death, his friend and fellow scoffer, George Jean Nathan, whose judgment of *Lazarus Laughs* Eugene O'Neill once contended could not be taken seriously because the drama critic was "lacking in all religious feeling," succumbed to the lure of Rome and joined the Catholic Church. After writing forty books and countless articles for more than thirty periodicals, Nathan's hand was paralyzed by arteriosclerosis. Undaunted by his affliction, the dean of American drama critics dictated his memoirs to an amanuensis at the request of his friend Arnold Gingrich of *Esquire*. On April 8, 1958, at the age of seventy-six, Nathan died in his old apartment at the Royalton with his wife Julie Haydon beside him.

Six weeks afterward, James Branch Cabell succumbed to a cerebral hemorrhage at his home in Richmond, Virginia. In 1964, his widow Margaret Freeman Cabell edited his letters with the assistance of Padraic Colum. The book, which was entitled *Between Friends*, with a preface by Carl Van Vechten, was published by Harcourt, Brace and World.

Before his death on December 21, 1964, Carl Van Vechten was fond of boasting that he had not left New York City since 1949. At eighty-four, he was still active. Having successfully completed one career as a music critic and another as a novelist, in his riper years he had achieved an enviable reputation in a third field as a portrait photographer. He rose at six A.M. and worked for five or six hours every day in the darkroom of his apartment at 146 Central Park West, where he had photographed celebrities from Mahalia Jackson to Mencken.

After the death of Blanche Knopf in 1966, Alfred, Sr., continued to carry on alone at Alfred A. Knopf, Inc., which under the terms of the merger with Random House he still runs as an independent fief, turning out books under the classic Borzoi imprint. His son Alfred A. Knopf, Jr., is now one of the executives of Atheneum Publishers and father of three children.

Until he suffered a series of heart attacks in 1965, August Mencken busied himself with tasks as varied as Henry's were. Two years before, Johns Hopkins Press had published his scholarly study of *The Railroad Passenger Car*. Between building detailed models of the pyramids and working on his new book, *The Design and Construction of the Pyra-*

mids, he turned out a series of rollicking tales. One has only to read his "The Fair Chanteuse," "The Reluctant Bride," and "The Glamorous Mrs. Kite" to realize that astringent humor was a characteristic of both the Mencken brothers and that, as Henry frequently said, some of his best ideas came from August. Since his sister Gertrude spends most of her time on her farm, Choice Parcel, near Baltimore, August kept open the family home at 1524 Hollins Street and carried on its hospitable traditions until his death in 1967. Charles Mencken, who was twenty months younger than Henry, died in the spring of 1956, shortly after the Sage's death, leaving his daughter Virginia Mencken Morrison and her son to carry on, if not the name, at least the Mencken line.

$\mathscr{A}$CKNOWLEDGMENTS

THE CONSTANT CIRCLE is based mainly upon unpublished letters, diaries, notes, and clippings in the Mayfield Collection in the University of Alabama Library, where a heavily documented and bibliographed manuscript of the book has also been deposited for the use of scholars.

To Dr. W. Stanley Hoole, librarian of the University of Alabama, I am indebted for permission to publish the materials, for his criticisms of the manuscript, and for the many courtesies of his staff, especially Mrs. William Terrill, Mrs. R. E. Johnson, Mrs. C. C. Jones, Mrs. W. E. Lamont, Mrs. Addie S. Coleman, Mr. Perry Cannon, and Mr. Joseph A. Jackson; to Mr. August Mencken and Mr. William Frederick of the Mercantile-Safe Deposit and Trust Company of Baltimore, Maryland, for permission to publish the letters of Sara and Henry Mencken, as well as for checking the manuscript; to Mr. Edwin Castagna, director of the Enoch Pratt Free Library, for giving me access to the Mencken Room there and for permission to quote from his "Long Warm Friendship: HLM-EPFL"; to Mr. Richard Hart and Mr. William Forshaw of the Humanities Department of the Enoch Pratt, Miss Betty Adler, editor of *Menckeniana*, and Mr. R. P. Harriss of the Baltimore *News-American* for their endless kindness in supplying information, answering queries, and reading the manuscript, thereby saving me from a host of errors; to Mr. William Dix, librarian of Princeton University, for permission to use the Mencken and Fitzgerald collections in the Firestone Library and for the many kindnesses of his staff, particularly Dr. Howard C. Rice, Mr. Alexander P. Clark, Mrs. Alden Randall, Miss Julie Hudson, Mr. Alfred Bush, and Mr. Charles Green; to Mrs. Mary M. Hirth, librarian of the Academic Center at the University of Texas,

295

for allowing me to use the Hergesheimer Collection there and for her unfailing helpfulness over a period of years; to Miss Sara D. Jones, librarian of Goucher College, for letting me see the Sara Haardt Mencken Collection there; to Mr. George H. Healy, curator of Rare Books at Cornell University Library, for permitting me to use its Mencken and Nathan materials; to Mr. W. H. Bond, librarian of the Houghton Library, for allowing me to quote from the Mencken, Fitzgerald, and Bradford materials by permission of Harvard College Library; to Mr. David R. Watkins, chief reference librarian of the Beinecke Library, for allowing me to use the Mencken, Fitzgerald, Van Vechten, and Sinclair Lewis Collections in Yale University Library; to Neda M. Westlake, curator of the Rare Book Collection at the University of Pennsylvania, for granting me permission to quote from the Dreiser, Mencken, and Weisburger materials there; and to Mr. Robert W. Hill, Keeper of Manuscripts, for showing me the unrestricted Mencken papers in the New York Public Library.

To the following, I am indebted for permission to quote from copyrighted and other material: Houghton Mifflin Company for *The Far Side of Paradise* by Arthur Mizener, © 1959 by Arthur Mizener; Charles Scribner's Sons for *Letters of James Gibbons Huneker*, © 1922 by Charles Scribner's Sons; Harold Ober Associates and Charles Scribner's Sons for *Save Me the Waltz* by Zelda Fitzgerald, © 1932 by Charles Scribner's Sons, and *The Letters of F. Scott Fitzgerald*, © 1963 by Frances Scott Fitzgerald Lanahan; University of Texas Press and Fidelity-Philadelphia Trust for *Ingénue Among the Lions*, © 1965 by University of Texas Press; William Sloane Associates for *Theodore Dreiser* by F. O. Matthiessen, © 1951 by William Sloane Associates; Mrs. Burton Rascoe for *Before I Forget* by Burton Rascoe, © 1937 by Doubleday, Doran, Inc.; Mrs. Joseph Hergesheimer for Joseph Hergesheimer's unpublished letters and autobiography; Mrs. George Jean Nathan for George Jean Nathan's unpublished letters and his character analysis of Mencken; Mr. Melville H. Cane for letters of Dorothy and Sinclair Lewis; Alfred A. Knopf, Sr., and *The Atlantic Monthly* for "For Henry with Love," by Alfred A. Knopf, Sr., © 1959 by The Atlantic Monthly Company, Boston, Mass. 02116; *Life* and Roger Butterfield for "Mr. Mencken Sounds Off," by Roger Butterfield, © 1948 by Time, Inc.; *The Yale Review* for "Mr. Mencken's Last Days," by Robert Allen Durr, © 1958 by the Yale University Press; *Comment* Magazine for

"The Fitzgeralds: Exiles from Paradise," Winter 1965; Ernst, Cane, Berner and Gitlin for *The Letters of Thomas Wolfe* edited by Elizabeth Newell, copyright 1956 by Edward C. Aswell, Administrator C.T.A.; Alfred A. Knopf, Inc. for *Mencken on Music* by Louis Cheslock and *Letters of H. L. Mencken.*

For permission to quote from their letters, thanks must go to Gerald Johnson, R. P. Harriss, Dr. Carl Dolmetsch of the College of William and Mary, Mrs. Margaret Cobb of Tufts University, Miss Mary Parmenter of Florida State College, Mary Ellen Chase, Louis Cheslock, Arnold Lohrfinck and Mrs. Charles Lappin. I am also indebted to Mrs. Frank Slater for the gift of her husband's sketch of H. L. Mencken and her permission to use it on the jacket; to Mrs. James Branch Cabell, Mrs. Ernest Boyd, Mrs. Edmund Duffy, Mr. Hudson Strode, and Dr. Carl Bode of the University of Maryland, Dr. Arthur Mizener of Cornell University, and Dr. Carlos Baker of Princeton University for supplying information and suggestions; and to Mrs. H. J. Finch, Mrs. Emil Stubben, and Mrs. H. E. Holcomb for typing the manuscript.

I am deeply grateful to my agent, Lurton Blasingame; Miss Virginia Cody; Mrs. Giorgio de Santillana; Mrs. H. H. Washburn and Professor J. B. McMinn of the University of Alabama; Dr. Joe Davis of Georgia State University; Professor Matthew J. Bruccoli of Ohio State University; Dr. Albert S. Johnson and Professor Stanley Rosenbaum of Florence State College; Dr. Sidney J. Landman of the University of Texas; Mr. Howard Webber of Western Reserve Press and Mr. Francis P. Squibb of the University of Alabama Press for reading and criticizing the manuscript.

Finally, to Mr. Richard Tucker Kennedy, senior editor of Delacorte Press, I owe a profound debt of gratitude for skill and patience in editing the manuscript.

$\mathcal{I}_{NDEX}$